GERMANY AND POLAND

From War to Peaceful Relations

W. W. KULSKI

GERMANY

SYRACUSE UNIVERSITY PRESS

AND **POLAND**

From War to Peaceful Relations

1976

Library of Congress Cataloging in Publication Data
Kulski, Władysław Wszebór, 1903–
   Germany and Poland : from war to peaceful relations.
   Bibliography: p.
   Includes index.
   1. Germany—Foreign relations—Poland. 2. Poland
—Foreign relations—Germany. 3. Germany, West—
Foreign relations—Europe, Eastern. 4. Europe,
Eastern—Foreign relations—Germany, West. I. Title.
DD120.P7K84   327.43'0438   75–42453
ISBN 0–8156–0118–2
ISBN 0–8156–0122–0 pbk.

In homage to my native city,

twice destroyed by the enemy and

twice reborn from the ashes.

W. W. Kulski, James B. Duke Professor Emeritus of Russian Affairs at Duke University, Durham, North Carolina, brings a lifetime of unique experience to this appraisal of Germany and Poland.

Educated in Warsaw and Paris, with degrees in international law, Dr. Kulski was a member of the Polish diplomatic service between 1928 and 1945. A delegate to the Conference on the Reduction and Limitation of Armaments, Geneva, 1932–33, he was later the Polish negotiator of the British-Polish Treaty of Mutual Assistance, August 1939, which formed the diplomatic basis for the British declaration of war on Nazi Germany. Also while in London, Dr. Kulski was secretary-general of the Inter-Allied Committee of Foreign Ministers on which all the European governments in exile were represented.

Throughout his career in Europe and the United States, Dr. Kulski has written many articles, reviews, and books on international relations, specializing in the Soviet Union and Eastern Europe. Particularly well known are *The Soviet Regime: Communism in Practice, De Gaulle and the World: The Foreign Policy of the Fifth French Republic,* and *The Soviet Union in World Affairs: A Documented Analysis, 1964–1972,* all published by Syracuse University Press.

Contents

Preface

The purpose of this book is to depict for the reader the successive stages in the development of relations between the Federal Republic of Germany and Poland up to the present time. Since the problems arising in these relations cannot be understood without knowledge of historical background, the book opens with a concise résumé of the thousand-year-long history of relations between the German and the Polish nations, condemned by their geographical proximity to live side by side, either in amity or in mutual hatred.

Even a slight knowledge of present-day European politics makes it self-evident that Poland may not deviate in its foreign policy from the signposts of Soviet policy. Also, the Federal Republic can modulate its own policy toward Poland only in tune with its over-all policy toward the USSR. Hence, I had to take into consideration the Eastern policies of the Federal Republic. As the result, this book is also a history of the successive policies of the FRG toward the Soviet Union and the whole Soviet bloc.

This book is different from most other Western publications devoted partly or mostly to the same subject, for the simple reason that most Western authors do not know Polish and do not use Polish source materials. It is, I believe, the merit of my book that it is founded on both German and Polish sources. This might be helpful also to German readers, especially those who sincerely want to achieve a reconciliation between the two nations, because such a reconciliation is impossible without full knowledge of the views of the other party.

My own competence for writing a book of this kind rests on two pillars: my former diplomatic experience and, of course, my research in German and Polish sources. As a Polish diplomat (1928–1945), I had ample opportunity to watch the German policies toward Poland, including those of the period of the Weimar Republic, characterized by the intention to revise the Western Polish frontiers, and that of Nazi Germany, bent eventually on the destruction not only of the Polish state but also of the Polish nationality. I was able also to observe during my diplomatic service the American, British, French, and Soviet policies toward Poland. Hence, I am completely familiar with the German-Polish problem in its manifold aspects.

If I have to disclose my personal feeling, I may only say that I hope that the time will come when the big Polish neighbors, Germany and Russia, will find it possible to conceive of their relations with Poland in the spirit of truly good neighborliness. This would be a true guarantee of peace in Europe.

I acknowledge with gratitude the financial assistance of the Senior Fulbright-Hays Program, the Joint Committee on East-European Studies of the American Council of Learned Societies, the Social Science Research Council, and the American Philosophical Society. That assistance helped me in carrying out research both in the Federal Republic of Germany and in Poland.

As was true regarding my former books, the research for this one was immensely facilitated by the generous and effective assistance of my wife, devoted companion of the happy and unhappy days of my life.

I also owe a debt of sincere gratitude to those numerous West German and Polish politicians, officials, and scholars whom I interviewed or who helped me in gathering the research materials.

W. W. KULSKI

December 1975
Durham, N.C.

Introduction

"Les morts gouvernent les vivants."
AUGUSTE COMTE

RECOLLECTIONS OF THE SECOND WORLD WAR

UGUSTE COMTE'S maxim, "The dead rule the living," has particular significance for German-Polish relations—relations which cannot be understood if the impact of history on the minds of the present generation in both countries is disregarded. This history is made up not only of the events of the Second World War and its aftermath, though these events would have heavily burdened mutual relations in any case. The Poles can hardly forget the unprovoked German attack on September 1, 1939, or the five and a half years of the cruel occupation regime, the time when the Germans treated them as sub-human beings, deported them to concentration camps or for forced labor, looted or destroyed their cultural treasures, razed to the ground their capital, Warsaw, and eventually, after their retreat before the Soviet troops, left behind a devastated Poland and six million dead (half of them Jewish and another half Christians) who had been exterminated in the Gestapo prisons and concentration camps. In fact, Poland suffered proportionately the most among all countries invaded by Nazi Germany, not excluding the Soviet Union.

The Germans cannot easily forget the aftermath of their military defeat: the expulsion from postwar Poland of millions of their countrymen, expellees who had swollen the numbers of other millions who fled from Poland in fear of advancing Soviet troops, and the Polish annexation of the former German territories east of the Oder-Neisse line. Most of these expellees and refugees now live in the Federal Republic of

Germany. They and many other citizens of the FRG find it extremely difficult to accept the existence of Poland's western frontier on the Oder-Neisse. They remember the historical maps of Imperial Germany within its 1914 frontiers, which included that part of Poland acquired by Prussia in consequence of four partitions (in the eighteenth century and at the Congress of Vienna in 1815), and they themselves or their parents lived in the Weimar Republic within its Versailles frontiers, not to mention the frontiers of Nazi Grossdeutschland which included almost the whole territory inhabited in the majority by Poles.

It is true that time is a great healer. Young Poles did not live under the German occupation, and their feelings toward the Germans are less inimical than those of their parents. Young Germans born in the Federal Republic, even the descendants of the refugees and expellees, are also much less inclined than their parents to think about the recovery of the former German territories as a practical proposition; the FRG has become their homeland, and they do not find attractive the idea of going back to the former homeland of their ancestors, even if this were possible.

One cannot figure out the feelings of East Germans, immediate neighbors of Poland, because the German Democratic Republic forbids the expression of any anti-Polish sentiments, both countries belonging to the Soviet bloc. One can only guess that a great many East Germans feel in their hearts a strong resentment against the Poland which has annexed the nearby former German territories, territories which they, so to speak, see across the Oder-Neisse frontier. However, this study is limited to West German–Polish relations only.

Polish and German recollections of the recent past reveal a psychological factor which does not make mutual reconciliation easy. There is no analogy between this problem and that of the postwar French-German reconciliation. The notion of the "hereditary enemy" arose in Germany only in response to the Napoleonic invasion, while the same notion appeared in France only after the French defeat in the 1870–71 war and the loss of Alsace-Lorraine. Moreover, the German occupation of France was mild if compared with the occupation regime in Poland or the Soviet Union. The Poles, unlike the French, were at that time faced with the prospect of the gradual extermination of their educated classes and of the final extinction of their nation in the event of German victory. Not only the Vichy regime but also a high proportion of Frenchmen collaborated with the German authorities and fared relatively well.[1] Hence, French-German reconciliation was an easy task. It is significant that soon after the end of hostilities General de Gaulle, the leader of anti-German resistance, accepted the concept of reconciliation and later, as President of the Fifth Republic, decisively contributed to friendly cooperation between the two countries. The reconciliation was due, among other things, to the belief in both countries that, while they fought as enemies in the two World Wars, neither won anything by its hostility. France lost its rank as a world power, while Germany emerged from those wars not only with much less national territory, but divided into two states. Germans and Frenchmen concluded that it was more reasonable to live together as peaceful and friendly neighbors.

THE POLISH VIEW OF THE GERMAN

German-Polish history is replete with conflicts during its one-thousand-year length. The Poles were faced at times with the hostility of the whole so-called Roman Empire of the German Nation, but mostly with the military and political eastward push at their expense by East Germans—the East German princes, the Order of Teutonic Knights, the Electorate of Brandenburg, and eventually the Kingdom of Prussia. Hence, either all Germans or only the immediate East German neighbors were alternately viewed by the Poles as their enemies. The Middle Ages and the later centuries until the time of the unification of Germany in 1870 left to the Poles a mixed view of the German. This confused view, reflecting the actual history of quarrels primarily with the East Germans, is best illustrated by the fact that two Germans, Saxon Electors Augustus II and Augustus III, were elected Polish kings in the eighteenth century. It is true that their reigns coincided with the worst period of political and cultural decadence of Poland, and that Augustus II toyed with the idea of partitioning his Polish kingdom among its neighbors. Nevertheless, the Poles, who had undertaken the complete reform of the state just prior to the second and third partitions, called the Saxon family to the Polish throne which was to be dynastic and hereditary. The Saxon king appointed by Napoleon to be the Grand Duke of the Warsaw Grand Duchy (a short-lived Napoleonic creation) was popular in the country. Hence, one cannot say that the Polish view of the German was by that time unfriendly, since the Poles equally disliked their three immediate neighbors, Russia, Austria, and Prussia, who had partitioned Poland.

The quarrels with the East Germans left behind for both nations the impression of the German eastward drive (*Drang nach Osten*). This concept reflects the history of gradual German expansion eastward, first by the conquest of Western Slavs, later by the conquest of Polish and other Eastern territories. Eventually Prussia reached the River Vistula and beyond and included former Polish provinces. This territorial heritage was preserved by the united German Empire. For the Poles the eastward drive meant the gradual loss of national territory and eventually the extinction of the Polish state at the time of the three partitions. For the Germans, the same drive was a great political and cultural venture, a historical achievement of the German nation.

This drive and the partitions reminded the Poles of the greatest threat they experienced in their history: German-Russian cooperation at their expense. They remembered that the Brandenburg Electors cooperated with the Grand Duchy of Moscow at a time when Poland was assailed simultaneously by several enemies in the second half of the seventeenth century; that Prussia continued to work together with Russia at the time of the partitions, that it did so again at the Congress of Vienna which partitioned Poland for the fourth time; that the political friendship in the nineteenth century between Prussia and later the German Empire, Russia, and Austria, was founded on their shared desire to guarantee mutually the preservation of their Polish spoils; that the Weimar Republic and the Soviet Union cooperated politically and militarily because of their unfriendliness toward independent Poland; and finally, that Nazi Germany and the Soviet Union agreed in August 1939 on the fifth partition of Poland.

This was the Polish nightmare for centuries. This nightmare disappeared with the German attack on the Soviet Union and the high cost for the Russians of the German invasion and occupation (over twenty million dead and the devastation of the western parts of the USSR). The Second World War left the legacy of a new historical phenomenon, mutual animosity between the Germans and the Russians. For the Russians it arises from the recollection of the cruel German policy toward them; for the Germans, from the loss of vast Eastern territories imposed by the USSR, and the division of Germany into two states maintained by Soviet fiat. For the first time in their history the Poles feel secure regarding Germany, sheltered as they are by the Soviet alliance and by the division of Germany. This allows them to look at the Germans with greater equanimity.

History left another recollection to the Poles. In 1791 Poland, still independent, concluded with Prussia an alliance against Russia, hoping to be freed of the overbearing Russian protectorate. This alliance was repudiated by Prussia soon after, in order to proceed with the last two partitions, undertaken in concert with Russia. In 1934 Poland concluded with Nazi Germany the ten-year pact of non-aggression in the hope of remaining neutral in German-Soviet quarrels. Five years later it fell victim to German aggression in violation of this pact and soon after was again partitioned between Germany and the USSR. This recollection would not incline the Poles to engage in agreement with Germany in a policy hostile to Russia, if such a policy were conceivable under the present circumstances, which it obviously is not.

All the Germans, not only the East Germans, began to be regarded by the Poles as their enemies only after the chancellor of a unified German Reich, Otto Bismarck, inaugurated an anti-Polish policy intended to eradicate national feelings among the Polish subjects in the former Polish provinces annexed by Prussia. This policy and the stubborn Polish resistance against attempts to Germanize them or to change the proportional relationship between Polish inhabitants of those provinces and the government-sponsored new German settlers, gave rise to an intense feeling of mutual animosity between the two nations. After Poland had recovered its independence in 1918, it was confronted with the hostility of the Weimar Republic, which resented the fact that the Polish-inhabited provinces, annexed at the time of the partitions, had been restored to the Poles and lost to Germany. In Germany the Versailles frontiers were considered unbearable. It is a paradox of history that the Federal Republic of Germany, almost until the conclusion of the Warsaw Treaty of 1970, insisted on the right of Germans to recover the same Versailles frontiers (frontiers of 1937) which the Weimar Republic had denounced as a blatant injustice. Of course, those frontiers were much better than those which were fixed in consequence of the Second World War, which Hitler had begun in the name of revision of the Versailles frontiers.

The history of mutual relations left another legacy. The Teutonic Knights; Frederick the Great, the initiator of the partitions of Poland; and Chancellor Bismarck, the founder of a unified Germany, are for the Germans great historical figures. Their names evoke in Polish minds the worst periods in their own history. Even Gustav Stresemann, the Foreign Minister of the Weimar Republic, who is hailed in the Federal Republic as a great statesman, is remembered in Poland as a man who intended to isolate Poland and force it to accept the revision of the Versailles frontiers. These interpretations clash with each other.

Other viewpoints also present obstacles on the road to true reconciliation. The Polish impression of the German is not flattering. The German appears in the Polish view as an overbearing and often aggressive neighbor who trampled the Poles under his heavy boots during the Nazi occupation and also as one who tried for several centuries to enlarge his national territory at Polish expense. The German view of the Pole is not flattering either. The Poles are viewed as culturally inferior and politically and economically inept. This image is the reflection of the eastward drive and serves retrospectively as its moral and political justification. Of course, no nation likes to be treated as being of lower quality, and the Poles are certainly no exception. André Malraux once said: "To say it all, I do not want them to look at me with contempt . . ."; this is relevant for the Polish reaction as well. Viewpoints of this kind do not help in mutual friendly understanding.

THE WARSAW TREATY

In short, history has heavily mortgaged present German-Polish relations. Does this mean that the Warsaw Treaty of 1970 has no significance for the future of these relations? This would be an incorrect conclusion. The Brandt-Scheel government was the first West German government to acknowledge the existence of the Oder-Neisse frontier and to promise in that treaty not to contest the validity of that frontier for the duration of the existence of the Federal Republic. The territorial claims were renounced, eliminating one former irritant in mutual relations. More important, as long as Poland remains the ally of the Soviet Union and as long as Moscow considers the preservation of the Oder-Neisse frontier as being in its own national interest, the Poles feel sure that no one can endanger their territorial integrity. The division of Germany, supported by the USSR, represents another guarantee of the integrity of the present Polish territory. The FRG, separated from Poland by the GDR and by twenty divisions of a nuclear superpower, cannot, even if it wanted to, practically challenge the survival of the Polish western frontier as it now exists. Incidentally, this points out another area of discord between the German and Polish views. No West German government will ever renounce its aspiration one day to see Germany unified in one state, while the same unification and the emergence of a very strong great power on their western frontier are hardly prospects to cheer up the Poles. At the present time, they feel secure behind the shield of the Soviet alliance and the division of Germany and can look at their relations with the Federal Republic with greater equanimity than would be true otherwise. This is the positive factor in the relations between the FRG and Poland.

Another positive factor is the Polish need for the extension of economic cooperation, be it in trade or joint ventures between West German private corporations and Polish state enterprises. Poland needs this economic cooperation with all advanced capitalist states and in particular with the FRG, the most important West European state insofar as the Polish economy is concerned.

The conclusion of the Warsaw Treaty will certainly stimulate cultural exchanges. As a matter of fact, the West Germans have demonstrated an interest in Polish cultural achievements, especially in literature and music, to a much greater extent than the Weimar Republic had done, while the Poles have always been familiar with German cultural achievements. Hence there exists a foundation for the favorable development of cultural relations. German visitors, who now find no obstacles in coming to Poland, will discover that Poland has an old culture which continues to flourish, that the Poles have been able to reconstruct their land, including the annexed former Eastern German territories, after enormous wartime devastations, with no outside assistance, and, in short, that the Poles are neither culturally inferior nor economically inept. The former unfavorable image might be gradually altered. Polish visitors to the FRG might discover that present-day Germans are very different in their outlook from the Nazi Germans they encountered during the Second World War; their view of the German might also be improved. With the coming new generations in both countries and their more frequent contacts, two former viewpoints might gradually be replaced by new ones.

This is not to say that one can expect miracles. For instance, the Poles have raised the question of damages to be paid to Polish victims of Nazi concentration camps and to forced Polish laborers who were deported during the period of occupation. If the standards for evaluating these damages were to be computed by what the Federal Republic has paid to Israel and to individual Jewish victims, the total would run into billions of German marks. The Poles also resent the fact that West German legislation continues to consider as West German citizens all former German citizens now of Polish citizenship if they or their parents were German citizens prior to the Second World War and if they inhabited Polish-annexed territories at that time. This law extends even to those former German citizens who feel that they are Polish. The FRG would like to repatriate from Poland all the people who consider themselves Germans. The Poles not only question whether all those who want to be repatriated are truly Germans, but they are also reluctant to see the outflow to the FRG of skilled manpower. Hence, the two governments dispute the number of people entitled to repatriation.

Moreover, there remains a profound difference between the two political regimes. The Polish regime, although incomparably more relaxed than the Soviet (relatively greater freedom of expression, private ownership of land by the peasants, and an uneasy coexistence between the Party and the Roman Catholic Church), cannot admit an unrestricted flow of West German and generally Western ideas which could undermine its stability. In addition, friendly Polish overtures to the FRG cannot go further than the Soviet Union would tolerate. The bitter Hungarian and Czechoslovak experiences (in 1956 and 1968) have taught the Poles that they may not diverge from the Soviet pattern of relations with the FRG or other states. The Warsaw Treaty could be concluded only because the Soviet Union had signed its Moscow Treaty with the FRG several months earlier. Only because the Soviet Union found to its own interest the normalization of relations with the FRG could Poland also move in the same direction.

The barometer of Polish-German relations does not as yet point to sunny weather, but it no longer predicts storms.

GERMANY AND POLAND

From War to Peaceful Relations

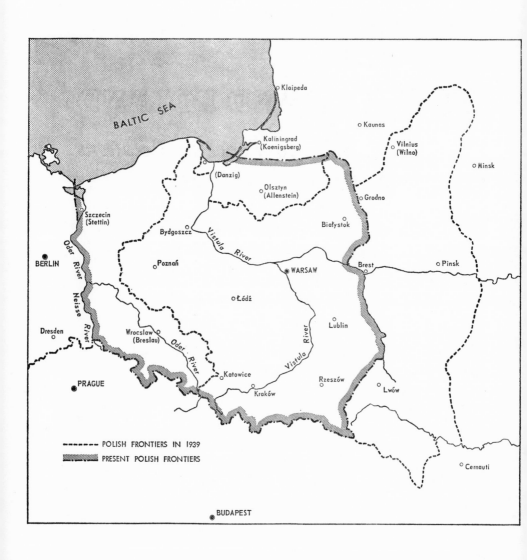

BALTIC SEA

Klaipeda

Kaunas

Kaliningrad
(Koenigsberg)

Vilnius
(Wilno)

Minsk

(Danzig)

Olsztyn
(Allenstein)

Grodno

Szczecin
(Stettin)

Bydgoszcz

Białystok

Oder River

Neisse River

BERLIN

Poznań

Vistula River

WARSAW

Brest

Pinsk

Dresden

Łódź

Lublin

Wrocław
(Breslau)

Oder River

Vistula River

PRAGUE

Katowice

Rzeszów

Lwów

Kraków

Cernauti

- - - - - POLISH FRONTIERS IN 1939

▨▨▨▨ PRESENT POLISH FRONTIERS

BUDAPEST

History

THE EASTWARD AND WESTWARD DRIVES

SINCE THE SECOND WORLD WAR West Germans and Poles have been advancing all sorts of arguments—historical, ethnic, legal, and even archeological—in their dispute over the former East German territories annexed by Poland. These debates of a highly emotional nature have been observed with indifference by the governments of third states who have been interested in the German-Polish postwar quarrel only to the extent that this quarrel might affect their own national interests. What the Germans and the Poles have forgotten is the stark fact, evidenced by the history of international relations, that the stability of a disputed frontier has always depended not on the correct or incorrect arguments of the parties concerned but on the international distribution of power. Whatever the validity of German and Polish arguments, Poland's Oder-Neisse frontier has survived to the present day and has every chance to continue to exist simply because its guarantor, the Soviet Union, is a nuclear superpower.

If one wants to understand the present condition of German-Polish relations, investigation cannot be limited to the problem of the Oder-Neisse frontier. One must become acquainted with the long past of these relations which began to be recorded in the tenth century, when the Polish state emerged in recorded history because of Polish conversion to Christianity. This thousand-year-old history lives in both German and Polish minds.[1]

One may look first at the much longer history of German-Slavic relations as they developed during a period of some fifteen hundred years. Prior to the collapse of the West Roman Empire under the Germanic push, the map of Central and Eastern Europe looked like a mosaic of Germanic, Celtic, and Slavic tribes living together without any definite frontiers between them. Germanic tribes resided among Slavic and Celtic tribes on the lower sectors of the Rivers Oder and Vistula and in what now are Silesia and Czechoslovakia and could be found as far as the Black Sea coast. Everywhere they had other ethnic neighbors.

The ethnic configuration was radically changed by the Germanic assault on the tottering Roman Empire. The Germanic tribes moved westward and southward in the process of conquering Roman territories. The territory between the Rivers Elbe and Oder became an empty space into which the Slavic tribes rushed. During the fifth to seventh centuries the Slavs occupied that territory and settled at several points even beyond the Elbe. This was the Slavic drive westward. For a time a wall of Western Slavic peoples, living between the Elbe and the Oder, was erected. Then in the tenth century this wall began to crumble gradually under the reverse impact of the German drive eastward. Step by step the various West Slavic peoples had to accept German rule. German military progress was marked by the creation of new German principalities and the erection of new German bishoprics. Since the Western Slavs remained pagan at the time of the German assault, they could not count on the support of already Christian Poland. They tried to save themselves by aligning at times with the Poles against the Germans or at others with the Germans against the Poles. The inability of Western Slavs to form one state and the bitter quarrels between the Poles and the Czechs greatly facilitated the success of the German drive between the Elbe and the Oder. By the end of the twelfth century the conquest of Western Slavs was completed, and by the end of the thirteenth century those Slavs were Germanized. Their descendants and the German settlers provided the ethnic foundation for those East Germans who later were to be called Prussians.

The final result was a direct political and ethnic proximity between the Germans and Poles. The German drive eastward continued this time at the expense of the Poles. It ended in the eighteenth century with the partitions of Poland. The final result can be seen by a glance at the map of the German Empire, as erected in 1871. Its eastern frontiers extended far beyond the lower Vistula and, of course, beyond the Oder.

This centuries-old German eastward drive ended with the German defeat in the First World War in which Germany and Russia fought as enemies. That war marked the beginning of the second Slavic westward drive. A Polish state was again erected. The Czechs escaped German-Austrian control by forming their own Czechoslovak state. This westward Slavic drive was interrupted by Hitler with his ambitious eastward drive not only against the Czechs and the Poles but also against the Russians. The German defeat in the Second World War renewed the Slavic westward drive, this time in the form of Soviet expansion. All the former German territories east of the Oder and Neisse were annexed by Poland and the Soviet Union, while the German populations either were expelled or had fled earlier in fear of the advancing Soviet armies. These expulsions also took place in Czechoslovakia and Hungary. The German retreat was not only political because of the shrinkage of German state territory but also ethnic following the outflow of Germans from Eastern Central Europe. Moreover, the former West Slavic habitat now being solidly German, the German Democratic Republic became a Soviet protectorate.

If one were to look back at those eastward and westward historical tides from the perspective of fifteen hundred years, one might ask tentatively whether history has found its equilibrium on the Oder-Neisse frontier, between the ancient Slavic boundary on the Elbe and the later German boundary on the Vistula. This question will be answered by the future distribution of international forces.

The impressive political and cultural German eastward drive was due, first, to German effort but secondly to the lack of cohesiveness of Slavic resistance. Western Slavs fought among themselves and were not supported by either the Poles or the Czechs. The Polish-Czech quarrels also played into German hands. Polish-Russian disagreements and wars led to German-Russian cooperation and, finally, in the second half of the eighteenth century, to the partitions and disappearance of the Polish state. Afterward the Germans and Russians had the same interest in keeping the Polish nation partitioned, and the reappearance of the Polish state in 1918 again provided a reason for Soviet-German cooperation (the other reason was the post–World War I inferior status of a defeated Germany and of the "outcast" Bolshevik Russia), its final result being the Soviet-German agreement in 1939 to proceed with another partition of Poland.

The German attack on the Soviet Union radically changed the course of history. The Russians paid for it with over twenty million dead and the devastation of their western territory. Hitler produced a new historical phenomenon: mutual Russian-German animosity and distrust between the two peoples which had hardly existed even during the periods of divergent foreign policies of the two states as, for example, following the conclusion of the German-Austrian and Russian-French alliances or during the First World War and even at the time of Hitler's tirades against bolshevism (1933–38). The net results were the Soviet and Polish annexations of the former German territories and the division of Germany itself. A bloc of countries controlled by the Soviet Union faced the Germans. The Soviet alliance offered a guarantee to the Poles and Czechs against a renewal of the German eastward drive.

THE MEDIEVAL PERIOD

Poland entered recorded history in the tenth century with the conversion to Christianity of its then ruler Mieszko, who united various Polish tribes under his scepter. A document, written in A.D. 991–92 and called *Dagome Judex,* mentions the extent of his realm's territory. The frontiers reached the Baltic Sea and the Carpathian Mountains, the River Oder up to its mouth, and in the east the River Bug. In other words, Mieszko's state was situated between the West Slavic and East Slavic territories and roughly corresponded to the extent of the present-day Polish state, except for the configuration of the eastern frontier which did not advance in Mieszko's time as far east as it does now. In the northeast the territory known much later as East Prussia (now divided between Poland and the Soviet Union) was inhabited by the Prussians, cousins linguistically and ethnically of the Lithuanians and the Latvians. These Prussians were conquered in the thirteenth century by the German Order of Teutonic Knights and were either exterminated or Germanized. Their German conquerors eventually adopted the name of the conquered.

Mieszko maintained good relations with the German emperors who claimed to be the successors of the Roman emperors. In fact, German kings were crowned as Roman emperors and hence considered themselves to be the superiors of all European rulers. Mieszko acknowledged this claim regarding his own realm. His son, Boleslav the Brave, was stronger than his father and was fortunate in finding a friendly partner in Emperor Otto III, who freed him from this feudal allegiance and promised to intervene in his favor in Rome so that the Pope would allow Boleslav to be crowned as the first king of Poland. Boleslav was crowned king in 1025, this ceremony expressing his wish to be independent of the German emperor. Greater warrior than statesman, Boleslav tried to extend his realm in all directions. He occupied parts of the West Slavic territory beyond the Oder and parts of the Czech territory, and waged war against the Eastern Slavs. The political result of these conquests was the siding of the West Slavs and the Czechs with the Germans and the first German-East Slavic cooperation in history. This happened at a time when Boleslav's relations with Otto III's successors turned into mutual hostility. His lasting success was the acquiring of papal assent to the erection of the Gniezno archbishopric, independent of German ecclesiastical control. Its jurisdiction extended then and for several later centuries to the territory of Mieszko's realm.

The results of Boleslav's imprudent policy of extending his conquests beyond his father's realm appeared soon after his death. His son, Mieszko II, had to face attacks by Germans, Czechs, and East Slavs. After his defeat, due also to the revolt of his brothers, Poland's position was not visibly improved for quite a time, in spite of the interlude of Boleslav the Bold's reign, until the accession to the throne of Boleslav the Wrymouth (twelfth century) who restored his country to its former position.

Boleslav the Wrymouth's last will opened a disastrous period in Polish history. He divided his realm among his sons. His sons did the same so that eventually one kingdom was replaced by dozens of small principalities, independent of each other though all of them ruled by members of the Piast dynasty whose ancestor was Mieszko I. The disappearance of a strong governmental center in the middle of the twelfth century and its continued absence until the middle of the fourteenth century coincided with the final defeat of the Western Slavs and the German advance toward and beyond the Oder. It was also the time of the drive by the German Brandenburg and the Order of Teutonic Knights to cut off Poland from the Baltic coast, and of the loss of Silesia to the Czechs. The Polish-German struggle was to remain in essence the Polish struggle against Brandenburg and the Teutonic Knights until these two merged into the Kingdom of Prussia, which finally won the battle in the second half of the eighteenth century.

It was one of the several Polish Piast princes, Konrad of Masovia, who invited the Order of Teutonic Knights (one of the crusading orders forced to flee to Europe in the face of the Moslem reconquest of the Holy Land) to settle north of the boundaries of his principality. His principality was the victim of recurrent invasions by the pagan Prussians, and he intended to find in the Teutonic Knights a shield of security. The

Knights came in 1230 and by 1283 conquered the Prussian land (more or less what was later called East Prussia). They refused all allegiance to the Polish princes and started their expansion this time at the expense not of the pagan Prussians but of the Christian Poles. They conquered Gdańsk (Danzig) and the Baltic coast west of the lower Vistula, reaching Brandenburg's Baltic coast. This territorial link between the two German states effectively separated Poland from the sea.

At the time when the last but one Piast, Wladyslaw the Short, reunited Poland and was crowned king in the fourteenth century, his realm was much smaller than that of Mieszko I. It did not include the Baltic coast or Silesia where the princes of the Piast dynasty continued to rule but acknowledged the suzerainty of the Czech kings. All the military and political efforts of Wladyslaw and his son, Casimir the Great, to recover the Baltic coast or Silesia failed. Silesia remained under non-Polish rule, Czech or German, until 1945, except for a part of Upper Silesia which Poland obtained in 1921.

The successful German eastward drive in these later Middle Ages was accompanied by peaceful cultural and ethnic advance. German settlers were coming east of the Oder not only to the territories already under the rule of Brandenburg and the Teutonic Order, but also, at the invitation of the various Piast princes, especially to Silesia but also to central and southern Poland. They were welcomed as contributors to the economic development of the country. With them came German religious orders. The ethnic frontier between the Germans and the Poles began to shift eastward as the result of this peaceful penetration. Formerly Polish cities such as Wrocław (Breslau), Szczecin (Stettin), Gdańsk (Danzig), Toruń (Thorn), even Poznań and Cracow as well as smaller Silesian cities were Germanized. The deterioration of the Polish position between Mieszko I's time and the fourteenth century was formidable. The West Slavic protecting wall entirely disappeared. Poland itself was surrounded in the north, west and southwest by the German states: in the north and the west by Brandenburg and the Teutonic Knights, in the southwest by Silesia, part of the Czech crown's possessions; this crown was borne by the Czech kings of German descent who were often at the same time German emperors. The process of Germanization of the former Polish lands was to go on, except that it was stopped in the fourteenth and fifteenth centuries in what remained of the Polish kingdom. However, the image of Poland as it was under the first Piasts was not forgotten by the Poles. This image was to play a great political role following the Second World War.

THE SHIFT OF POLISH INTEREST TO THE EAST

The Polish state, consolidated by the two last Piast Kings, Władysław the Short and Casimir the Great, was soon to enter its period of greatness. Casimir's nephew, Louis, king of Hungary, succeeded him in Poland. On Louis' death one of his daughters, Hedvig, inherited the Polish crown. At that time the Poles considered the Teutonic Order, supported by the German Empire, as the main threat to the territorial integrity of their kingdom. The northeast Teutonic drive also menaced the Grand Duchy of Lithuania, at that time a great power in Eastern Europe. The Lithuanians profited from the Tartar-Mongol invasion of the East Slavic (future Russian, Ukrainian, and Byelorussian) territory and extended their own dominion far into the east. The fourteenth century frontiers of their grand duchy included the present Ukrainian and Byelorussian republics and in addition the most western provinces of the present Russian republic. These frontiers lay not far from Moscow. The Lithuanians were not yet threatened by the Muscovite drive to reunite all East Slavic territories under Russian dominance, but Teutonic military actions threatened to cut them off from the Baltic coast, from which Poland had earlier been cut off. Thus the two states, Poland and Lithuania, found a common interest in a joint effort to halt the advance of the Teutonic Order.

The solution was found in the marriage between Queen Hedvig and the Lithuanian Grand Duke Jagiello, who became the Polish king and the founder of a new dynasty that raised Poland to the status of a great power. The dynastic union between its two neighbors was a challenge to the Teutonic Order, which was in fact a northern German state. Finally, war broke out during which the Poles and the Lithuanians, supported by East Slavic regiments of the Grand Duchy, Czech volunteers, and Tartar detachments, defeated the forces of the Teutonic Order decisively in 1410 at Grunwald (in German: Tannenberg). The military might of the Order was broken, and its anti-Polish and anti-Lithuanian drive was halted. The date of that historical battle, 1410, is remembered by both Poles and Germans but, of course, with different emotions. However, the Polish northern frontier remained unchanged until the next war (1454–66) waged between Poland and the Teutonic Knights. This time Poland, supported by the German gentry and burghers who chose Polish dominion in preference to the oppressive rule of the Order, was successful in regaining its access to the Baltic Sea. The Order's territory was divided into two parts: the lands lying west of the

Vistula and a part of the province east of that river (Ermland or in Polish *Warmja*) became Polish and were later called Royal Prussia; most of the Order's territory east of the Vistula remained its domain, but the Order had to acknowledge Polish suzerainty. Danzig became an autonomous city owing its allegiance to the Polish kings. Poland recovered the Baltic coast and was to retain it until the eighteenth-century partitions.

The union with Lithuania bore visible fruit. It bore other fruit, later fatal for Poland—namely, the new Polish interest in the struggle with the Grand Duchy of Moscow and its successor, the Russian Empire, over the Eastern territories, controlled by Lithuania at the time of the union between the two states. The decision, which looked obviously beneficial in the fourteenth and fifteenth centuries, eventually produced results which no one expected at that time.

The long Polish-Teutonic feud left behind a legacy of national viewpoints. On the one hand, the immense success of the Eastern drive, due to a large extent to the exertions of the Order, bred in the German mind a sense of superiority regarding all Slavs, particularly the Poles. On the other hand, a hostile image of Germans appeared in Polish minds. Had they not lost much of their Piast patrimony because of German encroachments, mostly due to the expansion undertaken by the Teutonic Knights whom a Polish prince had invited to come to Eastern Europe? One can trace back to the fifteenth and sixteenth centuries the Polish saying: "As long as the world remains the world, the German will not be brother of the Pole." The mutual animosity between the two peoples subsided gradually after the consolidation of the Polish northern and western frontiers following the war against the Teutonic Order, 1454–66. The Polish-German feud later revived as a struggle between the Poles and the Hohenzollerns who took over the lead in the Eastern drive.

In the meantime, all Polish efforts to recover Silesia in the fifteenth–seventeenth centuries proved fruitless. Eventually Silesia, as a part of the Czech lands, became the domain of the German Hapsburg dynasty after its members had ascended the Czech throne.

THE HOHENZOLLERNS

The Reformation brought about the dissolution of the Teutonic Order, and East Prussia became the secular domain of the Order's last Grand

Master, Albrecht von Hohenzollern. From that time it was called Ducal Prussia in contradistinction to the Polish province on the Baltic called Royal Prussia. The other Polish neighbor, Brandenburg, was ruled by another branch of the Hohenzollern family.

The first East Prussian duke, Albrecht, was recognized as such by the Polish king on the condition that he and his successors would hold their domain as a Polish fief. He had to pay public homage to the Polish king as his suzerain in 1525. This opened the crucial question as to whether Ducal Prussia should return to the Polish crown after the extinction of Albrecht's family or whether the other branches of the Hohenzollern dynasty would be the successors. The Polish kings, pre-occupied with their wars with the Grand Duchy of Moscow over those East Slavic territories originally conquered by the Lithuanians, committed the fatal mistake in the sixteenth and seventeenth centuries of allowing the other branches of the Hohenzollern dynasty to inherit Albrecht's domain. Eventually, princes of that branch of the family who had ruled in Brandenburg since 1415 became also the dukes of East Prussia. The Brandenburg Elector, John Sigismund, paid homage in 1618 to the Polish king as the first ruler in Ducal Prussia of his branch of the Hohenzollerns. Although Prussia remained legally a Polish fief, Poland was confronted with the same neighbor in the north and the west. One could foresee even at that time that the Hohenzollerns would try to cut off Poland from the Baltic Sea in order to unite their two domains across Polish land.

This prospect became real because of the decline of Poland, which began following the so-called deluge in the second half of the seventeenth century. The term "deluge" is used by Polish historians in reference to the time when Poland was assaulted on all sides by its enemies and when the Swedes occupied almost all Polish lands. Why the Swedes? The wars between Poland and Sweden broke out because of a dynastic quarrel between the Catholic Polish kings of Sweden's Vasa dynasty and the Protestant Swedish kings of the same dynasty. The other reason was the struggle over control of the northeastern Baltic coast of the present Estonian and Latvian republics which, of course, did not exist at that time.

Poland was impoverished by enemy looting and devastation. After the "deluge" it reemerged within practically the same frontiers but immensely weakened. It ceased to be a great power. This political decline was unfortunately accompanied by a cultural decline, arrested only in the middle of the eighteenth century, and by internal disorders. The other consequence of the "deluge" was the concession made in 1657 to the Brandenburg Elector, Frederick William, who was freed from his former vassal obligations regarding Ducal Prussia. From that time the Hohenzollerns ruled that domain as sovereigns. His successor, Frederick, was crowned king to mark the new international status of Prussia, the new name given to all Hohenzollern possessions. What remained was to unite Brandenburg and East Prussia by cutting off Poland from the Baltic Sea. This could be accomplished only through cooperation with the Grand Duchy of Moscow, which was soon to be known as the Russian Empire. This cooperation between two neighbors of Poland began in the seventeenth century and was to last, in spite of mutually hostile intervals, until the Nazi assault on the Soviet Union in 1941. Poland, weak itself, was confronted with the hostility of two of its neighbors, themselves emerging as great powers. The prospect of partition hung over Poland. The only obstacle in the eighteenth century was the fact that, beginning with Emperor Peter the Great, Poland became in fact a Russian protectorate. The question was whether Russia would consent to a partition which would mark the regression of its own influence in Eastern Europe.

THE PARTITIONS

The third neighbor, Austria, eventually joined the two other powers in the partitions despite the fact that in 1683 Vienna had been saved by Polish troops under the Polish king, John III Sobieski, from being conquered by the Turks. The Austrian Hapsburgs demonstrated the truth of the maxim that gratitude was unknown in international politics. They were to demonstrate it once again by their hostility to Russia in spite of decisive Russian military assistance in quelling the Hungarian revolt against the Hapsburgs in 1848–49.

Empress Maria Theresa reluctantly decided to take part in the partitions because of pressure by her son, Emperor Joseph II, and other advisers, but she made a prophecy on this occasion: "The partition of Poland will eventually cause the downfall of the whole [Austrian] Monarchy and of the Holy [German] Empire."[2] Whatever she had in mind at that time, her prophecy proved true, though it is impossible to establish a causal relationship between the partitions and the events of the twentieth century. The restoration of Poland in 1918 coincided with the fall of the Hapsburg monarchy, and the second restoration in 1945 was soon after followed by the loss of East German territories and the partition of Germany itself into two states.

The initiator of the first partition was Frederick the Great, a military genius and a skillful statesman. He conquered all of Silesia from Austria. This marked the beginning of the Prussian policy of Germanization of that land. The Polish population at that time still survived in spite of several centuries of non-Polish rule. Ethnic Poles lived east of the Oder in Lower Silesia and formed the mass of population in Upper Silesia. Beginning with the Prussian conquest, the Polish ethnic frontier gradually began to recede.

In 1770 Frederick II proposed to Catherine II, the Empress of Russia, that they proceed with the partition of Poland. Catherine, deeply involved in her Turkish wars, accepted the proposal. Austria joined the two other powers. The first partition took place in 1772 and gave to the Prussian Hohenzollerns the land connecting Brandenburg and East Prussia; Poland lost its access to the Baltic Sea except for the city of Danzig, which remained under Polish protection.

The beginning of the reign of Frederick II's successor, Frederick William II, seemed to be of good portent for Poland. Prussia was bent on a foreign policy independent of Russia. It concluded an alliance with Poland against Russia in 1790. This alliance was important for the Poles who, culturally regenerated, were proceeding with vital political and social reforms in order to make of their country a modern state with a strong central government and a strong army. This objective could be reached only by thwarting Russian opposition and terminating Russian influence in Poland. For a moment it seemed as though Poland, given a necessary respite, would once again become a viable state. Catherine II decided to solve the problem by reaching an accommodation with Prussia. The Polish ally, Prussia, and Russia proceeded in 1793 with the second partition. Prussia gained Danzig and some of the western Polish provinces. The Prussian alliance proved fatal.

Polish military resistance, led by Thaddheus Kościuszko, a hero of the American War for Independence, failed in the face of the overwhelming superiority of the Russian and Prussian troops, soon joined by Austrian troops. The whole country was occupied. The third and final partition in 1795 extinguished the Polish state, one of the oldest in Europe. The new Russian frontier as traced in 1795 corresponded roughly with the present Polish-Soviet frontier, except for Eastern Galicia which fell to the Austrians. A large part of the Polish population remained in those territories annexed by Russia, and great Polish cultural centers passed under Russian rule. However, the ethnically Polish provinces were shared in the three partitions between the two German states, Prussia, and Austria. Warsaw became a Prussian provincial city, while the other capital of Poland, Cracow, came under Austrian rule.

What were the reasons for the partitions? One was the weakness of the Polish state, due to domestic causes. This argument, used by the partitioning powers, was, however, no longer valid at the time of the partitions, because at that time the Poles were reforming their state and society and, given the necessary time, would have rebuilt a viable state. Actually the reforms carried out by the last generation of independent Poles prompted their neighbors to hasten the partitions. The other reason was the desire of the partitioning powers to aggrandize their dominions with a low, if any, degree of military effort. The Poles looked at the partitions as an act of force, immoral and unjust. From that time, they dreamed of restoring their state. This in turn consolidated the friendship among the three partitioning powers. They had the same interest in holding to their territorial acquisitions and thwarting Polish attempts to regain their own state.

THE GRAND DUCHY OF WARSAW AND THE CONGRESS OF VIENNA

Napoleon's victories over the three partitioning powers brought to the Poles a partial and ephemeral restoration of their national statehood. Napoleon created the so-called Grand Duchy of Warsaw in 1807, out of the main part of Prussian acquisitions in 1772–95. Warsaw and Poznań were again placed under Polish administration. Danzig became an autonomous city under French protection. In 1809 defeated Austria was forced to cede to the Duchy the main part of its acquisitions in 1772–95. Altogether 4.3 million Poles lived under their own government between 1809 and 1812. It is interesting to note that the Poles did not resent Napoleon's decision to place his ally, the king of Saxony, on the ducal throne. They remembered that their last Constitution of 1791, which replaced the elective by a dynastic monarchy, called the Saxon family to the Polish throne. They hated the Prussians and Austrians but evidently not the other Germans.

The very existence of the Duchy of Warsaw was a challenge to the partitioning powers, and it could survive only as long as Napoleon's military star was shining. His defeat in 1812 ended the Duchy's life.

However, its fleeting existence dashed to the ground the hopes of the partitioning powers that the name of Poland would be extinguished forever. The Polish problem was on the agenda of the Congress of Vienna (1814–15) and was to remain of interest to European chanceries throughout the following hundred years. The Paris Peace Conference, which followed the First World War, had to deal with that problem. Likewise the United States, Britain, and the Soviet Union had to do so during and following the Second World War. Each time the great powers had to take into account Polish aspirations, at least to some extent.

The Congress of Vienna was the first such meeting to consider the existence of the Polish nation. The immediate question was what to do with the former Duchy of Warsaw: was it to remain within its Napoleonic frontiers under the scepter of the Russian Emperor Alexander I, or were Prussia and Austria to recover at least a part of the Polish territories seized in the partitions? Alexander's ambition to become the Polish king within the territory of the Warsaw Grand Duchy was supported by Prussia, which was to be compensated by the annexation of the whole kingdom of Saxony. Opposition came from Britain, Austria, and France. Britain, preoccupied as usual with the Continental balance of power, dreaded a Russian advance far into Central Europe. Austria shared the same fear and wanted no Prussian aggrandizement north of its own frontiers. It is more difficult to explain the French position. Talleyrand, the main French delegate, helped Austria and Britain in the effort to cut down the territory of the former Warsaw Grand Duchy. Eventually Alexander I had to accept a compromise solution: the western part of the Duchy went to Prussia and the southwestern part to Austria. The central part with Warsaw was erected into the so-called Polish kingdom to be ruled by the Russian emperors. Prussia annexed only northern Saxony but was compensated by a vast territory on the Rhine. France now had a common frontier with Prussia. It was to pay a heavy price for Talleyrand's misjudgment; Prussian troops, helped by other German troops, crossed the Rhine in 1870 and inflicted a crushing defeat. France lost Alsace-Lorraine, annexed by the German Empire which was founded in 1871.

The Congress of Vienna guaranteed to the Poles that the Polish Kingdom, united with Russia by the same dynasty, would be an autonomous constitutional state, that the Poznań province would have self-government under Prussian rule, and that the ancient Polish capital, Cracow, would become a republic under the protection of the three partitioning monarchies. Polish territory was partitioned for the fourth time, but the existence of the Polish nation was acknowledged by the Vienna Congress.

It took the partitioning powers only a few decades to discard concessions made to the Poles. Our purpose being to survey German-Polish relations, we may mention only marginally that the autonomy of the Polish kingdom was terminated by Russia after the Polish insurrection in 1830–31, and every trace of Polish cultural and political rights was swept away following the second insurrection in 1863–64. By its neutrality Prussia helped Russia to suppress the two Polish insurrections. Russian Poland was ruled thereafter as just another province of the Russian Empire until the outbreak of the First World War. Prussian Poland also lost its autonomy and was soon faced with Prussian efforts to Germanize that part of Poland. The same was true of Austria, which absorbed Cracow in 1846 and also followed the policy of Germanization. Actually, the Austrian regime was the most oppressive of the three in the first half of the nineteenth century.

THE POLISH WESTERN COMPLEX

The short-lived Duchy of Warsaw left a legacy to the Poles. They regained their statehood, owing to French military victories. This created two complexes in Polish minds. The one, which seemed to be a daydream until 1914, consisted of the hope that another general European war would bring them independence. The other was the widespread conviction that they would be liberated by the Western powers. The three partitioning powers were linked together by having the same interest in preserving their hold on the Polish provinces; this left little room for the hope that the Poles could find support in any of the three capitals. But people who despair find their moral strength in hope against all hopes. Salvation was to come from the West, principally France.

This Western complex was rooted in a misconception. What was forgotten was that the Western powers—whether France, Britain, or later the United States—had no direct interest in the East European zone. The problem of the Poles and other East Europeans was seen in the Western chanceries only in relation to their policies toward the great powers, Germany, Austria until 1918, and Russia. Depending on the times, the Western powers remained indifferent to Polish aspirations, as they did between 1815 and the outbreak of the First World War, or became interested in the Polish problem only in light of their German and Russian policies. This naked fact remains true today and for the same reason. Poland appears to the West always as a subordinate factor in overall policies toward Germany and Russia.

This proposition can be illustrated by Western attitudes toward the present Polish western frontier. In 1945 the Germans were regarded with resentment and suspicion, and the concept of the Grand Alliance still survived. The United States and Great Britain acceded at the Potsdam Conference to the Soviet proposal that Polish administration should extend to the Oder-Neisse. The former East German provinces were not included within the occupation zones of any of the great powers, while the latter agreed that ethnic Germans should be expelled from Poland. In September 1945 the Allied Council for Germany interpreted the Potsdam decision to provide that the expulsions should include the Germans from both prewar Poland and the former East German territories east of the Oder-Neisse. In other words, the United States and Britain implicitly accepted the Oder-Neisse line as the Polish western frontier since it was inconceivable to sponsor mass expulsions of Germans from a territory destined eventually to return to Germany.

Soon after, the Cold War began. Both the American and British governments started to contest the validity of the Polish Oder-Neisse frontier. France broke out from the united Western front when General de Gaulle inaugurated a policy generally independent of the United States. He declared in 1959 that a reunited Germany should remain within the present frontiers, including the eastern frontiers. His own and all later French official statements clearly meant the recognition of the Oder-Neisse frontier. However, the United States and Britain continued to support the West German view that a future peace conference, attended by the government of a reunited Germany, should review the German-Polish frontier. The fact that neither the FRG nor the two Western powers could modify that frontier against Soviet wishes brought about a change. During the sixties, neither Washington nor London questioned the existence of the present western frontier of Poland. Finally, détente in Europe, greatly helped by the policies of President Nixon and German Chancellor Brandt, brought about American and British acceptance of that frontier, at least for the duration of the existence of the FRG.

All these successive modifications in Western views had nothing to do with Western-Polish relations, but were dictated by Western policies toward the USSR and Germany. Of all the great powers, only Germany and Russia have always had a direct and vital interest in Poland and in Eastern Europe generally.

DEVELOPMENTS IN THE SECOND HALF OF THE NINETEENTH CENTURY

While the Polish situation started to deteriorate quickly during the second half of the nineteenth century, both under Prussian (later all-German) and Russian rule, new developments in Austria brought an unexpected improvement. Austria, defeated by France in Italy in 1859 and by Prussia in 1866, had to make domestic concessions to some of its various non-German nationalities (actually the majority of the population). Hungarians received equal treatment with German Austrians in 1867. The Austrian Empire, formerly ruled predominantly by Germans, became the Austro-Hungarian Dual Monarchy. The Poles were granted self-government in Austrian Poland (Galicia), which became the only part of Poland where Poles were not discriminated against and had full cultural liberty. Moreover, Poles from that time started to play more than a minor role in Vienna itself, sometimes occupying important positions in the Austrian government. Austria was looked at with sympathy by the Poles, who could expect nothing from Russia or Germany.

The unification of Germany in 1871 had a decisive influence on the Polish view of the Germans. Until that time they saw their enemy in Prussia. Now they were confronted with the hostile policies of the all-German government. The distinction between the Prussians and other Germans lost its former meaning. However, the foreign policy of the German Empire was to open new and hopeful vistas for the Poles. Bismarck committed a fateful error in 1878 and 1879 by siding with Austria against Russia. The former pattern of close cooperation among the three partitioning powers was broken. After the partitions, they had been united by their desire to retain their Polish provinces. Except for the short interlude at the Congress of Vienna, this political cooperation between the three powers had continued throughout most of the nineteenth century. The Austro-Russian competition in the Balkans was to undermine this cooperation. Bismarck sided against Russia and with Austria in 1878 at the Congress of Berlin, which dealt with the Balkan question. In 1879 he concluded an alliance with Austria. It is true that in 1887 he negotiated the so-called re-insurance treaty with Russia, but this equivocal policy could not be continued indefinitely. After Bismarck's dismissal, William II denounced the re-insurance treaty. Germany sided definitely with Austria against Russia which had no choice but to conclude a counter-alliance with France. Eventually, this led to the emergence of the two mutually hostile coalitions: the Triple Alliance of Germany, Austria, and Italy versus the Triple Entente of Russia, France, and Britain. The partitioning powers were aligned with either of the two opposite camps. The former Polish dream of a liberating European war seemed now to become quite realistic.

THE ETHNIC FRONTIER

How was the ethnic Polish-German frontier fluctuating during the post-partition period and until the First World War? One must, first of all, note that any nationality can fully maintain its collective identity and protect itself against encroachments by another nationality only if its members live within a state controlled by their own nationality. The Poles had been deprived of that instrument, the nation-state, since the thirteenth century in regard to Silesia and since the eighteenth-century partitions in regard to the whole territory which they inhabited. Germanization could proceed unhampered in the Austrian and Prussian parts of Poland. A governmental commission in Vienna had said in 1790 (following the first partition) that "the true interest of the Austrian Monarchy demands the gradual transformation of the Polish population into a German one . . . in other words, its denationalization." This policy was followed by the Austrian government until the 1870s, though without noticeable success. The problem was far more serious in Prussian Poland.

Prussian policy employed two weapons: Germanization of the Poles and colonization by German settlers of the provinces detached from Poland. The ethnic situation was rather complex prior to the partitions because German-speaking people lived in Poland and Polish-speaking in Prussia (in the southern belt of East Prussia and in Silesia). Frederick II started the consistent policy of Germanization in Silesia after having conquered it from Austria. This policy was followed by his successors. Polish-speaking people completely disappeared by the middle of the nineteenth century in Lower Silesia. They continued to form the bulk of the population in Upper Silesia until the process of industrialization, followed by urbanization, started to have its linguistic effects. Germans began to come to the Silesian cities, while many Poles, who were leaving their villages to become industrial workers or miners, were gradually adopting the German language. Moreover, the Polish-speaking Upper Silesians, who lived for centuries separated by a political frontier from the country of their ancestors, had a very feeble awareness of belonging to the Polish nation. Only in the second half of the nineteenth century could one observe a new phenomenon, the growth of Polish national consciousness among the Polish-speaking Upper Silesians.

The population of Royal Prussia (called West Prussia after 1772) was ethnically mixed in 1772, at the time of the annexation by Prussia. For lack of statistics one can only presume that the population there was half Polish and half German-speaking. In the other Polish provinces annexed by Prussia in the eighteenth century and retained after the Napoleonic Wars (Western Poland) the Poles were the dominant part of the population though a sizeable German-speaking minority existed. The influx of German officials and settlers following the partitions increased the percentage of ethnic Germans everywhere.

Bismarck, in his capacity first as Prussian Prime Minister and later as German Chancellor, has been the subject of contradictory opinions on the part of German and Polish historians. As the unifier of Germany he fully deserves the foremost place in the German pantheon. He was an enemy of the Poles and is seen as such by Polish historians. This points out the impossibility of completely harmonizing German and Polish history textbooks. Other examples abound. For instance, how can German and Polish historians agree on the historical role of the Teutonic Knights or of Frederick II, the initiator of the partitions of Poland but also the hero of the German eastward drive?

Bismarck was right in thinking that the restoration of an independent Poland would immediately raise the problem of the return to Poland of the territories seized in the eighteenth century. He said at the time of the Polish insurrection against Russia in 1863: "The resurrection of an independent Polish state between Silesia and East Prussia with its logical demand for the Posen province and the mouth of the Vistula, indispensable for the Polish independence, would present a constant threat to Prussia. In addition to Posen and Danzig Poland would soon turn toward Silesia and East Prussia. The maps, which express the dreams of the Polish insurgents, include Pomerania as a Polish province with access to the Oder." The events which followed the Second World War proved him right.

Bismarck saw remedy in the Germanization of Polish-speaking Prussian subjects in order to preclude future Polish claims. A Prussian Colonization Commission was created in 1886 with the task of buying large Polish and German estates and distributing them to the imported

German peasants. However, the results of the activity of that Commission between 1886 and 1915 were not impressive. Polish was eliminated altogether as the language of instruction in all Prussian schools. Other measures were taken to put pressure on nationally conscious Poles. The effect was the usual one. Whenever a national group is subjected to discrimination and pressure it responds by stronger feelings of national identity. This happened also in Prussian Poland where the Poles began their peaceful self-defense by forming all sorts of associations, economic and cultural.

According to official German statistics of 1910, the Upper Silesian population was divided into 53 percent Polish-speaking and 40 percent German-speaking, the remainder speaking other languages, mainly Czech. The distribution of languages was different in the cities from that in the villages. Of the urban population 70.5 percent spoke German; 68.1 percent of the rural population spoke Polish. According to the same statistics, 68.1 percent of the population in the Posen province spoke Polish, and in the other province of pre-partition Poland, the Bromberg province, 50.3 percent used Polish. In West Prussia, annexed by Prussia in 1772, the Germans dominated, by 71.1 percent in the Danzig province, and by 58.8 percent in the Marienwerder province. Of course, these statistics included the German officials and military men, stationed in those various provinces.

The Germans were alarmed in the decades preceding the First World War by what they called the *Ostflucht,* the flight from the East, seeing in it the threat to their ethnic eastern frontier. This phenomenon was due to economic reasons. The rapid industrialization of Western Germany after 1840 attracted large emigrations from Eastern Germany. During the period of 1840 to 1910 the total of emigrants from the Eastern provinces (East and West Prussia, Pomerania, Posen, and Silesia) reached the figure of 3,728,000. A number of those emigrants went overseas, mainly to the United States, but over 2.5 million resettled in Western Germany. Polish-speaking people participated in both emigrations but less than the German-speaking people. A Polish minority suddenly appeared in the Rhineland and Westphalia and eventually, prior to the First World War, numbered half a million persons. Their descendants continue to live there, some still retaining their national consciousness.

The gap in the East German agricultural labor force had to be filled mainly by Polish seasonal workers coming from Russian and Austrian Poland. The Germans saw in this movement of population a Polish ethnic offensive.

Industrialization in Upper Silesia had the opposite effect. Many Polish-speaking Upper Silesians, who were coming from the rural areas to become industrial workers or miners and were surrounded in their new habitat by the German-speaking urban population, began to adopt the German language and eventually acquired the German national consciousness—hence the great number of Upper Silesians with Polish family names who felt or feel that they are Germans.

The ethnic struggle between the Germans and the Poles was based on mutual fear. The Germans were told by their politicians and intellectuals that they were threatened by the Slavic flood, in particular Polish. The Poles resented German efforts at Germanizing their countrymen. Incidentally, the policy of Germanization and discrimination brought about the rebirth of national consciousness among most of the Polish-speaking Upper Silesians, as proved by the events which followed the First World War.

THE FIRST WORLD WAR

The European war broke out in 1914. It revived international interest in the Polish question as the Napoleonic wars had done. The partitioning powers fought in opposite camps. Since Britain and France were allied with Tsarist Russia, the Poles could only adopt either pro-Austrian or pro-Russian orientation. This they did. Those who favored the Russian orientation hoped that a victorious Russia would annex the Prussian and Austrian provinces held by the Central Powers, and that a united Poland would be ruled by the Romanov dynasty as an autonomous unit, like the Polish kingdom had been between 1815 and 1830. They did not receive much encouragement from the tsarist government until the time when Russian military defeats forced that government to be more accommodating.

The pro-Austrian orientation, which expected the victory of the Central Powers, consisted in the hope that Austria, friendly to the Poles, would annex Russian Poland and unite it with Austrian Poland as an autonomous entity. The Austro-Hungarian monarchy would then be transformed into a triune monarchy with Austrians, Hungarians, and Poles as co-masters. This concept implied the renunciation of claims to the German-held Polish provinces.

Tsar Nicholas II conceded only on December 25, 1916, that a Russian victory would bring about a free Poland composed of Russian,

German, and Austrian parts but ruled by his dynasty. This promise freed the hands of the Western powers. President Wilson said in his message of January 22, 1917, that "a united, independent and autonomous Poland should exist." The British and French governments also started showing an active interest in the Polish question. The Provisional Russian government, formed after the first revolution of February 1917, declared on March 30, 1917, that an independent Poland, linked to Russia by a military alliance, should be created from all the territories inhabited by the Polish ethnic majority. The second revolution of October 1917 was followed on August 29, 1918, by cancellation by the Bolshevik government of the partition treaties. Actually, the conclusion of a separate peace treaty with the Central Powers on March 3, 1918, in which Soviet Russia renounced all claims to Russian Poland, the civil war, and foreign intervention, silenced the Russian voice in inter-Allied councils.

In the meantime, Germany and Austria started to compete with Russia in using the Polish card to their advantage. They did it reluctantly due to the cautious German attitude. The Austrians were the weaker partner and were steadily losing influence. On November 5, 1916, the two governments published a proclamation which promised to erect Russian Poland into a constitutional monarchy. On September 15, 1917, they allowed for the formation of a Polish government for Russian Poland with an extremely limited domestic autonomy. The Austrian solution was discarded, and the unification of Russian and Austrian Poland was no longer taken into consideration. Actually, the German government and the Military High Command considered a German solution which would make of Russian Poland a German protectorate but within a territory smaller than that which existed prior to the outbreak of the war. A large belt along the former German-Russian frontier was to be cut off and annexed by Germany. Germany was reluctant till the end to concede anything meaningful to the Poles. By 1917 the pro-Central Powers orientation lost former adherents among the Poles.

RESTORATION OF THE POLISH STATE

The weakening of Russia, the disintegration of the Austro-Hungarian monarchy, and the military defeat of Germany left the solution of the Polish problem to the Western powers. The wildest hopes of former

Polish generations were fulfilled. The partitioning powers were unable to prevent the resurrection of the Polish state after the lapse of one hundred and twenty-five years. The Polish eastern frontiers were finally determined after the war with Soviet Russia in the Peace Treaty concluded in 1921. The western frontiers were to be determined by the Western powers in the treaty of peace to be concluded with defeated Germany.

The point of view of the United States was determined in Point 13 of President Wilson's famous message of January 8, 1918: "An independent Poland should be erected. It should include the territories inhabited by the uncontestably Polish population, should have a free and secure access to the sea, and its political and economic independence and territorial integrity should be guaranteed in an international treaty." The American attitude was friendly to Polish claims in accordance with Wilson's belief in the principle of free determination for European nationalities.

France was even more sympathetic, because France thought that Poland would be a sort of counter-weight to Germany as a substitute for Russia, whose Bolshevik government was thoroughly disliked in Paris.

Britain followed the same policy which it had observed at the time of the Congress of Vienna. In 1814–15 the British ally, Russia, appeared to be the strongest among the victors, and its territorial acquisitions in Poland should have been limited in the name of the Continental balance of power. The British government now considered France, its ally, as the dominant power on the Continent since the victory over Germany. French influence in Eastern Europe should be restrained insofar as possible, while the power of Germany should be preserved as a counter-weight to France. The net result was that Britain acted as a brake on French and American endeavors to allocate to Poland the former German provinces and free access to the Baltic Sea. Later events proved the British error in the prognostication of the future European balance of power. France, exhausted by the war, never became a dominant power. Germany, soon after its defeat, started emerging as a factor that eventually dominated the European scene. During the Second World War the British people had to pay for the mistake committed by their government in 1918–20. The two world wars, which in Europe were German wars, undermined British strength and contributed to the disintegration of the British Empire and the downgrading of Britain's international status which we witness today.

The American-French-British tangle resulted in the disappointment of former Polish hopes. The decision regarding the Polish northern frontier created a situation ominous for Poland. Danzig, which initially was to be incorporated into Poland, was erected into a Free City, ruled by its German population who resented Polish economic rights there and the cutting off of political ties to Germany. One could have foreseen that Danzig would eventually become a bone of contention between Poland and Germany. It is true that Poland received a narrow access to the Baltic Sea, a sort of corridor between Germany on the one hand, and Danzig and East Prussia on the other. Whoever knew history could predict that Germany, like Prussia in former times, would try to eliminate that corridor and cut off Poland from the Baltic. Otherwise, the new Polish-German frontier followed the 1772 border line but with several pieces of territory remaining with Germany.

The fate of two German provinces was to be decided by plebiscites: Upper Silesia and the southern belt of East Prussia, where large Polish-speaking minorities existed. The East Prussian minority, the so-called Masurs (the descendants of Polish emigrants from Masovia, the central part of Poland) were Protestants and thus distrustful of a predominantly Catholic Poland. Upper Silesia presented a different problem. A portion of Polish-speaking Upper Silesians considered themselves loyal Prussians. They distinguished between the two allegiances: the one to the ethnic group and the other to the state. However, the majority of Polish-speaking Upper Silesians proved their ardent wish to be united with their countrymen in Poland by staging three armed insurrections against the German administration and by fighting desperate battles against the German so-called volunteer brigades (in 1919, 1920, and 1921).

The year of the plebiscite in the southern portion of East Prussia, 1920, was the worst time for Poland. It was the year of the Polish-Soviet war, marked until the middle of August by Polish defeats. It seemed on July 11, the date of the plebiscite, that the whole of Poland would be overrun by Soviet troops and a Soviet regime installed. This certainly influenced the results of the plebiscite. In any event, these results were in sharp contrast to the data of the official German census of 1910. In one of the plebiscite districts 97.8 percent voted for Germany while 43.72 percent had declared Polish to be their language ten years earlier. In the other district 92.4 percent cast their ballots for Germany, while 15.94 percent had said in 1910 that Polish was their language.[3] Another German census taken in 1925 listed 110,456 Polish-speaking people in the plebiscite area, but only 14,927 people voted for Poland in 1920. This contradiction was due not only to the uncertain position of Poland in July 1920 but also to the fact that Protestant

Masurs had no strong feeling of community with the Catholic population of Poland itself. Another factor was the several centuries of life under German rule. The ancestors of these Masurs came originally from central Poland as immigrants to East Prussia, which had never been an integral part of Poland. They had been converted to the Protestant religion at the time of the secularization of the Teutonic Order.

The results of the plebiscite in Upper Silesia, which took place in 1921, also contrasted with the figures of the census in 1910. This census listed 1,250,000 Polish-speaking people and 880,000 German-speaking (adults and minors). Yet 706,820 (59.6 percent) of ballots went to Germany and only 479,414 (40.4 percent) to Poland.[4] These results were due to two factors: the weakness and uncertain future of the Polish state, reborn only two and a half years earlier, and the many centuries of political separation of Upper Silesia from Poland. A sizeable portion of Polish-speaking people felt a strong allegiance to the German state. Both in East Prussia and in Upper Silesia the language proved not to be an infallible index of national feelings. This was confirmed in 1925 when a new German census listed 542,508 persons in the German part of Upper Silesia as Polish-speaking.

The Western powers, after consulting the League of Nations, decided to divide Upper Silesia according to the results of the plebiscite in each of particular counties. One part was allocated to Germany and another to Poland.

The reborn Polish state found itself in a precarious position. First, at least one-third of its population was composed of national minorities (Germans, Ukrainians, Byelorussians, Lithuanians, and Jews). Germans themselves accounted for 750,000 persons. The original number of Germans in the former Prussian provinces amounted to 1,134,000, but this figure included the military people stationed there and state officials. After the Polish annexation of those provinces, 378,055 military men and officials left. Another 225,000 Germans opted for Germany and also left Poland. Hence, 530,945 Germans remained there; the remainder of 750,000 Germans lived in the other parts of Poland which had not belonged to Germany prior to the First World War.

The weakness of Poland was due to the existence of national minorities who resented being ruled by the Poles and to bad relations with its two big neighbors. The Soviet Union was not happy with the Polish eastern frontier (this was the legacy of the century-old Polish-Russian feud over the allegiance of Ukrainians and Byelorussians, a feud inherited from the fourteenth-century union between Poland and Lithuania). However, the Soviet government never officially voiced any demands for the revision of the frontier. The two countries mutually disliked each other's regimes. To say the least, the relations were distrustful and cool.

THE WEIMAR REPUBLIC

Relations with Germany were in much worse shape. None of the German political parties, including the Communist Party, was reconciled to the new eastern frontier. All the successive governments of the Weimar Republic hoped for the return, total or partial, of the former Prussian territories. The least they wanted was the reincorporation of the Free City of Danzig, of the so-called Polish corridor, and of the Polish part of Upper Silesia. Some among the politicians and generals, in particular General Hans von Seeckt, Commander-in-Chief of the German army, thought that the best solution would be the total disappearance of the Polish state. As the Poles were unanimous in refusing any territorial concessions, the territorial feud poisoned mutual relations throughout the existence of the Weimar Republic.

The paradox of German-Polish relations following the Second World War consisted of the fact that the governments and political parties of the Federal Republic voiced for many years a claim for a return to the 1937 frontiers, *i.e.*, to the boundaries established after the First World War, which the Weimar Republic had considered unacceptable. Of course, the 1937 frontier was incomparably better for Germany than the Oder-Neisse frontier. However, this claim by the Federal Republic ignored the argument used by the Weimar Republic that East Prussia should not be separated by the Polish corridor from the main German body. Also the existence of the Free City of Danzig proved untenable. The restoration of 1937 frontiers was an unrealistic claim. Poland either had to have a secure access to the Baltic which meant that Danzig and East Prussia would be lost for Germany, or Poland would have to lose its access to the sea. Hitler tried to impose the latter solution and failed. The Soviet Union imposed the former solution, while taking for itself the northern part of East Prussia.

The difficulty in agreement by German and Polish historians on one version of history can be illustrated, among other things, by the respective estimates of Gustav Stresemann, for several years Foreign Minister of the Weimar Republic. His image in the Federal Republic is that of a venerated statesman. His skillful policy of friendly relations with the Western powers, including France, as well as with the Soviet Union, aimed at the international isolation of Poland. He hoped that Poland would then be compelled to retrocede Danzig, the corridor, and the Polish part of Upper Silesia. He also favored the tariff war against Poland, because, as he said, an impoverished Poland would have no strength to withstand German pressure. He remains in Polish minds a malevolent personality.

The official revisionist propaganda of the Weimar Republic was supported by the German press, the associations of those Germans who had left Poland after the First World War, various research institutes, and the government-backed organization for the protection of Germans abroad. It is interesting that the same pattern was revived after the Second World War with the associations of refugees and expellees from Eastern Europe and the several research institutes on Eastern Europe, all concentrating on the revision of the postwar frontiers.

During the existence of the Weimar Republic only a few of the better-known Germans showed any sympathy for Poland. Thomas Mann was one of them. Poles were presented in domestic propaganda as a nation of much inferior culture, politically anarchic, and economically inept. This sort of propaganda, inflaming German nationalism, contributed to the eventual success of the Nazi movement.

The existence of the German minority in Poland was also used as an argument for the revision of frontiers. The Polish minority in Germany, though also numerous, enjoyed no international protection except for those in Upper Silesia. The German minority were placed under the protection of the League of Nations wherever they lived in Poland. In 1919 the Western powers imposed on Poland a treaty on the international protection of minorities, believing that one could not trust Poland in this respect. They imposed no such treaty on Germany, except for Upper Silesia, because it seemed improper to treat a great power in this manner, but also because no one in the West expected that a cultured and law-abiding Germany would mistreat its minorities. History proved otherwise. It was Germany, not Poland, that exterminated millions of Jews, Poles, and other Europeans in its concentration camps.

The associations of the German minority, acting in agreement with the governments of the Weimar Republic, flooded the League of Nations with their complaints, whose purpose was not only to eliminate any Polish discrimination but also to keep the territorial problem open. If the Germans in Poland were unhappy, the logical alternative was to re-annex the territories which had belonged to Germany.[5]

NAZI GERMANY

The two nations felt during the interwar period that they were mutual enemies. However, Adolf Hitler's coming to power in 1933 seemed paradoxically to announce a change for the better in German-Polish relations. Poland was no longer the first item on the agenda as it had been under the Weimar Republic. Hitler, the most aggressive and nationalistic German politician, seemed to intend to improve relations with Poland.

He wanted to proceed step by step in his policy of expansion, and that expansion did not have to begin in Poland, as was generally believed in the West. His main objective had been defined in his *Mein Kampf*: "We stop the century-old German march toward Southern and Western Europe and turn our eyes toward the lands in the East. . . . If we talk now about new lands in Europe and our role in Europe, we must think in the first place about Russia and those peripheral states dependent on it." He knew that the medieval German push westward and southward left no permanent traces, while the eastward drive had greatly enlarged the German political and ethnic realm. He chose to be a modern Teutonic Knight, carving for the Germans a living space in the East. This concentration on the East would, he thought, save Germany from the peril of fighting the war on both the western and eastern fronts, the reason for German defeat in the First World War.

He declared Bolshevik Russia to be the main enemy of Germany. He stopped cooperation between the German and Soviet armed forces in 1933, overruling the contrary advice of his generals. This cooperation had begun soon after the conclusion of the Rapallo treaty between the Weimar Republic and the Soviet Union in 1922. It served the interests of both countries, because the German armed forces could bypass the restrictions imposed by the Treaty of Versailles on German armaments by using Soviet facilities for testing the forbidden weapons, while the Soviet armed forces benefited from German know-how. This cooperation had an anti-Polish undertone.

Nazi propaganda now poured invectives against bolshevism and the Soviet Union, and Soviet propaganda responded in kind. The sudden deterioration in German-Soviet relations broke for a time the former encirclement of Poland by its two big neighbors.

What was Hitler's design for Poland? It is not easy to be certain. Did he want to appease Poland for the time being while he was preoccupied with other tasks (the rearmament of Germany in 1935 in violation of the Treaty of Versailles, the occupation by the German army in 1936 of the Rhineland which the same treaty had demilitarized, the *Anschluss* with Austria in 1938, the annexation of the Czech Sudetenland in 1938, and finally the conquest of the whole of Czechoslovakia in the following year)? Or had he in mind a German-Polish alliance against the Soviet Union, as his emissaries often mentioned to the Polish government, while the settlement with Poland would be deferred until after the victory over Russia? He might have thought that he would then force the Poles to retrocede all or most former Prussian provinces in exchange for territorial compensation at the cost of vanquished Russia. During the Second World War he offered Odessa to Romania, the German ally. He could have offered the same access to the sea to the Poles, except that this would have been access to the Black instead of the Baltic sea. Whatever passed through his mind at one time might have evaporated at another time when he felt that Germany's international situation was stronger than before. Even if the Polish government had agreed to sign an anti-Russian alliance with Hitler, which they never envisaged, Poland eventually would have been the loser—loser in the case of a German defeat but also in the case of a German victory.

Hitler began negotiations with Poland six months after he became the Chancellor of Germany. On January 26, 1934, the two governments signed the declaration of non-aggression, valid for ten years, and on March 7 of the same year the tariff war, waged by the Weimar Republic, was ended. The Polish government had no reason to decline the German offer of non-aggression. This treaty and the formerly signed similar treaty with the Soviet Union provided at least on paper the guarantee that the two big neighbors did not intend to attack Poland separately or jointly. The conclusion of the declaration of non-aggression took the West by complete surprise. British and French public opinion was accustomed to thinking that Poland was the only or at least the first item on the agenda of German expansion. Moreover, it was inclined to believe that the Versailles German frontier with Poland was unfair and that the so-called Polish corridor should be restored to Germany for the sake of European peace. The fact that Poland, deprived of free access to the sea, would be dependent on German good will for its maritime trade did not deserve much attention. The Western press could not understand why the Nazi government reversed the policy of the Weimar Republic, and started speculating that the two governments had also signed a secret anti-Soviet alliance. In fact, no such understanding was reached between the German and Polish governments; Hitler had simply ordered his priorities differently. While he was advancing step by step in other directions, beginning with the open rearmament of his country, official German propaganda attacks on Poland ceased. The Soviet Union and bolshevism replaced Poland in the role of the Devil in the German drama.

The signature of the pact of non-aggression marked the beginning of illusions in Polish governmental circles. They believed that Poland with its non-aggression pacts, concluded with both neighbors, could remain neutral indefinitely in the German-Soviet quarrel. They even envisaged the formation of a neutral belt of states, starting with the Scandinavian nations and ending with the Balkan countries, a sort of wall between the two great powers. The then Foreign Minister Joseph Beck believed that the apparent change of heart in Berlin was due to the fact that Hitler himself, an Austrian, and most of his top collaborators, non-Prussians, did not nourish the traditional Prussian hatred of Poland and were sincere in their new policy of reconciliation. This short-sighted interpretation of Hitler's policy overlooked two facts: first, that Polish neutrality could not be indefinitely maintained and that Warsaw eventually would have to face the consequences of its refusal to join Germany in the march against the Soviet Union; second, that the aggressive and nationalistic regime in Germany would not remain silent forever regarding the territorial problem, especially the existence of Danzig as a Free City and of the Polish corridor separating East Prussia from the main body of Germany.

Actually, the first difficulties between Poland and Nazi Germany began to appear regarding the Free City of Danzig where the Nazi party came to power. This city had been placed under the protection of the League of Nations, which had to guarantee respect for Polish economic rights, among other things, the custom union with Poland and the Polish right to represent Danzig in international relations. However, the gradual loss of prestige by the League, from which Germany had withdrawn, undermined its actual power in Danzig. The Polish government thought that it could save the Polish position there by negotiating directly with Berlin, whose word was decisive for the Nazi government of the Free City. This new method worked for a time, but it implied Polish recognition that the fate of Danzig was a German-Polish problem. What the Polish government lost sight of was that the German population of the city wanted to be reunited with Germany, while Poland could not consent to lose its economic rights to a free access to the Danzig harbor. The other harbor, built in the meantime at Gdynia on the narrow Polish coast, could not replace the needed facilities of Danzig. An ominous threat of conflict appeared, casting its shadow on apparently normal

German-Polish relations. What was light-heartedly overlooked in Warsaw was Hitler's constant reiteration of his wish to reunite all territories inhabited by Germans. After all, the population of the Free City was German.

The Nazi regime, like that of the Weimar Republic, continued to be interested in the fate of the German minority in Poland. This became the object of frequent German-Polish conversations, since it could no longer be placed on the agenda of the League of Nations in the absence of Germany. This minority, unlike their countrymen in Czechoslovakia, was slow to succumb to Nazi propaganda. Eventually, however, it fell under Nazi leadership. It was to play the role of a fifth column prior to and during the German-Polish war and to assist the German occupation regime in its mistreatment of the Poles. The disloyalty of the German minorities to their states all over Eastern Europe was the reason for the postwar American-British-Soviet decision to expel them from Eastern Europe.

Polish illusions regarding Hitler's good faith were terminated soon after the German occupation of the Czech Sudetenland. The Anglo-French-German-Italian Munich agreement of October 1, 1938, which forced Prague to agree to this territorial cession, was immediately followed by the most deplorable decision by the Polish government to seize the Czech part of the Teshen area. This was as despicable as was the British-French decision to carve out Czechoslovakia for the benefit of Germany. Paris and London believed at that time that they were buying "peace in our time" at the expense of a small country. The two Western democracies sacrificed on the altar of their own national interests a democratic state in Central Europe and a French ally. This proved once again that Western policies toward the Eastern European nations were formulated in the light of their policies toward the great powers in that part of Europe, in this case the policies with regard to Germany. The Polish action alienated British and French public opinion which greeted the Munich agreement with a sigh of relief as proof that war had been averted, and could now vent its indignation on the sinful Polish behavior. Polish public opinion was divided. A part of it approved the action by their government but a part felt indignant that their country took part in the partition of a small neighbor. Those who approved remembered the old quarrels with the Czechs: the Czech military seizure in 1919 of a major part of the Teshen area prior to the decision by the great powers and at a time when Poland was only rising as an independent state and was facing a hostile Soviet Russia; the Czech refusal to form an anti-German alliance (the Czechs believed at

that time that Germany had a territorial quarrel only with Poland);
the inimical Czech attitude toward Poland at the time of the most
dangerous phase of the Polish-Russian war in 1920; Czech sympathy
for Russia which most Poles distrusted; and the existence of a large
Polish minority in the Czech part of the Teshen area. Eventually, the
Polish-Czech quarrels in 1938 and the preceding years benefited only
Germany, as their medieval animosity had done before.

A few weeks after the Munich agreement, on October 24, 1938,
Germany's Foreign Minister Joachim von Ribbentrop confronted the
Polish government with the German demands: the annexation of the
Free City of Danzig and the creation of the German extra-territorial
corridor across the Polish corridor. This German corridor would have
included the railroad lines and highways across Polish territory to provide a direct link with East Prussia. In exchange Poland would have
received the German guarantee, valid for twenty-five years, of its present
frontiers. Hitler reiterated these demands in January 1939 in a conversation with Minister Beck. The Polish government, now distrustful of
Hitler's ultimate intentions, rejected these demands on March 26, 1939.
It understood that if it accepted them, the next demand would be for
the conclusion of an alliance against the Soviet Union and participation
in the war as a German ally. No Polish government could have done
what public opinion unanimously would have opposed, namely, accept
German annexation of Danzig and the restriction on Polish sovereignty
in the maritime province. By March of 1939 the German-Polish war
looked certain.

However, March brought a change of heart in London. Hitler's
armies occupied Czechoslovakia in violation of the Munich agreement.
The British government realized that Hitler's word could not be trusted,
and that the appeasement policy bore bitter fruit. The former concept
of a moderate German expansion in Central Europe, each step agreed
upon with Britain, proved false. Suddenly it dawned on London that
Hitler had a plan of unlimited expansion. The British concept of the
Continental balance of power was in danger of collapsing. The British
government decided to use the Polish case as a warning to Germany.
In April 1939 it gave Poland a guarantee for the safeguard of its vital
interests. The two Western powers were hesitantly abandoning their
policy of appeasement, Britain by being bound to Poland by its guar-
antee, and France by its Polish alliance. The nature of the Polish-
German dispute changed. Hitler faced the prospect that a war against
Poland might become a European war. As his relations with the Soviet
Union were bad, he had to face the possibility of a two-front war, a war

which, as he said in *Mein Kampf*, should have been avoided by Imperial Germany. He tried up to the last day of peace to persuade Britain and France that it would be better to negotiate another Munich at the expense of Poland, but he failed. Eventually, he achieved agreement with the Soviet Union, thus avoiding the prospect of an eastern front.

Polish acceptance of the British guarantee provoked Hitler in April 1939 into denouncing not only the British-German naval agreement but also the Polish-German declaration of non-aggression, which had lasted five instead of ten years.

Poland was the first European country not to buckle under to Nazi German pressure. Further German expansion could no longer proceed peacefully, as it had done between 1938 and 1939. Poland—numerically, economically, and technologically, hence also militarily, much weaker than Germany—preferred to fight rather than surrender without honor. Its geopolitical situation was hopeless. The German armies after the conquest of Czechoslovakia (the Czech lands became a German protectorate, while Slovakia was erected into a German puppet state) were encircling Poland. They could strike simultaneously from the north (East Prussia), from the west (along the long German-Polish frontier), and from the south (German-occupied former Czechoslovakia).

The treaty of non-aggression of 1934 offered just as illusory a guarantee to Poland as had the Prussian alliance of 1790. In both cases the Germans broke their word. The friendly Polish policy toward Germany twice proved fatal. This is not forgotten in Poland to the present day.

The Second World War—Germans in Poland

THE EVE OF THE GERMAN ATTACK

THE PACE OF EVENTS quickened in August 1939. Hitler told his generals on August 22 that the military objective was the "total destruction of Poland." On August 23 he reached a generally unexpected agreement with the Soviet Union. The secret contacts between the two Polish neighbors started in April but did not yield tangible results until August because Hitler was reluctant to abandon his anti-Bolshevik stand. Only the growing probability of a western front finally decided him to enter into a compact with Moscow.

Stalin was conducting two parallel but contradictory negotiations in the summer of 1939. His government negotiated with Britain and France on an anti-German coalition. This was a sort of re-insurance in case the secret contacts with Germany should fail to produce any results. However, there was little that could incline Stalin to enter the war on the side of Britain, France, and Poland. He could foresee the ominous prospect of Germany concentrating its military effort on the eastern front, overrunning Poland, and advancing into Soviet territory. The Western powers could offer him no assurance of effective military help. He could not be sure that the Soviet Union would withstand the German onslaught. His regime might possibly collapse if the German armies were to occupy the main cities, and the Western allies, even if eventually victorious, would certainly have no interest in the reestablishment of this regime. Would Russia itself be saved from disintegration if the various non-Russian nationalities were tempted to overthrow

33

Russian rule owing to the German victory? Finally, the Western powers, committed at that time to respect for the independence of existing European states as a justification for their opposition to Germany, could offer Moscow no territorial gains, as, for instance, the Baltic republics.

The German offer was much more attractive. What Hitler wanted was only Soviet neutrality, and he was ready to pay for it with a handsome price: half of Poland, conquered by German military force, Estonia and Latvia (Lithuania was added in October in exchange for an extension of the German part of Poland), and the Romanian province of Bessarabia. Stalin could ensure peace to his country and, in addition, a large aggrandizement of its territory. He probably expected at that time that the war in the West would last for a long time, and that he would choose the appropriate moment to throw Soviet weight in the balance to reap new gains. Consequently, on August 23 the two governments signed the public treaty on Soviet neutrality, and a secret protocol which divided the Eastern European spoils according to the above-mentioned lines.

Hitler expected that the Western powers, taken aback by his agreement with Moscow, would now be inclined to negotiate another Munich, while he would dictate the terms of that Munich in view of the military victory in Poland. He gave the order to his armed forces to begin hostilities against Poland on August 26. It was a shocking surprise for him that on August 25 Britain signed a treaty of alliance with Poland, undeterred by the Soviet-German treaty. The war on the western front could not be avoided. This caused him to hesitate for a few days. He cancelled the date of the beginning of hostilities and tried again to persuade Britain and France of the necessity of forcing Poland to surrender without battle.

Britain was told that the German government expected the arrival next day, August 30, of a Polish plenipotentiary authorized to accept all the German demands. This was not an invitation to the Polish government to negotiate the terms of an agreement but an ultimatum to be accepted or rejected under the threat of war. The German demands went beyond those of October 1938:

1. Poland had to assent to the immediate German incorporation of the Free City of Danzig.

2. A plebiscite was to be held within the so-called Polish corridor to determine its future. This plebiscite was to be held not earlier than twelve months after Polish acceptance of the ultimatum. Those allowed to vote were to be those Germans and Poles who lived there on January 1, 1918, or had been born there prior to that date. This would allow

the vote to German officials and military men formerly stationed on the contested territory. Polish military personnel, police, and other officials were to quit the territory. The plebiscite was to be carried out under the supervision of Britain, France, Italy, and the Soviet Union. In case the results of the plebiscite were favorable to Germany, the Polish population was to be exchanged for German resettlers coming from the remainder of Poland.

3. In the meantime, *i.e.*, prior to the date of the plebiscite, Germany would build across the plebiscite territory its own railroads and highways to East Prussia and Danzig.

4. The two countries would conclude an agreement on the protection of their respective minorities.

This time Berlin offered no guarantee for the remaining Polish-German frontiers.

It was obvious that these demands, if accepted by Poland, provided for a plebiscite that would be prejudged in advance in favor of Germany. It left open the question of who would maintain order in the contested territory after the withdrawal of Polish authorities. In any event the Germans would enter the territory to build highways and railroads, probably under their own military protection. However, the Polish government was given time to do nothing, because its declared willingness to send a plenipotentiary to negotiate did not prevent Hitler on August 31 from issuing an order for the attack on Poland. The ultimatum was construed to justify the German attack in the eyes of the West. Hitler intended to destroy Poland. Even if Poland had been given time to accept the ultimatum, the Czech experience would have told the Polish government that the plebiscite would never be held. Hitler had begun to talk about the plebiscite in the Sudetenland in 1938, but ended by demanding an outright annexation.

THE GERMAN INVASION

In the early morning of September 1 the German armed forces began their unprovoked attack on Poland. German guilt for the outbreak of the Second World War on September 1, 1939, was established beyond any doubt, unlike the case of the First World War, regarding which historians argued responsibility for the outbreak from both sides.

The bulk of the German armed forces participated in the attack on

Poland. One and a half million German soldiers, supported by 1,400 warplanes, fought against much inferior Polish forces, composed of 840,000 soldiers without an adequate air cover and armed with inferior weapons. Yet the Polish army fought the desperate battles with valor. One could rightly estimate the courage and fighting spirit of the Polish soldiers only in June 1940 when it was possible to compare the September 1939 Polish performance with the French panicky retreat. Yet the French armed forces were both numerically and technologically much superior to the Polish forces. The difference between the two kinds of behavior was due to the Polish will to resist the invader and the French lack of that will. The Polish armies were retreating step by step when the Soviet forces entered Eastern Poland on September 17. Even so, the Poles, encircled on both sides, continued to offer resistance at several places. Warsaw fell only on September 27, and the struggle ended only at the beginning of October. Poland was conquered. The fifth partition took place, the two neighbors dividing the country between themselves.

In the meantime, Britain and France declared war on Germany on September 3. This did not help the Poles because their Western allies missed the opportunity of attacking the depleted German forces on the western front. France paid for it with its defeat in June 1940. However, Hitler now had to face the war in the West. Victory over Poland did not end the war.

THE GERMAN REIGN OF TERROR

Hitler's wrath turned against the Poles who had not surrendered meekly but had entangled him in a general war. They had to pay for this. On September 12 he said that his objective now was the extermination of the Polish nation. Although the war was not ended, he proceeded in violation of international law with the annexation of Danzig and of all Polish provinces lost by Germany following the First World War. Not satisfied with the reestablishment of 1914 eastern frontiers, he also annexed large slices of former Russian and Austrian Poland. The new German frontier ran close to Warsaw and Cracow. The remainder of German-occupied Poland was erected into a German-ruled General Government, a sort of homeland for the Poles.

The Western powers never recognized these annexations, but

Britain was inclined to accept the Soviet annexation of Eastern Poland in the hope that Russia would one day join Britain as an anti-German ally.

The war against Poland was certainly popular in Germany. Those few who had doubts were worried by something else, namely, the possibly disastrous consequences of the war against the West. The anti-Nazi conspirators, who eventually carried out the unsuccessful coup against the Nazi regime in July 1944, opposed that regime for two reasons: humanitarian revulsion against the atrocious and totalitarian methods of the Nazis, and the intention to save as much as possible for Germany from the forthcoming military disaster. After the United States joined the enemies of Germany in 1941 and after the German defeat at Stalingrad, it was clear that Germany would lose the war. The anti-Nazi Germans intended to form a democratic government which would conclude a negotiated peace with the victorious great powers. They even wanted if possible to retain the eastern frontier as it had been in 1914 insofar as Poland was concerned.[1] They continued to think, as the Weimar Republic had done, that the Versailles frontiers were unjust.

The Nazi regime had plans which went much further than mere territorial annexations. The Polish nation was eventually to disappear from Central Europe, and its educated classes were to be exterminated. Polish national culture was to be erased.

The five and a half years of German rule in Poland could rightly be called the reign of terror. The chief of the Gestapo and of the SS, Himmler, proceeded immediately after the end of hostilities with mass expulsions of Poles from the territories annexed by Germany. About 750,000 Poles were expelled to the General Government.[2] Their apartments and farms were taken over, of course with no compensation, by German settlers coming either from prewar Germany or evacuated from the Baltic countries by agreement with the Soviet Union, and later from other German-occupied Eastern territories. These resettlers had no compunction about taking over the expropriated Polish property. Poles from the annexed territories and also from the General Government were deported for forced labor in Germany. The German industrial managers and farmers treated them as slave labor since there was no appeal against mistreatment to any German authority. The total of that Polish labor force reached the figure of 2,460,000.[3] They had to wear an armband with the letter *P*. Seldom did they meet with any sympathy from the German population. Even the German Catholic Church remained silent, although the Poles were Roman Catholics. The Vatican and in particular Pope Pius XII also remained silent, although the fate of the Poles was well known and although several Polish bishops and thousands of priests died in German concentration camps. The Poles, like the Jews, were left to their own fate.

Poles and Jews were deported to the concentration camps, located partly in Germany, but mainly in German-occupied Poland. The Jews, inmates of those camps, faced certain death in the gas chambers. The Poles were condemned to a slow death by starvation and ill-treatment. A large number of them, men and women, were used by German doctors as guinea pigs in dangerous medical experimentation; if they survived, they remained crippled for life. Altogether, out of the prewar Polish population three million Jews and three million Poles were exterminated by the Germans in one or another way. This staggering figure was proportionately the highest human loss inflicted by the Germans on the occupied populations.

Of more than 27 million prewar Polish citizens who lived in German-occupied Poland and who were either Poles or Jews, 6,028,000 perished during the Second World War. This amounted to 22.2 percent of Poles and Jews who lived under the German occupation. The two countries which were next on this tragic list, Yugoslavia and the Soviet Union, lost more than 10 percent of their populations.

Only 644,000 Poles and Polish Jews died because of military hostilities. 5,384,000 perished in the Jewish ghettos, in the concentration camps and prisons, and in consequence of ill-treatment by the occupation authorities. After the war Poland had 590,000 invalids, mostly inmates of concentration camps, and 1,140,000 cases of tuberculosis as a result of malnutrition due to the occupation regime.[4]

Poles in the occupied country who had German names or were descendants of mixed marriages or lived in the historically contested ethnic areas such as Upper Silesia were forced to choose between the concentration camp and signing the lists of so-called *Volksdeutsche*, *i.e.*, members of the German nationality. Many refused and paid for it with their lives. The majority signed, having no alternative. About one million signed it voluntarily, but another 1.7 million signed only under threat although they felt themselves to be Poles. However, all these Germanization efforts failed, largely because of the relatively short time at the Nazis' disposal. In January 1944 the two nationalities in the German-annexed lands were represented by these figures: six million Poles and 1.7 million forcible *Volksdeutsche* against one million truly German *Volksdeutsche* and 720,000 German resettlers, who came from Germany itself or from the East.[5]

German plans for Poland increased in atrocity following the attack on the Soviet Union. Hitler committed the worst mistake of his political career by attacking neutral and economically collaborating Russia without provocation. He added a new enemy, while his war against Britain was far from ended and while the United States was ever closer to joining Britain. German-Soviet relations started to deteriorate after the German defeat of France. Stalin's hopes for a long duration of the western front collapsed. He was facing a powerful Germany, master of most of Continental Europe. Germany began its drive into the Danubian and Balkan areas, thus encroaching on Soviet interests. Soviet attempts to repeat the 1939 deal by dividing those areas into two spheres of influence were met with German refusal. Hitler decided to settle the matter by war. The German reign of terror was extended to occupied Yugoslavia and to the equally occupied western parts of the Soviet Union. He sowed the seeds of Russian hostility against the Germans. His attack on Russia was to prove a blessing for Poland, as the short-lived understanding between the two big neighbors was terminated. Eventually Poland was to reemerge as a state within new frontiers vastly expanded westward.

After the outbreak of the German-Soviet war, the Germans planned to erase the Polish nationality from its habitat. The *Generalplan Ost,* elaborated under Himmler's auspices on April 27, 1942, postulated the incorporation of even the General Government within the German Reich and the dismemberment of Russia. The Poles were to be deported en masse to Western Siberia so that no trace of them would be left in their own homeland. The German Empire, the "one-thousand-year Reich," was to extend to the Urals and the Caucasus. German hubris reached its zenith. At least twenty million Soviet citizens had to pay for it with their lives. They perished either on the front or in German concentration and prisoner-of-war camps, or they were simply shot on the spot. The war, which started as a war against Poland, turned into a general war against all Slavs.

Polish culture was to be destroyed by the extermination of the educated classes and by the looting of Polish collections of old manuscripts, books, archives, and objects of art. The occupants murdered 13,000 primary school teachers; 1,700 secondary school teachers; 1,000 vocational school teachers; 120 faculty of teachers' colleges; 700 teachers of extension schools for adults; 416 professors and other teaching staff of the universities; 177 librarians, archivists, and personnel at research centers; 639 historians of art, painters, sculptors, musicians, theatrical actors, literary writers, and journalists; 5,610 judges, procurators, and lawyers; 10,500 medical doctors, dentists, and public health personnel; 2,647 Catholic priests; and more than 30,000 other representatives of the intelligentsia.[6] These figures are staggering and prove what human cruelty may achieve with the help of modern efficiency and technology.

This dreadful record of "achievements" of the "superior race," of the killing of millions of Jews, Slavs, and other Europeans, is now forgotten in the West for three reasons: first, because the number of West Europeans of non-Jewish descent who perished in the Nazi camps was very small in comparison to Jewish and Slavic human losses; second, because the advent of the Cold War soon after the end of the shooting war caused the Western powers to look at the Federal Republic as a valuable ally, and an ally should be free of any stain; third, because of the assent in the early fifties by the West German government to pay to the state of Israel and individual Jewish victims or their families indemnities for the Jewish sufferings and deaths, a sort of blood money for 6,000,000 European Jews killed in the camps.

The German authorities took other measures to prevent the rebirth of the Polish intelligentsia. The Poles were to become a people of semiliterate workers and peasants whose only reason for existence was to serve their German masters. The Poles in the annexed territories were forbidden to attend vocational, secondary, and higher-learning schools. Polish children were permitted to attend primary school, but only up to the age of ten. Educated Polish people, if not exterminated, were deported to the General Government. Church services in Polish were forbidden, all Polish associations disbanded, and the publication of Polish books, periodicals, and newspapers was halted. Poles had no right to attend even German-language theaters and cinemas.

The situation in the General Government was not much better although the use of Polish was allowed. All secondary schools and universities were closed. Poles could attend only vocational and primary schools, the policy being that it would be enough for them to learn how to read and write and to master elementary arithmetic. Heinrich Himmler, who had the overall supervision of the treatment of the Poles, authored a memorandum on May 15, 1940, in which he outlined the program of education for the Poles. He said that Poles should learn how to calculate up to 500 and how to sign their names, but that they would not need to acquire the ability to read and write. They should be inculcated with the duty of obedience to the Germans. The German Propaganda Office defined the goal: "the Polish nation must no longer bear the name of a cultural nation within the European community of nations. Its existence as a nation must be ended." This was said about a nation traditionally Western-oriented in its cultural history, by the

Office of Propaganda which claimed that Nazi Germany was fighting against the Soviet Union to save the West from barbarian bolshevism.

Collections of value only to the Polish nation were systematically destroyed; other collections of world-wide cultural value were looted and transferred either to the German libraries and museums or to the private collections of Nazi dignitaries such as Hitler, Goering, Governor Hans Frank, or various Gauleiters in the occupied areas. German scholarly experts helped in making decisions. The decrees on the confiscation of public and private collections of documents, books, and objects of art were enacted in October and December 1939. Several examples will illustrate the effects of these decrees. In October 1944 all the collections of one of the greatest Warsaw libraries, including 60,000 old manuscripts, 200,000 old prints and music, including Chopin's manuscripts, several thousands of maps and atlases, more than 1,000,000 engravings, all of inestimable value, were burned. At the same time other collections in the Warsaw libraries and in private ownership were also burned by the German squads. In the Middle Ages only individual "heretical" books were destroyed by fire. The Germans caused the auto-da-fé of whole libraries only because these libraries belonged to a hated nation. The Polish state archives, covering several centuries, met with the same fate in November and December 1944.

Throughout the period of occupation, looted objects of art were shipped away. Paintings by Leonardo da Vinci, Raphael, Rembrandt, and other masters were looted as well as collections of antiquities, numismatics, antique furniture, Persian carpets, etc. Hans Frank made a gift to Hitler of thirty drawings by Dürer, robbed from the Poles. Monuments to great Poles in the cities were dynamited. The famous Royal Castle in Warsaw was razed to the ground. Of 175 prewar Polish museums, only thirty-three could be reopened after the end of hostilities.[7]

One example demonstrates the treatment of Polish scholars. On November 6, 1939, the Gestapo arrested 183 professors of Cracow University, founded in the second half of the fourteenth century and one of the oldest in Europe. They were immediately transported to the concentration camp in Sachsenhausen. Many of them died there or in other camps.

Such was the record of the cultural mission of the superior race.

POLISH RESISTANCE

The Polish underground and partisan movement was, side by side with those in the Soviet Union and Yugoslavia, the largest numerically and the most effective on the occupied Continent. Poles had no choice in the matter. Loyalty to the occupation authorities offered no guarantee of security, because no innocent Pole could be sure that he would not be deported either to a concentration camp or for forced labor in Germany. One of the frequent practices of the Gestapo was to close several blocks in the cities and to arrest haphazardly people who happened to be in the streets and to deport them without paying any attention to their "guilt" or lack of "guilt." The resistance movement helped the Allies in providing important information, disrupted German transports going East, and generally hampering the German war effort. German officials and soldiers could not feel secure in Poland.

Hundreds of thousands of other Poles, who fled abroad, enrolled in the Polish armed forces under Western or Soviet commands. Thousands of Polish fliers and mechanics helped in winning the air battle over Britain in 1940. Polish divisions fought in Northern Africa, Italy, and in the European battles following D Day, while those under the Soviet command fought their way, together with Soviet troops, up to Berlin. All in all, the number of fighting Poles in regular formations was superior in the closing period of the war to the number of troops which France could muster at that time.

The inhabitants of Warsaw, encouraged by the presence of advancing Soviet armies which had reached the other bank of the Vistula, rose in revolt in August 1944. The Soviet troops did not move to help. The poorly armed men, women, and even children resisted alone assaults by regular German troops for two and a half months, but they succumbed in this uneven battle. German detachments, ordered by Hitler, proceeded, after the Polish capitulation, with the systematic destruction of the city which was almost completely razed to the ground. What remained of the city of well over one million people, capital of Poland, was only heaps of ruins over the mass graves of hundreds of thousands of its inhabitants.

THE POLES REMEMBER

The German atrocities simply cannot be forgotten by the Poles, and recollection of them stands as an obstacle to a genuine reconciliation between the two nations. It would take a long time for present and future generations of Germans to convince the Poles by true proofs of their friendship and respect that they can trust their western neighbor. They cannot believe that the guilt was only that of Hitler, other Nazi chieftains, and the Gestapo. The thesis that all the crimes were committed by a small minority of Germans and only in the name of Germany is hard to reconcile with past reality. In the first place, how many Germans in 1939 opposed the war for the conquest of Polish lands? Did those Germans resettled in the annexed Polish provinces ignore the fact that they were taking over the property of expropriated and expelled Poles? Could the policy of occupation authorities be carried out without the active participation of hundreds of thousands of Germans, including the members of the Gestapo and the SS, scholars, and detachments of the regular army? Did not the millions of German soldiers stationed in Poland or going to and from the eastern front see the treatment reserved for the Poles? Did not the German industrial managers, engineers, workers, and farmers see the Polish slave laborers with their *P* armbands? Did other Germans never talk to their countrymen who worked in the concentration camps, and never learn at least something about the fate of the Jews, Poles, and other inmates? Did not all Germans hear the official Nazi propaganda about such subhuman beings as the Jews, the Poles, and other Slavs? How many German scholars refused their assistance in proving the German right to win *Lebensraum* at the expense of the Poles and other Eastern European nations?

THE YOUNG GERMAN GENERATION

Collective guilt for the action and inaction of the wartime German generation cannot be dismissed by glib talk about the Nazis as though they belonged to another nationality. Only the postwar generation is free of guilt. They and their children could build a new bridge to their contemporaries in Poland without being distrusted by the Poles. What the Poles expect from that young generation is actual proof of their forsaking any ambition to reopen the quarrel with Poland under more favorable circumstances than those of the present. What the Poles want is only to be left in peace, and to be sure that the Germans will never again try to encroach upon their frontiers.

The role of the young generation of Germans in the difficult task of reconciliation depends on education. This in turn depends on their school teachers and schoolbooks. Young Germans will not take a fresh look at their eastern neighbors if they are hindered by a hateful image of these neighbors. Yet the West German textbooks leave much to be desired in this respect. Two West German authors have mentioned many examples of textbooks intentionally hostile to the Poles.[8]

3

The Origin of the Oder-Neisse Frontier

VIEWS OF THE LONDON POLES ON POSTWAR
FRONTIERS

THE POLES, unlike most Frenchmen following their surrender in June 1940, never lost the hope that Germany would eventually be defeated and Poland liberated. It was hard to nourish this hope during the worst period of the war, following the German victories in the West while Britain alone among the great powers continued to fight. But the Poles needed this hope to sustain their spirit of resistance against German attempts to wipe the Polish nation out of existence. The outbreak of the German-Soviet war and the joining of the Americans with Britain and the Soviet Union in the anti-German coalition provided solid arguments for the Polish expectation that Germany would eventually lose the war.

The large resistance movement in Poland was directed by the Polish government in exile in London, recognized not only by the United States and Britain but after the summer of 1941 and until 1943 also by the Soviet Union. The government in exile and the underground political organizations in occupied Poland were studying the problem of desirable solutions for the Polish-German territorial problem. There was general agreement that the Versailles frontiers were untenable. While the Weimar Republic wanted to build a land connection with East Prussia by cutting off Poland from the Baltic coast, the Poles in London and in occupied Poland were thinking about another logical solution—namely, the annexation of East Prussia and Danzig in order to secure a truly safe access to the sea. They also wanted to make this access more secure by pushing the German-Polish frontier on the Baltic coast westward and fixing it somewhere between the mouths of the Vistula and the Oder. Only a minority of Poles in the resistance movement, notably the organizations uniting the Poles from the German-annexed western provinces, were bolder in claiming that the frontier should reach the lower Oder and possibly the Lusatian (Goerlitzer or Western) Neisse. Finally, the London Poles also wanted to annex the German part of Upper Silesia.

The relatively limited Polish aspirations in the West were due primarily to another territorial problem, one involving the Soviet Union, but also to the doubt as to whether Poles could resettle large German territories or whether millions of Germans would remain within the new Polish frontiers. Moscow wanted to retain almost all of prewar Eastern Poland, acquired in 1939 by agreement with Nazi Germany. The Poles considered it outrageous that they should be asked to pay the Soviet Union for its participation in the war against Germany. They wondered indignantly why the country which was the first to oppose Nazi Germany with arms in hand should lose its territory to another ally. Moreover, they feared that a victorious Soviet Union might not respect Polish independence but impose a pro-Communist government. Hence, they considered that they were facing two enemies: Germany and the Soviet Union.

This attitude could not meet with any sympathetic understanding in London and Washington. For these two capitals Germany was the only enemy, while the Soviet Union, which bore the main and heavy burden of the land struggle against powerful German armies in 1941–44, until the Anglo-American invasion of the Continent, was a very important ally. These discrepant views were typical of Polish-Western relations. What the Poles could not understand, neither at that time nor in their earlier history, was the fact that the Western powers always formulated their policies toward Eastern Europe and in particular toward Poland only in consideration of their relations with Germany and Russia. The Paris Peace Conference (1919–20) was the only exception, due to an unusual set of circumstances. At that time the Western allies were facing a defeated former enemy, Germany, and looked with hostility at Bolshevik Russia. Polish distrust of the Soviet Union during the Second World War could find no sympathy in the West. The Poles were to be disappointed in their hopes that Britain and the United States would support their claim to recovery of Eastern Poland with its two very important Polish cultural centers, Vilno and Lvov, and its almost four million Polish inhabitants, a large minority amidst the Ukrainian and Byelorussian majorities.

However, Polish resistance to accepting the Curzon Line as the eastern frontier not only alienated Moscow and found no Western support but had a determining influence upon Polish western territorial claims. The London government in exile, supported in this respect by the home resistance organization, rejected the thesis of compensation, accepted by the three allied powers, that Poland should be compensated for the loss of Eastern Poland by vast acquisitions of territory at the expense of Germany. The Poles continued, therefore, to limit their western demands to the annexation of East Prussia, Danzig, greater access to the Baltic coast, and the German part of Upper Silesia, thus asking less than the three powers were ready to adjudicate to Poland in the West.

THE SOVIET CONCEPT OF THE WESTERN
POLISH FRONTIER

The concept of the Polish frontier running along the lower Oder river up to its confluence with the Lusatian (Goerlitzer) Neisse and then along that river to the Czechoslovak frontier, arose among the pro-Soviet Poles and their protector, the Soviet Union. After its decisive Stalingrad victory, the Soviet Union began to be seriously interested in the Polish western frontier. Assuming that the Soviet wish for a "friendly" government in postwar Poland were to be realized, Moscow could rightly consider that that frontier would be in a sense the Soviet western frontier. The pro-Soviet Polish organization was encouraged to claim German territories to an extent much exceeding the London claims, while, of course, renouncing any claim to Eastern Poland. The views of Moscow and of the pro-Soviet Poles gradually acquired much greater weight in Western capitals than those of the London government. They coincided with the American and British opinion that after the war Poland should occupy a territory located between the Curzon Line and the western frontier, moved greatly toward the West.

The so-called Union of Polish Patriots, formed in Moscow, stated in its Manifesto of June 1943 that postwar Poland should annex East Prussia, Danzig, and the German part of Upper Silesia. This claim did not differ from the London one but was to be enlarged with the progress of Soviet offensives and the advent of Soviet troops in the Polish territory west of the Curzon Line. The representatives of the Union of Polish

Patriots, received at the Kremlin on March 16, 1944, stated that the Polish western frontier should follow the Oder, with Stettin becoming a Polish city. On July 26, 1944, the Polish Committee of National Liberation, formed in Soviet-occupied Poland, concluded an agreement with the Soviet government by virtue of which it accepted the Curzon Line, while the Committee and the Soviet government agreed that the Polish western frontier was to follow the lower Oder river, beginning with its mouth and leaving Stettin on the Polish side, and then the river Neisse up to the Czechoslovak border (East Prussia was to be divided between Poland and the USSR). This agreement left open the question as to which Neisse was to be the frontier line since the Oder had three confluents by that name. This meant that Moscow had not yet decided whether to grant to Poland Lower Silesia with its capital Breslau (Wrocław).

In August 1944 Stalin told the then Polish Prime Minister of the government in exile, Stanisław Mikołajczyk, that the Polish frontier should be "in the East the Curzon Line; in the West the frontier should follow the rivers Oder and Neisse and should include East Prussia." A few months later he told another Pole, Oscar Lange, then a professor at the University of Chicago and known for his sympathetic attitude toward the Soviet Union, that "we talk among us Russians about granting to Poland not only Danzig but also Stettin. Poland should claim not only East Prussia and Upper Silesia but all the German territories up to the Oder, including Stettin." He added, however, that he was not sure whether Poland should get Breslau.

THE FRONTIER ON THE ODER AND THE
LUSATIAN NEISSE

The Soviet position was clarified at the Yalta Conference where Stalin and Molotov asked Britain and the United States to agree to the western Polish frontier along the rivers Oder and Lusatian Neisse. This allowed the Polish Government of National Unity, formed in Warsaw under the auspices of the three great powers (the United States and Britain withdrew their recognition of the London government at the beginning of July 1945), to express the official Polish point of view at the Potsdam Conference. Its representatives stated, by agreement with the Soviet government, that in compensation for Soviet-annexed Eastern Poland, Poland wanted to receive the German territory up to the lower Oder and the Lusatian Neisse, therefore including Lower Silesia but excluding northern East Prussia with the city of Koenigsberg, regarding which the three great powers had agreed that it should be granted to the Soviet Union. The argument advanced by the Polish representatives was that Poland would lose in the east 180,000 square kilometers and should be compensated by 110,000 square kilometers of German territory. The theory of compensation was much later abandoned by the Polish government, which had to accept the Soviet view that Soviet annexation of prewar Eastern Poland was legitimate in any event on the ground of its population being mostly Ukrainian and Byelorussian. Warsaw then began to use a different historical argument for recovery of former Polish western territory, ruled by the first Piasts and later conquered by the Germans.

In fact, Polish annexation of the former German territories, like the parallel Soviet annexation of part of East Prussia, was founded on military conquest, the usual decisive factor in the modification of a contested frontier. German acquisition of the eastern territory had also been due to the military factor. The advancing German frontier in the East was formed owing to the military exertions of the Teutonic Knights and the Brandenburg Hohenzollerns. The same was true at the time of the Polish partitions, when the partitioning powers could do what they wanted because of their superior military force. Eventually, Nazi wartime annexations of Polish territory were possible only because of Polish military defeat. Now the distribution of military power was reversed in the relation not between Poland and Germany but between the Soviet Union and Germany. Incidentally, the same military factor played the decisive role in the establishment of the state of Israel and its occupation of Arab lands after the 1967 war. Military force, not any historical or ethnic arguments, has always been the main factor in settling the problem of contested frontiers. The varying fate of Alsace-Lorraine, for instance, between its conquest by Louis XIV and the present time, was also determined by respective French and German military fortunes. Decisive Soviet military superiority established the Oder-Neisse frontier and has maintained it since 1945.[1]

VIEWS OF THE THREE GREAT POWERS:
TEHERAN AND YALTA CONFERENCES

The territorial aspirations of the London or of the pro-Soviet Poles played a very minor role in the final decisions regarding Poland's western frontier. The decisive role was played by the three allied great powers. The Soviet position was finally clarified by the time of the Yalta Conference (February 1945). The Western views evolved until the end of the Potsdam Conference.

President Roosevelt, Prime Minister Churchill, and Generalissimo Stalin held their first meeting November–December 1943 in Teheran. Stalin's request for Soviet annexation of northern East Prussia with the city of Koenigsberg was accepted by the two Western statesmen. They also assented to Stalin's proposal that Poland should receive the remainder of East Prussia and all the German territory up to the river Oder as well as the German part of Upper Silesia on both sides of the Oder. Stalin did not mention the name of the Western Neisse because he was not yet ready in 1943 to grant Lower Silesia to Poland. The later inter-allied debate about the Eastern and the Western Neisse rivers involved in fact the question of whether Lower Silesia with the city of Breslau should or should not be allocated to Poland.

The question of the transfer of population was also mentioned at the Teheran Conference in very general terms, but always in relation to the territories to be lost by Germany. It was also at that conference that the three chief executives tentatively agreed that the eastern frontier of Poland should follow the Curzon Line, somewhat better than the German-Soviet frontier fixed in 1939. The Polish annexations at the expense of Germany were linked to Poland's territorial losses in the East; the concept of compensation was accepted. Churchill illustrated this concept of moving the Polish homeland westward by saying: "Poland might move westward, like soldiers taking two steps 'left close.' "[2]

Churchill, in his statement to the House of Commons on December 15, 1944, said: "The Poles are free, so far as Russia and Great Britain are concerned, to extend their territory, at the expense of Germany, to the West. . . . The transference of several millions of people [Poles from east of the Curzon line] would have to be effected from the East to the West or North, as well as the expulsion of the Germans, from the area to be acquired by Poland in the West and the North. For expulsion is the method which, so far as we have been able to see, will be the most satisfactory and lasting."[3]

More than fourteen months passed prior to the second meeting of the three chief executives at Yalta in February 1945. At that time they could be sure that Germany, fighting now in Europe on the western and eastern fronts, would be finally defeated. They had to think about the postwar situation. The President relied on his hope that American-Soviet cooperation would survive the common victory. The British Prime

Minister had doubts on that score and thought in terms of the traditional British policy of balance of power. Russia was about to emerge as the strongest power on the continent and hence as a threat to that balance. Whatever the Russian regime and whatever the name of its leader, Alexander I or Stalin, Russia in 1814–15 as in 1945, although an ally, was viewed as a possible future adversary. Stalin, like Alexander I, wanted to get for his country the fruits of victory, gained at a very high price.

These views influenced the stand of the three leaders regarding the Polish frontiers. The two Western leaders had no direct stakes in Poland. Their opinions depended on their relation to the Soviet Union and, by implication, to postwar Germany. Churchill said in his memoirs: "Great Britain had no material interest of any kind in Poland."[4] At the Yalta Conference President Roosevelt mentioned a domestic consideration, important personally to him, namely, millions of Americans of Polish descent whose votes for the Democratic Party he did not want to lose owing to his stand on the Polish question.[5] Neither Western leader considered that the national interests of his country were involved in Poland.

The Polish problem looked quite different to Stalin. Poland was not a distant country; it was an immediate neighbor of Russia. Located between Russia and Germany, the other great power with vital interests in Eastern Europe, its future international orientation was linked in his mind with the question of Russian security. His Polish concept had taken a definite shape prior to the Yalta Conference. First, he wanted a pro-Soviet Polish government—which he had already established in Soviet-occupied Poland following the rupture of relations with the London government—to be recognized by the two Western powers. This "friendly" government, controlled in fact by the Polish Communists, offered a guarantee that the Soviet Union would have a preponderant voice in shaping Polish policies. Western influences would be wiped out. Second, the Poles should be gradually reconciled to the loss of Eastern Poland by a generous territorial compensation at the expense of defeated Germany. Stalin made up his mind regarding the extent of that compensation during the interval between the Teheran and Yalta Conferences. The Polish western frontier should follow the line of the Oder and Western Neisse with the cities of Stettin and Breslau adjudicated to Poland. Third, Poland, ruled by a "friendly" government, would become a Soviet security bulwark. The Oder-Neisse frontier would be not only a Polish frontier but also the second Soviet security frontier. Fourth, Polish annexation of vast German territories would erect an insurpassable wall between the Poles and the Germans, while Poland would have to rely on the Soviet alliance against future German territorial claims. The only possible postwar Polish orientation would be pro-Soviet.

Of course, one can now exaggerate the impact of the Oder-Neisse frontier on German-Polish relations. If one were to assume for the sake of the argument that the three great powers had decided to restore the 1937, *i.e.*, the Versailles Polish-German, frontier (none intended to do so), the Polish-German territorial quarrel would have gone full circle back to what it had been at the time of the Weimar Republic. The Germans would have resented the existence of a Free City of Danzig with its German population wanting to be reunited with Germany, of the Polish Corridor, cutting off East Prussia from the main German body, and the partition of Upper Silesia. The Oder-Neisse frontier had only the effect of aggravating the Polish-German frontier quarrel.

Stalin asked again at Yalta for the partitioning of East Prussia between his country and Poland. He laid claim to the northern part of East Prussia with the cities of Koenigsberg and Tilsitt, arguing that Russia needed an ice-free port. Thus the Soviet Union was to become an accomplice of Poland in annexing the German territories. The two countries would have similar interest in opposing future German territorial claims. It seems that the trauma of the war made him lose any hope for future Russian-German cooperation. In 1939 he himself had tried to revive the historically traditional scheme of cooperation against Poland and suffered the sudden German attack on his own country at the end. At Yalta he did not conceal his distrust of all Germans, including the industrial workers. Hence Stalin substituted the concept of Russian-Polish cooperation for that traditional scheme. Hence he laid to rest the chronic Polish nightmare of partition by the two big neighbors.

The debate at Yalta revolved around two questions: what kind of Polish government could be recognized by all three powers (at that time the United States and Britain were still recognizing, though reluctantly, the London government, while the Soviet Union had installed its own government in Poland); and what should the postwar frontiers of Poland be? The two questions were related in British minds. Britain was willing to concede a better western frontier to a Polish government which would not be an obedient Soviet satellite than to a pro-Soviet government. Neither the United States nor Britain intended to quarrel with the USSR regarding the Polish-Soviet frontier, which Moscow wanted to be more or less the same as the Soviet-German frontier fixed in October 1939. Britain proposed to substitute the Curzon Line, which was somewhat better for Poland. Stalin rather quickly accepted the British proposal, to which the President also rallied after an unsuccessful attempt to wrest from Stalin the retrocession to Poland of the city of Lvov and the neighboring oilfields. Agreement on the Polish-Soviet frontier was reached fairly quickly.

The real debate centered around the exact extent of territorial compensation in the West. Stalin tried hard to obtain Western assent to the Polish boundaries which he favored. He met with no opposition regarding the Curzon Line as the Polish-Soviet frontier. He failed, however, to win a tripartite agreement on the Oder-Western Neisse frontier. Churchill was ready to go along with the Oder frontier but not with the Western Neisse. In other words, he wanted to leave Lower Silesia with Breslau to Germany. He agreed in all discussions with Stalin that the Germans should be removed from the territories which would be granted to Poland.

Churchill fought at Yalta for a truly independent Polish government but failed because of Stalin's resistance and lack of adequate American support. What he wanted was a Poland where British influence would coexist with the Soviet. The nature of the future Polish government influenced the British position regarding the western frontier, as Secretary of State for Foreign Affairs Eden frankly stated in his letter to the Prime Minister: "We need not make the same concessions to the Lublin [pro-Soviet] Poles which we were prepared to make to M. Mikolajczyk [a former Prime Minister of the Polish government in exile, favored by the British government as a man who would not be blindly obedient to Moscow]."[6] The problem of respective British and Soviet influences in postwar Europe was a factor in the British attitude toward the extent of Polish territory. Another British government at the Congress of Vienna had stated that it would have accepted a Poland with a much larger territory than the Duchy of Warsaw if free of Russian influence, but fought against the preservation of the territorial integrity of the Duchy because Russia wanted to unite it with itself.

The American President was annoyed by the Polish problem which was casting a shadow on American-Soviet relations. He said at Yalta: "Poland has been a source of trouble for over five hundred years."[7] It is impossible to guess why he mentioned five hundred years. Poland was causing no trouble in the fifteenth century either to the United States, which did not exist at that time, or to any Western power. However, former and contemporary Western statesmen could perhaps have agreed with him regarding the period following the partitions and ending with the Second World War, because the Polish problem was causing trouble in Western relations with Germany and Russia.

The President was ready to go along with the British view that the Polish western frontier should extend to the Oder but not to the Western Neisse.[8] Churchill noted that Roosevelt "agreed that Poland should receive compensation at the expense of Germany, including that portion of East Prussia south of the Koenigsberg line, Upper Silesia, and up to the line of the Oder; but there would appear to be little justification for extending it up to the Western Neisse."[9] Roosevelt contemplated the transfer of populations in relation to German-Polish frontier modifications.[10]

Stalin, confronted with British-American opposition, decided to postpone the joint decision on Poland's western frontier. He probably thought that his bargaining position would be stronger later, after the Soviet occupation of Eastern Germany.

The three leaders finally agreed to say in their public communiqué that "the Eastern frontier of Poland should follow the Curzon Line . . . [and] Poland must receive substantial accessions of territory in the North and the West."[11] Judged by the tenor of debates at Yalta, the three governments were in agreement on the division of East Prussia between Poland and the Soviet Union and on extending the Polish frontier to the Oder. The matter left in suspense was the fate of Lower Silesia.

Stalin won a victory regarding the composition of the future Polish government to be recognized by all three powers. It was agreed that the Provisional Government formed in Poland under the auspices of the Soviet Union would be enlarged only by the addition of other Poles residing in Poland or abroad. That reorganized government was formed under the auspices of the three great powers a few months later, but the Polish Communists continued to be its decisive factor. That government was then recognized by Britain and the United States, while they withdrew their recognition from the London government. It was the new government that was to submit Polish territorial claims at the Potsdam Conference.

THE POTSDAM CONFERENCE

The third allied summit meeting at Potsdam (July–August 1945) took place after the end of hostilities in Europe. The Polish question again figured on the agenda. The three heads of government could no longer postpone their decision regarding the Polish-German frontier because they needed to know the outward limits of their zones of occupation in Germany.

Stalin came to Potsdam with the firm intention not to yield regarding the Oder-Western Neisse line. He was now in a stronger position, not only because the contested territory had been occupied by Soviet troops but also because his views could be supported by the Provisional Polish Government of National Unity, recognized at the beginning of July 1945 by the United States and Britain. He was sure that that government, dominated by Polish Communists, would support his own views.

President Truman continued at that time his predecessor's policy of friendly American-Soviet relations. By contrast, Prime Minister Churchill was preoccupied with the problem of the postwar Continental balance of power. He faced a situation less favorable than that of 1814–15, when the British government could rely on two great powers, Austria and France, to support its resistance to the Russian annexation of the whole Grand Duchy of Warsaw. Churchill now had to reckon with the possibility that in a few years the United States would withdraw its troops from Europe, while France and the other West European countries looked very weak by comparison to the victorious Soviet Union. He had hardly any doubt that Poland and the rest of Eastern Europe would become part of the Soviet zone of influence. The vital question for him was to stop the Soviet Union as far east as possible. Therefore, the Polish western frontier should not be pushed too far west.

It seemed paradoxical to people who did not know the traditional British policy of maintaining the Continental balance of power that Britain, a Polish ally since 1939, should have agreed easily to the amputation of Polish prewar territory up to the Curzon Line, but opposed too great an extension westward of the Polish frontier at the expense of the enemy, Germany. Yet this seeming paradox was easy to explain. British policy in 1939 and 1945 was formulated always in relation to its policy toward Germany and the Soviet Union. Britain granted to Poland its guarantee against Nazi Germany in 1939 because London had decided, following the German occupation of Czechoslovakia, that Hitler's expansion should be stopped, if necessary by war. The Polish-German conflict of the time provided London with the opportunity for making public its new policy replacing the former policy of appeasement that had misfired. The British guarantee to Poland was the result of the new policy toward Nazi Germany.

Britain, which fought Germany alone in 1940–41, greeted the Soviet Union, attacked by Germany, as a most welcome ally in June

1941. If the Soviet Union wanted to have Eastern Poland, it should have it. Poland was to be compensated by the annexation of some former German territory. But by 1944–45 the Soviet Union appeared to be the new threat to the European balance of power. Hence, the Polish western frontier had to be advanced westward less than Britain had been willing that it should be earlier. Polish interests played no role in all these British decisions.

Churchill told President Truman in his letter of May 11, 1945, that "Poland would be completely engulfed and buried deep in Russian-occupied lands. . . . The territories under Russian control would include the Baltic provinces, all of Germany to the occupational line [the western line of the Soviet zone of occupation], all Czechoslovakia, a large part of Austria, the whole of Yugoslavia, Hungary, Roumania, Bulgaria to Greece. . . . This constitutes an event in the history of Europe in which there has been no parallel." He concluded that, if this were to happen, there would be "very little hope of preventing a third world war."[12] He had in mind war against the Soviet Union. President Truman did not share Churchill's apprehensions at that time. He was to rally to his point of view only in 1946.

In another letter, addressed on May 12, 1945, to President Truman, Churchill used the term "iron curtain" to describe Soviet-occupied Eastern Europe, and expressed his fear that the Russians might "advance if they chose to the waters of the North Sea and the Atlantic."[13] His prediction that Eastern Europe would become the Soviet sphere of influence proved to be true. However, the United States eventually decided to remain in Europe and to protect Western Europe. The balance of power was restored.

At the time of the Potsdam Conference, Truman did not share Churchill's apprehension and refused to meet him prior to the conference because this "would give the Russians the impression that we were 'ganging up' on them."[14] The views of the two Western powers were clearly different at that time.

Joseph E. Davies, sent by the President in June 1945 to confer with Churchill, reported that he "was shocked beyond words . . . by so violent a change in his [Churchill's] attitude toward the Soviets." He mentioned to Churchill the statement by a British officer that "the British and American Armies should not stop, but go right through and clear up the Red Army and destroy the Soviet menace." "The Prime Minister again berated the Communists and expiated on the Communist 'menace' vigorously." "He was bitterly hostile to the Soviets," and "he is doggedly maintaining the classic British policy in Europe."[15]

American experts fully understood the motivation of the British policy: "Traditional British policy in Europe has been, of course, that of preventing any one state from dominating the continent. . . . Heretofore, there have always been several strong European powers providing the basic elements for this policy. Upon the ending of the war, however, this situation has completely changed in that Russia is left as the sole great power on the Continent, a position unique in modern history. Britain accordingly feels that Russia will dominate the Continent. . . . There is no longer power to balance."[16]

The British government was thinking in 1943 and even more in 1944–45 about a unified Western Europe under British leadership as a counterbalance to Soviet-dominated Eastern Europe. General Smuts, the South African Prime Minister, publicly formulated this British idea on November 25, 1943, at the time of the Teheran Conference, and it was again mentioned to the United States prior to the Potsdam Conference.[17]

Stalin was aware of the British distrust. He told Harry Hopkins, sent by President Truman to Moscow prior to the Potsdam Conference, that "he did not intend to have the British manage the affairs of Poland and that is exactly what they want to do."[18] There is a grain of truth in this overstatement. The British wanted to retain some influence in Poland. They pressed the Polish soldiers under their command and the Polish civilians in Britain to return to Poland for two reasons: to get rid of them, but also in the hope that they would retain a pro-British sympathy and would counter the Soviet influence. The American view was somewhat parallel to the British: "While this Government may not want to oppose a political configuration in Eastern Europe which gives the Soviet Union a predominant influence in Poland, neither would it desire to see Poland become in fact a Soviet satellite and have American influence there completely eliminated."[19]

It is difficult to understand how the two Western governments expected to preserve some influence in Poland while they recognized a Polish government controlled by the pro-Soviet Polish Communists.

In any event, Stalin considered Churchill as his adversary at Potsdam. He told representatives of the Polish government after the British elections, which had resulted in the fall of Churchill's government, that "Churchill did not trust us and in consequence we could not fully trust him either."[20] This mutual distrust caused the bitter British-Soviet debate at Potsdam over the Polish western frontier.

Stalin came to Potsdam firmly intending to obtain assent by the two Western powers to the Oder-Western Neisse frontier. His position was much stronger at that time than at Yalta. His troops had overrun not only the contested East German territories but all of Eastern Germany up to the river Elbe, *i.e.*, the Soviet zone of occupation, assigned to the Soviet Union by the three-power agreement. He could do whatever he liked in the territory east of the Oder-Western Neisse. He did it by turning over the administration of that territory gradually to the Polish authorities. His task was made easier by the mass flight of the majority of Germans, in fear of the Soviet military advance, and also by the earlier mass evacuation of Germans by the retreating German military forces. This allowed the Soviet government to encourage the Poles to resettle in the territory, mostly abandoned by the Germans.

One of Stalin's first statements at Potsdam was to recall the results of the Yalta Conference: "At Crimea [Yalta], the President [Roosevelt] and Mr. Churchill suggested the line should be along the Oder until it joined the Neisse. I insisted on the western Neisse. Under Churchill's plan, Stettin [lying west of the Oder] and Breslau would remain German."[21] However, both Western governments intended, prior to the Potsdam Conference, to allocate to Poland less than the Oder line allowed.

Britain was ready to concede "the Free City of Danzig, East Prussia south and west of Koenigsberg, Oppeln Silesia [German Upper Silesia], and most of the eastern portions of German Pomerania."[22] In other words, the Polish Baltic coast would end somewhere between the mouths of the Vistula and the Oder. This was a *volte-face*, since Britain had been ready before to accept the Oder line, while opposing only the Western Neisse line. Sir Alexander Cadogan, the then Permanent Under-Secretary at the British Foreign Office, told his American colleagues on July 14, 1945, that "his government had never approved any cessions to Poland beyond those listed above, and expressed opposition to the Oder-Neisse line."[23] This was a diplomatic lie. Sir Alexander himself wrote a letter on November 2, 1944, on behalf of his government in response to a question asked by the Polish London government, in which he said: "You have enquired whether His Majesty's Government were definitely in favour of advancing the Polish frontier up to the line of the Oder, to include the port of Stettin. The answer is that His Majesty's Government do consider that Poland should have the right to extend her territory to this extent."[24] What happened in the meantime was the growing British apprehension that Poland would be engulfed within the Soviet zone of influence, and that the Soviet Union would become the dominant power on the continent.

The initial American stand was the same as the British, namely, that Poland should receive that part of East Prussia which was not allocated to the Soviet Union, Danzig, the German part of Upper Silesia, and an extended Baltic coast up to a point located somewhat between the Vistula and the Oder. The briefing papers, prepared in advance of the Potsdam Conference, also recommended that the United States might eventually concede the Oder line but should resist the inclusion of Lower Silesia and hence the Western Neisse line.[25]

In effect, the Soviet view differed greatly from the British and the American, much more than had been true at Yalta. As the debates at Potsdam were to prove, Stalin had to fight mainly against Churchill, while President Truman acted as a mediator.

All three governments were in agreement from the start of the conference that East Prussia should be divided between Poland and the Soviet Union with the Koenigsberg area going to Russia.[26] The discussion centered around the western Polish frontier. The Soviet stand was defined as "the line west of Swinemünde to the river Oder leaving Stettin on the Polish side, further up the river Oder up to the estuary of the river West Neisse to the Czechoslovak frontier."[27] Stalin invariably defended that stand at the conference, until he eventually obtained Western assent. His arguments were three. First, that Poland should receive compensation for the territory lost to Russia. Second, that the Germans living east of that line had fled, and the territory was being resettled by Poles. He maintained at first that no Germans were left.[28] Later on, the representatives of the Polish government, invited to come to Potsdam to submit their point of view, conceded that one and a half million Germans still remained. Stalin then accepted that figure.[29] Third, he told the Western powers that the Soviet military authorities, faced with the flight of Germans and the incoming of Poles, had no choice but to turn over the contested territory to Polish administration.[30] He did not conceal that he was creating an accomplished fact regarding the future line of the Polish Western frontier: "The more ready we were to let the Polish administration function, the more we were sure that the Poles would receive the territory to the west. I do not see the harm of permitting the Poles to set up administration in territories in which they are to remain."[31]

THE OFFICIAL POLISH REQUEST

Since the three great powers had agreed at Yalta to seek the opinion of the reorganized Polish government, the representatives of that government were invited to come to Potsdam. They talked to the three great-power delegations and submitted a long memorandum in support of their claim to the Oder-Western Neisse frontier. Their arguments were as follows:

1. The demographic and economic arguments were in line with the concept of territorial compensation for the loss of prewar eastern Poland, annexed by the Soviet Union. This concept was also accepted by the three powers. The Poles said that the lost eastern territory amounted to 180,000 square kilometers out of the prewar 380,000 square kilometers of Polish territory, while the German territory east of the Oder-Western Neisse was not larger than 100,000 square kilometers. Hence the postwar Polish territory would be smaller by 80,000 square kilometers. While Poland would lose 20 percent of its prewar territory, Germany would lose 18 percent. The population in Poland would be smaller than prior to the war by seven million people, but the Polish representatives said that the exchange of territories would make for a nationally homogeneous population, while more than one third of prewar Poland had been composed of national minorities.

American sources calculated that Poles east of the Curzon Line in 1931 numbered 3,842,000 in the total population of over 10.5 million. The majority of that population was made up of Ukrainians and Byelorussians (about 5.5 million) and Jews (about 890,000).[32]

The delegates of the Polish government, bound in this respect by agreements with the Soviet Union, said that the almost four million Poles from prewar eastern Poland would have to be evacuated. At that time these Poles were living either east of the Curzon Line or in other parts of the Soviet Union, to which very large numbers of them had been deported by the Soviet authorities in 1939–1941. The Polish delegates also mentioned that about two million Poles deported to Germany during the war as forced laborers, about one million Polish prisoners-of-war in Germany, and thousands of Polish soldiers under the British command, as well as Polish civilians who had fled from Poland to the West in fear of the Nazis, would also have to resettle in postwar Poland. Altogether the Polish government was confronted with the problem of resettlement of more than seven million Poles. They could not be absorbed within the overpopulated prewar Polish territory drastically reduced by the three powers' decision to grant the eastern half of Poland to the Soviet Union. Hence the Polish government needed the East German territory for the resettlement of those seven million Poles.

The Polish representatives argued that even prewar Poland was overpopulated with its average density of 83 persons per square kilometer, a high density for a mostly agricultural country. In order to maintain only that density, Poland needed 314,000 square kilometers, while its prewar territory was reduced by the Soviet annexation to only 204,000 square kilometers. The area east of the Oder-Western Neisse line with its 105,000 square kilometers would restore the prewar balance between the total population and the available land surface. They pointed out that the postwar population amounted to 26,000,000 but had a very rapid natural increase rate of 250,000 new births every year.

The Polish memorandum recalled that prewar Poland had suffered from over-population. About 4,000,000 were landless and in fact unemployed peasants. This is why about 2,500,000 Poles emigrated abroad during the period of 1919–1939. Moreover, 431,000 Polish agricultural laborers had to go to East Germany in 1927–38 as seasonal farm workers, to replace those East Germans who were emigrating to industrialized Western Germany. This East German emigrating trend, which had begun about 1850, continued even under Hitler in spite of Nazi efforts to stop it. 448,000 persons left East Germany for West Germany during the period of 1933–39. What the Polish representatives intended to convey was that there was a secular trend of East Germans emigrating westward and being replaced by Poles.

This raised the question of the population of the prewar German territory east of the Oder–Western-Neisse line, how many Poles lived there, and how many Germans remained in 1945. The figures offered by the Poles, the British, and the Americans differed widely. According to the Polish memorandum, the total prewar population amounted to about 8,000,000. Prime Minister Churchill claimed at Potsdam that that figure should be 8,500,000.[33] The American figure of about 10,000,000 probably included German military personnel and German officials in addition to the permanent population. The American sources included in that population the Polish minority of 712,000 people.[34] The Poles claimed that the population remaining east of the Oder-Neisse line amounted to 3,500,000, 1,500,000 being German and 2,000,000 of Polish descent.

The conference was confronted with these divergent figures. The confusion was increased by the Nazi policy of resettlement. The Germans during the war not only annexed vast areas of prewar Poland but expelled Poles from these areas and resettled Germans in them. According to the American sources, half a million German settlers were brought from the Baltic countries and other parts of Eastern Europe, and another half a million from Germany proper.[35] It was unknown at the time of the Potsdam Conference how many of those Germans had fled and how many still remained east of the Oder-Neisse line. Parenthetically, the policy of resettling Poles and Germans was initiated by the Nazi regime which uprooted both Poles and Germans from their centuries-old homelands in order to Germanize Western Poland. This and the disloyalty of German minorities in Eastern Europe during the war, when they helped the German occupation authorities in oppressing the native population, brought about the demand of the Polish, Czecho-slovak, and Hungarian governments to expel all Germans from their postwar territories. This idea had been accepted in principle by the United States and Britain. Prime Minister Churchill said at the Yalta Conference that the expulsion of six million Germans from the territories to be annexed by Poland would be "manageable."[36] He was to change his view at Potsdam. He then began to worry about the uprooting of millions of Germans for two reasons; one was humanitarian and the other, the fear that the Western zones of occupation could not feed large numbers of expelled Germans. He never objected to the uprooting of millions of Poles to be evacuated from the territory east of the Curzon Line.

2. Also in line with the concept of compensation, the Polish government mentioned in its arguments the economic losses suffered because of the Soviet annexation of Eastern Poland (oil and natural gas fields, agricultural lands, forests, pastures, etc.). These losses could be counter-balanced by the acquisition of resources in East German territories. The exchange of agricultural Eastern Poland for the much more industrial-ized East German provinces and broad access to the Baltic Sea with its ports would enable Poland to change its economic orientation from the prewar, which was mostly agricultural, to an industrial-agricultural and maritime orientation.

3. The Poles also invoked historical rights to the lands east of the Oder-Western Neisse line: the cradle of the Polish state, as it had emerged in the tenth century in recorded history, was located there and in the present western provinces of Poland; and the Oder-Neisse frontier had existed until the middle of the twelfth century, the time when the Germans started gradually to advance eastward. They said that Poland, unable to recover the lost territories in the West, began by the end of the fourteenth century to acquire an eastern orientation and was gaining territories in the East. The inter-war Poland "was a compromise between Eastern and Western orientations." "Circumstances now have changed radically." They meant by this that the Soviet Union had put an end to the former Eastern orientation by annexing Eastern Poland. Hence, Poland had to return to its historically initial Western orientation by

pushing its western frontier westward to what it had been in the first centuries of its existence.

4. Finally, the Polish representatives said that Poland, which had suffered so much during the period of German occupation, had the right to a moral reparation, and also, having experienced German aggressiveness, needed the shortest possible strategic frontier in the west. The Oder-Western Neisse line would form such a frontier.[37]

CHURCHILL'S STAND

The Polish-Soviet proposals for the Oder–Western Neisse frontier met with Churchill's vigorous opposition. As we have seen, he came to Potsdam in a mood completely different from the one he displayed at Teheran or even Yalta. His prospective enemy was no longer defeated Germany but the Soviet Union, the former "gallant ally." He might have thought of Germany as a future Western factor in the Continental balance of power. Poland, now under the Soviet protectorate, had to be prevented from acquiring too much German territory. Retreating from the former British view that the Polish western frontier should reach the estuary of the Oder, he said at Potsdam that the Oder line "was a very rough description . . . an approximate line."[38] Stalin reminded him that he, Churchill, and President Roosevelt had agreed at Yalta on the line which would begin at the estuary of the Oder and would follow the Oder until its junction with Eastern Neisse, while he, Stalin, had preferred the line of Western Neisse.[39] Churchill was carried so far in his debate with Stalin that he exclaimed that "Poland is now claiming more territory than she gave up,"[40] although the contrary was true if the exchange of territories was to be measured in square kilometers.

Churchill used two arguments in his opposition to the Oder–Western-Neisse frontier. His main argument was that one should not move 8.5 million Germans from the disputed territory. He assumed that that was the number of prewar Germans living there, although he admitted that probably only 2.5 to 3 million still remained east of the Oder-Western Neisse.[41] His argument regarding the displacement of 8.5 million Germans, whether they were already in other parts of Germany or in the contested territory, had interesting implications. He understood that the agreement of the three powers at Potsdam regarding any western line of Polish administration could hardly be undone at the future peace conference. Whatever that line, it would probably become the final frontier. He was not reassured by the agreement of all three powers that the final decision on the German-Polish frontier would have to be reserved to the peace conference. He said that "if the settlement of the question were delayed, the present local situation would be consolidated, Poles would be digging themselves in and taking effective steps to make themselves masters of this territory."[42] He was not wrong in his prediction. Hence, he wanted the Germans who had fled in fear of advancing Soviet troops to "be encouraged to come back."[43] He must have realized that if 8.5 million Germans were again resettled in the contested territories, it would mean the return to the ethnic situation that had existed in 1939. The Poles would be confronted with the following alternative: either to resign themselves eventually to small border rectifications, allowing them much less even than what Churchill was ready to accept at Potsdam, or to annex a larger territory with a very big German minority longing for revision of the frontier.

While advocating the return of 8.5 million Germans, Churchill did not mind the expulsion of almost 4 million Poles from the former Eastern Poland annexed by the Soviet Union, because "the British had accepted in principle the transfer of the population from east of the Curzon Line."[44] In his war memoirs he wrote: "Moving three or four million Poles was bad enough. Were we to move more than eight million Germans as well?"[45] He added that "The British had grave moral scruples about vast movements of population."[46] He did not have these scruples at Yalta when he thought that moving six million Germans was "manageable." In contrast to his position regarding Polish frontiers, he assured Stalin of British support for the Soviet annexation of the Koenigsberg area.[47]

The problem of removing Germans was further complicated at Potsdam by demands of the Czechoslovak and Hungarian governments for the removal of millions of Czech-Sudetenland Germans (2.5 million) and of several hundred thousands of Hungarian Germans.

Churchill's other argument against the transfer of Germans was that it would create insuperable difficulties in the Western zones of occupation, where the expelled and refugee Germans from the East would be added to the existing population and would aggravate the already difficult problem of food supplies.

Churchill stated in his war memoirs that eventually he would have conceded at Potsdam the Oder-Eastern Neisse line, but would rather have broken the conference than agreed to the Western Neisse line.[48] Did he want to use the issue of the Western Neisse as an occasion for precipitating open discord between the allies and thereby involving the United States in his anti-Soviet policy of balance of power? His statement about "the terrible issue of the German-Polish frontier"[49] in the postwar period sounds retrospectively like an un-British overstatement, especially in the light of the German-Soviet and German-Polish treaties of 1970.

THE AMERICAN PROPOSAL

President Truman rather seldom but calmly intervened in the passionate Churchill-Stalin debate. However, he, like Churchill, expressed his unpleasant surprise at being confronted with an accomplished fact, the Soviet grant to Poland of a large piece of Germany.[50] He asked Stalin whether the territory transferred to Polish administration should be considered a fifth zone of occupation under the authority of the Allied Council for Germany.[51] Stalin denied that the territory would be either a Polish zone of occupation or part of the Soviet zone. He wanted to limit the jurisdiction of the Allied Council to a Germany which would end at the Oder-Western Neisse, which he understood as the Polish western frontier. The President did not insist. He stressed, however, that his constitutional powers did not allow him to agree to any final frontiers, which should be determined in a peace treaty to be approved by the United States Senate. Both Churchill and Stalin agreed with him that the final decision on frontiers should be deferred to the peace conference.

Eventually, on July 29, the American delegation submitted to the Soviet delegation a proposal by virtue of which, "pending the final determination of Poland's western frontier, the former German territories east of a line running from the Baltic Sea through Swinemünde, to west of Stettin to the Oder and thence along the eastern Neisse to the Czechoslovak frontier, including that portion of East Prussia not placed under the administration of the Union of Soviet Socialist Republics in accordance with the understanding reached at this conference and including the area of the former free city of Danzig, shall be under the administration of the Polish State and for such purposes should not be considered as part of the Soviet zone of occupation in Germany."[52]

The use of the term "former" in relation to the territories placed under Polish administration implied that the American government did not expect that the future peace conference would return these territories to Germany. It was also clear that Stettin, located on the western bank of the Oder, would also be placed under Polish administration. This detail did not appear in the final text of the three-power decision, but the intention remained the same. The Soviet delegation refused to accept this American proposal, insisting on the Western Neisse line.[53]

Then something happened during the following twenty-four hours. American official sources offer no explanation. It is possible that the result of the British elections had to do with the shift in the American position. With Churchill gone and replaced by the new Prime Minister Attlee, the Americans probably did not expect to meet with a fierce British opposition to a new American proposal. The British delegation might have been consulted on that proposal or not; American sources remain silent on this point. Anyhow, the American delegation on July 30 submitted to the Soviet delegation an amended proposal whereby Eastern Neisse was replaced by Western Neisse.[54] The Soviet delegation could only express its gratification.[55] The British delegation put up a short show of resistance, Secretary of State for Foreign Affairs Bevin stating that his instructions obliged him to ask for the line of Eastern Neisse. He also asked unsuccessfully to extend the authority of the Allied Council to the whole territory placed under Polish administration. Finally the British delegation gave up, faced as it was with a united American-Soviet front. The three delegations then approved the amended American proposal which did not mention Stettin, but it was understood that that city was to be included, as stated expressly in the first American proposal.[56]

The three delegations also agreed on the transfer of Germans from Poland, Czechoslovakia, and Hungary. The Allied Council on Germany clarified the matter of what should be understood by "Poland" by agreeing in November 1945 to the transfer of Germans also from the territory east of the Oder and Western Neisse. It is more than probable that this was also the understanding of the three powers in August 1945. If so, they must not have expected that the future peace conference would change the Polish western frontier as they had defined it at Potsdam. Otherwise, it would have been foolish to transfer a few million Germans still residing east of the Oder-Neisse line, while expecting that they would return in case the peace conference should modify the German-Polish frontier.

THE DECISION

The final joint communiqué, accepted on August 2, 1945, by the three powers, stated the following regarding the former East German territories and the transfer of German population:

VI. CITY OF KOENIGSBERG AND THE ADJACENT AREA.

The Conference examined a proposal by the Soviet Government that, pending the final determination of territorial questions at the peace settlement, the section of the western frontier of the Union of Soviet Socialist Republics which is adjacent to the Baltic Sea should pass from a point on the eastern shore of the Bay of Danzig to the east, north of Braunsberg-Goldap, to the meeting of the frontiers of Lithuania, the Polish Republic and East Prussia.

The Conference has agreed in principle to the proposal of the Soviet Government concerning the ultimate transfer to the Soviet Union of the City of Koenigsberg and the area adjacent to it as described above subject to expert examination of the actual frontier.

The President of the United States and the British Prime Minister have declared that they will support the proposal of the Conference at the forthcoming peace settlement. . . .

IX. POLAND. . . .

. . . B. The following agreement was reached on the western frontier of Poland: . . .

. . . The three Heads of Government reaffirm their opinion that the final delimitation of the western frontier of Poland should await the peace settlement. The three Heads of Government agree that, pending the final determination of Poland's western frontier, the former German territories east of a line running from the Baltic Sea immediately west of Swinemünde, and thence along the Oder River to the confluence of the western Neisse River and along the western Neisse to the Czechoslovak frontier, including that portion of East Prussia not placed under the administration of the Union of Soviet Socialist Republics in accordance with the understanding reached at this conference and including the area of the former free city of Danzig, shall be under the administration of the Polish State and for such purposes should not be considered as part of the Soviet zone of occupation in Germany. . . .

XIII. ORDERLY TRANSFERS OF GERMAN POPULATIONS.

The Conference reached the following agreement on the removal of Germans from Poland, Czechoslovakia and Hungary:
"The Three Governments, having considered the question in
all its aspects, recognize that the transfer to Germany of German
populations, or elements thereof, remaining in Poland, Czechoslovakia and Hungary, will have to be undertaken. They agree that
any transfers that take place should be effected in an orderly and
humane manner."

The remainder of decisions on the transfers instructed the Allied
Control Council in Germany to examine the problem with special regard
to the question of the equitable distribution of the transferred Germans
among the several zones of occupation. The Polish, Czechoslovak, and
Hungarian governments were requested to suspend expulsions pending
the Council's instructions.[57] The problem of Polish and Soviet frontiers
was placed on the same footing, in respect to the final determination
at the peace settlement.

On his return home President Truman said in a radio address to
the nation on August 9, 1945: "The territory the Poles are to administer
will enable Poland better to support its population. It will provide a
short and more easily defensible frontier between Poland and Germany.
Settled by Poles, it will provide a more homogeneous nation."[58] This
comment could be interpreted to mean that the President considered
the Oder-Neisse line as a final Polish frontier.

What remained was to inform the French government, representing
the fourth occupying power. French Foreign Minister Georges Bidault
told Secretary of State James Byrnes on August 23, 1945, that "the
temporary but probably permanent in actual fact" western frontier of
Poland, as determined at Potsdam, did not meet with any objections on
the part of his government.[59] His prediction was to be confirmed by
later events, including the Soviet-German and German-Polish treaties
of 1970.

The Poles owed the Oder–Western-Neisse frontier to Stalin's per-
severance at the Potsdam Conference, to the final concession made by
President Truman, and to the fall of Churchill's government.

The Poles, now living in a smaller territory than before the war,
nevertheless gained one important advantage, a nationally homogeneous
population in contrast to what had been true prior to 1939. The Polish
census of 1931 listed 30.9 percent of the population as declaring use

of a non-Polish language: 4,442,000, Ukrainian; 2,723,000, Yiddish (3,113,000 declared to have the Jewish religion); 989,000 Byelorussian; and 741,000, German. The smaller minorities such as the Lithuanian, Czech, and Hungarian did not exceed the figure of 150,000. The Ukrainian and Byelorussian minorities became parts of the population of the Soviet Union together with the territory east of the Curzon Line. The Germans exterminated almost the whole Jewish minority, while the remnants emigrated later to Israel or other countries. There are now probably not more than 10,000 persons who consider themselves of Jewish nationality. The Germans either fled in fear of advancing Soviet armies or were expelled in the postwar years. What remains now is the question of whether a few hundred thousand persons of Polish descent feel like Germans or Poles. This is the subject of current controversy between the German and Polish governments, the German government wanting to repatriate all former German and now Polish citizens who declare themselves as ethnic Germans. This German insistence is politically interesting, because no government would request the repatriation of its countrymen if it had any hope that the territory they inhabit would eventually return to the country of their language and nationality. The Polish government disputes the West German figure of ethnic Germans remaining in Poland, and this is the substance of the controversy.

4

After Potsdam

THE CONTROVERSIAL MEANING OF THE POTSDAM DECISION

THE POTSDAM DECISION was legally far from clear; soon after, it produced controversy between Poland and the Soviet Union on the one hand, and the Federal Republic of Germany, the United States, and Britain on the other, regarding the exact meaning of that decision. The German and Western argument was that the question of the final German-Polish frontier was left open until the peace settlement. The Federal Republic claimed that the German frontiers remained legally those of 1937, *i.e.,* as they existed prior to Hitler's annexations. The Soviet and Polish governments advanced the opposite argument that the decision was in fact final and that the mention of the future peace settlement referred only to a formal approval of what was decided at Potsdam. The confusion was due, among other things, to the use in the Potsdam decision of two terms: "determination" and "delimitation." *Determination* meant a decision on the substance, *i.e.,* the peace settlement could change the line of the German-Polish frontier by, for instance, the retrocession to Germany of a part of the area placed under Polish administration. *Delimitation* meant something entirely different, namely, the fixing on-spot of the exact running of the frontier otherwise established. The Potsdam decision did not include a detailed map of the western limit of the area placed under the Polish administration, although each great power delegation had general maps at its disposal at Potsdam. It did not raise serious questions regarding the

71

line of the rivers Oder and Western Neisse, but unintentionally did not mention the cities of Swinemünde and Stettin, both located west of the Oder.

On the one hand, the serious nature of the controversy at Potsdam regarding the Eastern or Western Neisse indicated that the three powers did not seem to expect that the peace settlement would change what they decided at Potsdam. On the other hand, the reservation that the final determination of the Soviet frontier in East Prussia and the Polish western frontier should be reached in the peace settlement gave something of a provisional and temporary flavor to their decision.

THE POLISH THESIS

The Polish lawyers began immediately to assemble an array of arguments to prove that the Potsdam decision was final:

1. The three great powers had the legal authority to determine finally the future German frontiers because of the German unconditional surrender and the taking over by the Allied occupying powers of supreme authority over Germany. On June 5, 1945, the four occupying powers (the United States, Britain, the USSR, and France) issued in Berlin the Declaration in which they said that they had assumed supreme authority over Germany and that they would later determine the German frontiers. It is true that the same Declaration mentioned the 1937 frontiers of Germany to indicate the territorial extent of their authority, just as the Allied statement of the same date also mentioned the 1937 frontiers for the purpose of dividing occupied Germany into the four zones of occupation. In the case of both allied pronouncements the Allies were saying that they did not consider the territories annexed by Nazi Germany since 1938 as part of the defeated country they were occupying. In neither case did they state the intention to maintain the 1937 frontiers in the postwar period. Moreover, the Potsdam document, later in date, never mentioned the 1937 frontiers. That document in effect restricted the territory of Germany in the east to the Oder-Western Neisse line because it withdrew the lands placed under Polish administration from the authority of the Allied Control Council. These lands were removed from the area of the Soviet zone of occupation but were not erected into a Polish zone of occupation. The Potsdam decision did not place any restrictions on the rights of Polish administering authorities. The three great powers seemed to think on August 2, 1945, therefore, that their assignment of the territory east of Oder-Neisse did prejudge the matter insofar as the future peace settlement was concerned.

2. This seems to be confirmed by their Potsdam decision to transfer the German population from Poland. If any doubt was left as to what "Poland" meant regarding the extent of territory, this doubt was dispelled on November 20, 1945, by the decision of the Allied Control Council. The Council, on which the three great powers present at Potsdam and France were represented, decided to resettle Germans from Poland, Czechoslovakia, Hungary, and Austria in occupied Germany. 3.5 million Germans were to be deported from Poland. The Allied Control Council for Germany decided that "the entire German population to be moved from Poland (3.5 million persons) will be admitted to the Soviet and the British zones of occupation in Germany."[1] Since the total number of Germans in prewar Poland was about 750,000, it was obvious that the four great powers had in mind principally Germans still living between the prewar Polish western frontier and the Oder-Neisse line. The decision of the Allied Control Council clarified the meaning of "Poland" in the Potsdam decision.

The Polish argument continues by saying that no one in his senses would assent to and help in the deportation of millions of Germans from their homes east of the Oder-Neisse, if he had any doubts that the territory in question would ever return to Germany.

3. The Potsdam decision used such terms as "Western frontier of Poland" in the sub-title, and "former German territories" as well as "the former free city of Danzig." This was another proof that the three powers considered those territories lost to Germany. Moreover, they would not have debated so seriously and sometimes even passionately, as in Churchill's case, the problem of contested territories, if they thought that their decision would be only temporary, especially in view of the fact that they expected at that time to meet at a peace conference rather soon after the Potsdam Conference.

4. Polish lawyers usually overlook in their comments on the Potsdam decision the word "determination," and insist on the meaning of "delimitation," another term used in the same decision. They say that the peace conference was left with only the right to proceed with the demarcation on the spot of the frontier already determined at Potsdam.[2]

CHANGES IN THE ETHNIC COMPOSITION OF THE POPULATION

Much more important than any legal arguments were the firm Soviet support of the Oder-Neisse frontier and the thorough change in the ethnic composition of the population in the Polish-annexed former East

German provinces. This change was brought about by the German-ordered evacuation of German civilians from the territories to be invaded by Soviet troops, the mass flight of other Germans in fear of those advancing troops who were taking their revenge for the cruelties of the Nazi occupation of Soviet lands, the expulsion of millions of still other Germans in consequence of the Potsdam decision on the transfer of the German population, the later departure of most of the other remaining Germans owing to their repatriation to Germany, and, finally, the re-settlement of several million Poles. The net effect of all these events was the replacement of the German population by Poles, whose present number is equal to the prewar figure of the German population. The Polish-German ethnic boundary now corresponds to the Oder-Neisse political frontier, except for the current Polish-German dispute about the exact number of ethnic Germans still remaining, whom the Federal Republic would like to repatriate. The German and Polish figures differ greatly. Probably a few hundred thousand persons, former German citizens and now Polish citizens, would now claim to be ethnic Germans if given free option.

The prewar population of the former East German territories annexed by Poland and the Soviet Union amounted to 9,559,900 persons. This was the figure according to the German general census of the population taken on May 17, 1939.[3] The census included within the above figure 212,322 persons who were only temporarily stationed in those territories, namely, soldiers and persons doing compulsory labor service. Deducting these, the figure for the permanent population stands at 9,347,578. To reach the final figure for the prewar population of the territories annexed by Poland, one must add the population of the Free City of Danzig, which was not part of the German Reich in May 1939 and was not included in the German census (404,000), and deduct the prewar population of the Soviet-annexed Koenigsberg area (1,187,200). In this way we arrive at the conclusion that the prewar population of the Polish-annexed German provinces east of the Oder-Neisse line numbered 8,564,378. This much is certain. What is controversial is the number of the Polish minority within that permanent population. Some postwar German sources quote the figures taken from the results of the census of May 1939. According to that census, approximately 65,000 persons declared that their language was other than German, i.e., Polish, a Polish dialect, or Polish and German. Only about 10,173 persons dared to declare their Polish nationality.[4]

The figures of the census, taken under the Nazi regime and at the time of open conflict with Poland, cannot be seriously considered.

Obviously those German citizens who acknowledged the use of a language other than German or, even worse, that they belonged to the hated Polish nationality, knew that the penalty would be confinement to the concentration camp.

The Polish authors contrast these low figures with the results of the German censuses taken at a time when the German authorities did not have recourse to terror. The census of 1910 listed 1,020,500 persons as speaking Polish or Polish and German. The census of 1925 gave the figure of 663,004, and the census of 1933, 437,894. Assuming that the Germanization process made progress between 1910 and 1933, even a sceptic would have to admit that at least 437,894 persons were not German-speaking but used Polish or one of the Polish dialects. This is admitted by the postwar official publication of the Federal Republic which states that some 450,000 persons either spoke Polish or were bilingual prior to the outbreak of the Second World War.[5] What is contested by that publication is the number of Polish-speaking or bilingual people who also felt that they belonged to the Polish minority, a controversial matter which cannot be proved either way in a conclusive manner. What is certain is that before the war there was a sizeable Polish minority residing between the 1939 Polish frontier and the Oder-Neisse line.

The population statistics became unreliable later on, until the first postwar Polish census of February 14, 1946.[6] What happened in the meantime was the war, with its human losses due to enemy air bombing, to the frontline deaths of those inhabitants of the territories East of Oder-Neisse who were enlisted in the German armed forces and in the last stage of war in the *Volkssturm,* to which all Germans between the ages of 16 and 60 were called up for the last fight, and to the casualties among civilians because of the German-sponsored hasty evacuation of civilians just prior to the Soviet military advance and the desperate and panicky flight of other civilians during that advance. Any guess-estimates are complicated by the increase in the prewar population by perhaps one million Germans from Western and Central Germany who, beginning in 1942, had fled east of the Oder-Neisse to escape Allied bombing of their native cities and industrial regions. The losses of the German armed forces were no longer registered after January 1945, because of the quick retreat of German armies in a less than orderly way. Hence, one cannot be sure how many German soldiers, recruited east of the Oder-Neisse, actually perished. It is also unknown for certain how many of them died in Soviet prisoner-of-war camps. Since the German armies made a desperate resistance to the Soviet advance in the last months of the war, these losses and the losses suffered by the *Volkssturm* must have been very great. German estimates for military and civilian losses due to the war vary greatly and are only guess-estimates. However, these estimates agree that the human losses among the population of the territories east of the Oder-Neisse were proportionately higher than in the remainder of Germany. This was due to the heavy losses in the *Volkssturm*, which included people enlisted at the last moment and poorly trained, the forcible and hastily improvised government-sponsored evacuation of civilians, and, finally, the disorderly and panicky flight of other civilians.

West German sources assume that at least 656,000 soldiers from the Eastern territories died because of military hostilities.[7] This is a guess because of the lack of official statistics beginning with January 1945. In any event, all German sources agree that the population of the Eastern territories suffered heavier military casualties proportionately than the population of Western and Central Germany because more recruits were called up from those mostly agricultural regions, while a relatively high proportion of industrially necessary manpower was exempted from military service in the industrialized parts of Germany. East German peasants were replaced by forcibly imported foreign agricultural laborers. The other reason for proportionately heavier human losses of the population of the Eastern territories was enlistment in the *Volkssturm*, which Hitler ordered to be formed on October 18, 1944. This *Volkssturm* suffered proportionately much heavier casualties than the regular armed forces in the last-ditch resistance to the Soviet advance. It seems that the figure of military losses among the population of the Eastern territories (565,000 out of the total of 3,760,000 for Germany) which has been given in West German official statistics is too low and unreliable since no one knows the figures after January 1945.[8] Probably 800,000 or 900,000 would be closer to the actual losses.

The civilian losses of the same population must have been very great during the last stage of war. By Hitler's orders, several cities east of the Oder-Neisse were made into fortresses which were desperately defended to protect Berlin until the last moment. Only a part of the civilian population of those "fortresses" had been evacuated prior to the assault by Soviet troops. The Soviet offensive, which was to end with the capture of Berlin, had begun on January 12, 1945. The Nazi authorities ordered the forcible evacuation of civilians from the localities threatened by the Soviet advance often at the last moment prior to their capture by Soviet troops. The civilians, if reluctant to leave, were forced to do so under the threat of force.[9] This evacuation was frequently chaotic because of orders being given at the last moment.[10] The transports were haphazard. Trains, ships, trucks, buses, and peasant horse carts transported the refugees westward. Many of them trekked on foot. It was a flow of disoriented refugees, reminiscent of the Dutch, Belgian, and French refugees in 1940. The evacuation turned into a catastrophe in the winter months of 1945. There were a great many deaths due to cold and lack of food, mostly among the aged, sick, and children. However, no one registered the civilian losses which were also due to Soviet bombing of evacuee trains and to deaths of those civilians who were caught between the fighting lines.

Staggering losses, perhaps amounting to a half million, occurred among the civilians from East Prussia who were assembled around Elbing (Weichsel Haff) in the hope that they would be evacuated by ships. This tragedy took place in the worst winter months of January and February 1945. The evacuees were killed by enemy air-bombing, others perished from cold, were stampeded by the panicky crowds, or were drowned during the thaw at the end of February while attempting to reach the ships by walking on ice. Still other refugees who boarded German ships in Danzig and Gdynia perished when the ships were torpedoed, bombed, or struck the mines. At the same time other civilians were killed during the Hitler-ordered defense of cities such as Breslau, Danzig, Glogau, Koenigsberg, Elbing, Kolberg, and several others. The losses among the old, women, and children were greater than they would have been otherwise, because the able-bodied men, conscripted in the *Volkssturm,* could not accompany their families.

The five million Germans (among them were wartime resettlers from the German Reich and from Eastern Europe) who were evacuated or fled on their own from the Eastern territories suffered tremendous casualties but reliable statistics are lacking.[11] Many of them, already exhausted, died later in Western and Central Germany during the last stage of the war.

No one knows how many Germans died of hunger or exhaustion during their desperate trek westward; how many were frozen to death; how many were drowned in the Vistula Haff or in the Baltic while their ships were sunk; how many perished in the "fortress" cities or from bombs or, finally, while caught in Soviet-German crossfire.

In any event, some 3.5 million Germans, according to Polish sources, remained east of the Oder-Neisse line by the end of hostilities. According to the West German and East German censuses of 1950, there were 4,422,900 refugees and resettlers (expelled by virtue of the

Potsdam decision) from the Polish and Soviet-annexed former German territories in the Federal Republic, 150,000 in West Berlin, 2,212,363 in the German Democratic Republic, and 55,249 in East Berlin, altogether 6,840,512.[12] Of the 3.5 million Germans who remained east of the Oder-Neisse, some 200,000 were expelled by the Polish authorities in June and July 1945, and 3,190,000 were expelled following the Potsdam decision. Hence approximately 100,000 Germans, acknowledged as such and not as Polish autochthons, still remained in Poland by the end of 1950.

Assuming that these figures are correct (they include the refugees and expellees from Danzig), and taking into account that the Poles claimed that over one million of the prewar population declared themselves to be Poles and were not expelled, the total surviving population of the territories east of the Oder-Neisse amounted in 1950 to approximately 7,840,000 persons, living in various parts of what was prewar Germany. This would mean that 1939–45 military and civilian casualties amounted to over 1.5 million among the prewar population of Polish and Soviet-annexed territories. Those who accept this figure claim that military casualties amounted to 600,000 and the civilian losses to 900,000.

The statistics are unreliable. For instance, in 1945 the Poles estimated the remaining native population of the Polish-annexed lands to be 3.5 million. The Allied Control Council for Germany allowed the expulsion of 3.5 million Germans by its decision of November 1945.[13] Actually only 3,390,000 were expelled, while 1,017,086 prewar inhabitants were allowed to remain because the Polish authorities claimed that they were Poles. Approximately 100,000 Germans considered as such by the Polish government were not expelled. Hence, the total population that remained after the end of hostilities must have numbered 4,407,000 persons, not 3.5 million. It is true that a great many had returned to their former domiciles after the end of hostilities before the Soviet and Polish authorities stopped this eastward trek. One has to suppose that either over 900,000 persons returned or that the 3.5 million figure, estimated by the Polish authorities for 1945, was short of several hundred thousands.

The Polish authorities proceeded at the beginning of 1946 with verification of the nationalities of the prewar population remaining east of the Oder-Neisse, in order to be sure who were Germans among them, to be expelled, and who were Poles, allowed to remain. The criteria were as follows: Polish descent as indicated by the family name, blood relation to Polish families, assent to the education of children in the

Polish spirit, knowledge of the Polish language, etc. This procedure wavered between two extremes: on the one hand, the Polish government did not want to retain a large German minority in Poland, and on the other hand, it hoped that many families, already Germanized, would be re-Polonized under the Polish regime. After verification 1,017,086 persons were declared to be Poles or, as they were called, autochthons. The bulk of them (867,105) resided in Silesia.

This verification was unreliable for two reasons. First, the Polish authorities wanted to re-Polonize as many as possible of those inhabitants who were of Polish descent. Second, the so-called autochthons did not enjoy complete freedom in declaring their true nationality; many must have feared that if they opted for the German nationality, they would be expelled. This is the origin of the present German-Polish controversy regarding the present number of autochthons (German citizens prior to 1945 who are now Polish citizens) who feel that they are German. The original number of the prewar population declared in 1946 to be autochthon Poles was later reduced by their repatriation to either part of Germany. Their number in December 1948 amounted to only 935,830.

Regular repatriation to the FRG began in 1955 by agreement between the West German and Polish Red Cross organizations and has continued to the present day. It has been carried out as a humanitarian reunion of families, the prewar German citizens now residing in Poland being allowed to join their relatives, even very distant relatives, in the Federal Republic.

According to the data given by the German Red Cross to the author, 399,415 persons were repatriated to the Federal Republic between 1955 and May 1972. Assuming that the natural increase has been counter-balanced by the repatriation to the German Democratic Republic (both figures are unknown), the remainder of the so-called verified autochthons should be now about 600,000. German and Polish claims regarding the nationality of these autochthons are absurd. The West Germans claim that all of them are ethnic Germans, relying on the Nazi-held 1939 census and disregarding the results of the 1933 census which listed almost 480,000 persons as speaking Polish or being bilingual. The Poles claim that all the autochthons are Poles since they were verified in 1946, although that verification was unreliable. What one may assume is that many verified autochthons genuinely felt Polish at that time, and that the children of many others were later re-Polonized by education in Polish schools.

The feelings of the so-called autochthons, who sincerely felt by the end of the war that they were Poles, were badly hurt on contact with the newly-installed Polish authorities and with the Polish settlers who were pouring in from the territory of prewar Poland. They were often discriminated against because both the authorities and the incoming Polish settlers treated them as Germans for various reasons: their having been German citizens, their having served in the German armed forces, their different ways of life, and their local dialect which sounded strange in the ears of Poles from Poland. The bitter experience of being discriminated against in spite of their acknowledgment of Polish nationality at the time of the verification left its traces. Another factor was dislike of the socialist system introduced by Poland. All this played its role in the later desire of many autochthons to be repatriated to Germany.[14]

The controversy cannot be solved by recourse to statistics, because the Polish statistics do not mention the nationality of Polish citizens. Using a sort of Solomon's judgment, one may perhaps assume that some 250,000 to 300,000 autochthons feel that they are ethnic Germans and would be willing to be repatriated to the Federal Republic. The question is further complicated by the economic attraction of the prosperous Federal Republic. How many former German citizens might be Poles who are ready to declare themselves ethnic Germans for the sake of going to the Federal Republic where they expect to have higher living standards than in Poland? A German journalist admitted recently: "Doubtless not all the applicants [for emigration] are Germans by extraction or native tongue, and in a number of instances the motive behind their desire to emigrate will merely be the wish to improve in the West their economic situation."[15] This is further complicated by the fact that almost all of those autochthons live in Upper Silesia, which was detached from Poland six centuries ago. Their ancestors had lived under Czech, Austrian, and Prussian governments; consequently, in many cases the present descendants might be uncertain of their allegiance to either Poland or Germany and be guided in their choice by sheer opportunism.

Except for the autochthons, all of whom the Polish government claimed as Poles, and perhaps one hundred thousand self-avowed Germans who were allowed to remain, the prewar population of the former German territories either perished during the war, or went to Germany west of the Oder-Neisse as the result of Nazi-ordered evacuation and spontaneous flight, or of the Potsdam-ordered expulsions. The void began to be filled in 1945 by the inflow of Polish settlers. The census of December 3, 1950, found that 2,792,714 immigrants had come from central Poland, 1,553,512 from Soviet-annexed prewar eastern Poland (in spite of the later second repatriation in the fifties, Soviet statistics still register about 1.5 million Poles living in the USSR), and a few hundred thousands returning from Germany and the West (forced laborers, inmates of the concentration camps, soldiers who served under the British command, and so on). The total population of 5,855,000, including the autochthons, was predominantly Polish in 1950. Owing to the very high birth rate (the average birth rate in the late forties and fifties was generally high in Poland but lower than in the annexed Western and Northern territories), the population grew very rapidly. In 1955 it amounted to 6,738,000, in 1960 to 7,618,000, in 1965 to 8,210,000, and in 1968 to 8,500,000, i.e., it reached the prewar figure.

The natural increase (the difference between the figures for births and deaths) during the years 1945 to 1969, amounted to 3,540,000. During the same period of time 4,890,000 children were born alive. Today over half of the population are natives, i.e., born in the Northern and Western territories as these territories are now called.[16]

The high birth rate, the highest in Europe at that time (late forties and fifties) was due to two factors: the general tendency in Poland of instinctive biological nature to compensate for the enormous war-time losses, and the younger composition of the population in the Northern and Western territories, due to the average younger age of the Polish settlers. Only in the sixties did the birth and natural increase rates begin to fall rapidly in Poland (a general phenomenon observed in all economically advanced countries, including the Federal Republic of Germany, where in 1973 the number of deaths exceeded by 100,000 the number of births, the United States, and the Soviet Union). Still the figure of birth rate for the Northern and Western territories was higher in 1968 than in the rest of Poland (17.1 per thousand versus 15.9 per thousand).

The frequency of marriages also has been higher in those territories than the national average. Mixed marriages helped to merge the various segments of the population (the autochthons, the immigrants from former eastern Poland, and the settlers from central Poland). This in turn strengthened the process of integration of the autochthons.[17]

According to the Polish Statistical Yearbook for 1970, the total population of the Northern and Western territories numbered 8,575,000 persons (the total Polish population at that time was 32,589,000, an increase of 8,659,000 by comparison to the figure for 1946). Thus, over 25 percent of Polish citizens live in the Northern and Western territories. In spite of the fall in the natural increase rate, the Polish population in general and its portions in the Northern and Western territories continue to grow. For instance, 546,900 births were registered in Poland in 1970. The Polish natural increase in 1970 was 8.5 per thousand as compared with 3 per thousand in the Federal Republic of Germany and a loss of population in the German Democratic Republic (−3 per thousand).[18] The rapid fall in the birth rate will not affect the rate of natural increase for quite a time, because the high birth rate in the late forties and fifties is now reflected in the high proportion of young people; half of the population is below thirty years of age.

REHABILITATION OF ANNEXED TERRITORIES

What the Poles found in 1945 in the former Eastern German territories was not the lively and prosperous economy of prewar years. The military hostilities of the last months of the war left behind immense destruction. Several cities, erected by the retreating Germans into "fortresses" and often defended for quite a long time, including Breslau, Danzig, and Gdynia, lay in ruins. The outflow of millions of evacuated, westward-fleeing, and expelled Germans left factories, mines, and agricultural homesteads abandoned. The following table illustrates the material losses:

Destroyed or heavily damaged property in percentages of the prewar condition:

Urban housing	40
Rural housing	28
Industrial equipment	50
Horses	90
Cattle	92
Hogs	96
Sheep	97
Railway tracks	63
Railway rolling stock	97
Bridges	50
Farms	27.5[19]

The immense task of reconstruction faced a Poland itself bled white by the war. Of prewar national wealth 38 percent was lost (33 percent of industries, 35 percent of agricultural production, 28 percent of forests, 50 percent of public transportation, 30 percent of housing). Six million persons dead and 590,000 totally or partially incapacitated must be added to this sad balance-sheet of the Polish territory between the 1939 western frontier and the new eastern frontier. The work of reconstruction was further hampered by disproportionately high losses among educated people and skilled manpower, as well as by the lack of educational facilities under the German occupation. There was no external assistance, such as the Marshall Plan for Western Europe, including West Germany. The Poles could count only on themselves.

What is amazing is not only the present and visible results in Poland in general and in the Northern and Western territories in particular, but also the great effort to reconstruct or repair historical buildings (castles, palaces, churches, etc.). Poles, intent on affirming their national identity after the Nazi challenge, attached a special importance to those reconstructions, which are visible not only in rebuilt Warsaw but also in several other places, including Szczecin, Wrocław, and Gdańsk. The Poles seemed to want to proclaim the truth of the initial verse of their national hymn: "Poland exists as long as we live." This effort to reconstruct or repair historical buildings, which continues without interruption, has resulted in the emergence of many specialists whose services were also used abroad, for instance, in Florence after the great flood, in Trier (FRG) where an ancient cathedral is being renovated with their assistance, and in Munich where they renovated one of the medieval gates of the city.

Gradually, year after year, the economy of the Northern and Western territories was rehabilitated, expanded, and integrated within the Polish national economy. These territories, with their 33 percent of total national territory and about 26 percent of national population, now provide 30 percent of the national production. Industrial output amounts to 25.8 percent of the national. Among several branches of that production are energy (30 percent of the national figure), coal (20 percent), brown coal (73.4 percent), metallurgy, machine-building, computers, railroad rolling stock, chemical, non-ferrous extraction of zinc and copper (important copper deposits were discovered by Polish geologists), and other industries. In other words, the acquisition of those territories greatly helped Poland to become an industrial nation.

Historically, Poland had not been a maritime nation. Only after the recovery of independence in 1918 and the acquisition of the narrow strip of the Baltic coast in 1920 did the Poles fully understand that their independence, especially economic, depended partly on their full use of maritime facilities. At first they thought that they could rely on the facilities provided by their economic rights in the Free City of Danzig, but they learned very soon that the Senate of that City did not intend to cooperate. Hence, the Polish government of the time came to the conclusion that the country also needed another port, one located on the Polish coast. The port and city of Gdynia were built where before there had been only a fishing village. This first Polish effort to provide an opening to the sea was brutally interrupted by German aggression in 1939.

The annexation of the former German territories gave Poland a coast 312 miles long with the three main harbors at Gdańsk (Danzig), Gdynia, and Szczecin (Stettin). This spurred national effort, which included big investments and the training of skilled maritime personnel.

The results are visible today. Poland has three main shipyards in Gdańsk, Gdynia, and Szczecin which built various ships of a total tonnage of about 700,000 tons in 1972 (74.3 percent were exported). It must be said that these shipyards were able to expand gradually, beginning with the immediate postwar years, owing mainly to Soviet orders. The Soviet Union has been and remains the main customer, but there are other customers such as Norwegian, French, Chinese, West German, Brazilian, Colombian, Bulgarian, and Romanian. For example, in 1972 the Szczecin shipyard was building tankers for Norway, each of 28,000 tonnage, and the Gdynia shipyard, two cargo ships for Sweden of 55,000 tons each, and a series of tankers for the Soviet Union, each of 105,000 tonnage (the maximum tonnage for ships navigating through the Danish straits). One of the specialties of Polish shipyards is fishing vessels; Poland occupies second place in the world in this respect, Japan taking the first place.

The three main harbors are being constantly improved. A new port is being built in Danzig, the so-called Northern Port. The Polish ports handled about 41 million tons of incoming and outgoing shipments in 1972. All in all, 150,000 persons are engaged in various maritime activities, while two million persons work at inland industrial enterprises whose operations are totally or partly related to the maritime industry, such as shipbuilding and ship repairing. In 1972 vessels and ship fittings amounted to 30 percent of all Polish exports.

The Polish merchant fleet was made up of 279 ships with an overall tonnage of 2,336,927 in 1973. This tonnage has increased each year and should reach 3.5 million tons by 1975. This effort to expand the national merchant fleet is caused by the fact that up to the present, 55 percent of Polish maritime imports and exports have been handled by foreign ships, a strain on national resources. The national fleet includes

160 deep-sea fishing vessels which operate in the North Sea and the Atlantic Ocean.[20]

Agriculture of the Northern and Western territories provides Poland with 30.3 percent of the national total for wheats, 25.8 percent for potatoes, 30.7 percent for cattle, and 26.2 percent for milk. The productivity of that agriculture is greater than the national average for two reasons: the average plot of the individually-owned farm is much larger than the national average, and the percentage of large estates (the state farms) is also much higher than the national.

The educational record is also impressive. To mention only the universities and equivalent higher-learning schools, ten of them existed prior to the war and had a total enrollment of 6,200 students. 80,664 students were enrolled in the academic year 1970–71 at the now existing twenty-seven universities and comparable schools. The educational importance of annexed territories can be measured by the following figures for the Polish cities with the highest number of schools of higher-learning: Warsaw and Cracow, eleven schools; Wrocław and Poznań, eight; Gdańsk and Lodz, six. Several research centers are located in the territories.

Wrocław has become one of the main Polish cultural centers, side by side with Warsaw and Cracow. Generally, the northern and western territories have a lively cultural life, as exemplified by the existence of twenty theaters, three operas, three comic operas, and seven symphonic orchestras. They are the home of the well-known folklore song-and-dance ensemble "Śląsk" ("Silesia"), and of no less known theaters: Jerzy Grotowski's Laboratory Theater and the Pantomime Theater, both having their headquarters in Wrocław.[21]

This necessarily very brief glance at the record of less than thirty years of Polish administration of the northern and western territories explains why the Poles firmly believe that they now have a moral right to those territories.

5

The Adenauer Era

WAS THE WAR LOST?

THE SHOCK of complete military defeat and the fear of retribution for the crimes committed by the Nazi regime against foreign peoples did not last long in Germany. The disintegration of the Grand Alliance and the beginning of the Cold War soon after the Potsdam Conference reassured the Germans who lived in the Western zones of occupation. The skillful policy of Konrad Adenauer, the first Chancellor of the Federal Republic, who succeeded in integrating Western Germany within the European Community and the North Atlantic Alliance, and in appeasing Israel and the Diaspora Jews by huge indemnities for the Nazi genocide, restored the good name of Germany. The so-called economic miracle, helped by the Marshall Plan and American investments, resulted in making West Germany one of the most prosperous countries in the world and economically the most powerful in Western Europe. The armed forces were rebuilt, and the *Bundeswehr* became the strongest army in Western Europe. It seemed that the traces of defeat were erased except for the division of Germany into two mutually hostile states and for the loss of eastern territories. All this helped West Germans almost to forget the Nazi record and the military debacle.

It was somewhat difficult to reconcile the economic prosperity, greater than that of victors such as Britain and France, and the important role played by the Federal Republic in international affairs, with the fact of total military defeat. The West Germans lived in a world of their own make-believe as though they bore no responsibility for what

87

had occurred during the Second World War. The division of their nation and the loss of eastern territories were felt as completely undeserved injustices, inflicted on them by the Soviet Union and Poland. The Cold War with its ideological propaganda against communism stimulated this emotional atmosphere. The Federal Republic, to use Chancellor Adenauer's words, proclaimed itself the shield of the Western world against communism. The unification of the country and the recovery of the lost lands appeared as valid goals for the whole West in the process of rolling back communism. Since Poland annexed almost all of those lost provinces and was ruled by a Communist government, it became the main target for West German propaganda. That propaganda also attacked the Soviet Union, but there was a sort of unspoken hope that Moscow would one day see reason and make a deal at the expense of Poland. At the same time, those German politicians who were the most vocal in demanding the return of the lost provinces were trying to convince the non-Communist Poles that a return to the 1937 frontiers would coincide with the liberation of their country from the communist regime. Some of the rightist scholars reminded the Poles of their eastern mission, as though the German return to the 1937 frontiers would also mean for Poles the recovery of eastern Poland, annexed by the Soviet Union. It was never spelled out how a weak Poland could recover former eastern Poland, or why the Germans had any interest in favoring the Poles over the Ukrainians and the Byelorussians.

The bitter German-Polish controversy was in full swing. It was bitter because the Germans, who in the postwar decades formed the political and intellectual elites in West Germany, remembered other times. They were young at the time of the Weimar Republic and could recall not only the 1937 frontiers but also the nostalgia at that time for the 1914 frontiers. They remembered the Nazi period when so many of them were rejoicing in Hitler's first external successes such as the *Anschluss* with Austria or the absorption of the Czech Sudetenland. They witnessed an unprecedented period in German history when their nation controlled almost the whole European continent. It is true that those victories were followed by debacle, but it had taken the French a long time to forget the Napoleonic glories in spite of Waterloo and enemy occupation. In both cases, the same generation saw both the summit of power of their nation and the abyss of its defeat.

Psychologically, it was far from easy to become reconciled to a situation in which Poland, defeated in 1939 and silenced for five and a half years, now governed the former eastern provinces of Germany. On top of everything, those provinces were lost to a nation traditionally considered culturally inferior and economically and politically inept.

Even the fiercest former opponents of the Nazis did not find it easy to think of Danzig as Gdańsk or Breslau as Wrocław, just as their Polish contemporaries did not find it easy to forget that Lviv was earlier Lwów and Vilnius, Wilno.

REFUGEES AND EXPELLEES

These bitter feelings were stimulated daily by the ubiquitous presence of the refugees and expellees from Eastern Europe, mostly from the Polish and Soviet-annexed lands and from the Czech Sudetenland. Every fifth citizen of the Federal Republic was a refugee or expellee. These refugees and expellees claimed the right to return to their homelands (*Heimatrecht*), something they could achieve only after revision of the frontiers. Their propaganda was financed by the federal and state governments of the Federal Republic, supported by the political parties for whom their votes were important, encouraged by various research institutes and individual scholars who supplied arguments legal or historical, and disseminated by the mass media. The young generation was taught at school of the right of Germany to recover the lost territories, while educational programs in many cases perpetuated the traditional image of the Pole as an inferior human being. A psychological chasm divided the Germans and the Poles.

NEGOTIATION FROM THE POSITION OF STRENGTH

The governments of the Federal Republic had no precise plan as to how to regain the former eastern provinces. They only nourished the hope that the greater military superiority of the Atlantic Alliance at the time of American nuclear ascendancy and, later on, the Soviet-Chinese quarrel, would eventually force the Soviet Union to come to the negotiating table and make a deal at the expense of Poland. The American position of negotiating from the position of superior strength became the West German position also. The West German population was told by its ruling elites that it should await patiently the X Day when the lost territories would be returned.

No official explanation was provided as to how to avoid, after recovery of the 1937 frontiers and the reestablishment of the Free City of Danzig, the repetition of the difficulties which had arisen with Poland over the Polish corridor and the Free City. In fact, the desired reestablishment of the 1937 frontiers was to be only the initial legal position for future negotiations with the Soviet Union about less favorable frontiers. American and British statements regarding the Potsdam decision indicated that the United States and Britain would support a modification of the 1937 frontiers in favor of the Soviet Union and Poland. It was clear to the West German politicians that at least East Prussia and Danzig were lost and probably more than that unless a catastrophe should overtake the Soviet Union. However, the constantly repeated slogan of "1937 frontiers" was breeding false hopes among average West Germans.

WESTERN SUPPORT FOR FRONTIER REVISION

The claim for the revision of Polish frontiers found Western support. West Germany was an important element in the policy of containment of the Soviet Union. Hence, the West Germans had to be given reassurance that the Western powers were not bound by any obligation to consider the Polish western frontier as finally adjudicated by the Potsdam decision. One of the first signals of the beginning Cold War was given by Secretary of State James F. Byrnes in a speech made on September 6, 1946, significantly in Stuttgart:

> At Potsdam specific areas which were part of Germany were provisionally assigned to the Soviet Union and Poland subject to the final decisions of the Peace Conference. . . . The heads of government agreed to support at the peace settlement the proposal of the Soviet government concerning the ultimate transfer to the Soviet Union of the city of Koenigsberg and the area adjacent to it. We will certainly stand by our agreement. With regard to Silesia and other eastern German areas, the assignment of this territory to Poland by Russia for administrative purposes had taken place before the Potsdam meeting. The heads of government agreed that, pending the final determination of Poland's western frontier, Silesia and other eastern German areas should be under the administration of the Polish state and for such purposes should not be considered as a part of the Soviet zone of occupation in

Germany. However, as the Protocol of the Potsdam Conference makes clear, the heads of government did not agree to support at the peace settlement the cession of this particular area. . . . As a result of the agreement at Yalta, Poland ceded to the Soviet Union territory east of the Curzon Line. Because of this, Poland asked for revision of her northern and western frontiers. The United States will support a revision of these frontiers in Poland's favor. However, the extent of the area to be ceded to Poland must be determined when the final settlement is agreed upon.[1]

The Secretary of State was telling the German people that the Koenigsberg area was lost forever but that the Polish western frontier should be revised in their favor though not to the extent of a return to the 1937 frontiers. However, his speech legitimized the West German claim to a revision of the Polish-German frontier. The target of the speech was the American adversary, the Soviet Union, but Poland, so to speak, was to pay the price for the Western-Soviet quarrel.

The position taken by Secretary Byrnes was confirmed by his successor, George C. Marshall, in his radio address of April 28, 1947.[2] This stand was contested by the American ambassadors in Warsaw who advised the Secretary of State that it would alienate Polish sympathy for the United States. The first postwar ambassador, Arthur Bliss Lane, although bitterly critical of the Polish Communists and their brutal suppression of the opposition, told Secretary Marshall on April 29, 1947 (Bliss Lane was at that time no longer ambassador in Warsaw): "I disagree with the views which you expressed in your broadcast last night on the matter of the boundary between Poland and Germany. . . . My main preoccupation is the effect of our apparent present policy on our long-term relations with the Polish people. The effect on the Polish people of your predecessor's Stuttgart speech was apparently not taken into account at the time. . . . Yet Mr. Byrnes' speech was damaging . . . to the prestige of the United States in Poland." Ambassador Lane added in his conversation with the Secretary of State on May 9, 1947, "Since we had allowed the Poles to evacuate the Germans from this territory, they were justified in thinking that we did not intend to change the frontier."[3]

The Secretary of State admitted in the same conversation that "our chances for changing the Polish frontier were very slender."[4] What he intended to achieve was not so much the actual revision of the frontier as influencing West German public opinion by giving them yet another important reason for siding with the United States against the Soviet

Union. He and Ambassador Lane looked at the problem from two different points of view. Ambassador Lane had in mind American-Polish relations; the Secretary of State looked at the problem from the global point of view of adverse relations with the Soviet Union.

Mr. Lane's successor in Warsaw, Ambassador Stanton Griffis, said in his dispatch to the State Department of August 18, 1947: "You are perfectly aware, of course, that the one subject on which all Poles, whether here or in the United States, are united is the question of the Western borders. . . . I believe that a final settlement of this question in favor of the Poles would weaken the position of Russia as the Poles would no longer fear the loss of Russian support on the all-important border question."[5] His remark was well taken. The Poles knew that they could not hope to recover prewar eastern Poland since the Western powers were in agreement with the Soviet Union on this subject in spite of the Cold War. The loss of Western support for their western frontier meant to them that they could rely only on the Soviet guarantee.

The American stand was reaffirmed on June 8, 1950, namely, that the United States had never recognized the Oder-Neisse line as the final Eastern German frontier. Dean Acheson, Secretary of State at the time, said the same on April 8, 1952. This view was modified officially only following the conclusion of the West German–Soviet and Polish treaties in 1970.

The British government fully supported the American stand. The first signal was given by Winston Churchill, at that time the leader of the opposition, in speeches made in 1946 at Fulton, Missouri, and in Zurich, where he stated that if he had remained Prime Minister until the end of the Potsdam Conference, he never would have accepted the Oder–Western Neisse border. Very soon after, this became the official position of the British government, as evidenced in official statements made at various times. Secretary for Foreign Affairs Ernest Bevin expressed on October 22, 1946, and on May 15, 1947, support for the stand taken by American Secretaries of State Byrnes and Marshall that the Potsdam decision was not final, and that the western frontier of Poland should be determined in a peace settlement. Winston Churchill, again the Prime Minister, declared on January 1, 1948, that the British government did not accept the Western Neisse as the Polish frontier. On April 14, 1949, the British occupation authorities instructed that the West German maps should indicate the 1937 frontiers as continuing to be the German frontiers. The same view that Britain did not recognize the Oder-Neisse frontier was restated in 1950, 1959, and

1961, and was modified publicly only following the conclusion in 1970 of the Moscow and Warsaw treaties.

The French position fluctuated until 1959. Bidault, the French Foreign Minister, declared on April 4, 1947, that his government would not oppose the eventual recognition of the Oder-Neisse frontier. But on July 7, 1950, the French Foreign Ministry aligned its position with the American and British; it declared that the French government considered that the German territory existed within the 1937 frontiers. The French High Commissioner for Germany, François-Poncet, declared on January 1, 1951, that the German Eastern frontiers were not yet finally determined. The same view was formulated on October 10, 1951, by a spokesman of the French Foreign Ministry who said that France considered the Oder-Neisse line provisional and that the final frontier of a united Germany should be determined in a peace treaty. The American, British, and French Foreign Secretaries agreed on September 28, 1955, that the settlement of German frontiers should be decided in a future peace treaty.

However, France did not wait until 1970 to recognize the Oder-Neisse frontier. The French position was radically modified by General de Gaulle in his capacity as President of the Fifth Republic. He declared on March 25, 1959, that he favored the reunification of Germany but on condition that a unified Germany would remain within its present western, *eastern*, northern, and southern frontiers. He reaffirmed French recognition of the Oder-Neisse frontier on the occasion of his visit to Poland in September, 1967. In one of his speeches he referred to Poland "inside the frontiers which are and must remain her own," while he said in another speech: "I see Poland, which possesses a compact territory without allogenuous elements, with clearly justified and clearly marked frontiers, to which frontiers, moreover, France has always given her full agreement since 1944."[6] His mention of the year 1944 was a reference to his approval, in his capacity as the head of the French Provisional Government, of the Oder-Neisse frontier on the occasion of his official visit to Moscow. His successors, Georges Pompidou and Giscard d'Estaing, have never deviated from de Gaulle's position.

Beginning with the late fifties and even more in the sixties, the American, British, and French press departed from the official position of their governments and started to advise the Federal Republic to recognize accomplished facts in the interest of European peace.

Beginning at least with the sixties, the United States and Britain understood that American-Soviet nuclear parity precluded the existence of even "slender chances" for a modification of the status quo in Central Europe, including the reunification of Germany and the modification of the German eastern boundaries. The status quo was implicitly accepted. But neither government could openly disagree with the revisionist claims of its West German ally.

THE SOVIET STAND

The third great power present at the Potsdam Conference, the Soviet Union, never varied in its firm support of the Oder-Neisse frontier. This was part of the general Soviet policy regarding the maintenance of the Central European status quo, which included, insofar as Moscow was concerned, the existence of two German states, this precluding reunification, the status of West Berlin as a separate entity but not a part of the Federal Republic of Germany, and the Sudetenland being an integral part of Czechoslovakia. The Soviet government had several occasions on which to state its point of view. For example, V. Molotov, then Foreign Minister, said on April 9, 1947, that "the decision of the Potsdam Conference regarding the western frontiers of Poland is final and not liable to revision." On January 10, 1959, the Soviet government sent a draft of the peace treaty with Germany to all its wartime allies. Its Article 8 said that "the frontiers of Germany shall be the same as of January 1, 1959." Article 9 asked Germany to renounce all rights and claims to the former German territories east of the Oder-Neisse line and to recognize that those territories were transferred to Polish sovereignty. The treaty of friendship and mutual assistance between the Soviet Union and Poland, concluded on April 8, 1965, stated in its Article 5 that "the High Contracting Parties . . . reaffirm again that the inviolability of the state frontier of the Polish People's Republic on the Oder and the Lusatian Neisse is one of the fundamental elements of European security."

This Soviet view has remained the same to the present day.[7]

THE VATICAN

The Holy See was also involved in the Polish-German territorial controversy. Its traditional policy had always consisted in not recognizing any modification of frontiers until such time as the two states concerned agreed on such modification. For lack of any agreement on the matter between Poland and the Federal Republic, the Vatican refused to do two things: first, to redraw the boundaries of dioceses to make them coincide with the new western Polish frontier, and second, to appoint to those dioceses regular ordinary Polish bishops. As a consequence, the former German bishops were replaced by provisional Polish so-called Apostolic administrators, while the boundaries of the former German dioceses continued to cut across the frontier line. This was the situation until the summer of 1972. The Polish Catholic hierarchy constantly requested the Vatican to proceed with the redrawing of boundaries of the dioceses and with the investiture of regular Polish bishops. But the Holy See was caught between two fires. On the one hand, the immense majority of the Polish population continued to remain practicing Catholics to an extent far greater than the low Western European percentages of regularly practicing though baptized Catholics. These Polish Catholics felt bitter about the reluctance of the Vatican to recognize the western frontier. The communist government never failed to point out in domestic propaganda against the Catholic Church its lack of influence in Rome and the allegedly hostile attitude of the Vatican regarding Polish territorial integrity.

On the other hand, Rome was under the strong pressure of the prosperous West German Catholic Church to continue its policy of nonrecognition. This pressure was reinforced by the fact that the Federal Republic was governed by the Christian Democrats supported by the German Church. The problem was not too troublesome to Pope Pius XII, known for his German sympathy and his fierce hostility to Communism, the Soviet Union, and Eastern European Communist governments. It became a delicate matter for his successors, Popes John XXIII and Paul VI, who inaugurated a different policy of trying to find a *modus vivendi* with the Soviet and Eastern European governments in the hope of improving the lot of Catholics living under these governments. Yet, they could not jettison the precedents of the Holy See's policy. In consequence, the stand of the Vatican was not different from that of the United States and Britain.

THE GÖRLITZ (ZGORZELEC) TREATY AND THE GDR

Poland could only respond to the West German territorial claims by its own counter-propaganda and refusal to establish diplomatic relations. According to the Soviet bloc, there were two successor states of the former German Reich, the Federal Republic and the German Democratic Republic. The Oder-Neisse frontier divided Poland from the GDR. It was, therefore, of practical importance to arrive at an agreement with the immediate German neighbor who had no choice in the matter, being a Soviet ally.

Otto Grotewohl, the Prime Minister of the newly formed German Democratic Republic, stated in his first governmental declaration on October 12, 1949, that "the Oder-Neisse frontier is for us the frontier of peace."[8] However, this recognition of the frontier between the two socialist states was probably not easy to make. In 1946 and 1947 the East German communists still supported the point of view of the other German parties that the Oder-Neisse frontier was not definitive. Their press organ *Neues Deutschland* stated on September 14, 1946, that "the SED [The United Socialist Party of Germany] is opposed to any diminution of the German territory. The eastern frontier is provisional only and may be determined only at the Peace Conference with the cooperation of all victorious great powers."[9] The future President of the GDR, Wilhelm Pieck, declared at a press conference in Munich on March 13, 1947, that "the SED rejects as it did before any modification of the frontiers."[10] The future Prime Minister of the GDR, Otto Grotewohl, said on March 9, 1947, at a meeting in Frankfurt that "the SED disapproves the frontier line in the East as much as the planned new settlement of the frontiers in the West."[11]

These statements reflected the then communist hopes that they would play a major role in a Germany which was not yet divided into two states. By 1949 the division of Germany into two states was an accomplished fact. The SED had to change its stand in view of the forthcoming integration of the GDR within the Soviet bloc and the need to straighten out its relations with another Soviet ally, Poland. Beginning with 1949, the slogan that the new eastern frontier of Germany was a frontier of peace between the two nations was coined and has been repeated until the present day.

The Chairman of the Central Committee of the Polish United Workers' Party (Communist Party), Bolesław Bierut, sent a letter to Wilhelm Pieck, President of the GDR, on October 14, 1949, in which he warmly greeted the creation of the GDR because, among other things, the new Republic had declared that the Oder-Neisse frontier was a frontier of peace.[12] These and other mutually friendly messages were followed on July 6, 1950, by the signature in Zgorzelec (Görlitz), the frontier town, of the East German–Polish treaty on their common boundary.[13] Article One of the treaty said that "the High Contracting Parties agree that the established and existing frontier running from the

Baltic Sea along a line west of Swinemünde and then along the River Oder up to the confluence of the River Lusatian Neisse and along the Lusatian Neisse to the Czechoslovak frontier, constitutes the state frontier between Poland and Germany." The preamble of the treaty mentioned that that frontier had been determined in the Potsdam agreement.

This formulation supported the legal Polish view that the Oder-Neisse frontier had been determined at Potsdam, and that there was no need for a German confirmation of the validity of the frontier. This is why Article One was so drafted as to make it clear that the GDR only acknowledged the existence of the frontier, already validly determined in 1945 by the three great powers.

The Görlitz treaty seemed to solve the problem insofar as Poland was concerned. The Polish government rejected the claim of the FRG that it could speak on behalf of all Germans, and considered that there were two coequal German states, one of them an immediate Polish neighbor, hence legally empowered to settle the territorial problem. Of course, the matter looked different politically since the FRG was an incomparably more influential state than the GDR, and its contestation of the validity of the Polish western frontier influenced the attitudes of other nonsocialist states, in particular the United States and Britain. The revisionist stand of the FRG could not be ignored but was one of the reasons for the close ties between the GDR and Poland. On January 27, 1951, the GDR and Poland signed in Frankfurt-on-the-Oder the agreement on the final delimitation of their frontier.

The existence of the GDR has great importance for Poland. First, it recognized the western frontier without any reservations, unlike the FRG in 1970. Second, its existence means the perpetuation of the division of Germany which in turn guarantees Polish security. Władysław Gomułka, at that time the First Secretary of the Polish Party, said as much on February 15, 1958, in an interview with the London *Times*: "It would not be a misfortune if Germany continued to be divided still for some time to come. . . . Let us assume that unified Germany should become a great military power, armed with nuclear weapons. It would become a great European power. . . . Certain people there [West Germany] do not conceal their claims to our Western Territories. Taking this into account, we must view the problem of unification of Germany more cautiously than the western countries."[14]

The Polish government, like the Soviet and other East European governments, approved in advance the decision of the GDR, taken on August 13, 1961, to erect the Berlin Wall, because "the security of frontiers of the German Democratic Republic is also one of the fundamental guarantees . . . of the security of the Polish Oder-Neisse frontier."[15]

On March 15, 1967, the two governments concluded a treaty of friendship and mutual assistance, a bilateral alliance superimposed on their existing obligations resulting from the regional Warsaw Treaty of 1955 (a treaty linking together the Soviet Union and all its East European allies).[16] Article 3 of that treaty stated that "the territorial integrity of both states as well as the inviolability of the Oder-Lusatian Neisse frontier of the Polish People's Republic and of the frontier between the German Democratic Republic and the Federal Republic of Germany, are of fundamental importance for European security." Article 6 restated the general thesis of the Soviet bloc that "West Berlin is considered by the High Contracting Parties a separate political entity."

The two governments are bound together not only by the coincidence of their state interests and the same ideology but also by economic ties. The GDR is the second trade partner of Poland, the Soviet Union being the first.

Judged by official documents and statements, the relations between the two states are cloudless. However, beneath the official surface the feelings of the two populations are not exactly warm. The East Germans are not happy to encounter the Polish frontier not far east of Berlin. The Poles are aware that the inhabitants of the GDR are Prussians, traditionally their worst enemies among the Germans. In spite of all the efforts of the two governments, unpleasant incidents frequently occur between private citizens when one is visiting in the other's state.

Relations with the FRG have remained one of the most important external problems of Poland. W. Gomułka conceded this in a speech he made on October 6, 1969: "Poland, bound to the GDR by the alliance and close cooperation, is not opposed to a normalization of relations with the other German state, the Federal Republic of Germany. This could be accomplished only on the foundation of recognition of existing reality, existing frontier, and of respect for sovereignty and territorial integrity."[17] Poland had to wait for more than twenty years (1949–70), filled with mutual bitter recriminations, for this to happen.

CLAIMS OF THE EXPELLEE ORGANIZATIONS

The first outcry against the loss of Eastern territories and the expulsion of ethnic Germans from Eastern Europe came quite naturally from those Germans who themselves had been expelled, had fled, or had been evacuated by the Nazi authorities, *i.e.,* who had lost their homelands for one or another reason. Among them were those ethnic Germans who had been evacuated from various East European countries on Hitler's orders and resettled mostly in the German-annexed Polish western provinces. Their resentment was directed against the Soviet Union and Poland, which did not allow them to remain in the homes they had taken over from expelled and expropriated Poles.

The list of Nazi German international agreements and unilateral German decisions regarding the evacuation of ethnic Germans from the various East European countries is as follows: the German-Estonian agreement of October 10, 1939, and the German-Latvian agreement of October 30, 1939; the German-Soviet agreement of November 11, 1939, on the evacuation of Germans from Soviet-annexed eastern Poland; the German-Soviet agreement of September 5, 1940, on the evacuation of Germans from Soviet-annexed formerly Romanian Bessarabia and Northern Bukovina; the resettlement by order of the German occupation authorities of Germans from the southeastern part of the General Government, carried out in September and October 1940; the German-Romanian agreement of October 20, 1940, on the evacuation of Germans from South Bukovina and Northern Dobrudja; the German-Soviet agreement of January 1, 1941, on the evacuation of remaining Germans from Estonia, Latvia and Lithuania; the German-Croatian and German-Serbian agreements of October 6, 1942, and the simultaneous unilateral evacuation by the Nazi authorities of Germans from Slovenia and Bosnia; the German-Bulgarian agreement of October 13, 1942; the evacuation of ethnic Germans from the Ukraine by German authorities in 1943; and, finally, the evacuation of other Germans from Hungary in October 1944. It is estimated that, all told, about 1,100,000 ethnic Germans were evacuated by the Nazi authorities from various parts of Eastern Europe.[18]

These ethnic Germans, evacuated by the Nazi authorities without any pressure by the governments of the countries where those Germans lived, were resettled mostly in the annexed Polish western provinces to ensure their Germanization. They now claim the name of "expellees" as though they had been expelled by foreign governments from their ancestral homelands. Another category of "expellees" consists of those millions of Germans whom the Nazi authorities evacuated from the German Eastern territories which were to be occupied by the Soviet armies, or who had fled on their own. For a few years following the end of war different names were used, and they were correct: the refugees, expellees, and war victims, but eventually the name used for all was "expellees." This change in name shifted the blame for the wartime evacuations of Germans by the Nazi authorities to the Soviet, Polish, Czechoslovak, Hungarian, and other East European governments although these governments bore the responsibility only for the postwar expulsions.

Whoever was responsible for their fate, the ethnic Germans from the East who found themselves in occupied Germany west of the Oder-Neisse line felt the loss of their prewar homes bitterly. Their initial bitterness was deepened by the unfriendly attitude of the native German population who were themselves facing all sorts of acute shortages immediately following the war, including the housing shortage in the allied-bombed cities. It took several years for the "expellees" to become integrated into the West German economy and society. One of the arguments used for the West German claim against the Oder-Neisse frontier was that the Federal Republic could not possibly accommodate the population, greatly increased by the influx of Germans from Eastern Europe, and needed the greater living space provided by the 1937 frontier. This argument was corroborated by another, namely, that the Poles could not settle and rehabilitate the former German eastern territories. Eventually both arguments lost their force. The Federal Republic became so prosperous that it could offer employment to all its citizens, including those who had come from Eastern Europe, and began to feel manpower shortage. The remedy was found in bringing in foreign workers from Southern Europe (Italians, Spaniards, Yugoslavs, Greeks, Turks, etc.) who numbered about 2,400,000 in 1973. At the same time, the Poles resettled the former German territories and rebuilt the war-devastated economy.

Beginning with 1946, the expellees and refugees started to organize themselves for the protection of their interests in the Western zones of occupation. In July 1946 the ethnic German scholars and publicists who were refugees or expellees from Eastern Europe founded the so-called "Göttinger Arbeitkreis," the first such institution to become the scholarly mouthpiece of refugees and expellees. On April 29, 1950, another such research center for Eastern Central Europe was founded in Marburg on the Lahn, the Johann-Gottfried-Herder Institut, to be followed by the creation of other research institutes of the same kind, all of them providing arguments for the revision of the Oder-Neisse frontier.

On October 29, 1946, the total number of refugees and expellees from Eastern Europe, including the former East German territories annexed by Poland and the Soviet Union and the Czech Sudetenland, numbered over 10,000,000 in the four zones of occupation. The total number of refugees and expellees from Eastern Europe in the Federal Republic alone reached the figure of 8,300,000 persons at the end of 1953 (this total included the former inhabitants of the Soviet and Polish annexed territories and of the Czech Sudetenland), and the total number of refugees from the GDR was about 2,000,000.[19]

On December 4, 1946, the Germans expelled from the Sudetenland raised the claim, which was to become the claim of all refugees and expellees from Eastern Europe, of having the right to return to their former homeland (the *Heimatrecht*). This *Heimatrecht* was coupled with another right, that of self-determination. In other words, the mass return of ethnic Germans would have meant the modification of the postwar ethnic composition of Eastern Europe. The revision of Eastern frontiers would follow logically, while the returning Germans in the Sudetenland would claim the right at least to a cultural and political autonomy if not the union of the Sudetenland with Germany. In effect, the *Heimatrecht* implied the shifting eastward of the German frontiers to the 1937 line and the rebuilding of German minorities in Eastern Europe. The changes in the German political and ethnic frontiers which took place after the war would be erased.

The activities of the expellee and refugee organizations were legalized by the American occupation authorities on May 18, 1947; the former prohibition of the open existence of those organizations was lifted. The British occupation authorities did the same on September 11, 1947. These American and British decisions were followed by the multiplication of organizations of refugees and expellees, such as those from Danzig, Sudetenland, Pomerania, East Prussia, Hungary, West Prussia (the interwar Polish northern province), Vistula-Warta (the interwar Polish western province), Lower and Upper Silesia, Brandenburg (its part annexed by Poland), Baltic countries, Bessarabia, the Soviet Union, etc. All these organizations claimed the *Heimatrecht* and protested against the postwar political and ethnic status quo.

These vindications were unrealistic for the simple reason that their realization would necessitate the military defeat of the Soviet Union and its East European allies. Yet the successive governments of the Federal Republic and the West German political parties had to cater to these claims, because the expellees and refugees represented one-fifth of the West German voters. Their organizations eventually united in an over-all union which was to become one of the Federal Republic's most powerful lobbies. Several dozens of officials of these organizations were also Bundestag deputies sitting on the benches of all three main West German parties. Since the conclusion of the Eastern treaties by the Brandt-Scheel government, these deputies can be found exclusively on the benches of the opposition parties, the Christian Democrats and the Bavarian Christian-Social Union. However, Brandt's Eastern policy was followed by political decline in the power of the expellee organizations.

Another reason for that decline is the rise of young generations much less interested in the political program of the expellees. The lapse of time and integration within the prosperous economy of the Federal Republic made the *Heimatrecht* sound hollow because the refugees and expellees in fact lost the desire to return to their former homelands. Although West German legislation made the status of "expellee" hereditary so that children, grandchildren, and all the future descendants of authentic refugees and expellees might remind West Germans of the loss of the Eastern territories and the former existence of German minorities in Eastern Europe, those children and grandchildren do not evince much interest in the former homelands of their parents and grandparents.

NO RECOGNITION OF THE ODER-NEISSE FRONTIER

The West German politicians, once allowed to express their views freely in the Western zones of occupation, began to contest the validity of the Oder-Neisse frontier. The future first Chancellor of the Federal Republic, Konrad Adenauer, spoke for all political parties when he declared in March 1949 in Geneva that Germany would never recognize the Oder-Neisse frontier. Kurt Schumacher, the leader of the Social Democratic Party, had said the same on January 28, 1947, and so had the leader of the Free Democratic Party, Franz Blücher, in September 1945. This was to become the official point of view of the Federal Republic until 1970.

At the same time the Polish political exiles' organizations abroad and their press unanimously supported the validity of the Oder-Neisse frontier in spite of their fierce opposition to the communist regime in Poland and to the Soviet Union. Also, the Polish Catholic hierarchy, often quarreling bitterly with the communist government, agreed with the latter government that the former East German territories were to be retained as an integral part of Poland. The Polish bishops expressed this view most solemnly in a letter they addressed to the German bishops on November 18, 1965, while the bishops of both countries were present in Rome on the occasion of the Second Vatican Council. They recalled Polish historical and other arguments regarding the former East German territories and stated that the Oder-Neisse frontier was a problem of survival for Poland. (See also Chapter 7.)

Thus, the Polish-German territorial controversy divided the Germans, Catholic and Protestant, Christian Democrat and Socialist, from the Poles, Catholic and communist, living in Poland or abroad.

ADENAUER'S OBJECTIVES

Immediately following the foundation of the Federal Republic of Germany in September 1949, its first government, headed by Chancellor Konrad Adenauer, formulated the main guidelines of its foreign policy. That policy was to be active in the West and passive in the East. These guidelines were important, because they remained valid for some twenty years. First, the Federal Republic claimed from its very beginning that it was the only legitimate German state. The German Democratic Republic, created in October 1949, was called contemptuously the Soviet Zone of Occupation, *i.e.,* an administration imposed by the Soviet occupation authorities and subservient to the Soviet Union. Chancellor Adenauer said on October 21, 1949, that "the Federal Republic of Germany is, until the achievement of complete German unity, the only legitimate state organization of the German people . . . [and] feels itself responsible for the fate of 18 million Germans who live in the Soviet Zone. . . . The Federal Republic is the only one empowered to speak for the German people."[20] The denial to the GDR of the status of another German state implied the refusal to negotiate any equal agreements with it, and the claim that German reunification might take place only through the incorporation of the GDR into the FRG. It meant too that the GDR could not conclude any valid international agreements, and that third states should not establish regular diplomatic relations, to which only the FRG was entitled, with the GDR.

Second, Chancellor Adenauer stated on September 20, 1949: "We cannot under any circumstances accept the unilateral separation of these territories [east of the Oder-Neisse line] by the Soviet Union and Poland. . . . We shall not stop voicing in an orderly legal way our claims to these territories." He added that the expulsion of ethnic Germans from these territories was carried out in violation of the Potsdam agreement.[21] He claimed, in other words, in agreement with the contemporary American and British view, that the Potsdam agreement had established only a provisional administrative line and that the FRG had the right to raise a claim for the return of the eastern provinces. His remark regarding the expulsion of Germans meant that the Potsdam agreement authorized the Poles to expel Germans only from prewar Poland but not from the former East German territories. He ignored the decision to the contrary made by the Allied Control Council in November 1945. What he implied, therefore, was the right of the expellees to return to their former homes since they had been illegally expelled. The Görlitz Treaty, concluded in 1950 by the GDR and Poland, was illegal by definition since the GDR was not a state and could not speak on behalf of any Germans.

On September 27, 1951, the Chancellor clarified what he understood by the reunification of Germany: "The union of the territory of the Soviet Zone with the Federal Republic will be the first step toward the reunification of Germany."[22] It was obvious that the second step should be the incorporation of the former Eastern territories within the FRG, already enlarged by the territory of the GDR.

This stand was supported by all German parties. For instance, one of the leaders of the Social Democrats, Herbert Wehner, submitted a resolution to the Bundestag on September 14, 1950, in which he stated: "The German people see in the recognition of the Oder-Neisse Line [a reference to the Görlitz treaty], in the justification of inhuman treatment of German prisoners of war and displaced persons, in the disregard of the fate and the right to homeland of the expellees, crimes against Germany and mankind. The German Bundestag denies the right to act in the name of the German people to all who are responsible for these crimes and who support the incorporation of Germany into a system of foreign domination."[23] The Christian-Democratic Union, the Bavarian Christian-Social Union, the Social Democratic Party and the Free Democratic Party voted for the resolution.

The Bundestag treated the government of the GDR as traitors and criminals. The same resolution required the Federal government to institute criminal proceedings against "all persons who participate in crimes against mankind in the Soviet Zone of occupation."

Finally, the Constitution of the Federal Republic of May 23, 1949, extended its validity in Article 23 to the city of Berlin (West and East Berlin) and to the other parts of Germany following their union with the FRG (presumably the GDR and the former Eastern territories east of the Oder-Neisse Line).[24] The operation of Article 23 regarding Berlin had to be suspended at the request of the three Western occupying powers, which feared that the inclusion of Berlin in the FRG would undermine their rights of occupying powers *vis-à-vis* the Soviet Union and deprive them of the right to defend West Berlin against Soviet encroachments. This point of view was maintained by the Western powers in later years as well, and confirmed in their agreement with the Soviet Union on West Berlin, concluded in September 1971.

WESTERN SUPPORT FOR THE FRG

This stand of the Federal Republic clashed head on with the Soviet and generally Eastern European point of view. For the USSR and its allies, the Potsdam agreement finally and irrevocably determined the Oder-Neisse frontier. Hence, the Soviet and Polish annexations of the former East German territories were legitimate; West Berlin was not a part of the FRG; the GDR was another and equal German state which had full capacity to act in international relations; and the FRG had no right to speak on behalf of all the Germans. This gulf dividing West German objectives in foreign policy from Soviet and East European objectives precluded any active Eastern policy on the part of the FRG. This did not particularly trouble Chancellor Adenauer who relegated the accomplishment of stated Eastern objectives to a future time when the circumstances would be more favorable. His immediate task was to rehabilitate the name of Germany and regain legal equality for the FRG through his policy of integrating the FRG within the Western community. His task was enormously facilitated by the cold war. He could be sure of a sympathetic Western attitude. On April 18, 1951, the FRG signed as an equal partner together with France, Italy, Belgium, Holland, and Luxemburg the treaty on the European Coal and Steel Community, the foundation stone for the future Common Market. The official West German publication notes that "by the end of 1949 [*i.e.*, prior to the outbreak of the Korean war] the first Western voices asked for an active German participation in the defense effort. . . . The initiative regarding the proposal for a German contribution to defense came, above all, from the Americans."[25] This participation was to be accomplished a few years later by the Western-sponsored rearmament of West Germany and its admission to the North Atlantic Alliance.

One of the prerequisites for Western integration of the FRG was the conclusion on September 10, 1952, in Luxemburg of an agreement between the FRG on the one hand, and the State of Israel and the

Presidium of the Conference on Jewish Material Claims on the other hand, on the payment of indemnities to Israel (3 billion dollars) and to individual Jews living in Diaspora (450 million dollars) for the Nazi genocide policy and its victims.[26] Jewish opposition to the acceptance of the FRG into the Western community was overcome.

The Western orientation of Chancellor Adenauer and his governments postulated that a united Western Europe and the superior strength of the West, in fact of the United States, would eventually force the Soviet Union to accept both the reunification of Germany and the revision of frontiers. He told the Bundestag on February 8, 1952: "We may regain Berlin and the German East only through a united Europe."[27] He said also on March 1, 1952, in a speech he made in Heidelberg: "When the West is stronger than the USSR, it will be necessary to explain to it that the present situation cannot last any longer, that it may not hold half of Europe in servitude, and that the East European problem must be settled anew."[28]

He visualized at that time a future united Western Europe standing behind the FRG which would also be supported by the superior might of the United States. The Soviet Union would have no choice but to make concessions.

ADENAUER'S ASSUMPTIONS PROVEN FALSE

The nuclear superiority of the United States and West European enthusiasm for a speedy economic and political union seemed in the fifties to justify the optimistic expectation of Adenauer's government. Later events were to prove that these expectations were mere illusions. The Soviet Union was to reach nuclear parity with the United States and could not be compelled to negotiate because of the Western position of strength. Former hopes for a rapid building of a Western European political union collapsed in spite of full success of the European Economic Community. The gradual economic integration of six member-states of the Common Market did not bring about their political and military integration. The official West German history of the foreign policy of the FRG correctly says: "Many steps and positions of German foreign policy which seemed to be practical or which were necessary in the fifties, might mean less in the light of ideas of the seventies."[29] Among other things, in the seventies the FRG could no longer rely on the former American promise of "massive nuclear retaliation," because "the more the United States was becoming vulnerable in the nuclear sense, the more 'the massive retaliation' in a serious situation was to lose its credibility."[30] By the same token, the West German concept of re-unification following free elections in the GDR (the free elections surely would have produced a pro-West German majority) and hopes for a revision of Eastern frontiers were also losing their credibility. It was becoming obvious that the Soviet Union was strong enough to make its veto credible.

THE TREATY ON GERMANY

The fifties were the time of continuing integration of the FRG within the Western community. On May 26, 1952, the three Western powers concluded the so-called treaty on Germany with the FRG. The Western powers undertook the obligation to support West German objectives regarding the East. Article 7 said: "The Federal Republic of Germany and the three Powers are united regarding the fundamental goal of their joint policy which is the peace-treaty settlement for the entire Germany, freely agreed upon and concluded between Germany and its former enemies. . . . They are also united regarding the fact that the final de-termination of frontiers of Germany must be postponed until that settle-ment."[31]

The three Western powers thus underwrote the West German claim that the Potsdam agreement had not solved the problem of Ger-man eastern frontiers, and implied that those frontiers should be modi-fied in favor of a unified Germany. The same treaty restored to the FRG its sovereignty, with some reservations. Article 2 reserved the rights of the three powers regarding the stationing of their troops within the FRG, the status of Berlin and the future of Germany as a whole, including reunification and a peace settlement. This meant that the FRG could not decide alone (for example in its negotiations with the Soviet bloc) the question of reunification, the problem of Eastern frontiers, or the status of Berlin. Any peace settlement would have to be negotiated with the participation of the three powers and presumably the fourth former occupying power, the USSR. Article 2 played an important role in the seventies.

West German rearmanent went through two stages. In the first, German participation in the so-called West European Defense Com-munity (joint West European armed forces) foundered on French opposition. The abovementioned treaty of 1952 was a sort of Western price paid for West German willingness to participate in the Western defense system, a price that had to be paid at that time because of the Social Democratic opposition to rearmament. The Social Democrats feared that the FRG's participation in the Western defense system would stiffen Soviet opposition to reunification.

The second stage consisted in the rebuilding of German armed forces which were to be incorporated within NATO, and in West German accession to the North Atlantic Treaty. On that occasion the three great powers and the FRG amended the 1952 Treaty by the so-called Paris agreement, concluded on October 23, 1954. (The FRG acceded to the North Atlantic Treaty several months later, in May 1955.) However, Articles 2 and 7 remained unchanged.[32]

While the three Western powers approved the West German objectives, the reunification and the revision of frontiers, they wanted to be sure that a rearmed Federal Republic would not entangle them against their will in a war with the Soviet bloc. This is why Chancellor Adenauer had to make the following pledge on October 3, 1954: "The Federal Republic of Germany accepts the obligation never to carry out by forcible means the reunification of Germany or the modification of present frontiers of Germany and to solve by peaceful means all the disputes that might arise between the Federal Republic of Germany and other states."[33] This obligation, undertaken *vis-à-vis* the Western allies, made meaningless the later West German offers of mutual renunciation of force, addressed to the Soviet Union and the Soviet allies.

FRG REFUSES TO ACCEPT THE STATUS QUO

On March 25, 1957, the FRG, France, Italy, Belgium, Holland, and Luxemburg signed the treaties of Rome, which created the European Economic and the European Atomic Communities. This completed Adenauer's main task of integrating the FRG within Western Europe and the Atlantic Alliance. He did not try to activate his policy regarding the Soviet bloc. Actually, the barriers erected earlier remained intact in the fifties. Adenauer declared on February 25, 1954: "The Federal Government must make it clear in words and deeds that Germans will never be reconciled with the division of Germany and will never put up with the existence of two German states."[34] On April 7, 1954, the Bundestag adopted a resolution that stated: "The Federal government, as the only democratic and freely elected German government, is the only one empowered to speak for all Germans."[35] The Bundestag said in another resolution, adopted on July 1, 1953, that "the supreme goal of the Federal government remains the reunification of Germany in peace and freedom. . . . The German people, according to numerous declarations by the Bundestag and the federal government, will never recognize the so-called Oder-Neisse frontier."[36] Chancellor Adenauer provided an answer on October 20, 1953, to the question of how these goals could be achieved: "There is no other way toward reunification but the one leading through European integration. . . . There is no doubt that the Soviets will not find themselves ready at all for the negotiations regarding reunification until, first, the approaching union of free peoples builds up the required premises."[37]

ESTABLISHMENT OF DIPLOMATIC RELATIONS WITH MOSCOW

The Chancellor hoped for negotiations from the position of superior Western strength, but even so, he had to be on speaking terms with Moscow in order to open negotiations in some undetermined future. Moscow came to his rescue by issuing its official declaration of January 15, 1955: "The Soviet Union maintains good relations with the GDR. The Soviet government is ready to normalize the relations also between the USSR and the German Federal Republic."[38] This offer could not be rejected because reunification could not be achieved without Soviet assent.

Chancellor Adenauer went to Moscow in September 1955 and, after several days of negotiations, agreed to establish diplomatic relations with the Soviet Union in exchange for only one Soviet concession, the promise to release the remaining German prisoners of war. He safeguarded the legal position of his government by sending two letters to the then Soviet Prime Minister Bulganin. In the first of these letters he expressed his conviction that the establishment of diplomatic relations would help in solving the problem of reunification of Germany.[39] In the other letter, sent to Bulganin on the day of Adenauer's departure from Moscow, the Chancellor stated:

> The establishment of diplomatic relations between the government of the Federal Republic of Germany and the government of the USSR does not mean the recognition of the present territorial possessions of either side. The final determination of frontiers remains reserved for the peace treaty. The establishment of diplo-

matic relations with the government of the Soviet Union does not mean any modification in the legal view of the federal government regarding its authority to represent the German people in international affairs and regarding the political situation in those German territories which remain at present outside its effective sovereignty.[40]

The latter letter was accepted by the Soviet government. This signified that it took cognizance of the West German reservations but certainly not that it shared them. Politically the two governments remained divided by the gulf of opposite views regarding the GDR, Berlin, and frontiers.

Following his visit to Moscow, on September 22, 1955, the Chancellor gave his interpretation of the significance of the visit. He said in a speech to the Bundestag that the establishment of diplomatic relations with Moscow was necessary because the USSR was one of the victorious powers without whose cooperation the reunification of Germany could not be achieved. However, he denied that the establishment of diplomatic relations either legalized the division of Germany (Moscow now had diplomatic relations with both German states) or changed anything in West German relations with the West ("Germany is a part of the West," he said). He cited his second letter to Bulganin as a proof that the FRG continued to claim its right to represent all Germans, to refuse to recognize, as he said, "the so-called 'GDR,' " and to deny the validity of Central European frontiers. As a matter of fact, the GDR was called in the official terminology "the Middle Germany," and the Polish and Soviet annexed territories, "East Germany." This terminology was apt to confuse Western public opinion for whom East Germany meant the GDR.[41]

Adenauer was right in his evaluation of the meaning of diplomatic relations with the USSR. For him these relations should not have been equated with friendly relations.[42] Mutual relations were to remain far from friendly until 1970.

THE HALLSTEIN DOCTRINE

What the establishment of diplomatic relations with Moscow implied was the risk that third states could now claim the same right as the one conceded by the FRG to the USSR of having embassies in both

German capitals. Adenauer precluded such a development by stating in the same speech to the Bundestag that "the federal government will also in the future regard as an unfriendly act the establishment of diplomatic relations with the 'GDR' by the third states with which the federal government maintains official relations."[43]

The establishment of diplomatic relations with the Soviet Union brought in its wake the so-called Hallstein doctrine, named for the then Under-Secretary for Foreign Affairs. A representative of the German Foreign Office explained on December 11, 1955, that, if a third state were to establish diplomatic relations with the GDR, the FRG would retaliate by various measures, including the rupture of diplomatic relations. Asked whether the FRG would make an exception for the East European states as it had done for the Soviet Union, the same representative replied that the USSR was one of the four great powers which could help in German reunification, while the Eastern European states could not be of any assistance in this respect.[44] The extension of validity of the Hallstein doctrine to the Eastern European states which unlike other third states had already had embassies in the GDR, erected a legal barrier which had later to be overcome by reinterpretation of the doctrine.

On June 28, 1956, the Foreign Minister, Heinrich von Brentano, confirmed that the federal government did not intend to establish diplomatic relations with the East European states. He also repeated that the federal government considered further that Germany existed legally within the 1937 frontiers, would not recognize any frontier modifications which had taken place since the war, and reiterated his government's insistence on the *Heimatrecht* of the expellees and their right to self-determination, while the final determination of frontiers should be postponed until the peace treaty.[45] The message thus given to the Soviet Union, Poland, and Czechoslovakia, was clear. The existence of the GDR and of new frontiers would not be recognized. Moreover, the millions of refugees and expellees should be readmitted to the Soviet and Polish annexed provinces and to the Sudetenland. They would then enjoy the right of self-determination, *i.e.,* to participate in the decision regarding the final destiny of the contested territories and to claim autonomy in the Sudetenland.

The spokesman for the Social Democratic opposition, Erich Ollenhauer, partly disagreed. He stated that his party favored the establishment of diplomatic relations with Poland and Czechoslovakia on the condition that this would not mean West German recognition of the division of Germany or of the existing frontiers.[46] He referred to the then-existing prospect of establishing diplomatic relations without any Polish preconditions. The rejection of Polish offers proved later on to be a grave error of the Adenauer government.

THE POLISH OFFER

Shortly following the Soviet offer to establish diplomatic relations with the FRG, the Polish government followed suit. On January 31, 1955, it declared that it was contemplating the normalization of relations with the FRG.[47] The Polish Prime Minister, J. Cyrankiewicz, restated the Polish willingness on March 16, 1955, and the First Secretary of the Polish Party, B. Bierut, did the same on July 6, 1955.[48] A Polish commentator explains that "the question of recognition by the FRG of the Oder-Lusatian Neisse frontier was not at that time a preliminary condition for the establishment of diplomatic relations. While proposing the normalization of relations with the FRG, Poland did not link this problem with any political conditions."[49]

It is worthwhile noting that the Polish initiative must have been taken in concert with Moscow, since it was taken prior to the October 1956 crisis in Polish-Soviet relations.

The October crisis in Poland did not influence the negative West German attitude although the new Polish leader, W. Gomułka, expressed again on June 5, 1957, his willingness to establish diplomatic relations without any preconditions.[50] Since the conciliatory attitude of Poland in the years 1955–57 did not produce any results, the Polish government stiffened its own attitude in the fall of 1957. It stated that it would establish diplomatic relations with the FRG only if the FRG would recognize the Oder-Neisse frontier.[51] This new position was to remain unchanged in the following years. The door which Warsaw tried to open in 1955 and 1957 remained closed, first by the FRG and after the fall of 1957 until 1970 also by Poland. The Adenauer government lost the opportunity. The Brandt government established diplomatic relations but under more onerous conditions.

In the meantime, Soviet-German relations did not improve. Both governments maintained opposite stands regarding German reunification, the GDR, Berlin, and the German frontiers. Even if the USSR had contemplated the reunification, which it did not, it would have been discouraged from ever consenting to it by the agreement concluded on July 29, 1957, between the Foreign Ministers of the FRG and the three Western powers, which expressly reserved for a unified Germany the right to remain, if it wanted to, in NATO.[52] The Soviet government would have to be incredibly foolish to add the human and economic potential of East Germany to the opposite coalition.

The gulf dividing Bonn from Moscow was marked on December 20, 1957, by the statement made by the then Mayor of West Berlin, Willy Brandt, who claimed that his city was a constituent province of the FRG.[53] As a matter of fact, this view was never shared by the Western powers.

ATTITUDE TOWARD EASTERN EUROPE

The sanction of the Hallstein doctrine was applied to Yugoslavia on October 19, 1957. That country, which had normalized its relations with the Soviet Union in 1955, established diplomatic relations with East Berlin in 1957. The FRG broke off its relations with Belgrade although Yugoslavia was not otherwise unfriendly toward West Germany and steered a policy of uncommitment to either bloc, Soviet or Western. The same was done in 1963 regarding Cuba.

However, the problem of East European countries was different since they had had embassies in East Berlin prior to the emergence of the problem of their relations with the FRG. The West German government was free either to make an exception of them, as it had done of Moscow, or to extend its doctrine to include Eastern Europe. As we have seen, it preferred to do the latter.

Toward the end of the fifties the West German Foreign Office seemed to be ready to offer to the East European countries agreements on the renunciation of the use of force. The official history of the foreign policy of the FRG, printed in 1972, published for the first time a confidential proposal made by the Foreign Office on July 20, 1959, to offer such agreements to Poland and Czechoslovakia. This proposal also contained reservations which stated that the disputed questions that existed between the FRG and Poland and Czechoslovakia would be solved only by peaceful means, and that the agreements would not imply the modification of the legal views of the parties.[54] The existence of that proposal was mentioned by Foreign Minister von Brentano in a conversation with a German journalist but was never offered to Warsaw or Prague because of "the domestic political constellation."[55] This rather cryptic reference to the domestic situation in the official history of German foreign policy probably meant that the expellee organizations were opposed to this kind of mild proposal although it would only have confirmed the obligation undertaken by the FRG toward its Western allies.

THE JAKSCH REPORT

The political power of the expellee organizations was demonstrated by the report to the Bundestag of its committee on foreign relations on June 9, 1961. The report was submitted on behalf of all the three main political parties by the Social Democratic deputy Wenzel Jaksch, who was also one of the main leaders of the expellee organizations. It included among other things all the allegations of those organizations and their statistics regarding the prewar and postwar numbers of ethnic Germans in Eastern Europe and in the former German territories. Thus, the number of Germans in prewar Poland was increased to 963,000, and the total in all of prewar Eastern Europe, to 8,852,000. Almost the whole autochthon population in the former German territories annexed by Poland was declared to be German. The total number of ethnic Germans in 1961 in the whole of Poland was stated to be 1.2 million persons, thus disregarding the repatriation in the fifties of a portion of them to the FRG and the GDR. The report mentioned also that all the autochthons (whether they felt themselves to be Germans or Poles) were officially considered by West German legislation as West German citizens although they had acquired Polish citizenship in the meantime.

The report conceded that the autochthons, whom it claimed as ethnic Germans and as citizens of the FRG, remained principally in Upper Silesia (about 700,000), while about 180,000 lived in other parts of the Polish-annexed lands. These figures for various parts of the former German territories amounted altogether to 880,000. The report further claimed that 300,000 ethnic Germans still remained in the prewar territory of Poland. These inflated figures were taken from the claims of the expellee organizations. The report stated that the committee had consulted those organizations.[56]

The three main political parties aligned their positions with those of the expellee organizations. This did not help in relation to Poland.

END OF THE COLD WAR

However, the sixties brought new international developments. On August 13, 1961, the GDR, with full support of the whole Soviet bloc, erected the Berlin Wall, thus preventing the continuation of mass flights of East Germans, which had been a sort of demographic hemorrhage. The division of Germany was strengthened by this measure. The Cuban crisis in the fall of 1962 convinced the two superpowers that they must avoid any policies which could possibly lead to a nuclear catastrophe. The cold war or at least its most inflamed stage was coming to an end. The Soviet Union gained nuclear parity, *i.e.*, could respond to American "mass retaliation" by an equally devastating second strike against the United States. The expectation of negotiating with Moscow from a position of strength became invalid. These new developments were well described in 1972 in the official history of German foreign policy:

> The cold war . . . was followed by a cool peace. . . . The acute forms of the East-West opposition receded, therefore, more to the background. . . . While it was relatively easy in the fifties to find orientation in world politics owing to the opposition between the two big blocs . . . now the number of "unknown" foreign factors increased. . . . One understood that a modification, favorable for the West, in East-West relations was to be expected not from a direct confrontation between the East and the West, particularly not in the situation of "nuclear parity," but rather from other developments taking place outside the realm of direct European confrontation. . . . The experience confirmed that the Federal Republic could protect its foreign interests at least in relation to the East only to the extent that its Allies were ready to identify themselves with the objectives and methods of German policy. . . . This global development influenced (at first it hardly was seen) the internal situation in the Federal Republic. Here was growing a generation . . . for whom in many cases the process of rethinking . . . brought about a painfully felt renunciation of cherished, quite understandable and historically well-founded political ideas. The doubt regarding the possibility of success of a "policy of strength," often seen in a simplified manner, was coming to the fore. . . . At the same time the fear was emerging that some of the Allies might be ready to implement the policy of detente, if an occasion were to arise, at the cost of the Federal Republic. Public opinion began to ask itself whether one should not have recourse to new methods in order to build up a more satisfying attitude toward Eastern Europe.[57]

In other words, German public opinion began to realize that Adenauer's assumptions in the fifties proved to be erroneous. The Soviet Union could not be forced to make concessions. The boycott of the Eastern European states did not bring anything useful to the FRG. The trend among the Western allies toward finding a *modus vivendi* with the Soviet Union could lead to the diplomatic isolation of the FRG. A new, more flexible policy had to be found. This new Eastern policy was formulated mainly by Foreign Minister Gerhard Schroeder, especially after the replacement of Adenauer by the new Chancellor Erhard.

The Erhard-Schroeder Eastern Policy

A POLICY OF THE POSSIBLE?

MINISTER GERHARD SCHROEDER began his career as the Foreign Minister in the last Adenauer government by warning against the German inclination to overlook realities and indulge in wishful thinking. He said on June 4, 1962: "We Germans unfortunately did not always possess in our history a detached view of our possibilities and limitations, and let our sight be dimmed by emotions, wishes or political dogmas. . . . I think that German foreign policy must be deduced from the real conditions. We must conduct a foreign policy of the possible, not of the impossible."[1]

However, this call to realism did not bring about the admission that the objectives of the fifties were unrealistic given the international distribution of power. The GDR remained the Soviet Zone of occupation, and the frontiers continued to be contested. Nevertheless, the passive or rather negative attitude toward the East European countries was at last abandoned. Schroeder's freedom of action in this respect was limited by the resolution which the Bundestag adopted on June 14, 1961:

> The federal government shall seize every existing opportunity to achieve the normalization of relations between the Federal Republic and the East European states without the surrender of vital German interests. It should strive to develop further the existing relations with those states in the economic, humanitarian, spiritual

117

and cultural realms. It should take into account in building up relations with Poland the particular psychological factors which burden German-Polish relations, and it should always assert, on the occasion of the eventual establishment of official contacts, the necessary international law reservations in relation to such countries which deported parts of the German population or keep German territory under their provisional administration.[2]

The reservations made by the Bundestag meant that the federal government should continue to contest the validity of the Oder-Neisse frontier and should be mindful of the right of refugee and expellee Germans to return to their former homelands. The Bundestag realized that Poland would not consent to establish diplomatic relations under such conditions, and confined its recommendation to the establishment of informal economic and cultural relations with Poland and the other Eastern European states.

COMMERCIAL MISSIONS AND THE MUNICH AGREEMENT

Minister Schroeder had to move forward within these confines. He proposed to Warsaw the exchange of commercial missions in view of the fact that the two countries already had rather lively trade. The negotiations with Poland began in November 1962 and ended on March 7, 1963, with an agreement for such missions. The FRG was officially represented in Warsaw for the first time, if only by a commercial mission. However, the successive heads of the German mission always had a high diplomatic rank and were professional diplomats.

Similar missions were established in 1963 and 1964 in Bucharest, Budapest, and Sofia. Only Czechoslovakia refused, on account of a difference of views with Bonn as to the date of invalidity of the 1938 Munich agreement by virtue of which the Czech Sudetenland had been annexed by Germany. The Czechoslovak government maintained that the Munich agreement was null and void on the date of its signature. Bonn conceded that the agreement was invalidated only in March 1939 by Hitler's military occupation of Czechoslovakia. Adenauer's successor, Chancellor Ludwig Erhard, tried to reassure the Czechs in his statement of June 11, 1964, in which he declared that the FRG, of whom Czechoslovakia was the only immediate Eastern European neighbor, had no territorial claims against that neighbor, and considered the Munich agreement as torn up by Hitler himself.[3] This reassurance did not appease Prague. The Czechs feared that if the Munich agreement should be acknowledged as valid in 1938, it could be used later by the Germans to claim that Germany had the right to the Sudetenland. This fear was related to the free activities in the FRG of the German expellees from the Sudetenland and their claim to the *Heimatrecht*. Prague was not certain that a future possibly powerful Germany would not officially support this *Heimatrecht*. If the Germans were to return to the Sudetenland and should claim the right to self-determination as their expellee organizations were doing, the next step would be for Germany to ask, as in 1938, for the cession of that part of Czechoslovakia. This is why they preferred to say that the Munich agreement had no justification even in 1938. The FRG had a different preoccupation. If the Munich agreement were to be considered null and void from its inception, then the Sudetenland Germans, who had been declared German citizens after the German annexation in 1938 and who had served the Third Reich, could be considered by Prague as traitors to Czechoslovakia and be prosecuted if they visited the country of their former allegiance. Millions of Sudetenland expellees lived in the FRG and had been its citizens since the war. This quarrel lasted until 1973 when a formula satisfactory to both sides was established in the German-Czechoslovak treaty of that year. Previously, in 1968, Prague had consented to an exchange of commercial missions, at the time of the Czech "spring."

THE HALLSTEIN DOCTRINE AND EAST EUROPE

The establishment of commercial missions in the East European capitals raised the question of whether it had affected the Hallstein doctrine. Minister Schroeder, in a conversation with a German journalist on March 7, 1963, assured him that this was not true because those missions were not empowered to perform any diplomatic or consular functions.[4] However, six months later, on November 4, 1963, he expressed a deliberate doubt regarding the extension of the Hallstein doctrine to the East European countries: "The so-called doctrine initially did not include the attitude to be taken regarding the Communist countries which already had diplomatic relations with Pankow [the GDR] simply because of their Communist regimes. The extension [to East Europe] of the thesis, that originally had been differently understood, took place more or less automatically in the course of time."[5]

Two years later Schroeder openly abandoned rigid interpretation of the doctrine. He said in an article published by *Foreign Affairs* in 1965: "We may establish diplomatic relations with the East European countries just as well as we have done it with the Soviet Union." He added that "our right to the exclusive representation of Germany in the world would neither be endangered nor prejudiced."[6] What he seemed to say was that the FRG would make the same exception for the East European countries as it had for the Soviet Union, because all those countries had erected their embassies in East Berlin prior, not after, having established diplomatic relations with Bonn. His reservation could have been expressed in the same way as Chancellor Adenauer had expressed it to Moscow, by sending to each East European country with which diplomatic relations were to be established unilateral letters regarding the West German claim to represent all Germans. Since the East European governments could do the same as Moscow had done in 1955 and maintain their own point of view regarding the existence of another German state, the GDR, the divergence of views would not be an obstacle to diplomatic relations. But the time passed when the East European countries, in particular Poland, were ready to establish diplomatic relations without any preconditions. Hence, the FRG had to be satisfied with the channel of commercial missions.

The new interpretation of the Hallstein doctrine, which would allow the establishment of diplomatic relations with Eastern Europe, was supported on March 22, 1965, by the Minister for All-German Affairs, Free Democrat Erich Mende, who said: "We [Free Democrats] were and are of the opinion that those states which had at no time any choice regarding the recognition or non-recognition of the Zone [the GDR] because of their compulsory belonging to the Soviet Empire, should not be included within the purview of the doctrine."[7]

ROMANIA

This restrictive interpretation of the doctrine not only reflected the new willingness to establish diplomatic relations with the East European countries but also the real prospect of doing so with Romania which had begun to steer a new course in foreign affairs, independent of the Soviet Union. The Romanians visited Bonn in the summer of 1966 and gave the FRG to understand that they would gladly exchange embassies.[8] In September 1966 the West German Minister for National

Economy, Schmücker, paid a visit to Bucharest in turn, the first such official visit to any East European capital. He had warm talks with the Romanian First Secretary, Nicolae Ceaucescu, and Prime Minister Maurer regarding future relations, including diplomatic.[9] It was in this context that Minister Schroeder said on August 13, 1966: "The claim of the Federal Republic of Germany to represent all Germans does not preclude the establishment of diplomatic relations with the East European states."[10]

In other words, the Erhard government was ready to establish diplomatic relations with all Eastern European states, including Poland, but this time, unlike in the middle fifties, neither Poland nor other East European states were inclined to respond. Romania was an exception, but this raised a problem for the FRG, actually debated in 1966 and 1967. Was it prudent to begin with Romania, at that time the only out-of-step Soviet ally? Would it not lead to a deterioration in relations with the Soviet Union? However, the temptation to cultivate friendly relations with the dissident Soviet allies was too great. Diplomatic relations were established with Romania in 1967 and rather warm relations with Czechoslovakia were cultivated in 1968. Moscow, alarmed by this kind of Eastern policy, which not only was not concerted with Moscow but could be interpreted as aiming at the dislocation of its bloc, eventually reacted sharply and for this and other reasons intervened in Czechoslovakia. This intervention terminated the West German policy of differentiated relations with the East European countries which in effect bypassed not only the GDR but also the Soviet Union and Poland.

ACTIVE EASTERN POLICY

In any event, Minister Schroeder wanted to initiate an active Eastern policy. He said on June 28, 1963: "We do not want to isolate ourselves from the East European peoples. . . . We wish rather to conduct a policy which we have already started. . . ."[11] He could move with greater freedom following the replacement of Adenauer by Ludwig Erhard as Chancellor in October 1963. Erhard stated in his first speech to the Bundestag on October 18, 1963: "It must remain the goal of our policy to help in terminating the cold war."[12] His government was aligning itself with the attitudes of its Western allies but he still believed that "the German problem is one of the main reasons of world tensions, and one cannot hope that these tensions would be reduced if the German problem were to remain unsolved." This meant that the West should subordinate its policy of detente to the solution of the problem of German reunification. Later on the West German governments had to reverse this thesis in order to be in step with the Western allies. The detente was declared to be the precondition for reunification. However, Erhard was not as optimistic as Adenauer had been in the fifties that reunification would come soon: "It is clear for all of us that great difficulties have to be overcome on the road toward the reestablishment of German unity. This road may be long and thorny. It will cost us renunciations and material and psychological sacrifices. . . . At the end of this road, according to the federal government's conviction, a peace treaty must emerge, freely negotiated and concluded with a freely-elected all-German government. The final frontiers of Germany, which remains according to the valid legal point of view within its frontiers of December 31, 1937, may and must be determined in that treaty and only in it."[13]

TERRITORIAL SACRIFICES?

This was an important statement because it seemed to indicate a more flexible position, although the allusion to "renunciations" and "sacrifices" was far from clear. What it seemed to imply was the expectation that Germany would have to pay with territorial losses for its reunification. As a matter of fact, none other than former Chancellor Adenauer told the Israeli newspaper *Haarets,* on October 29, 1964, that Germany might accept a territorial compromise at the peace conference.[14]

Chancellor Erhard again mentioned the same willingness to make "great material sacrifices" as a price for reunification in an American radio interview, "Face the Nation," on November 1, 1963. He reiterated it in a joint communiqué, published on October 5, 1966, at the end of his visit to President Johnson: "The reunification will demand our sacrifices, even if these sacrifices alone should not suffice to bring the reunification."[15] But he could not afford to lose the electoral support of the expellee organizations. Hence he reassured them on March 22, 1964: "We do not renounce . . . [the claim] to the territories which are the ancestral homeland of so many of our German brothers and sisters."[16] These assurances given to the expellee organizations could not be reconciled with the official stand, formulated in the so-called peace notes of

March 25, 1966: "the government of a unified Germany might have to recognize Eastern frontiers other than those of 1937."[17]

Several other West German politicians made similar hints. In effect, the German political elite at last had enough courage to tell the citizens of the FRG and in particular the refugees and expellees that the hope of returning to 1937 was a dream, and that they should be prepared for territorial losses as the price of reunification. This was obvious at any earlier time since the Western powers, while contesting the finality of the Oder-Neisse frontier, always had stressed that the 1937 East German boundaries must be modified in favor of the Soviet Union and Poland.

Dr. Barzel, then the chairman of the Christian-Democratic Union and Christian-Social Union parliamentary group, admitted to the American Council on German Affairs in a lecture given on June 16, 1966, that "if someone were to ask what the frontiers of a reunified Germany should be in the east, the Western positions would not be unanimous."[18] He and other German politicians knew that President de Gaulle had said in 1959 that a unified Germany should remain within the present frontiers, including the Oder-Neisse frontier. Barzel could not possibly forecast what the American and British attitudes would be if the USSR were to agree unexpectedly to talk about the settlement of the German question. Would they still insist on a territorial compromise as they had done in the late forties and fifties or would they agree to the Oder-Neisse frontier? Neither Washington nor London could bind itself to any formula in advance of unforeseen events. This weakened the West German position.

The leader of the right-wing Bavarian Christian-Social Union, Franz-Joseph Strauss, took a different view from Erhard's government but one closer to the aspirations of the expellee organizations, of which he was the beloved hero. He refused to talk about any sacrifices because he said that "whatever price one might now mention, he will not obtain the Soviet assent to reunification." He did not believe that the USSR would consent to reunification even under a Communist government because it would not like to have such a great power on its Western frontiers. Hence, he preferred, like Adenauer in the fifties, to postpone reunification until such time as Western Europe should form a true political and military union which would act as a magnet for Eastern Europe. Then this union, he implied, would force the USSR to consent to reunification and to a change in Central European frontiers. He believed the FRG should have a very active Western policy while remaining passive in the East.[19]

Foreign Minister Schroeder, perhaps having in mind the territorial problem, once again on April 3, 1964, called for a realistic outlook:

> We can talk rationally about our foreign policy only if we take into account . . . the powers and possibilities of our state in the world political situation as these powers and possibilities actually are. History teaches us that a foreign policy would fail if it did not see or did not want to see the incompatibility between the objectives and the possibilities. . . . When we want to discuss our future course of action, we must look at the political forces and trends in the world. The outlook is anything but reassuring. . . . I do not deduce from what I have said that we should return to methods of the cold war. On the contrary, the West should continue to contribute to detente. . . . Hence, we strive to improve our relations with the East European states and to normalize them as much as possible. . . . We do not expect any surprising political successes from our East European policy. . . . We have in fact often enough declared that the final line of German Eastern frontiers should be determined peacefully and without the use of force in a peace treaty with the whole of Germany. . . . The expulsion of millions of our Eastern countrymen from their homelands was a great injustice. We shall not repay it, however, with a new injustice.[20]

What he rather clearly implied was that the FRG did not expect the restoration of the 1937 frontiers, since the peace treaty would determine the line of future frontiers. He also seemed to imply that the Poles, settled since the war in the territories, most of which he hoped would eventually be returned to a unified Germany, would not be expelled but allowed to remain though under German sovereignty. This was a step forward, although neither the Soviet Union nor Poland was ready to make any territorial concessions. Taking into account this fact and the nuclear power of the Soviet Union, his Eastern policy was still far from realistic.

MOSCOW

In any event, on October 15, 1964, Chancellor Erhard conceded that "the key to reunification lies not in Bonn but in Moscow."[21] This was true. Moscow, however, maintained its position that Germany was divided into two coequal German states, was far from willing to sacrifice the GDR, claimed that West Berlin was a separate political entity, and stood by its guarantee of the inviolability of the Oder-Neisse frontier. The Soviet key was well turned in the lock. Insofar as Poland was concerned, Warsaw observed with suspicion the new West German Eastern policy and the contradictions between the statements made to the expellees and other rather flexible statements regarding the future Eastern frontiers. It had no reason to accept the concept of a territorial compromise. Moreover, it entertained a serious doubt as to whether a unified, hence very powerful, Germany would consent to make territorial sacrifices, and, if it did, would not later ask for a return to the 1937 or better frontiers. The deadlock between the FRG and the USSR and Poland was complete.

In July 1964 the Soviet First Secretary and Prime Minister, Nikita Khrushchev, sent his son-in-law Alexei Adzhubei, editor-in-chief of *Izvestia,* to Bonn. Adzhubei had talks with Chancellor Erhard and other German politicians and, according to rumors, made indiscreet statements. He reached an agreement with Erhard on the forthcoming visit of his father-in-law. What Khrushchev wanted to achieve remains an enigma even today. Chancellor Erhard revealed only that the topics of conversation would be the problem of Germany and that of Berlin.[22] Was Khrushchev ready to make concessions at the expense of the GDR? Was his attitude one of the many reasons for his downfall in October 1964? In any event, he never visited Bonn, and direct Soviet-German negotiations took place only in 1970. The Moscow Treaty of 1970 contained no Soviet concessions regarding the GDR or Poland.

DIFFERENTIATED APPROACH TO EAST EUROPE

Minister Schroeder explained the assumptions and objectives of West German policy in the abovementioned article in *Foreign Affairs* in 1965. He said, among other things, that it was no longer possible to consider the East European states as mere Soviet "satellites" since they were subjects of international relations in their own right. He once again declared the West German intention to normalize relations with them "without surrendering vital German interests." He conceded that Eastern Europe still remained a *"terra incognita"* for the FRG and that he heard voices (see below p. 128) which were of the opinion that "we should

consider the reunification of Germany less as a programmatic requirement of our policy, but rather as a historical process which should be
left to the healing hand of time." He rejected this view as "unrealistic,"
but the Brandt-Scheel government was to adopt it in the seventies. He
also reassured Moscow in the same article that the more flexible West
German Eastern policy was neither directed against the Soviet Union
nor was its aim to alienate the East European states from each other or
from the USSR. He added that "our policy toward the individual East
European states will be further differentiated." This obviously meant
that the FRG intended to improve its relations with some of those states
more than with others. This approach was to be taken by the next Kurt
Kiesinger and Willy Brandt government of the great coalition. That
government bypassed the GDR, Poland, and in effect also the USSR,
and tried or did establish diplomatic relations only with the dissident
Soviet allies, Romania and Czechoslovakia. Moscow interpreted that
approach as an unfriendly policy and an attempt at dislocating its bloc.
It feared this kind of active Eastern policy of the FRG much more than
the passive attitude of Adenauer which did not hurt Moscow's interests.

PEACE NOTES

Since none of the Eastern European countries (except Romania) intended to respond to Schroeder's foreign policy by establishing diplomatic relations, the federal government decided to adopt a different approach which would be in tune with the policy of detente followed by its
Western allies. It unearthed the secret memo of the Foreign Office
written in 1959, and sent so-called peace notes to all governments with
which the FRG entertained diplomatic relations. These identical notes
mentioned that relations with Poland could not be normalized because
Poland demanded the recognition of the Oder-Neisse frontier, while the
FRG continued to insist that Germany legally existed within the 1937
frontiers until such time as the government of a unified Germany "would
recognize other frontiers."[23] This wording indicated that the FRG expected to make territorial sacrifices as a price for reunification. The
notes reaffirmed the West German view that Hitler himself had torn up
the Munich agreement and that the FRG had no territorial claims regarding Czechoslovakia. Finally, the federal government offered to exchange
with the Soviet Union, Poland, Czechoslovakia, and other East Euro-

pean states, declarations of mutual renunciation of threat or use of force for the settlement of disputed questions.

This proposal was immediately rejected by the Soviet Union and its allies for various reasons. One of them was that the acceptance of the German proposal would isolate the GDR, which was excluded from the West German offer as not being a state in the FRG's understanding. Second, the FRG had already undertaken the same obligation toward its Western allies not to use force either for reunification or for the modification of Eastern frontiers (see p. 108 above). The new declarations would have added nothing of practical value for the Soviet bloc, which knew that the Western allies would restrain the FRG from using force and thus unleashing a general war. Third, such declarations would deprive the Soviet Union of its right under Articles 53 and 107 of the Charter of the United Nations.[24] These articles exempted members of the United Nations, including the USSR, from the obligation of Article 2 of the Charter to refrain from the threat or use of force in international relations, insofar as the Second World War enemies were concerned. The Western powers considered articles 53 and 107 dead letters. But the Soviet Union reminded the FRG several times of the existence of those Articles although it was impossible to visualize a forcible Soviet action against the FRG, a member of the North Atlantic alliance, without its provoking a general war which the USSR did not contemplate. The Soviet government renounced its claim to the validity of Articles 53 and 107 only in the 1970 Moscow treaty, concluded with the FRG. Fourth, Poland did not intend to enter into any political agreement with the FRG without renunciation by the FRG of its contestation of the Oder-Neisse frontier. Moreover, the Polish government was afraid that the renunciation of the use of force for the solution of disputed questions might possibly imply that the problem of the Western frontier was a disputed matter. Practically speaking, Warsaw did not need a West German reassurance because Poland was separated from the FRG by the territory of the GDR and, more important, by more than twenty Soviet divisions stationed on East German territory. Direct attack by the FRG was out of the question as long as Poland was protected by its alliance with the nuclear superpower and by the existence of the GDR. Finally, the Poles remembered their recent experience with the German-Polish agreement of non-aggression of 1934, which was valid for ten years but was broken by German military attack five years after its signature. They had no trust in such paper guarantees.[25]

The peace notes proved to be the wrong approach. Rejected by the Soviet bloc, they led nowhere.

THE SOCIAL DEMOCRATS

The Social Democrats, at that time the opposition party, adopted a contrasting attitude to both the views of the Erhard government and even more to Strauss's opinion. They did not want to wait patiently until the advent of Day X when a sudden change in international circumstances would force the USSR to make concessions. Incidentally, on March 23, 1966, former Chancellor Adenauer mentioned the Soviet quarrel with China as a factor that should compel the USSR to secure its European rear by making concessions presumably to the FRG.[26]

But the Social Democrats did not believe in miracles. Egon Bahr, a close friend of Willy Brandt and at that time head of the West Berlin press office, said in a lecture on July 15, 1963:

> The first consequence of the extension to Germany of the [American] strategy of peace is the exclusion of the policy of everything or nothing, of either free elections [in the GDR] or nothing, either an all-German freedom of decision or a hard nay. . . . All this is not only hopelessly antiquated and unworkable but also senseless from the point of view of the strategy of peace. It is clear today that reunification will not be a single act which will take place because of a historical decision on a historical day at a historical conference but will be a historical process with many steps and many stops. . . . Any policy which aims at a direct overthrow of the regime [in the GDR] is hopeless.

If such a policy were followed, then "we should have to wait for a miracle, and this is no policy at all."[27] This was a new departure even for the Social Democrats. Bahr advised, probably in agreement with Brandt, undertaking a new policy toward the GDR in search of a workable *modus vivendi,* although without recognizing it as a coequal German state. This view clashed with the Christian Democratic opinion. Minister Schroeder rejected Bahr's view as "unrealistic" (see p. 126 above).

Willy Brandt took the ball which Bahr had started to roll, and said in a lecture on June 11, 1964: "The two world powers are interested in preventing a nuclear confrontation. They must, therefore, strive to reduce tensions. . . . This means the end of the policy of either everything or nothing. This policy is now more hopeless than ever. . . . One may at last calmly say that reunification may be visualized only in relation to a wide-reaching modification in Western-Eastern relations. . . .

We have had enough of declamations and proclamations. We must now proceed with small steps and strive for gradual change."[28]

This conciliatory attitude toward the GDR led Brandt to delineate what he considered a practical policy toward Eastern Europe. He did this in a memo forwarded in August 1964 to Secretary of State Dean Rusk (published only on January 25, 1965): "It is in the Western interest to support the independence of East European nations. . . . The national consciousness in the East European states and the trend toward independence express themselves in an increasing self-interest. This trend must be taken into consideration. . . . The differentiated development [in Eastern Europe] makes it necessary to develop a differentiated attitude regarding each Eastern European country."[29]

This was in a nutshell the foundation of the policy he favored later on in his capacity as Vice-Chancellor and Foreign Minister of the great coalition government. It led him to bypass Moscow, the GDR, and Poland, with which he could not find a common denominator, and to seek better relations with Romania and equally dissident Czechoslovakia, and, he hoped, with Hungary and Bulgaria. This policy foundered with the Soviet occupation of Czechoslovakia, and in turn forced him as Chancellor to seek a direct understanding with Moscow and Warsaw.

However, in 1966 Brandt was ready to adopt a conciliatory attitude toward the problem of the Oder-Neisse frontier. As the leader of his party, he told the Dortmund congress of Social Democrats on June 1, 1966, that sacrifices which the Germans would have to make would be the price to be paid for the war which Hitler had begun and had lost. He warned that the usual territorial claims were formulated in an unrealistic manner as though "we had the territories east of the Oder-Neisse." In this sense we "do not have the territories east of the Oder-Neisse." This was much more than any Christian Democratic politician would say. He dropped the usual term of the Soviet Zone and called the GDR the other part of Germany with which a *modus vivendi* had to be sought.[30] This new attitude toward Poland and the GDR was to guide his policy as Chancellor much later. At the same Congress another Social Democratic leader, Helmut Schmidt, warned that an uncompromising policy toward the East would end in isolating the FRG internationally, that reunification would demand sacrifices regarding the Eastern frontier, and that one could not hope to win trust and understanding of neighboring peoples without readiness to reach compromises.[31]

It was becoming obvious in the sixties that the former unity of views among West German political parties was ended, and that the Social Democrats were ready to go farther than the Christian Democrats.

This had an impact on the Eastern policy of the great coalition government that succeeded the Erhard government by the end of 1966.

THE RESULTS OF SCHROEDER'S NEW OUTLOOK

One cannot say, in spite of the failure of the peace notes, that the Erhard-Schroeder Eastern policy did not bring about a change in West German attitudes toward Eastern Europe. Quite a few shibboleths of the Adenauer era were discarded. The Hallstein doctrine was reinterpreted and hence the door to diplomatic relations with East Europe was opened. The dogma of the return of a reunified Germany to the 1937 frontiers was abandoned by the hints that sacrifices would be required as a price for reunification. First official contacts with the East European capitals were established in the form of commercial missions. Schroeder's call to realism was in itself a call for an active Eastern policy, *i.e.*, rupture with Adenauer's passivity.

After the fall of Erhard's government in 1966 and its replacement by the government of great coalition of Christian Democrats and Social Democrats, the field was open for further experimentation with an active Eastern policy. Schroeder's advice to try a differentiated approach to the various East European countries was to be followed by the new government until it had to be abandoned after Soviet intervention in Czechoslovakia. This in turn gave birth to the entirely new Eastern policy of the Brandt-Scheel government. In any event, the concept of an active Eastern policy, originating with Schroeder and radically reinterpreted by Brandt and Scheel, eventually led to the Moscow and Warsaw treaties.

7

The Eastern Policy of the Great Coalition Government

FORMATION OF THE KIESINGER-BRANDT GOVERNMENT

BETWEEN 1949 and 1966, Christian Democrats ruled the FRG either alone or in coalition with the Free Democrats. The latter party proved to be difficult by forcing the replacement of Adenauer by Erhard as Chancellor, and by causing the fall of Erhard's government by its withdrawal from the coalition. In the meantime, the concept of a great coalition of the two main parties was gradually maturing. The Christian Democrats hoped thus to ensure a greater stability in the FRG, while the Social Democrats were ready to join the federal government from which they had been barred since the foundation of the Federal Republic.

The Social Democratic Party had its own reasons for joining the great coalition government. It intended to demonstrate to the electorate that it was a moderate left-center party which could be trusted with governmental responsibilities. It could prove this only by being a part of the government. It abandoned its previous opposition to such aspects of Adenauer's policy as accession to the North Atlantic Alliance and West German rearmament, which it had considered at that time as an obstacle to Soviet acceptance of the reunification of Germany. At its Godesberg congress in 1959 it abandoned its traditional commitment to Marxism. This was more of a reassuring gesture to the electorate than anything else, since the Social Democrats, even prior to the First World War, had been a reformist party working within the German constitutional frame-

131

work, had contained the November 1918 Revolution within the bounds of democracy successfully, and had proved their law-abiding nature during the existence of the Weimar Republic. The official repudiation of Marxism, which did not mean much to the party anyhow, was intended to show the electorate that the Social Democrats had nothing in common with communism, in particular East German communism. It was meant also to tell the nation that their party was not only the party of the working class but that it wanted to represent the interests of other segments of the society. They intended to instill in the minds of the electors that they were a party similar to the British Labour Party, undogmatic and with appeal to almost all social strata, a sort of cautious reformist party.

Since the Christian Democrats had been more successful at the polls ever since the foundation of the Federal Republic, the Social Democrats could not expect that they would be able to form the government by themselves in 1966. Their only chance of becoming a part of government was to join the Christian Democrats in a coalition. They had first manifested their readiness to do so in 1961 but met with a favorable Christian Democratic response only in 1966.

The new government was formed in December 1966. It was headed by Chancellor Kurt Kiesinger (CDU), while Willy Brandt (SPD) became Vice-Chancellor and Foreign Minister.

UNCERTAIN CONTENTS OF THE EASTERN POLICY

This great coalition government had to find a common denominator for a joint foreign policy. There were no difficulties regarding the Western policy, but the Eastern policy represented a potential source of trouble. Although the divergences of views between the Christian Democrats and the Social Democrats were eluded for a few years by lame compromises within the government, these divergences appeared fairly soon in the different nuances of statements made by Chancellor Kiesinger and Vice-Chancellor Brandt.

One should add that the sixties was the period of soul-searching in Germany. People began to ask whether the former foreign policy had not led the FRG into a blind alley, and whether it was not an illusion to expect a change in the status quo in any foreseeable future.

EXCHANGE OF LETTERS BETWEEN THE
GERMAN AND POLISH BISHOPS

The debate regarding relations with Poland was stirred up by an exchange of letters between the Polish and German bishops attending the Vatican II Council in Rome. The Polish bishops took the initiative by sending a letter to the German bishops on November 18, 1965. This letter came after a period of strong criticism by the German Catholic Church of the attitude of the Polish Church regarding the Oder-Neisse frontier. During the summer and fall of 1965 the Polish hierarchy had celebrated the twentieth anniversary of the incorporation of the Western and Northern provinces (former East German territories) by solemn services in former German cities such as Stettin (Szczecin) and Breslau (Wrocław). Kardinal Doepfner, the president of the assembly of German bishops, expressed the dissatisfaction of German Catholics.[1] The German public was surprised to see, soon after the Polish-German ecclesiastical polemic, the Polish bishops' letter, and the reply of the German bishops.

The Polish bishops did not yield regarding the question of the Oder-Neisse frontier but the tone of their letter was cordial and conciliatory. The letter began by inviting the German bishops to take part the following year in the Polish Church's celebrations of the millennium of Polish conversion to Christianity (incidentally, the German bishops who had accepted the invitation did not receive Polish visas and could not come). Then the letter traced the history of Polish Catholicism, starting with the decision of Pope Sylvester II in the eleventh century to erect the Polish ecclesiastical organization with the archbishopric in Gniezno (close to Poznań) and bishoprics in Cracow, Wrocław, and Kołobrzeg. This was a clear allusion to the Polish nature in the Middle Ages of the cities called Breslau and Kolberg by the Germans, and did not please the German bishops. However, the Polish bishops also mentioned periods when the two churches and the two nations had cooperated, in particular in the Middle Ages. While enumerating the long list of Polish saints, the bishops mentioned also the name of Father Maximilian Kolbe, a Polish Franciscan priest who had offered to be murdered in the Auschwitz concentration camp in place of the designated victim, the father of a family to whom he hoped to return. The martyrdom of Father Kolbe was to be honored in Rome a few years later by his beatification. The Polish bishops called the period of wartime German occupation "the dark night" for Poland, when six million

Polish citizens were murdered by the German authorities, including two thousand Catholic priests and five bishops. They wrote: "Every German uniform, not only that of the SS men, provoked a nightmarish fear among the Poles and was the source of hatred of the Germans. . . . After all that happened in the past, alas the very recent past, one cannot be surprised that the whole Polish nation . . . still looks with distrust at its immediate Western neighbors."

The Polish bishops also mentioned more ancient history which had left bitter memories in Polish minds. They said that the Teutonic Knights "converted the natives in the Slavic North and in the Prussian and Baltic countries by fire and sword. They became for centuries a burden, horrible and compromising to the highest degree for European Christianity, for their symbol, the Cross, and for the Church in whose name they acted. . . . On the territories settled by the Teutonic Knights were born those Prussians who compromised generally everything German in the Polish lands. The following names represent the Teutonic Knights in the historical development: the Prussian Albrecht, Frederic called the Great, Bismarck, and eventually as the summit Hitler." Obviously, the German bishops were not particularly pleased with this Polish version of their national history, in which the Teutonic Knights, Albrecht—the first prince in East Prussia—Frederic the Great, and Bismarck were considered national heroes. This part of the Polish letter in itself indicated, whatever the bishops' intention, the enormous difficulty in reaching a true reconciliation between the two nations. History itself had accumulated too many obstacles which could not be easily overcome.

The Polish bishops reiterated the general Polish view regarding the frontier problem: "The Polish western frontier on the Oder and the Neisse is, as we understand well, a very bitter fruit of the last mass extermination war, as are likewise the sufferings of millions of German refugees and expellees. . . . The majority of that [German] population left those territories in fear of the Russian front and fled to the West. . . . For our country . . . [that frontier] embodies the question of its existence." Thus, the loss of the territories and the sufferings of German refugees and expellees were linked to the war which the Germans had started and which in Poland they had turned into a war of mass extermination. The Oder-Neisse frontier had to remain because it was a matter of Poland's existence. Again, this part of the Polish letter could hardly please the German bishops who supported the then prevailing West German view that the frontier had to be changed in favor of Germany.

However, the Polish bishops implicitly acknowledged Polish responsibility for the expulsion of East Germans, because they solemnly called out: "Let us try to forget. . . . We stretch our hands to you, who sit on the benches of the Council that is about to end; and we forgive and we ask you also to forgive."

It was this call to mutual forgiveness that provoked strong criticism in Poland. Did not such a call to mutual forgiveness place on even scales the murder of six million Polish citizens and the horrors of German occupation with the loss by Germany of Eastern territories and the expulsion of East Germans? The usual Polish view was expressed by the Polish Vice-Minister for Foreign Affairs, Józef Winiewicz, who was confronted on his first visit to Bonn in 1970 with a question related to the expulsions. He answered by saying that he could not bring with him the six million Polish dead to give the proper reply.

The German bishops responded on December 5, 1965. They conceded that "the Polish nation experienced many horrors inflicted by the Germans and in the name of the German nation. . . . We understand that the period of German occupation left a burning wound which is not easy to heal even with the best will. . . . This is why we also ask for forgetfulness, more, we ask for forgiveness." Then the German bishops recalled the problem of East German refugees and expellees and their right to the former homelands, but they admitted that they understood the significance of the former German territories for Poland and for the young Poles born there, who considered those territories as their own homeland. However, they refrained from any statement which would commit the German Church regarding the present or future German-Polish frontier.

In reading the two letters, one wonders whether they contributed much to Polish-German reconciliation. Faced with criticism at home, on February 15, 1966, *i.e.,* a few months after their return from Rome, the Polish bishops issued a pastoral letter in which they explained: "They [the bishops] never opened a debate regarding our Oder-Neisse frontier because we consider our present [territorial] possessions as a matter of 'to be or not to be' for our state. . . . We recalled [in the letter] the injustices inflicted on our nation." They explained the words, "We forgive and ask for forgiveness," as the expression of the Gospel teaching: "Love your enemies, be good to them who hate you." "We had the Christian courage to tell the German people what their sins were regarding our nation. . . . Has the Polish nation any reason to ask its neighbors for forgiveness? No doubt it has not! . . . But we considered that, if even a single Pole did not deserve to be called a man, if even one Pole in history committed a reprehensible act, we should have reason to say: 'We ask for forgiveness.' Only then we shall better understand that part of the Lord's prayer: 'Forgive us our trespasses, as we forgive them that trespass against us.' "

This pastoral letter was a retreat from the tenor of the letter to the German bishops. However, the exchange of letters between the bishops stimulated the West German debate regarding the problem of relations with Poland.

THE NEW TREND IN THE FRG

The German Protestant Church went further than the Catholic Church. Its famous memorandum, published at the end of October 1965, called the expulsion of East Germans "a lawless act," but related it to German moral responsibility toward German neighbors for what the Nazi regime had done to them. The memorandum recalled the demographic and economic changes which had taken place in the Eastern territories since the war and seemed to concede that these territories were vital for Poland. It stated, among other things, that "the heritage of evil past imposes on the German nation a particular obligation of respecting in the future the rights of the Polish nation to life and of leaving to that nation as much territory as it needs for its development. . . . The resettlement of the East German population and the fate of Eastern German territories are part of the misfortune which the German nation suffers . . . as a punishment for its guilt [for starting the Second World War]. . . . The readiness to bear the consequences and to offer reparation for the committed lawless acts must be an important and integral part of German policy in respect to our Eastern neighbors."[2]

The memorandum, unlike the letter of the German bishops, was attacked by the expellee organizations as a betrayal of the German cause. Nevertheless, the memorandum contributed to the debate. Several German intellectuals such as K. Jaspers, K. Barth and G. Mann, the son of Thomas Mann, and several journalists, including the editors of *Der Spiegel* and *Der Stern,* favored recognition of the territorial status quo.

The new trends in public opinion were evidenced by the polls of opinion carried out by the Allensbach Institute of Research on Public Opinion. The new attitudes were noticeable not only among the population at large but also among the refugees and expellees. In 1953, 77 percent of those refugees and expellees believed that they would return to their former homelands. In 1965 only 34 percent held that view, while 76 percent admitted their complete integration within the FRG. The answers to the crucial questions asked of the West German population showed a noticeable trend toward the acceptance of the status quo. The question of whether one should be reconciled to the present Polish-German frontier was answered in the following way:

	In 1951	1956	1962	1964	1967	and	1968
Yes	8%	9%	26%	22%	47%		51%
No	80%	73%	50%	59%	34%		32%
No opinion	12%	18%	24%	19%	19%		17%

Answers to the question of whether the Eastern territories were or were not lost forever were as follows:

	In 1953	1959	1962	1964	1967	and	1968
No	66%	35%	29%	25%	20%		16%
Yes	11%	32%	45%	46%	56%		68%
No opinion	23%	33%	26%	29%	24%		16%

The third question was whether one would be willing to resettle in the Eastern territories if they were returned to Germany. The answers were as follows:

I. For the whole West German population

	In 1967	and in 1968
No	74%	80%
Yes	14%	11%
No opinion	12%	9%

II. For the natives of West Germany

	In 1967	and in 1968
No	80%	85%
Yes	8%	7%
No opinion	12%	8%

III. For the refugees and expellees

	In 1967	and in 1968
No	59%	59%
Yes	30%	29%
No opinion	11%	12%

These answers indicated the trend toward the acceptance of the Oder-Neisse frontier and also a growing reluctance among the refugees and expellees to envisage a return to their former homelands. They also revealed that the adamant attitude of the expellee organizations was not shared by the majority of those whom they claimed to represent. This in turn influenced the positions of both the SPD and the FDP.

THE NEW EASTERN POLICY

The great coalition government started by continuing the Eastern policy of Erhard's government while introducing a few innovations.

It is impossible to single out that part of the Eastern policy which related directly to Poland, because the Polish problem was only a part, admittedly an important part, of the whole policy. Neither Bonn nor Moscow and Warsaw regarded the Polish aspect of the policy as something independent of the other segments.

Chancellor Kiesinger outlined the Eastern policy in his first governmental declaration, made on December 13, 1966, in the Bundestag. He reminded parliament of the peace notes which the preceding government had sent to all governments with which Bonn entertained diplomatic relations. He reiterated the willingness of the FRG to exchange declarations on the renunciation of force with the Soviet Union and the Eastern European states as well as to establish diplomatic relations with the latter states.

He included in his declaration the following statement regarding Poland: "There is a strong desire in wide strata of the German people for a reconciliation with Poland whose sorrowful history we have not forgotten, and whose claim to live finally within a state territory with secure frontiers we understand now better than in former times because of the present fate of our partitioned people. However, the frontiers of a reunified Germany may be determined only in a settlement freely agreed upon with an all-German government. This settlement should create the foundation for peaceful and lasting good-neighbor relations which both peoples could approve."[3]

The Chancellor did not ask for a return to the 1937 frontier but pointed out in effect that the future frontier would have to be a sort of territorial compromise, a view firmly rejected by the Soviet Union and Poland. He conceded that his countrymen had not understood the bitter nature of the former Polish situation until their own country was in turn partitioned. Parenthetically, the Poles had felt desperate throughout the nineteenth century not because they did not have secure frontiers but because they had no frontiers of their own, having been partitioned among their three neighbors, including the Germans. On the whole, his statement regarding the Polish western frontier did not differ from what the Erhard government had been saying.

The Chancellor reassured Prague that the Munich agreement was no longer valid but that the FRG must protect its own citizens who had been Czechoslovak citizens prior to the date of that agreement. He reaffirmed the right of the FRG "to speak on behalf of the whole German people," but used a new term while referring to the GDR. It was no longer the Soviet Zone but "the other part of Germany," with which his government was ready to establish closer contacts, without, however, recognizing the GDR as another German state. This was a step forward, but it could not lead to a *modus vivendi* with the GDR which insisted on being recognized as a co-equal German state.[4]

The first governmental declaration of the great coalition should not have left any expectation in the minds of Christian Democrats and Social Democrats that any political accommodation was possible with the Soviet Union, Poland, and the GDR. What the new government probably expected was to produce the impression among the Western allies that the FRG's policy was becoming flexible and moving somewhat in the same direction as their own policies of building bridges toward the Soviet Union and its allies. The new government also hoped that this building of bridges was possible in regard to those Soviet allies who would be willing to respond and in doing this to bypass Moscow, Warsaw, and East Berlin in their own policies toward Bonn.

The official history of German foreign policy notes that there were fears in Bonn at that time that if the FRG were to remain the last bastion of the cold war, it would run the danger of being isolated among its own allies.[5] Vice-Chancellor Brandt conceded in an interview on July 2, 1967, that "harmony with our allies did not exist in the last years of the small coalition. We ran the danger of being isolated."[6] Walter Scheel, the leader of the opposition Free Democratic party said the same on April 2, 1968: "We are in a period of detente in Europe. But this policy of detente is not ours; it is the policy of detente between the USA and the USSR."[7]

THE SOVIET STAND

The Soviet government did not limit itself to propaganda attacks. It conducted negotiations in the period 1967–69 with the great coalition government regarding renunciation of the use of force, but insisted that any agreement in this area should include other matters such as the inviolability of existing frontiers, including the Oder-Neisse and the FRG-GDR frontiers; the recognition of the GDR as another co-equal German state; the renunciation by the FRG of its claim to represent all the Germans; the existence of West Berlin as a political entity separate from the FRG; the nullity of the Munich agreement since its inception; and signature by the FRG of the treaty on non-proliferation of nuclear weapons.

One may wonder why Moscow talked with Bonn while insisting on the demands which it knew Bonn was not prepared to accept. The only plausible explanation is that it intended to instill in West German minds that only the acceptance of its own views regarding the preservation of the Central European status quo would open the prospect of an agreement with the Soviet Union. Was it a superfluous exercise? Not quite, if one considers the ongoing debate in West Germany at the time on a realistic Eastern policy, and also if judged by what Moscow achieved a few years later in negotiations with the next German government.

What is more difficult to understand is the Soviet insistence on Articles 53 and 107 of the United Nations Charter, the validity of which Moscow claimed would not be affected even by an agreement on the renunciation of force. Yet Vice-Chancellor Brandt was correct when he said on September 4, 1968: "The Atlantic Alliance to which we belong protects us in any conceivable case of intervention."[8] The only explanation that makes sense is that Moscow insisted on its right of intervention by virtue of the so-called enemy clause of the Charter in order to keep in reserve the renunciation of that claim as a concession to be made if Bonn should be ready to accept the status quo. This actually happened in 1970.

THE QUESTION OF THE STATUS QUO

But the great coalition firmly held to the traditional West German objective of achieving a modification in the status quo, although Vice-Chancellor Brandt frankly conceded in December 1967: "I know that the

Soviet government is not interested under the present circumstances in any fundamental change in the status quo."[9] Chancellor Kiesinger stated the matter quite correctly on August 25, 1968: "The problem is as follows. The Soviet Union wants as a minimum to maintain the status quo in Europe. . . . We must seek to change the status quo because only then can we achieve the reunification of our people."[10]

With the West German and Soviet policies clashing head on, there was no prospect of any arrangement with Moscow. Yet Bonn wanted to pursue its goal of exchanging the declarations on renunciation of force with such East European countries as would be willing to do so. Perhaps Bonn hoped in 1967 that Poland would agree to conclude this sort of non-aggression pact. If Poland had agreed, it might have been deterred by the calculation of a West German writer who wrote in an article published by the respected periodical *Europa Archiv:* "The renunciation of force will not mean the renunciation of legal claims, but, to the contrary, will amount to their being upheld and perhaps ever strengthened, because one would renounce thereby not the [future] settlement of the dispute regarding legal claims but only the use of illicit means for the settlement. The attempts to make legal claims prevail by political and diplomatic means would remain licit. . . . The partner would admit, by making the statement on the renunciation of force, that the problem, which should not be settled by the use of force, continues to require a solution."[11]

This clever legal argument did not escape Polish and Soviet attention, but certainly did not increase their trust in the new Eastern policy.[12] Moscow could not be appeased by mere reassurances such as Vice-Chancellor Brandt offered on June 5, 1968: "It would be foolish and unrealistic to make a policy which would be directed against the Soviet Union. It would be equally illusory to want to make use of some differences between Moscow and its allies."[13] This is exactly what preoccupied Moscow at that time. It suspected that the new Eastern policy aimed at exploiting conflicts between the USSR and some of its allies and thus at undermining its influence in Eastern Europe.

The Soviet Union considered the division of Germany and the existence of the GDR integral parts of the status quo, while the objective of the Eastern policy was to achieve eventually the reunification by merger of the GDR with the FRG. Poland was also interested in the maintenance of the division of Germany, the existence of the GDR, a Soviet ally, being the best guarantee for its Western frontier.

Chancellor Kiesinger in vain reassured the USSR on January 27, 1967: "Insofar as the Soviet Union is considered, it should not fear that the inauguration of normalization of our relations with the other Eastern neighbors is directed against it."[14] This is precisely what Moscow feared. The Soviet government told Bonn in a memorandum of July 5, 1968, that mere agreements on the renunciation of force which did not recognize the status quo would "legalize in an international law form the refusal to recognize the results of the Second World War."[15] The USSR also insisted that the FRG should conclude an agreement on the renunciation of force with the GDR in the same kind of international treaty as Bonn was ready to make with the other Eastern European countries. It stated on October 12, 1967, that this was an important matter since the frontier between the GDR and the FRG was the only place where the danger of the use of force could arise.[16] The Kiesinger-Brandt government refused to make such an agreement for fear that a regular treaty would imply the recognition of the GDR as a state. It was ready only to issue together with the GDR simultaneous unilateral declarations on the renunciation of force.

This and other divergences of view between Bonn and Moscow had the expected result. Chancellor Kiesinger said on June 23, 1967, that the Eastern policy evoked only a hostile Soviet reaction: "The Soviet Union waited for a few weeks following the formation of the government and then answered with massive attacks against us."[17]

REUNIFICATION

The reunification of Germany remained the first objective of Eastern policy although the great coalition government admitted that this would be a long process, which could be accelerated only by the Eastern policy. Chancellor Kiesinger on June 17, 1967, said in a pessimistic vein: "Time does not work for us."[18] Neither was Brandt unduly optimistic when he declared on January 8, 1967, "No one may pull back the wheel of history. . . . It is clear to our people that the reunification demands a long process."[19]

In any event, the Kiesinger-Brandt government abandoned the former thesis that reunification should precede European detente and be its precondition. Kiesinger said on November 4, 1967: "There was a time when we said: First reunification and then the detente. This would be a politically impossible alternative if we continued to say so at the present time."[20] Brandt said the same in his article in *Foreign Affairs* (April, 1968):

Our political goal has changed in one fundamental point. Previously, we and our allies assumed that an arrangement with the Soviet Union and a bridging of the political-power conflicts in Central Europe were unthinkable unless the problem of Germany's division was solved first. . . . Today, our policy is based more strongly on the interrelatedness of the German problem and European development generally. It concentrates on the improvement of the present climate of distrust, tension and conflict. This means that a long and arduous road lies ahead of us. . . . Preconditions should not be put in the way. . . . German policy today is based on the assumption that the overcoming of division of Germany will be a long process whose duration no one can predict.[21]

This new long-term view of the problem of reunification did not entail either the abandonment of the West German claim to be the spokesman for all Germans, including those living in East Germany, or willingness to recognize the existence of another German state. The former dogmas remained unchanged in this respect. Kiesinger said on February 1, 1967, "The federal government is the only one empowered and obliged to speak on behalf of the whole German people."[22] He added on June 23, 1967: "While we have expressed less often than before the claim to the sole representation [of all the Germans] or, better, the right to the sole representation, this is not because we have given up our legal point of view."[23]

THE GDR

On April 11, 1969 Chancellor Kiesinger said, "It is not most important in the final analysis whether this or the next generation will achieve this [the reunification]. What is important is that our people itself does not give up."[24] What he had in mind was the prospect that West Germans would eventually get used to the division of Germany, while East Germans would accept the existence of the GDR as something as natural as the existence of another German-speaking country, Austria. Both major parties conceded, however, through their spokesmen, Kiesinger and Brandt, that the division of Germany might last for a long time. Both feared that the former policy of simply ignoring the GDR by contemptuously referring to it as the "Soviet Zone" or the "Pankow regime," while considering only the four former occupying powers as the valid interlocutors regarding reunification, would only help the East German regime to keep its population isolated. The building of the Berlin Wall stabilized that regime by cutting off the main escape route for the East Germans. The question arose as to whether these East Germans would not develop a mentality quite different from that of their West German countrymen and would not acquire a separate national consciousness similar to the Austrian. It appeared that the most important task of the Federal Republic was to preserve the unifying German national consciousness in both parts of Germany. This could be achieved by broadening contacts of all sorts with the GDR and by reaching some kind of *modus vivendi* with that other German state. The great coalition government faced the problem of eating their cake and having it. On the other hand, it was willing, unlike former German governments, to seek a *modus vivendi,* while on the other hand, it held to the former position that the GDR could not be recognized as a state. This was a problem of squaring the circle since the GDR refused any *modus vivendi* unless it was recognized as a coequal German state. One could observe, however, a difference in the approaches of the Chancellor and his Vice-Chancellor. The former was willing to call the GDR "another part of Germany" or the "GDR" in quotation marks, while Brandt referred to the GDR without quotation marks. It was becoming clearer with the lapse of time that any recognition of the GDR as a state was out of the question for Kiesinger, while Brandt only refused to recognize it as a foreign state.

However, on June 13, 1967, Chancellor Kiesinger consented to answer a letter of May 20, 1967, from the GDR Prime Minister, Willi Stoph. Even the styling of the address of that answer was interesting; Willi Stoph was addressed as the Chairman of the Council of Ministers but there was no mention of the name of the state where he performed his official functions. Thus the problem of recognition was bypassed. Willi Stoph proposed in his letter the normalization of relations between the two German states but conditioned this normalization on the mutual renunciation of force, the recognition of the existence of the frontier between these two states, the acceptance of the right of both the FRG and the GDR to have diplomatic relations with third states, the renunciation by the FRG of its claim to speak on behalf of all Germans, and the annulment of West German restrictions on trade with the GDR.[25] All these demands were fully supported by the Soviet Union.[26]

Chancellor Kiesinger rejected these demands as amounting to the recognition of the GDR and maintained the claim of the FRG to representation of all Germans.[27] The two German governments remained at loggerheads after this exchange of letters.

In the meantime, Vice-Chancellor Brandt was undergoing an evolution in his concept of relations with the GDR. On December 14, 1966, he still expressed the view, shared by the Chancellor, that contacts with the GDR should not mean "any recognition of another German state."[28] But on October 13, 1967, he made a different statement: "The international law recognition of the 'GDR' is out of the question. This is not a matter for negotiations or talks."[29] He reiterated the same thought on November 22, 1967: "We are not willing to recognize the international law existence of another German state. The Chancellor and I have said more than once that one cannot deny the existence of a political system of a particular kind in the other part of Germany, and that the Constitution of the Federal Republic is not valid there. This does not mean that the German territory on the other side of the Elbe is a foreign country for us."[30]

What seemed to be implied was that he refused to recognize the GDR as a state foreign to the FRG, as for example France or Spain was foreign, but was not reluctant to recognize the GDR as a state of the same German nation. The March 21, 1968, resolution of the Social Democratic Congress held in Nuremberg implied the same thing: "The renunciation of the use of force with the GDR [without quotation marks] must take into account the fact that the two parts of Germany may not become mutually foreign subjects of international law. . . . The interests of the German and European peoples urgently demand cooperation between the two parts of Germany. . . . It is incontroversial that the Germans in both parts of the country belong to the same nation. Both governments can and must, however, conduct negotiations and try to reach an agreement which would not discriminate against either party. . . . The international law recognition of the GDR is out of the question."[31]

Brandt in his article in the April 1968 issue of *Foreign Affairs* conceded that "the other part of Germany is also a reality. . . . Our new policy means that we are prepared to arrange our relationship with the other part of Germany in a way different than has been the case hitherto. We have, however, made it clear that international legal recognition of that part of Germany . . . is impossible."[32] He continued in the same vein in his statement of April 18, 1969: "We must tell him who denies the existence of the GDR: the reality is different. We say similarly, the reality is different, to him who says to the contrary that international law recognition of the GDR would solve our problems and would make friends of the enemies of German unity."[33] He admitted that the Hallstein doctrine, aiming at the international isolation of the GDR, did not help: "The *modus vivendi* between the two parts of Germany is a problem that must begin with a minimum of good understanding and be developed further in a patient way. This cannot exclude also the difficult matter of international relations which was earlier handled possibly in a radical and in any case an undifferentiated manner with the surgical knife of the so-called Hallstein doctrine." Yet he was not yet ready to allow third states to establish diplomatic relations with East Berlin, because he added, "The recognition of the GDR by third states will be viewed by us as an unfriendly act as long as the GDR will not modify its intransigent and malevolent attitude in inter-German relations."[34] Finally, he said on July 31, 1969, "We have repeatedly stressed that, without prejudice to the different political fundamentals on German territory, one must seek to reach a settled coexistence between the two parts of Germany on the basis of equality of rights and non-discrimination."[35]

The evolution in his mind seemed to indicate that he would be ready to recognize the GDR as a coequal German state but not as a foreign state. Yet he allowed his party to vote in the Bundestag on September 25, 1968, together with the Christian Democrats, for a resolution which restated the old position: "Our allies and the overwhelming majority of peoples have manifested the view that they see the federal government as the only German government which is free and legally formed. This government speaks also for those with whom it has hitherto been denied cooperation. The recognition of the other part of Germany as a foreign country or as a second sovereign state of the German nation may not be considered."[36] He evidently did not want to disrupt the great coalition for the sake of his own views one year ahead of the forthcoming elections.

As long as the great coalition existed, relations with the GDR remained unchanged. This was a matter of great importance to the Polish government, which considered the existence of the GDR as a guarantee of the safety of its western frontier.

THE FRONTIER WITH POLAND

The great coalition government clearly did not expect that a peace settlement with a unified Germany would restore the 1937 frontiers. Chancellor Kiesinger admitted this in his reiterated suggestions that the FRG and Poland could talk now about a territorial compromise in order to prepare the ground for the future peace settlement. He told the expellees on April 29, 1969: "Of course, we should not close our eyes to the fact that many politicians in the western world are of the opinion that the renunciation of the Eastern German territories is the price the Germans have to pay for the war begun and lost by Hitler. We do not share this view as we do not share the naïve romanticism of renunciation on the part of certain Germans. I have already often told our expellees from their homelands that what is today should not remain as it is, but that what once was could not simply be again as it was."[37] Following this line of thought, he told Warsaw at a press conference held on November 3, 1967: "We want . . . the problem of frontiers to be settled first in a peace treaty concluded with an all-German government. . . . This does not preclude, for example, that one could not imagine joint deliberations prior to such a peace treaty about a solution which would be acceptable for both peoples."[38] He repeated on April 2, 1968:

> One could object to us that this constant allusion to the peace treaty with an all-German government is only an [empty] phrase and means only the postponement of the whole problem [of frontiers] to *"Ad Calendas Graecas."* This is why I have said on appropriate occasions that, while the question may be solved first in a peace treaty with an all-German government, this should not hinder Poland and us from sitting together earlier and exchanging ideas regarding the future solution. Moreover, we have always sought, everyone in his own way, to point out to the Poles how we envisage the contours of the future settlement since we cannot anticipate a future perfect solution. . . . Nobody among us thinks that the seven million Poles over there, almost half of them born there, should experience what our expellees experienced, namely, that they should be driven away as cattle.[39]

The Polish government was not tempted by these suggestions. It held adamantly to its position that the Oder-Neisse frontier was final whatever the FRG might say. It felt secure in this view, because it coincided with Soviet opinion. Assuming for the sake of the argument that Warsaw were willing to conclude with the FRG an agreement on a territorial compromise, it could not be sure at all that a powerful unified Germany would be willing to honor such an agreement. As a matter of fact, it could cite Chancellor Kiesinger's statement of March 20, 1967: "One can point out that the attempts to anticipate solutions failed in past history because the expected political situation did not materialize."[40]

The program of the Christian Democratic Party in November 1968 restated the old position: "It remains the task of German policy to represent . . . the rights [of the expellees and refugees]. The question of the German Eastern frontiers may first be solved in an internationally legal way in the peace treaty."[41]

The Social Democrats took a different approach on March 21, 1968, at their Nuremberg congress. Their resolution, adopted by the congress, stated: "This [Eastern] policy will be the more successful the more clearly we express our will to respect and recognize the existing frontiers in Europe, in particular the present Polish western frontier, until such time as the German frontiers will be finally determined in a peace-treaty settlement, frontiers which could be considered right and lasting by all concerned."[42]

This resolution, which certainly did not please the Christian Democrats, was the seed from which the German-Polish treaty eventually grew in 1970. The treaty said basically the same thing, namely, that the obligation to respect and recognize the Oder-Neisse frontier was undertaken by the FRG for the duration of its existence, i.e., until the reunification of Germany. This formula was acceptable to Poland although its meaning was interpreted differently by Bonn and by Warsaw.

Brandt stated his point of view even more clearly in his article in *Foreign Affairs* (April 1968): "The present borders of Poland can be recognized for the period for which the Federal Republic can commit itself, i.e., until a peace settlement."[43] He repeated on July 31, 1969: "As I said in Godesberg [at the Social Democratic congress], it cannot be our task to chase after illusions or to wait for miracles. . . . We have proposed [to Poland] the exchange of declarations on the renunciation of force and stated that we will be ready to include expressly therein the problem of frontiers."[44]

He declared on June 10, 1968: "We consider reconciliation with Poland a task of historic rank. Once we reach it, not only will a dark chapter be closed but also something will be achieved that can be compared only with the German-French reconciliation. But strong obstacles still exist. . . . The Federal Republic of Germany has no territorial claims. Moreover, because of German partition, we have no common frontier with Poland. We have declared that we respect the present frontiers and include them in the renunciation of force."[45]

This was a clever though historically incorrect statement. The FRG claimed the right to speak on behalf of all Germans, and this is why it considered the Görlitz treaty, concluded in 1950 between the GDR and Poland, as null and void. In spite of the obvious fact that there was no common frontier between the FRG and Poland, it contested the Oder-

Neisse frontier allegedly on behalf of all Germans. If a West German government were to abandon its claim to represent all Germans and recognized the GDR as another coequal German state, as his own government would do in the seventies, then his thesis would become valid. The FRG, speaking only on its own behalf, could declare that it had no territorial claims against Poland and leave the question of frontier to a future unified Germany.

The Polish government sensed that there were differences of views between the two partners of the great coalition and that a large part of West German public opinion stood behind Brandt and his Social Democrats. This is why the Polish First Secretary, Władysław Gomułka, made his speech on May 17, 1969. He started by denouncing the Eastern policies of Chancellors Adenauer, Erhard, and Kiesinger, but noted that Kiesinger abandoned the claim to the 1937 frontiers. He further observed:

For some time now trends have been appearing in definite quarters in the German Federal Republic which seem to indicate intentions slightly different [in] programming Bonn's Eastern policy. . . . I have in mind first of all certain statements by the leaders of the West German Social Democratic Party at its congresses in Nuremberg and Bad Godesberg as well as other public declarations, especially those made by the FRG Vice-Chancellor, Mr. Brandt. . . . The position of Chancellor Kiesinger vis-a-vis the question of frontiers . . . has not changed to this day. . . . Representatives of the Social Democratic Party in that government take their own position on certain important matters of Bonn politics; the latter [position] does not fully correspond to the position of their coalition partners. . . . There are . . . signs of differences of view on the question of the FRG's attitude towards the German Democratic Republic and on the problem of Bonn's Eastern policy. . . . Chancellor Kiesinger did not confirm the formula of the Minister of Foreign Affairs and Vice-Chancellor of his government on the recognition of existing frontiers in Europe. In fact, the formula has been repeated only by the SPD members of the coalition government. One should not underrate the fact that from a political point of view the Nuremberg SPD formula on the recognition by the FRG of the Oder-Neisse frontier represents a step forward if compared to the position expressed on the subject by all the FRG governments. At the same time we have to realize fully that every interstate agreement between Poland and the FRG if based on that formula, even under its most favorable interpretation for us, could not contain more than a de facto recognition of the Oder-Neisse frontier by the FRG and only a temporary one, *i.e.,* until a peace treaty with Germany is concluded. Therefore, assuming even that the Bonn government should adopt the Nuremberg formula of Vice-Chancellor Brandt, this would actually change nothing in the present state of affairs. A change can only come about if the FRG government unreservedly recognizes the existing frontier of Poland on the Oder-Neisse as final and inviolable. . . . Poland will never conclude a treaty with the FRG on the Oder-Neisse frontier which would depart from the Zgorzelec [Görlitz] Treaty concluded with the German Democratic Republic. . . . If West Germany wishes to coexist peacefully with other European countries . . . [this] requires recognition of the borders established as a result of the Second World War, including in the first place the Oder-Lusatian-Neisse frontier, renunciation by the FRG government of the illegal claims to exclusive representation of the German people, *i.e.,* recognition of the other German state, the GDR, and signing of the treaty on non-proliferation of nuclear weapons.[46]

Gomułka did not reject out of hand Brandt's conciliatory stand. He seemed to imply that Poland would be ready to negotiate with him but maintained the traditional Polish view that the FRG must recognize the Oder-Neisse frontier as final. In 1970 he accepted a compromise formula which the FRG and Poland were able each to interpret differently.

Chancellor Kiesinger responded coolly to Gomułka's speech, repeating his earlier position that the frontier problem could be solved only in a peace treaty, while the FRG and Poland could now only talk about a territorial compromise.[47] By contrast, Brandt responded positively on May 20, 1969, and on July 31, 1969, saying that the declarations on the renunciation of force would include the problem of the frontier and adding that "we have noted with interest Gomułka's words of May 17."[48]

In any event, as long as Brandt was only a Vice-Chancellor and could do nothing without the approval of his Christian Democratic partners, the deadlock in relations with Poland remained. Brandt was enabled to move forward only after the September 1969 elections and the formation of his own small coalition government.

THE DISSIDENT SOVIET ALLIES

The Kiesinger-Brandt Eastern policy in the years 1966–1969 met with negative response in Moscow, East Berlin, and Warsaw. The great coalition government hoped to elicit better results in the other East European capitals. However, it could expect better results only in those capitals which were ready to part company with the Soviet, Polish, and East German policies. The success of its Eastern policy in relation to the dissident Soviet allies could not but provoke serious suspicions in Moscow, East Berlin, and Warsaw that Bonn intended to disrupt the solidarity of the Soviet bloc.

On December 28, 1966 Chancellor Kiesinger said, "We shall strive to achieve diplomatic relations with such states of the Eastern bloc as do not link those relations with any conditions unacceptable to us and which wish to have such relations."[49] The ground was prepared by the Erhard-Schroeder government with its restrictive interpretation of the Hallstein doctrine, which was said to be inapplicable to the Soviet allies, and with its first friendly contacts with Romania. Diplomatic relations with this dissident socialist state were established on January 31, 1967. This was not something of a nature to please Moscow. On June 23, 1967 Chancellor Kiesinger noted Soviet suspicions regarding his government's Eastern policy and said, "Perhaps the establishment of diplomatic relations first with Romania, no doubt the most independent partner of the Soviet Union, could have caused this erroneous interpretation and fear."[50] Vice-Chancellor Brandt rubbed salt in the Soviet wound by warmly espousing the Romanian policy of independence in foreign affairs on the occasion of his official visit to Bucharest on August 8, 1967: "Both parties are of the opinion that sound relations between states, as the foundation for a lasting peace and fruitful international cooperation, can develop only if respect is guaranteed for the principles of sovereignty and national independence, for the recognition of the right of each people to determine its own fate without external interference, for the equality of rights and mutual benefits."[51] He repeated in effect the very words of the Romanian First Secretary N. Ceaucescu, knowing full well that these words were a challenge to Moscow which expected its allies to follow its own foreign policy.

The great coalition government next faced the problem of relations with Yugoslavia. Since that country was internationally uncommitted, the USSR could not resent the exchange of embassies between Bonn and Belgrade. However, the problem was controversial domestically. Could the Hallstein doctrine be abandoned in this case at the risk of other states claiming the same right as Yugoslavia to have embassies in both East Berlin and Bonn? At the same time, the rupture of relations with Yugoslavia seemed unreasonable in retrospect, since informal relations were excellent. The government opted for political common sense rather than to abide by the Hallstein doctrine. On January 31, 1968, diplomatic relations were reestablished with Belgrade, which retained its embassy in East Berlin.

This created a precedent for other states. In May and June 1969 Cambodia, Sudan, Iraq, and Syria exchanged embassies with the GDR. The above-mentioned Arab states did not have embassies in Bonn, in retaliation for the pro-Israeli West German policy. But Cambodia did have an embassy in Bonn. The question arose as to whether the Hallstein sanction should be applied and diplomatic relations with Cambodia broken off. The West German government decided to apply a milder sanction by only revoking its ambassador and sharply reducing its economic aid to Cambodia. Obviously the Hallstein doctrine was gradually on its way out. Chancellor Kiesinger did not renounce the doctrine but adopted a flexible attitude on July 8, 1969, by saying, "We shall also in the future decide according to circumstances which measures we believe to be appropriate."[52] He knew that the Western allies would not establish diplomatic relations with East Berlin as long as the FRG refused to recognize the GDR as another German state. The practical question at that time was the attitude of the uncommitted states of the Third World. The former severe sanction of breaking off diplomatic relations having been discarded, Bonn could still effectively discourage those states from sending embassies to East Berlin by withdrawing its economic aid as it did in the case of Cambodia.

CZECHOSLOVAKIA

In 1967 and 1968 West German hopes centered around the three Soviet allies—Czechoslovakia, Hungary, and Bulgaria—the so-called non-controversial states which, unlike Poland, had no territorial dispute with the FRG. One must remember that the FRG declared several times that it considered the Munich agreement invalidated by Hitler's occupation of Czechoslovakia and that it had no claims to the Sudetenland.

The statements by Kiesinger and Brandt prior to Soviet intervention in Czechoslovakia prove that Bonn was in an optimistic mood regarding Prague, Budapest, and Sofia. Kiesinger said on February 3, 1967, in answer to a question by a West German radio commentator regarding the prospect of diplomatic relations with Prague and Budapest, "I certainly believe that this will come about. There are forces [an allusion to the Soviet Union] which want to make it more difficult or prevent it altogether, but I believe that the time is simply ripe for this policy of ours, and I trust also that our other Eastern neighbors will now take the same path."[53] Brandt was no less optimistic on October 13, 1967: "We have the impression that the governments of Hungary and Bulgaria share our wish for improved relations, although they do not consider that the time has yet come for the establishment of diplomatic relations for reasons regarding which I do not want to speculate."[54] The reasons about which Brandt did not want to speculate were Soviet influences which dissuaded both Sofia and Budapest from responding to West German advances. By 1968 it was fairly clear that only one East European capital might agree to establish diplomatic relations. That was Prague, in the full swing of its "spring" and of defiance of the Soviet Union.

It is beyond the scope of this book to discuss the domestic challenge which the Czechoslovak "spring" presented to the Soviet Union, with its concept of a humane and democratic socialism, a synthesis of socialism and democracy. But the Soviet Union was also confronted by the Czechoslovak challenge in foreign affairs. The matter was very serious from the Soviet point of view, more serious than the Romanian challenge. First, the Romanian Party, it is true, followed its own independent line in international affairs, but remained conservative in domestic affairs. Second, Romania, surrounded on almost all sides by the Soviet Union and its Hungarian and Bulgarian allies, could not effectively disrupt the Soviet bloc. Czechoslovakia was in an entirely different geopolitical situation, having common frontiers not only with the Soviet Union, Poland, the GDR, and Hungary, but also with independent-minded Romania and the capitalist FRG and Austria. It held the central strategic position within the Soviet bloc. Its dissidence was by far a more serious affair for Moscow than was that of Romania.

This is why Moscow observed with apprehension the Czechoslovak flirtation with Bonn in 1968. Moscow could not but feel apprehensive about the contrast between the unfriendly tone of Czechoslovak mass media regarding itself and the amicable references to the FRG. Voices were frequently heard in Prague asking for the normalization of relations with the FRG despite the fact that Moscow had been unhappy about the Romanian decision in 1967 and despite its efforts to keep its other allies in line. The Soviet government feared that what it called the selective coexistence favored by Bonn, *i.e.*, the normalization of relations with some of its allies while bypassing Moscow, Warsaw, and East Berlin, might possibly end in undermining its influence in Eastern Europe, in disrupting its bloc, and in opening the gate to West German influence. Yet the informal contacts between Bonn and Prague multiplied. Blessing, the president of the Federal Bank, Egon Bahr, a close confidant of Brandt and one of the highest officials at the Foreign Office, several Bundestag deputies such as the Free Democrat Walter Scheel, the Social Democrat Eppler, and Christian Democrats Müller-Hermann and Marx, visited Prague, which hoped eventually to welcome Brandt himself. It seemed that the normalization of relations was to be expected fairly soon. West German press comments reflected this expectation. Brandt himself challenged Moscow on June 10, 1968, by saying with regard to the possible normalization of relations with Czechoslovakia, Hungary, and Bulgaria: "Why should not members of the Warsaw Pact adopt their own particular attitude toward the Federal Republic and not be hindered in improving their relations with us? Everyone knows that . . . the former tensions could be reduced also by loosening up the fronts."[55] It was exactly this possible loosening of the Soviet front that Moscow feared. On June 7, 1968, Brandt, in an interview with *Die Zeit,* linked domestic developments in Czechoslovakia to the belief among the leading politicians in Prague that his Eastern policy was inspired by honest motivations. Chancellor Kiesinger remarked on April 2, 1968: "We have improved our relations with Czechoslovakia. Interesting and significant events have taken place in the recent weeks. I want to say today in this respect that our desire to build up the relations of good neighbors with all our eastern neighbors includes, of course, the wish that the domestic situation in those countries develop favorably and happily."[56] Thus he linked the expectation of better relations with Prague to the liberal trends in that country. He confirmed at a press conference held on July 5, 1968, that his government contemplated a visit to Prague by Foreign Minister Brandt but that it was not sure whether this should be done in view of possible adverse Soviet reactions.[57]

Not only Moscow but also East Berlin and Warsaw felt apprehensive. If Prague were to normalize its relations with Bonn, the FRG would have scored a great success in isolating the GDR. Warsaw was unhappy about the liberal trend in neighboring Czechoslovakia because it could have a contagious effect in Poland and the rest of Eastern Europe. It did not want Prague to establish diplomatic relations with the FRG while bypassing the question of Central European frontiers and ignoring the fact that Poland was not ready for the normalization of its own relations with West Germany. Moreover, the Poles, unlike the Czechs, not only had an open quarrel with the FRG over the Oder-Neisse frontier but had a different historical perspective. The Poles remembered their thousand-year history of disputes with the Germans, and the recent horrid experience of the German occupation. The Nazi occupation of Czechoslovakia was mild in comparison. Moreover, the Czechs were culturally much closer to the Germans than were the Poles because Bohemia had been a part of the medieval German Empire, because several German emperors had also been Czech kings, and because the Czechs had intermingled culturally with the Germans for many centuries. Any Czech attempt at improving relations with the FRG was looked upon with utmost suspicion, not only in Moscow but also in Warsaw and East Berlin. Budapest and Sofia had no choice but to follow the Soviet lead.

The top representatives of the Communist parties of the USSR, Poland, the GDR, Hungary, and Bulgaria met in Warsaw in July 1968 to examine jointly the situation in Czechoslovakia. They addressed a warning letter to the Czechoslovak Central Committee on July 18, 1968. It is sufficient here to quote those parts of the letter which related to the international implications of Czechoslovak policy:

> We cannot accept that hostile forces push your country away from the socialist path and create the threat of pulling Czechoslovakia out of the socialist commonwealth. This is not only your problem. This is the common problem of all Communist and Workers' parties and of all states united by alliance, cooperation, and friendship. This is a matter of common concern for the countries which have joined together in the Warsaw Treaty in order to ensure their independence as well as peace and security in Europe and to erect an unsurpassable barrier against attempts by imperialist forces of aggression and revanche. . . . The borders of the socialist world have been pushed into the center of Europe up to the Elbe and the Shumar Mountains. We shall never assent to the prospect of a threat to these historic achievements of socialism as well as to the independence and security of our peoples. We shall never assent to the prospect that imperialism might peacefully or not, from the outside or the inside, make a breach in the socialist system and change the balance of power in Europe to its advantage.[58]

It was obvious that the Soviet Union would not allow its allies, including Czechoslovakia, to follow in Romanian footsteps and formulate an independent foreign policy. It perceived a threat to the balance of power in the attempts by Prague to take its own stand regarding the FRG.

This warning was ignored in Prague. Eventually another conference of the top leaders of the five Communist parties met, this time together with the Czechoslovak leaders in Bratislava on August 4, 1968, and adopted a declaration which contained the following statement regarding international affairs: "The fraternal parties . . . again re-affirm their readiness to harmonize and coordinate their actions in the international arena. . . . We shall continue consistently to carry out the agreed policy on European matters which corresponds to the common interests of socialist countries and to [the requirements of] European security. We shall rebuff all attempts at a revision of results of the Second World War and at an infringement on existing European frontiers. We shall continue to insist on the nullity of the Munich agreement since its beginning. We shall resolutely support the German Democratic Republic."[59]

However, the Czechoslovak leadership was in no hurry to comply with the other parts of the Bratislava declaration regarding the reversal of its domestic policies. On August 21, Soviet, Polish, East German, Hungarian, and Bulgarian troops crossed the Czechoslovak frontiers. Czechoslovakia was compelled by military force to reintegrate into the fold of faithful Soviet allies.

COLLAPSE OF THE EASTERN POLICY

The West German government joined in the almost universal condemnation of Soviet intervention. It had not only moral reasons for doing so. Soviet troops were now for the first time stationed on Czechoslovak territory, including all along the Austrian and West German frontiers. The FRG now faced Soviet divisions not only in the GDR and Poland but also in Czechoslovakia, i.e., along its whole eastern frontier. Soviet intervention also meant that the other Soviet allies knew what kind of penalty was in store for them if they dared to follow an independent foreign policy. The Eastern policy with its attempts at bypassing Moscow, Warsaw, and East Berlin simply collapsed. Chancellor Kiesinger was confronted in an interview with the following statement by a radio commentator: "The events in Czechoslovakia force our government . . . to reexamine its policy. . . . The twenty-first of August [the date of the Soviet intervention] shook to its foundations the policy of building the bridges. . . . The critics of that policy say now, after the events in Czechoslovakia, that that policy has become a wreck because it had proceeded from illusions and had erroneously evaluated the realities." The Chancellor pointed out in his reply that the main reason for failure was opposition to the Eastern policy on the part of Moscow, Warsaw, and East Berlin.[60] He stated on September 25, 1968, that the Soviet Ambassador in Bonn had declared on September 2 that "no one will be allowed to break off even one member of the community of socialist countries." Kiesinger interpreted this statement as meaning that the GDR would have to remain within that community and that the Soviet Union considered the division of Germany to be final.[61]

Vice-Chancellor Brandt conceded on December 6, 1968, that "no one will doubt that the practical prospects [for the Eastern policy] have deteriorated because of the invasion of Czechoslovakia." The German journalist who was interviewing him deduced the conclusion in the form of a question: "Is the impression correct that, if negotiations with the East are possible, they are possible mainly or only with Moscow and in any event and for the time being not with the other states of the Warsaw Pact camp?" Brandt did not agree at that time but was to agree with this line of thought once he had become the Chancellor.[62] He would then remember his own statement of June 5, 1968: "All political actions must proceed from realities, from existing conditions, not from wishful thinking. Every policy that violates this principle risks becoming a wreck."[63] Actually, he frankly admitted on May 7, 1969: "We stand before a new phase of contacts and talks between the East and the West."[64]

He did not consider that a new Eastern policy should try to exploit the Soviet-Chinese quarrel as a negotiating card with Moscow.[65] He had two reasons for this view. First, the FRG could not afford to disagree with the United States which had not yet changed its own policy toward China. Second, he had no illusions that China could effectively help the FRG in its relations with the Soviet Union.

The expellee organizations resented the views of Social Democrats, which widely differed from their own. Their president, the Bundestag deputy R. Rehs, resigned from the SPD and joined the Christian Democratic Party as a sign of protest. Eventually all expellee leaders could be found only within the latter party, except for the chairman of the Silesian organization, deputy H. Hupka, who remained a member of the SPD until the ratification debate on the Moscow and Warsaw treaties; then he also joined the CDU. In effect, only the CDU and the CSU could rely on the electoral support of the expellee lobby. This was duly taken into account by the Christian Democrats, who opposed the ratification of those treaties partly in order to remain in the good graces of the expellee organizations. However, these organizations felt betrayed even by the Christian Democrats after the latter eventually abstained in the final vote on the treaties and thus allowed their ratification. Yet the general elections in 1972, from which Brandt and Scheel emerged victorious, proved that the expellee lobby was less influential than had been believed.

A NEW EASTERN POLICY?

The collapse of the great coalition's Eastern policy following the Soviet intervention in Czechoslovakia and the electoral campaign in 1969 (the general election took place in September of that year) stimulated further the ongoing debate on future relations with Eastern Europe in general and with the GDR and Poland in particular. The Catholic Church followed the lead of the Christian Democrats, the party it favored. But a group of Catholic intellectuals, called the Bensberger Kreis, issued in March 1968 a memorandum in favor of the recognition of the Oder-Neisse frontier. This memorandum was repudiated by the Catholic hierarchy. The Protestant Church adopted a different attitude at its congress, held in July 1969. It expressed a view similar to that of the Bensberger Kreis. Voices for the same view were being heard more and more frequently among the liberal intellectuals and in the mass media. West German public opinion was no longer united regarding policies to follow in relation to the GDR and Poland.

Several Social Democratic politicians favored a bolder Eastern policy. For instance, West Berlin Mayor Schütz wrote in an article in *Die Zeit,* published on June 27, 1969: "The Polish people must have security in the sense that nothing be changed in fundamentals. . . . The debate on frontiers and frontier lines led to the frightful Second World War and it leads to nothing good today; it can lead only to even greater destruction than twenty-five years ago. What then should be the goal of our policy toward Poland be today? . . . The agreement on the renunciation of force between the People's Republic of Poland and the FRG and the recognition of existing frontiers. . . . We want to proceed from what exists, to build up on what exists, not to violate the integrity of any state, not to encroach upon any frontiers."[66]

The majority of the opposition party, the Free Democrats, also was moving in the direction of a bolder Eastern policy. One of its officials, Wolfgang Schollwer, wrote in a study paper for his party (published in *Der Stern* on March 3, 1967):

> Two German states have been established . . . on German soil. . . . The elimination of the GDR is impossible either by vio-

lence or by negotiation. . . . The reunification of Germany . . . would lead to a total dislocation of forces in Europe and would disregard the fact that all European peoples deeply fear and try to prevent [the emergence of] a German national state with 75 million inhabitants and the strongest economy on the European continent. . . . The restoration of the status quo ante bellum is impossible or undesirable within either the European or German framework. . . . The German policy . . . leads to . . . the renunciation of the claim to the sole representation [of all the Germans] . . . , the renunciation of the claim to the German Eastern territories, and the acceptance of the present German eastern frontiers . . . , [as well as to] mutual support for the admission [of both German states] to the United Nations. . . . Today the former German Eastern territories are fully integrated within the Polish state; millions of Poles who live there were born in these territories and possess thereby the *Heimatrecht*. On the other hand, the expellees are fully integrated within the Federal Republic; this part of Germany has become their true new homeland.[67]

Rubin, the treasurer of the FDP, wrote on March 12, 1967:

It is true that Germany bears the guilt for the Second World War, totally lost and ended with unconditional surrender. It is true that friends and enemies are in agreement that the restoration of the German Reich within the 1937 frontiers is neither possible nor desirable. . . . It is true that Germany as a great power is the nightmare for the whole world. . . . It is true that the East and the West prefer for good reasons a divided rather than a reunited Germany. All our friends will not move a hand in favor of reunification. . . . There will be no reunification without the recognition of those facts which have occurred since 1945. He who wants reunification must recognize the Oder-Neisse line and take cognizance of the existence on German soil of the other Communist state with all the inevitable consequences.[68]

The leader of the FDP, Walter Scheel, stressed in his public statements the necessity of recognizing the existence of another German state. On January 31, 1968, he said:

All our neighbors, in the West and in the East, fear a new merging together of Germany. Practically, this [the policy of reunification] does not promise success since the GDR is integrated within the Eastern bloc as its essential and permanent part. . . . It is not a secret to the leaders of other parties that we have nowhere any support for the recreation of the German Reich. . . . Neither the Hallstein doctrine (whatever one understands by it) nor the frontier question of the old German Reich makes any sense. They have been used as arguments of the Cold War. Recognition or non-recognition have become meaningless words. . . . It is impossible to establish diplomatic relations with the Eastern bloc while having the isolation of the GDR as the objective.[69]

On September 25, 1968, in his repeated criticism of the Eastern policy of the great coalition, Scheel said:

I ask whether the federal government has always correctly esti-mated its own conduct *vis-à-vis* the role of the Soviet Union within the context of the Warsaw Pact? I must say here: can we spare the federal government the reproach of not always having taken into account the Moscow factor in its efforts for an under-standing with the states of the Warsaw pact? This applies equally to the establishment of diplomatic relations with Romania and Yugoslavia and also in a certain sense to our policy toward Czecho-slovakia. . . . He who considers the negotiations with Moscow as devoid of sense . . . and this at the time when Bonn has established diplomatic relations with Romania, who repeatedly postpones from one year to another the trip of the German parliamentary delega-tion to Moscow, who concentrates mainly on his contacts with those states of the socialist camp which have more or less serious differences of view with the Soviet Union, and who bypasses those states which have particularly close relations with Moscow, should not have been surprised . . . that the government of the USSR has formed, doubtless incorrectly, the view that Western Germany looks at its Eastern policy simply as a means to incite to revolt the states of the Soviet Union's *cordon sanitaire*.[70]

On December 14, 1968, he added:

An Eastern policy of bypassing the GDR is in any event impos-sible. We must make an effort to adjust our mutual relations on a contractual basis. The negotiation partners would be the GDR and the government of the GDR for the GDR on the one hand, and the government of the FRG on the other hand. There are many dis-cussions as to whether this would represent a recognition of sovereignty [of the GDR] in the eyes of international law. I hold all this for an abstract play [in words]. . . . One may certainly have doubts today as to whether this [German] unity can be a national-state unity. . . . We believe that the claim to the sole representation [of all the Germans] is not justified by anything. . . . If we do not advance this claim . . . then we in the Federal Republic do not have to discuss any frontier problem with Poland since we have no frontier with Poland but have a frontier with the GDR.[71]

The Free Democrats adopted an electoral platform on June 25, 1969, in which they declared themselves in favor of abandoning the claim to sole representation by the FRG of all Germans and the Hallstein doctrine, and proposed recognition of the existence of two German states, not foreign to each other, but each having the right to have diplomatic relations with third states.[72]

It became clear in 1968–69 that the Social Democrats could speak a common language with the Free Democrats regarding Eastern policy, rather than with the Christian Democrats. The image of a new coalition government was emerging, on condition that those two parties should gain a working parliamentary majority in the forthcoming elections.

Neither Moscow nor Poland remained blind to the new trend in Western Germany. Polish comment on the great coalition Eastern policy, published in 1972, was highly critical of that policy, as was to be expected, but was not totally negative. It acknowledged that the policy had ended the former immobility in the relations between the FRG and the socialist states, and represented the first step toward the later policy of the SDP–FDP small coalition government. The policy also helped in stimulating public debate in the FRG and getting a part of West German public opinion accustomed to the idea that the FRG should become reconciled with postwar realities. "In this sense 'the great coalition' prepared the public ground for an active Eastern policy of the 'small coalition' with Chancellor Brandt at its head." The Polish commentator noted that the Social Democrats were the main initiators of almost all the steps taken toward the socialist states by the great coalition in 1968–69. He ended his evaluation of the great coalition's Eastern policy by saying: "Generally speaking, the period of the government of 'great coalition' prepared the political and social ground for the policy of normalization of relations between the FRG and the socialist countries, initiated and realized by W. Brandt's government."[73]

8

Brandt's New Eastern Policy:
The Moscow Treaty

A NEW DEPARTURE

A S WE HAVE SEEN, the Eastern policies of West German governments evolved from the initial stand of Adenauer's chancellorship toward the different views of the great coalition government. This evolution related to such problems as the attitude toward the GDR, the Hallstein doctrine, relations with the East European countries, and the postwar frontiers. One could not say, therefore, that the Bonn governments stood still and upheld all the dogmas of Adenauer's era. Beginning with the Erhard-Schroeder government, the Eastern policy gradually became more flexible. The period 1963–68 could be called that of continuity and change. For instance, the GDR was no longer called simply the Soviet zone of occupation, nor did Bonn insist as before on a return to the 1937 Eastern frontiers of Germany. However, the change was not deep enough to encourage the Soviet Union, Poland, and the GDR to undertake serious negotiations with Bonn. The really new Eastern policy began only in the fall of 1969, following the general elections and the emergence of the small coalition government of Willy Brandt and Walter Scheel, *i.e.,* the coalition of Social Democrats and Free Democrats.

The Christian Democrats remained numerically the largest parliamentary group, but the Social Democrats and the Free Democrats together had a slim parliamentary majority. The Christian Democrats went into opposition for the first time in the history of the FRG.

Chancellor Brandt, supported by the Free Democrats, at last had a

163

free hand in formulating his own Eastern policy. This new policy was not a surprise to anyone who was familiar with the statements made by the Social Democrats and Free Democrats at the time of the great coalition. However, Brandt and Scheel could now afford to make explicit what had been at least partly implicit in their former statements.

The Christian Democrats were no longer compelled to make concessions to the Social Democrats, and could try to attract the sympathies of the nationalistic segment of West German public opinion by stiffening their attitudes regarding the Eastern problems. The new Eastern policy of the small coalition government ran immediately into the sharp opposition of Christian Democrats.

This new policy openly discarded several old shibboleths and quite naturally provoked very lively debates in the Bundestag and in public opinion at large in 1969–1972. It seemed for a time that the controversy over the Eastern policy would split West German public opinion to the same extent that the Dreyfus affair had done in France. Not many people realized that the majority of the West German electorate was ready to accept a radical shift in Bonn's policy toward the East. Actually, recognition of the GDR as another German state and of the Oder-Neisse frontier had been debated for quite a number of years and did not look as heretical as it had done in the fifties.

Yet the shift in the official policy was too great a shock for several governmental deputies, mostly the Free Democrats. Eventually they abandoned the government and crossed the aisle to join the Christian Democratic opposition. As a result, the governmental majority melted down and in 1972 amounted to only half of the parliamentary seats, while the other half belonged to the Christian Democratic opposition. This left the final decision regarding the fate of Brandt's Eastern policy to the opposition. To the surprise of many and the indignation of not a few, the Christian Democrats ensured the success of the Eastern policy by abstaining in 1972 in the crucial votes on the Moscow and Warsaw Treaties. This amounted to admission that no other Eastern policy was viable in spite of what the Christian Democrats had been saying before to the contrary.

BRANDT'S INITIAL STATEMENT

Chancellor Brandt made his first governmental declaration on October 28, 1969, thus opening the Bundestag debate. He said:

This government assumes that the questions which confront the German people as the consequence of the Second World War and of national treason by Hitler's regime may be answered only within the framework of a European peace order. However, no one can persuade us that the German people does not have the same right to self-determination which all other peoples have. The task of practical policy in the forthcoming years consists in preserving the unity of the nation by freeing the relations between the [two] parts of Germany from present restrictions. . . . Twenty years after the foundation of the Federal Republic of Germany and of the GDR we must prevent a further living apart of the [two parts] of the German nation and seek to reach a common life through a regulated side-by-side life. . . . An international law recognition of the GDR by the federal government may not be considered. Although the two states exist in Germany, they are not foreign countries to each other. Their mutual relations may be only of a special nature.

This statement made clear his main preoccupation. Unity of the German nation should be preserved and the drifting apart of its two parts must be stopped. Hence, the existence of the two German states must be recognized in order to improve their mutual relations and promote contacts between the citizens of both parts of Germany. The same preoccupation with the preservation of all-German national consciousness, in spite of the political partition of the country, dictated to Brandt his firm opposition to a recognition of the GDR which would be of the same legal kind as the recognition of any other state. He was willing to grant the recognition *sui generis* so that the two German states would not be considered foreign to each other as, for instance, Poland was to either of them. This subtle distinction between recognition under the rules of international law and that according to constitutional law was understandable to Bonn and to East Berlin, which continued to ask for recognition under international law. It was too subtle for the third states. For the latter states any recognition by the FRG would be interpreted as meaning that the GDR was a full-fledged member of the international community. Since Brandt was ready to concede to the GDR the right to be admitted to the United Nations at the same time as the FRG, the provision of Article 2 of the Charter of the United Nations which stated that "the Organization is based on the principle of the sovereign equality of all its members" would deprive the inter-German legalistic quarrel regarding the form of their mutual recognition of any practical sense for the third states. Yet the two German governments were to continue their legal quarrel until 1973 when a compromise formula, satisfactory to both parties, was finally found.

Brandt announced in the same speech that the Ministry for All-German Affairs would be renamed the Ministry for Inter-German Affairs. This was a conciliatory gesture toward the GDR. He also declared that his government was ready to conclude with the GDR an internationally binding agreement on the renunciation of force, similar to such agreements to be concluded with the Soviet Union and other East European countries.

The new Chancellor had this to say regarding relations with the Soviet bloc:

> The German people needs peace in the full sense of the word also with the peoples of the Soviet Union and all the peoples of the European East. We are ready for an honest effort in reaching an understanding so that the consequences of the disaster which a criminal clique had inflicted on Europe could be overcome. . . . We are free of illusions and do not believe that the task of reconciliation would be either light or could be rapidly completed. . . . The policy of reconciliation, which respects the territorial integrity of all partners, is, according to the strong conviction of the federal government, a decisive contribution to a detente in Europe. . . . [The Federal government] will answer the Soviet *aide-memoire* on the subject of renunciation of force and will propose a date for the negotiations alluded to by the Soviet Union. It will forward to the government of the People's Republic of Poland a proposal regarding the start of talks; this proposal will reply to Wladyslaw Gomulka's statement of May 17th, 1969. It will sign the Treaty on non-proliferation of atomic weapons as soon . . . as the still outstanding clarifications are forthcoming.[1]

The Chancellor had learned from his experience as Vice-Chancellor in the government of the great coalition. He knew that the former Eastern policy of trying to open the doors to Eastern Europe by contacting the dissident governments (Romania and Czechoslovakia) while bypassing Moscow, Warsaw, and East Berlin had proved fruitless. He decided to take an entirely new road by opening negotiations with Moscow, Warsaw, and East Berlin. His mention of territorial integrity was an offer to Moscow and Warsaw of some kind of recognition of their postwar annexations of former German territories. Both the Soviet and the Polish governments were soon to respond favorably. Actually, on September 12, 1969, the Soviet government had addressed to Bonn the *aide-memoire* mentioned by Brandt, in which it expressed its interest in the resumption of negotiations on an agreement on the renunciation of force.

SOVIET AND POLISH INTEREST IN AGREEMENTS WITH THE FRG

At that time the Soviet government was pursuing its policy of detente with the West, including the United States. Its purpose was to stabilize the status quo in Central Europe and to open an era of economic co-operation with the Western countries, in order to reinvigorate the lagging Soviet economy by greater trade and cooperation between Soviet indus-trial enterprises and Western private firms. It hoped that the importation of a better quality of Western machinery, the purchase of Western licenses, and the joint building of new Soviet enterprises with the assistance of "capitalist" Western firms would help to modernize Soviet economy. It was ready to pay for this cooperation with, among other things, supplies of oil and natural gas. As a matter of fact, the USSR and the FRG had already concluded an agreement on the supply of Soviet natural gas. The pipeline was completed in 1973, and Soviet natural gas began to be supplied to the FRG.

The FRG, with the strongest West European economy, had crucial importance for this policy. If the FRG were to recognize the Central European status quo, no other state would quarrel with it, while eco-nomic relations with the West German state had a great importance in themselves. Soviet eagerness to reach an agreement with the FRG was demonstrated in 1972 when the USSR agreed to the adoption by the Bundestag of a unilateral interpretation of the Moscow and Warsaw Treaties, which did not please Poland.

Brandt's mention of territorial integrity signaled to Warsaw that his government was prepared to recognize the Oder-Neisse frontier in some form. The road to Poland was open. This did not mean that Polish distrust was dispelled. For instance, a Polish journalist, familiar with German affairs, commented that Brandt was perhaps a more far-seeing nationalist than Adenauer. According to him, Adenauer seemed to be satisfied with West German integration within the Western community and the international isolation of the GDR at the risk of perpetuating the division of Germany. Brandt wanted gradually to pave the way toward German unity and prevent the split of Germany into two separate nations as well as states.[2]

BRANDT'S VIEWS

In another speech, made on October 30, 1969, during the Bundestag debate Brandt added, "The debate on the recognition [of the GDR] has seemed to me not only now but in past years a bit academic. This is because I learned a long time ago where the boundaries of power lay and how little one was served in actual situations by substituting formulas for reality." However, he was still opposed to recognition of the GDR by third states because this would make his forthcoming negotiations with the other German state more difficult. But he did not threaten these third states, in fact those of the Third World, with uniformly severe sanctions. He only said, "We shall solve each case according to our own interests."

Answering an accusation by the opposition that his government was abandoning the continuity of the former West German policy, he said, "It would be a misunderstanding to believe that continuity is nothing but the continuation of what has been."[3] In fact, his Eastern policy was a new departure and an abandonment of old dogmas.

His government signed the treaty on the non-proliferation of nuclear weapons on November 28, 1969. This appeased Soviet fears that the FRG might one day become a nuclear power and thus change the balance of forces in Europe. The USSR was fully able to uphold the political and territorial status quo in Europe whatever the West German policy should be. It had no visible means to prevent the FRG from acquiring a national nuclear force in the rather improbable case of its Western allies agreeing to it.

In December 1969 negotiations began with the Soviet Union.

Brandt again reassured the Bundestag on January 14, 1970, that his government did not consider the GDR as a foreign state and would not grant it international law recognition. On this occasion he offered his definition of patriotism: "Patriotism demands the recognition of what exists and an effort always to find out what is possible. It demands the courage to acknowledge the reality. This does not mean that one considers this reality as corresponding to his wishes or that he abandons the hope that it should be changed in the course of a long period of time." He stressed the importance of West German ties to West Berlin and the responsibility of the four powers for the whole city of Berlin. Eventually, he based the ratification of the Moscow and Warsaw Treaties on the condition of conclusion by the four powers of a satisfactory agreement on Berlin. This forced the USSR to make concessions on West Berlin in order to ensure West German ratification of the two treaties.

He added in the same speech that any agreement with the GDR must be based on the understanding by both German states that they would preserve unity of the German nation, but also on mutual non-discrimination, respect for their territorial integrity and respective frontiers, and the obligation of solving all disputes only by peaceful means.[4]

THE OPPOSITION ATTACKS

The Eastern policy of the new government was immediately attacked by the Christian Democratic opposition. Former Chancellor Kurt Kiesinger complained in a speech made on October 29, 1969, during the Bundestag debate, that he had been compelled to make concessions to his Social Democratic partners in the great coalition: "One must often achieve compromises in a coalition. One would often and readily do something else than what he may or must do together with the other [partner] . . . . As you know, it cost me many times very serious, very protracted and very tenacious struggles and debates." This meant that he had not felt happy even with the cautious Eastern policy of his own government. He added, however, that his party did not intend to renege on the Eastern policy of the great coalition and go back to its former views. He criticized the government for not having mentioned the right of the FRG to be the sole spokesman for the whole German nation, for its willingness to recognize the GDR as a state, and for its readiness to begin negotiations with Poland and Czechoslovakia while using ambiguous formulas as to the terms of agreements. He reminded the Bundestag that he, as Chancellor, had been ready for talks with Poland on finding a compromise solution for the Polish Western frontier, while reserving the final determination of that frontier to the peace treaty to be concluded by the future all-German government. Assuming that the new government might recognize the Oder-Neisse frontier, he exclaimed dramatically: "But, if you are ready to make concession which would be politically a gross imprudence in the present historical situation, which we, the Federal Republic of Germany, this High House and your government, have no right to make, and, moreover, which only the entire German people is competent to make, then, for Heaven's sake, do not conduct such negotiations at all." He finally expressed regret that the new government did not mention expressly the state reunification of Germany.[5]

Baron von und zu Guttenberg, representing the right wing of the opposition, the Bavarian Christian-Social Union, accused the government of breaking down the continuity of West German policy by its willingness to recognize the GDR as a state. He said, not without reason, "Show me anyone in the United Nations, anywhere in Africa, Asia and the Third World, who would understand the distinction between the refusal to recognize [the GDR] as a foreign country and the recognition as another state of the same nation."[6]

Rainer Barzel, rather moderate leader of the parliamentary opposition group, seemed to be just as much opposed to the new Eastern policy. In his speech on December 7, 1969, in the Bundestag debate, he repeated the statement already made by Kiesinger: "Germans and Poles wish to live within frontiers which would be freely agreed upon and which would be accepted by both peoples. The conversations about such frontiers are meaningful even prior to the conclusion of a peace treaty. The final settlement requires the assent of the [whole] German people." He went further than Kiesinger by demanding from Poland the concession to the Germans still remaining in that country of minority rights, and to all Germans the freedom of selecting their domicile. He must have known that Poland would never grant such minority rights after having bitterly experienced the effects of prewar international protection of its minorities and the wartime disloyalty of its German minority. His other demand amounted to the claim that the East German refugees and expellees should have the right to return to the former East German territories, a demand unpalatable to Warsaw. He mentioned the far-fetched figure of one million German-speaking Polish citizens, although he must have known the much lower figure cited even by the German Red Cross. His demands, never mentioned at the time of the great coalition, would effectively bar any negotiations with Warsaw.[7]

Chancellor Brandt responded in an interview of December 28, 1969: "It was clear to us at the time when we approached the Polish government that the European frontiers in general and the question of this particular one [Oder-Neisse] . . . could not be excluded from such conversations. . . . We know that this important topic will be discussed, and that the Polish side stated at the start that this is for them a sort of precondition."[8]

Responding to the opposition's claim that his government should seek state reunification of Germany, Brandt made a quite realistic statement in the abovementioned speech of January 14, 1970: "It should be clear to all of us that not many people in this world, except for our own people, would be enchanted at the prospect of unity between the sixty and the seventeen million men, between the one and the other economic potentials, not to mention the armies." This is why he thought that "the German people in its entirety cannot hope for a peace treaty in the fore-seeable time. . . . The Federal Republic remains a Western state because of its ties and convictions. The GDR remains an Eastern state because of its own ties and the will of its leadership. These are the facts."⁹ These facts precluded the possibility of a state reunification and allowed only for an effort to preclude the emergence of two separate national con-sciousnesses.

Former Chancellor Kiesinger had to concede in a speech made on January 15, 1970, during the Bundestag debate that "we all agree that reunification is not to be found around the corner. . . . We also believe that the solution of the German question is impossible in the future by our efforts alone since our shoulders are really too narrow for this task. . . . [But] our goal must remain the preservation and the restora-tion of the national and state unity of Germany. . . . You know that we reject this thesis [of the two German states]."¹⁰ This stand amounted to saying that the FRG should not take any steps to reduce the hostility between the two German states and should only continue to hope that one day the state unity of Germany would be restored somewhat. This kind of policy produced no visible results in the fifties and sixties and resulted in fact in the drifting apart in opposite directions of the two parts of the German nation.

Franz-Joseph Strauss, the leader of the Bavarian Christian-Social Union, insisted in the Bundestag debate on January 15, 1970, that German unity should be achieved under the roof of one state, presum-ably the FRG. He conceded, however, that the FRG had very small room for maneuvering and could not by itself achieve that state unity. He also admitted that a change in the existing situation could not be expected in the foreseeable future without a modification in the world's power distribution. What he meant was the hope that the West would become so much more powerful than the Soviet bloc that it could force Moscow to assent to the absorption of the GDR by the FRG. This was a stand similar to that of Adenauer's in the fifties. Judged by the actual distribution of power between the Western and the Soviet blocs, his view amounted to the expectation of a miracle. Being a clever politician, he must have realized that his stand would have meant the return to the fruitless policy of a bygone age. But his views appealed to the right wing portion of the West German electorate, for whom the petrification of the current situation seemed to be preferable to the acknowledgment of realities and the abandoning of old shibboleths.¹¹

Chancellor Brandt replied to this all-or-nothing thesis by stating on

January 16, 1970, also during the Bundestag debate: "The time will not stay put. . . . The relationship between the world powers has not remained unchanged. Who here would want to say that it has remained unchanged during the last twenty-five years? . . . I think that we must now resist stronger than before the temptation to accept formulas as reality."[12] He meant to remind the German public of the fact that the Soviet Union was not becoming weaker than it had been in the fifties, and that it had reached nuclear parity with the United States. Adenauer's policy of talking to Moscow from a position of strength proved futile. Moreover, Brandt knew well that the new Nixon American administration was embarking on a policy of seeking a detente with the USSR.

THE POLISH STAND

The negotiations with Warsaw were not expected to be easy. The Polish starting position was that the FRG should recognize the Oder-Neisse frontier as final so that no future German government, even that of a united Germany, could contest it. With such unconditional recognition by the FRG, combined with the unconditional recognition by the GDR in 1950, Poland could claim that a united Germany would be bound by them as the successor state to both the FRG and the GDR.

The Polish Prime Minister, Józef Cyrankiewicz, told the parliament on December 22, 1969, that his government had received a note from the German government on November 24 in which Bonn proposed to open negotiations. He stressed on this occasion that "the basis for a process of normalization in the relations between the FRG and Poland must be the FRG's recognition of Poland's western frontier on the Oder and Neisse as final and inviolable."[13]

One of the then leading Polish politicians, Marian Spychalski, reminded his countrymen on February 20, 1970, that nine million Poles lived in the former East German territories, and that economic production there was vital for Poland. Alluding to the first West German-Polish contacts in early February, he said firmly that the basic condition for the normalization of mutual relations was "the renunciation by the FRG's government of all territorial claims and the recognition of the present western frontier of Poland as final and in such terms which no German government could challenge in any circumstances."[14]

Finally, First Secretary Gomułka himself made a no less firm statement on May 9, 1970, choosing not without reason Wrocław, formerly Breslau, as the place to deliver his speech. He began by restating the Polish arguments which were meant to justify the annexation of former German territories. He said:

> The Polish nation made a great contribution to the victory over Nazi Germany. Over two million Poles fought against the German aggressor, arms in hand. Defeated in September 1939, bled white under the occupation, Poland took part in the final battle of the great war. . . . At that time Poland had about 600,000 men at the fronts. . . . Over 200,000 Polish soldiers fought in the Berlin operation. . . . In fact, the greatest result of World War II . . . was the establishment of Poland's western frontier on the Oder and the Neisse. It meant that that war resulted in cancelling the gains achieved during the thousand years of Teutonic *"Drang nach Osten."* . . . We have built up an industry in these territories which gives employment to more than 1,100,000 workers. This production is . . . about three times greater than in the German period. This production represents about 30 percent of the overall industrial production in the country. . . . They [the former German territories] supply almost half of the country's grain crop and over 40 percent of [state] potato purchases. Cities in the Western and Northern territories have become centers of dynamic development of Polish sciences, learning and culture. . . . Wrocław, with its eight academic schools and numerous institutions, is the third largest center of learning in the country. . . . More than half of the population of about nine millions living in these territories was born in People's Poland.[15]

Then he proceeded to define the Polish stand:

> We are ready and we desire normalization of relations, and for this reason precisely we are demanding of the FRG the unequivocal recognition of Poland's existing western frontier, established by the Potsdam agreement as final and inviolable, and guarantees that such recognition will be considered binding in all future agreements concerning peace and security in Europe. Any efforts to settle this problem by some kind of temporary agreement, recognizing the existing state of affairs until some future peace treaty, the conclusion of which has become unrealistic, cannot be accepted by Poland.[16]

Yet in the same year of 1970 Gomułka's government accepted a compromise formula, by virtue of which the Oder-Neisse frontier was recognized by the FRG only in its own name, *i.e.,* for the duration of the FRG's existence. This opened the question as to whether a united Germany would be bound by treaties concluded by the two German states. Why did the Polish government eventually accept this compromise solution? It might have been due to Soviet pressure. It might have been caused as well by a rather practical consideration. Whatever the formulation of the problem in a treaty with the FRG, the reunification of Germany would change radically the distribution of power in Europe. It could take place only with the assent of the Soviet Union which would presumably be so weak as to be unable to uphold its veto. Poland, left alone, could not in these circumstances defend its Oder-Neisse frontier or, as a matter of fact, any western frontier against a united, hence powerful Germany. The Polish-Western German controversy over the formulation of West German recognition was perhaps legally important but politically rather academic. Gomułka conceded as much in the same speech: "The inviolability and security of our frontiers will never in the slightest degree depend on their recognition or non-recognition by the FRG. They are guaranteed by Poland's alliance with the Soviet Union and all socialist countries."[17] This was the stark truth. As long as the USSR found that the Oder-Neisse frontier was in its own national interest, that frontier was secure. Neither the FRG nor the Western powers could modify it. Conditional recognition by the FRG had its value nevertheless. West German governments could not continue to question the existence of the frontier, while West German allies and the Vatican could deduce practical conclusions, favorable for Poland, from West German recognition. The official "revisionist" policy of the FRG would come to an end.

RETROSPECTIVE GERMAN HISTORY OF GERMAN-SOVIET RELATIONS

It is worthwhile to mention here the Brandt government's interpretation of Soviet-German relations during the twenty-five years following the Second World War.[18] According to that interpretation, the Soviet Union intended to ensure the survival of its military, ideological, and political conquests won during that war. The United States had respected this Soviet stand at least since the fifties by its implicit recognition of the boundary between the two zones of influence in Europe. The same interpretation claimed that it was doubtful whether the West German governments took into consideration these policies of the two super-powers in the fifties and even in the sixties. In the fifties the government of the FRG seemed to be convinced that the Soviet Union might eventually be compelled to agree to German reunification within the politically democratic state (the FRG) which, moreover, would remain a member of both NATO and the Common Market. This was to come about owing to Western military and in particular nuclear superiority. The 1970 official text commented that no one could now deny that American-Soviet nuclear parity had deprived that policy of any realism, and that the policy from the position of strength had failed.

The beginning of adjustment of the West German policy took place with the appointment of Gerhard Schroeder as Foreign Minister. However, the Erhard-Schroeder and the great coalition governments continued to refuse to recognize the state-like quality of the GDR and produced the impression that their Eastern policies intended to bypass and isolate the GDR. The great coalition government seemed to want to bypass the Soviet Union also. German-Soviet conversations in 1966–69 on a mutual renunciation of force were "an animated dialogue between the deaf." While Moscow wanted to include political matters in the agreement, Kurt Kiesinger's government intended to exclude those matters in a sort of abstract renunciation of force which would not acknowledge the political and territorial status quo. Eventually the Eastern policy of the great coalition was blocked by the Soviet Union.

The abovementioned official German interpretation of German-Soviet relations further supplies a short historical survey of Soviet-German relations and of the 1969–70 negotiations. It begins by reminding the readers of Chancellor Adenauer's statement of October 5, 1954, that the FRG would not seek to achieve by force the reunification of Germany or the modification of existing frontiers. This West German undertaking was incorporated in the Paris agreement of October 1954, concluded by the FRG with the United States, Britain, and France. This agreement reserved the rights of the three powers regarding Berlin and Germany as a whole until and including a peace settlement (Article 2), stated that the final determination of German frontiers must wait until such a settlement (Article 7, par. 1), and expressed the conviction of the contracting parties that a reunified Germany should be a democratic state, integrated within the West European community (Article 7, par. 2). Article 2 and the first paragraph of Article 7 of the Paris agreement played an important role during the German-Soviet and German-Polish negotiations in 1970.

In September 1955, on the occasion of establishing diplomatic relations between the FRG and the Soviet Union, Chancellor Adenauer sent a letter to Soviet Prime Minister Bulganin in which he expressed the hope that the diplomatic relations would help in the reunification of Germany. Bulganin agreed. Adenauer also sent a second letter to Bulganin in which he stated that the final determination of German frontiers had to wait until the peace settlement, and that the establishment of diplomatic relations did not change the West German legal view that the FRG was the only spokesman for the German people in regard to those territories which now were outside its actual jurisdiction. This second letter was silently accepted by the Soviet government, but the official Soviet agency TASS provided an answer. It stated that the Soviet government considered that there were two German states, the FRG and the GDR, while the German frontiers had been fixed in the Potsdam agreement. The FRG had jurisdiction only over its own territory. In other words, Adenauer's view was rejected.

Conversations with Moscow regarding the mutual renunciation of force were initiated by the Erhard-Schroeder government's peace notes of March 25, 1966. The Soviet government did not agree with the West German proposal for concluding such agreements between the FRG and the USSR and East European countries, because the German government was not ready to accept the Central European status quo as the foundation of such agreements. Only on September 12, 1969, did Moscow manifest a serious interest in opening the negotiations. The new Brandt-Scheel government responded on November 15, 1969, by expressing its willingness to start conversations. On December 8, 1969, the negotiations began in Moscow, Secretary of State Egon Bahr and Foreign Minister Andrei Gromyko representing the two parties respectively. One of the main controversies was the Soviet insistence on West German recognition of the immovability (finality) of the Central European frontiers while the West Germans were ready to accept only their inviolability (prohibition of non-peaceful attempts to change them). Eventually a compromise solution was found. The draft agreement of the treaty was ready in July, and Foreign Minister Scheel went to Moscow to wind up the negotiations and initial the treaty on August 7, 1970. A few days later, on August 12, 1970, the Moscow Treaty was signed by Chancellor Brandt, Foreign Minister Scheel, Soviet Prime Minister Aleksei Kosygin, and Foreign Minister Andrei Gromyko.[19]

THE MOSCOW TREATY

This treaty marked the turning point in West German-Soviet relations. It was also to serve as the foundation for following treaties concluded with Poland, the GDR, and Czechoslovakia. Its Article 2 stated that the contracting parties would solve their controversies exclusively by peaceful means and would abide by Article 2 of the United Nations Charter which obligated states to refrain from the use or threat of use of force. This Article amounted to Soviet renunciation of its frequently repeated claim to its continued right to take forcible action against the FRG by virtue of the so-called enemy clause in the United Nations Charter (Articles 53 and 107).[20]

Article 3 was of crucial importance. It stated that "the peace in Europe can be preserved only if no one questions the present frontiers." It continued:

> They [the contracting parties] undertake the obligation unreservedly to respect the territorial integrity of all European states within their present frontiers; they declare that they have no territorial claims against anyone and also that they shall not raise such claims in the future; they consider now and shall consider in the future as inviolable the frontiers of all European states as they are on the day of signature of the present Treaty, including the Oder-Neisse Line which forms the Western frontier of the People's Republic of Poland, and the frontier between the Federal Republic of Germany and the German Democratic Republic.

This obligation was, however, circumscribed by Article 4 which said that the treaty did not invalidate the former bilateral or multilateral agreements concluded by either party.[21] One can understand the meaning for the FRG of Article 4, if one looks at the notes which the West German government sent at the time of the conclusion of the treaty to the Soviet, American, British, and French governments, as well as at the official West German interpretation of Articles 3 and 4.

On the day the treaty was signed, Foreign Minister Walter Scheel sent a letter to the Soviet Foreign Minister in which he stated that the treaty did not contradict the FRG's political goal of German reunification and self-determination.[22] On August 7, 1970, the German government conveyed identical notes to the three Western powers, in which it stated that the Soviet-German treaty did not invalidate the rights of the four powers (the USA, Britain, France, and the USSR) regarding Germany as a whole and Berlin in particular because the peace settlement remained to be achieved. These notes mentioned a statement on August 6, 1970, by the Soviet Foreign Minister, who had agreed that the treaty would not encroach upon the rights of the four powers and that these rights were not the subject of German-Soviet negotiations. The three Western powers agreed with this point of view in their responses of August 11.

This meant, first of all, that the question of eventual reunification remained open for the FRG in spite of its obligation to respect the frontier between the FRG and the GDR. It also meant that West German recognition of the Oder-Neisse frontier did not prejudge its final determination at a future peace conference on Germany. In other words, Article 3 of the treaty was binding only on the FRG and for the duration of its existence, not on a reunified Germany and not on the four powers. The most the USSR could claim was that the FRG, as a participant in such a conference, would be bound by the treaty and could not claim different Eastern frontiers for a reunified Germany. The Western powers would still be free to adopt any position they wanted to regarding these frontiers.

Why did Moscow accept these West German reservations? First, it wanted the treaty as the central piece of its policy of detente with the West and as a diplomatic bridge to closer economic relations with the FRG. Second, it obtained in the treaty what it had wanted during the preceding twenty years, West German acceptance of the Central European political and territorial status quo. Third, it knew that the Brandt government, facing stiff opposition at home, could not undertake a broader obligation. Fourth, the USSR, as one of the four powers, had the veto over both reunification and the question of frontiers. Assuming the improbable, that the FRG and the GDR should agree on the restoration of German state unity, the USSR could interpose its veto as one of four powers whose rights were fully reserved by Article 4 of the treaty and by the simultaneous notes and statements. Moreover, this veto was enforceable by the twenty Soviet divisions stationed on East German soil.

The same is true regarding the Oder-Neisse frontier. Let us suppose the gathering of a peace conference, although the USSR has said many times that it does not want it. If one or all three Western powers proposed a change of that frontier, the USSR would not only refuse its assent by virtue of its being the fourth great power but could claim that the FRG, as one of the participating states, could not support such a

Western move, being bound by Article 3 for the duration of its existence. Neither could the GDR favor a change, being committed by the Treaty of 1950. This legal position of the USSR was not weakened by the Treaty of Moscow. In fact, the status quo, any status quo, may be changed only owing to a radical change in power relations.

It was mutually understood by the USSR and the FRG that the Moscow Treaty was to be a part of a whole, the other parts being the forthcoming treaties with the GDR, Poland, and Czechoslovakia. It was conceded by the West German party during the negotiations that an agreement with the GDR would be founded on the legal equality of both German states, their independence, mutual non-discrimination, their right to have diplomatic relations with third states, and their simultaneous requests for admission to the United Nations.[23]

The new Eastern policy was a far cry from the former stand of preceding West German governments. Chancellor Brandt was facing a long and stiff battle for the ratification of the treaty. He appealed to his countrymen in a radio broadcast from Moscow, telling them that nothing was lost by concluding the treaty that had not been lost a long time ago, and he assured them that the treaty did not diminish in any way the strength of bonds between the FRG and its Western allies.[24] He was to stress many times again that his Eastern and Western policies formed mutually interdependent parts of the over-all West German policy. He knew full well that the FRG could remain an equal partner of the USSR only if it continued to be strong enough, thanks to its military bonds with its Western allies and its ties to Common Market members.

WEST GERMAN INTERPRETATION

On July 15, 1970, Foreign Minister Scheel gave his interpretation of the forthcoming treaty by stating that the treaty would create a *modus vivendi,* founded on existing reality, but would not recognize that reality "in the sense of international law and hence would not legalize it."[25] This meant that the FRG's acceptance in Article 3 of existing frontiers not only did not entail recognition of the GDR as a foreign state, but also that the FRG refused to accept the Soviet-Polish thesis of the Oder-Neisse frontier as having been finally fixed at Potsdam. It also meant that the recognition of that frontier was *de facto* but not *de jure.* This should be remembered because the Bundestag, while giving its assent to the Moscow and Warsaw treaties, adopted a unilateral resolution in which it affirmed the same stand (see below). This unilateral West German interpretation was rejected by the USSR and Poland and was not, therefore, binding on them. Thus, the Moscow Treaty entered into force with opposite interpretations by the parties concerned.

After the signature of the treaty, the main German negotiator, State Secretary Egon Bahr, said, "Two states exist in Germany. It cannot be foreseen when this situation might change. . . . The frontiers which exist now must be respected and will remain inviolable even if we do not like them. . . . As long as the rights of the four powers subsist, the Federal Republic of Germany may not ignore them. It can not undertake the obligation to recognize the validity in international law of the frontier on German soil even if it wanted to do so. There is no peace treaty." Mentioning the situation in Berlin, he added that "the conclusion of the treaty will facilitate the negotiations of the four powers."[26] He thus alluded to the statement made on July 23, 1970, by Foreign Minister Scheel in his conversation with the Soviet Foreign Minister to the effect that the FRG would ratify the treaty only if the four powers reached a satisfactory agreement on Berlin.[27] This reservation gave the three Western powers the disguised right of veto. If they wanted to torpedo Brandt's Eastern policy, they had only to advance such claims regarding Berlin as the USSR could not possibly accept. In fact, this did not happen, and the four powers reached a mutually satisfactory agreement in 1971.

The official West German comment on the treaty stated that "an understanding with East Europe must begin with Moscow because it is impossible to reach it against the will of the USSR."[28] This view simply registered the reason for the failure of the great coalition's Eastern policy in 1968. The Moscow Treaty opened the doors to the other East European countries.

Egon Bahr said quite rightly that frontiers could be modified in a peaceful agreement reached by the two states concerned.[29] But neither the GDR nor Poland was in the mood to make such agreements.

The Social Democratic and Free Democratic parliamentary groups approved in August 1970 the governmental policy which led to the Moscow Treaty.[30] The opposition Christian-Democratic Union–Christian-Social Union parliamentary group expressed its reservations, which were to be expanded later during the Bundestag debates on the ratification of the Moscow and Warsaw treaties.[31] It was to be expected in

August 1970 that Brandt's Eastern policy would be fiercely attacked by the opposition.

The Brandt-Scheel government also was moving on the Polish front throughout 1970. However, it did not conclude the treaty with Poland until after the signature of the Moscow Treaty, abiding by its conviction that the latter treaty would be the key to unlock all the East European doors.

9

Brandt's New Eastern Policy: The Warsaw Treaty

THE GERMAN VERSION OF RELATIONS WITH POLAND

THE OFFICIAL West German commentary on the Warsaw Treaty offers the German version of Polish-German relations and the history of negotiations leading to the signature of that treaty.[1] It recalls that the Weimar Republic always wanted to revise in its favor the frontier with Poland as it had been fixed in the Versailles Peace Treaty. It wished in particular to regain the so-called Polish corridor, Danzig, and the Polish part of Upper Silesia. In other words, the Weimar Republic contested the validity of what the FRG had been calling the 1937 frontiers. This stand of the Weimar Republic clothed Hitler's attack against Poland with a sort of legitimacy in German eyes. However, he went much farther than the Weimarian claims. The agreements concluded with the Soviet Union on August 23 and September 28, 1939, and his military victory enabled him to annex not only the Free City of Danzig (September 1) and the Polish provinces lost by Germany following the First World War, but also large chunks of other Polish territory far beyond the 1914 frontiers of the German Empire. The remnant of Polish ethnic territory was placed under German administration (the so-called General Government). German commentary concludes: "Hence, the thesis of the uncontestable validity of the frontiers of December 31, 1937, which large circles of German public opinion formulated with an entirely subjective honesty but without the knowledge of objectively existing circumstances, had been invalidated in its every aspect at the beginning of the Second World War."[2]

The same official commentary retraces the history of the origin of the Oder-Neisse frontier, mentioning the fact that the USA, Britain, and the USSR considered the revision of the Eastern German frontier in favor of Poland as a compensation for the loss of Eastern Poland to the Soviet Union. It recalls that the Potsdam Conference excluded the East German territories placed under Polish administration from the Soviet zone of occupation, but reserved the final determination of the Polish Western frontier until the peace settlement. The commentary concludes: "The western Polish frontier along the Oder and the Western Neisse could have been regarded during the past twenty-five years as provisional in its formal aspect but it has become [in fact] one of the most durable and most secure of European frontiers owing to the normative force of facts."[3]

The same official publication continues with a historical survey of German-Polish relations since the Second World War and until the signing of the Warsaw Treaty.[4] It mentions the Polish annexation on May 24, 1945, of the former German territory east of the Oder-Neisse line, and the extension of Polish citizenship on May 10, 1946, and January 8, 1951, to all former German citizens who remained in that territory and whose Polish nationality had been verified by Polish authorities (the so-called autochthons).

Chancellor Adenauer said in one of his first official statements on September 20, 1949, that his government would never agree to Soviet and Polish annexation of East German territories, and would not cease to uphold the claim to those territories. On June 13, 1950, the Bundestag, all parties agreeing, declared the Görlitz frontier treaty, concluded between the GDR and Poland, illegal, and stated that the territories east of the Oder-Neisse continued to be part of Germany, the final frontier settlement having to wait until a peace treaty to be concluded with an all-German democratic government. On August 5, 1950, the organizations of East German refugees and expellees adopted their Charter in which they claimed the right to the former homeland (*Heimatrecht*), i.e., the right to return to their former homes in Eastern Europe, including the territories east of the Oder-Neisse frontier. Adenauer restated on October 20, 1953, that the German people would never recognize the Oder-Neisse frontier.

On February 18, 1955, Poland, following the Soviet example, announced the termination of the state of war with all of Germany and expressed its wish to have good-neighborly relations with the German people on the basis of the Oder-Neisse frontier.

On December 8, 1955, the German Red Cross made public its

agreement with the Polish Red Cross on the emigration to the FRG beginning with 1956 of those inhabitants of the Polish-annexed territory who claimed to be Germans. This was the beginning of the emigration which continued in the following years.

On January 10, 1959, the Soviet government published its draft of a peace treaty with Germany. Article 8 stated that the frontiers of Germany should remain as they were on January 1, 1959, and Article 9 asked Germany to renounce all claims to the territories east of the Oder-Neisse frontier. The then West German government rejected this Soviet proposal with a clear "no."

On July 10, 1960, Chancellor Adenauer stated in a speech addressed to the East Prussian refugees and expellees, that they had a right to their former homeland. This amounted to questioning not only the Polish annexation of its part of East Prussia but also the Soviet annexation of the northern part of the same province. Yet Adenauer knew that the Western powers had pledged their support for the Soviet annexation of the Koenigsberg area of East Prussia.

On June 14, 1961, the Bundestag adopted a resolution in which it expressed a wish to normalize relations with East Europe but "without paying the price of sacrificing vital German interests" or abandoning the German legal reservations. This implicit claim to a modification of frontiers marked in effect the end of Adenauer's era and of its uncompromising stand.

His successor, Chancellor Erhard, conceded on September 8, 1965, that "we consider as illusory the belief that the settlement of the German question [the reunification] could be obtained against the will of East European peoples."

The same German commentary reproduces the memorandum of the German Evangelical Church of October 1, 1965, the letters exchanged between the Polish and German bishops attending the Vatican II Council of November 18 and December 5, 1965, and the memorandum of March 2, 1968, by a group of Catholic intellectuals (the Bensberger Kreis), presumably to prove a change in West German attitudes toward Poland. The main point of those memoranda and of the letter of the German bishops consisted in the admission that German grief, caused by the loss of Eastern territories and the expulsion of East Germans, had to be counterbalanced by the recollection of sufferings of the Poles at the time of the German wartime occupation.[5]

On March 25, 1966, the Erhard-Schroeder government sent its peace notes with the offer of agreements on the renunciation of force, in which it conceded that Poland had suffered most during the Second

World War and expressed the desire to improve mutual relations. How-ever, the same notes stated that the solution of the frontier problem must await the peace settlement to be concluded with a reunified Germany, and that Germany continued to exist legally within its December 31, 1937, frontiers. The Polish government rejected the offer of an agree-ment on the renunciation of force because it held it to be meaningless as long as the FRG would not agree to the irreversibility of the Oder-Neisse frontier.

Erhard's successor, Chancellor Kiesinger, declared on December 13, 1966, that the German people wanted reconciliation with Poland and the establishment of diplomatic relations. He admitted the right of Poland to live within secure frontiers, but renewed the usual reservation that such frontiers could be finally determined only in a peace treaty, accepted by the government of a unified Germany. His Foreign Minister, Willy Brandt, sounded a different note on April 29, 1967, in his address to the expellee organizations: "We all shall probably agree that one should not indulge in false hopes regarding the possibility of imple-menting claims [otherwise] convincingly grounded."[6] On November 3, 1967, Kiesinger himself admitted the necessity of agreeing to a modifica-tion of the 1937 frontiers, because he proposed to the Polish government that they hold talks regarding a territorial compromise which would be confirmed later in the peace settlement. On March 18, 1968, Foreign Minister Brandt made another step forward by telling the Social Demo-cratic congress in Nuremberg, that "most [Germans] have forgotten that the bill for the lost war is still outstanding. . . . It is a fact that forty percent of people who live there [in the former East German terri-tory], were born there. And there is no one so deluded as to think of a new expulsion. . . . What does follow? The recognition of, or respectively respect for the Oder-Neisse line until a peace settlement. . . . All peoples should live in the secure certitude that their frontiers will not any longer be changed against their will."[7] Brandt, still in his capacity of Foreign Minister, responded favorably on May 20 to Gomulka's speech of May 17, 1969, by assuring Warsaw of his willingness to include the territorial question in an agreement on the renunciation of force. It was evident by that time that Brandt approached the problem of normalization of rela-tions with Poland in a spirit entirely different from his Chancellor's. It was becoming probable that the great coalition would not survive the approaching general elections.

Gustav Heinemann, the President of the Republic, offered his sup-port of Brandt's way of thinking in his speech on the occasion of the thirtieth anniversary of the German attack on Poland (September 1,

1969). He reminded his countrymen that Hitler wanted to "solve the Jewish question" and "impose German dominion over the Slavic peoples."

> Danzig and the corridor were only the prologue to the program of Great Germany and of German overlordship over the so-called Slavic subhuman beings. . . . We must not forget that over 55 million men in the whole world lost their lives during the Second World War. . . . What was achieved to our great satisfaction with France, our former "hereditary enemy," remains before us as a so far unsolved task in regard to our Eastern neighbors and in particular Poland, who in 1939 was the first victim of the surprise attack. Its number of war dead amounts to six millions, of whom 700,000 perished as soldiers while the remaining more than five million fell victims of a despotic extermination. . . . We must make a new beginning between us and our Eastern neighbors, above all Poland.[8]

NEGOTIATIONS WITH WARSAW

Soon after the formation of the government of the small coalition, negotiations between Bonn and Warsaw began, with the first contacts in November–December 1969. The actual conversations were conducted by G. F. Duckwitz, State Secretary at the German Foreign Office, and Józef Winiewicz, the Polish Vice-Minister for Foreign Affairs. The negotiations were far from easy, because the Polish side insisted on the recognition of finality of the Oder-Neisse frontier, while the German side was willing to grant a recognition limited in time to the duration of the FRG, which would not bind the future united Germany. The German government wanted also to receive a Polish commitment to the wholesale repatriation of all Polish citizens of German ethnic nationality. Warsaw refused to conclude any bilateral agreement because it feared that such a bilateral agreement would give the FRG the right of protecting those citizens vis-à-vis the Polish government. Finally a compromise was reached in November 1970. On November 18, Foreign Minister Walter Scheel, who had come to Warsaw for the final stage of negotiations, and Polish Foreign Minister Stefan Jędrychowski initialed the treaty to be called the Warsaw Treaty.

Chancellor Brandt, accompanied by Foreign Minister Scheel, in turn paid an official visit to Poland and on December 7, 1970, signed the treaty, which bore the signatures of Brandt and Scheel for the FRG and of Prime Minister Józef Cyrankiewicz and Foreign Minister Stefan Jędrychowski for Poland.

THE WARSAW TREATY

The Warsaw Treaty states in its preamble that the contracting parties are aware of the fact that the inviolability of frontiers and respect for the territorial integrity and sovereignty of all European states within their present frontiers are the fundamental conditions of peace.

Article One, of crucial importance, reads as follows:

> 1. The Polish People's Republic and the Federal Republic of Germany unanimously affirm that the existing frontier line, the course of which was established in Chapter IX of the decisions of the Potsdam Conference of August 2, 1945, as from the Baltic Sea immediately west of Swinoujście [Swinemünde] and thence along the Oder River to the confluence of the Lusatian Neisse River and along the Lusatian Neisse River to the Czechoslovak frontier, constitutes the western state frontier of the Polish People's Republic.
>
> 2. They confirm the inviolability of their existing frontiers now and in the future, and mutually pledge to respect unreservedly their territorial integrity.
>
> 3. They declare that they have no territorial claims against one another nor shall they advance such claims in the future.[9]

This Article, as we shall see, was to be interpreted differently by the FRG and Poland.

Articles 2 and 3 commit the two parties to abide by the Charter of the United Nations, in particular to settle their disputes exclusively by peaceful means and to promote the bilateral normalization of relations and mutual cooperation.

Article 4 reproduces an analogous provision in the Moscow Treaty, namely, that the treaty does not affect the validity of both parties' previous bilateral and multilateral international agreements. In November, immediately following the initialing of the treaty, the West German government sent identical notes to the American, British, and French governments, in which it stated that the German-Polish treaty would not encroach upon the rights of the four powers, that the Polish government had been notified of this German reservation, and that the FRG could negotiate only on its own behalf. The three Western powers approved this reservation in their answers.[10]

Article 4 and the exchange of notes between Bonn, Washington, London, and Paris made it clear that the FRG recognized the Oder-Neisse frontier only on its own behalf and only for the duration of its existence. The West German commitment was not to bind a reunified Germany. However, the FRG would be forbidden by Article One of the Treaty from raising territorial claims against Poland at the peace conference. The GDR, committed by the Görlitz Treaty, would be in the same legal position. Only the four powers or one of them could do so if they wanted to. The situation would be different if the peace conference took place *after* German reunification. According to the West German interpretation of the Warsaw Treaty, an all-German government, participant at the conference, would not be bound by the FRG's recognition of the Oder-Neisse frontier.

The signature of the treaty was accompanied by a unilateral Polish "information," addressed to the German party, regarding the repatriation to the FRG of Polish citizens of German nationality. This "information" was considered by the German government as a sort of counterpart of the Warsaw Treaty.[11] The statement is not reproduced, interestingly enough, in the Polish official collection of documents relating to the Warsaw Treaty.

The Polish "information" recalled that the Polish government recommended in 1955 to the Polish Red Cross that it reach an agreement with the German Red Cross on the reuniting of German relatives in Poland with their families in the FRG. The 400,000 persons of German nationality were subsequently allowed to leave Poland. However, the Polish government refused permission to citizens of Polish nationality who wanted to go to the FRG for economic reasons. The Polish government further stated its readiness to allow further emigration to either German state of persons of uncontested German nationality or of the descendants of nationally mixed families if they had manifested during the past years that they felt themselves to be German. This was to include those Polish citizens who had repudiated their former declaration of being Poles at the time of the verification of nationality of the so-called autochthons. This gave the right to any autochthon to annul his former declaration of being a Pole and to claim his German nationality with the accompanying right to leave Poland. The Polish government also stated that it did not accept the figure of prospective emigrants as given by the FRG. It was known that the German Red Cross claimed the total of Germans in Poland amounted to 600,000, because it included in this figure all former German citizens irrespective of their German or Polish nationality. At the time of the conclusion of the Warsaw Treaty the German Red Cross had applications from West German citizens who alleged that their 200,000 relatives still remaining in Poland wanted to join them in the FRG. The Polish Red Cross had only 80,000 direct applications from such relatives. In any event, the Polish government in its unilateral statement said that the total of prospective emigrants numbered only tens of thousands. It expressed its readiness to recommend to the Polish Red Cross that it remain in touch with the German Red Cross in order to cooperate regarding the emigration of Germans from Poland.

The Polish government went further than to consent to the reuniting of separated families. It also agreed in its statement to repatriate those Germans who had no relatives in the FRG but who claimed to be Germans in spite of their opposite declarations at the time of verification of the nationality of the autochthons. In other words, every person claiming to be a German would be offered permission to leave Poland. Politically, the Polish government should have felt happy because of the FRG's willingness to accept all Germans still remaining in Poland. No government consents to repatriate its countrymen from territory it intends to regain. The stand of the FRG confirmed that it did not hope ever to recover the territory east of the Oder-Neisse. Yet, Warsaw was not eager to commit itself to a wholesale emigration. First, it did not want to lose the skilled manpower. As the German Red Cross told this author, the implementation of the Five Year Plan was the obstacle. Second, Warsaw feared that former German citizens of undoubtedly Polish nationality might claim to be Germans for the sake of emigrating to the FRG, where prosperity seemed to offer them better living conditions. Dr. Wagner, the representative of the German Red Cross in charge of the repatriation of Germans from Poland, said on December 5, 1970, that the criteria to be used for determining the German nationality of Polish citizens would be the language used by the family and the ethnic nationality of parents.[12] The unilateral nature of the Polish statement left to the Polish government the discretionary power regarding permissions to emigrate which it would grant or refuse. One could expect that its attitude would be more or less liberal, depending on the general condition of German-Polish relations.

THE REACTIONS OF GERMAN POLITICAL PARTIES

The West German political parties aligned themselves on partisan lines regarding the Warsaw Treaty. J. F. Volrad Deneke, leader of the Free Democratic parliamentary group, spoke in favor of the treaty on November 16, 1970, the eve of its initialing by his party colleague, Foreign Minister Scheel. He reminded his countrymen of the partitions of Poland in which two Germanic states participated (Prussia and Austria), of the unsuccessful, as he said, Germanization policy of the German Empire toward its citizens of Polish descent, of Hitler's policy of a new partition of Poland, and of persecutions of the Poles during the German occupation. He also remarked that if a peace settlement for Germany had taken place prior to the outbreak of cold war, the territories east of the Oder-Neisse would have been lost by Germany, which would have been compelled to sign such a peace treaty. He also recalled that not only East Germans but also Poles from Soviet-annexed Eastern Poland had to abandon their former homes and resettle in new homelands. The Germans had to admit that they had lost the war, and hence had to accept the realities which followed that war. Poland had lost 22 percent of its prewar population during the Second World War and could not trust those Germans who wanted to continue the hostile tradition of anti-Polish policies of Imperial Germany and of the Weimar Republic. The right to the homeland could also be claimed by the Poles who now lived in the former German territories.[13]

The Social Democratic parliamentary group adopted a resolution supporting Brandt's policy toward Poland on November 19, 1970. It warned the refugees and expellees that no amount of entreaties or illusions could change the postwar situation, but called their attention to the fact that the treaty to be concluded with Poland would result in the reunion of separated families. The resolution concluded with the hope that the treaty would lead to a reconciliation similar to that with France.[14]

The opposition parliamentary group (the Christian Democratic Union and the Christian Social Union) adopted its own resolution in turn on December 4, in which it expressed its support of an understanding with Poland, but on the condition that the final determination of German frontiers be postponed till the peace settlement. According to that resolution, the treaty with Poland should only establish a *modus vivendi* which might take into consideration the existence of the Oder-Neisse line. It also asked for Polish concession of minority rights to the Germans still living there. The resolution was not couched in completely negative terms but manifested dissatisfaction with Brandt's approach to Poland.[15] The parliamentary battle over ratification had been joined even before the treaty with Poland was signed.

One of the federal ministers, Social Democrat Horst Ehmke, made a last-minute appeal to German public opinion on the eve of the signature of the treaty with Poland:

> What happened between 1939 and 1946 is beyond any description insofar as the extent and horror are concerned. At the end of those events both peoples stood bled-white, impoverished and expelled from the territories of their former settlements. Poland had lost large territories, and Germany had to give up to Poland almost one-fourth of its soil. . . . People found in the meantime work and bread in their new habitations. . . . This is equally true of Poles and Germans. . . . Koenigsberg, Breslau and Stettin as well as the beautiful territory between the Oder, the Neisse, the Vistula and Memel, remains for us an unforgettable German territory insofar as history and recollections are concerned. They belong [however] now and will belong in the future to Poland. This we cannot change. Whoever believes that he should preserve the hope for a change or that he should bring up young people in such a manner that they should await a change, should know that he plays the game of war.[16]

Most of the Bundestag deputies, including a good portion of Christian Democrats, agreed in private conversations that the East German territories were lost without any hope of recovering them. Some of them hoped at the most that final assent to that loss would be the price to be paid for the reunification of Germany.

GERMAN INTERPRETATION OF THE TREATY

Yet even the Brandt-Scheel government wanted to leave a free hand to a reunified Germany, probably in the hope that unforeseeable future developments might perhaps allow that reunified Germany to reclaim the territory beyond the Oder-Neisse frontier. This could only add to the reasons why Poland did not want the reunification to take place.

West German interpretation of the scope of the Warsaw Treaty was clearly stated by Foreign Minister Scheel in an official publication, printed after the signature of the treaty:[17]

> The Third Reich tried even to annihilate the biological substance of the Polish nation and in any event wished to degrade it to the level of a helot community. The Polish state, resurrected after the Second World War . . . , came into existence only after frontier shifts and migration of peoples. Not only did the burden fall upon the Germans but upon millions of Poles as well. No one can wonder that, after these experiences, the frontier question has plainly become the cardinal question for Poland. Every attack on the integrity of her national territory must have been felt as an attack on her very existence. The trauma of having to be a "state on the wheels" is very close to the fear of non-existence. For Poland the desire of every state for "secure frontiers" has a particular significance. . . . For Poland, the mere renunciation of force for the securing of the future is not enough; it can help but little for the present, since Poland does not feel threatened by the Federal Republic of Germany. . . . Thus, anyone who wants German-Polish understanding must immediately concern himself with the frontier question. . . . Anyone who does sidestep it [this question] must take into account that there just can be no reconciliation. . . . Anyone who wants to 'keep open' the frontier question under all circumstances must ask himself what he hopes to achieve if force as a means of changing frontiers is excluded in every respect. A peaceful change is conceivable neither now nor in any foreseeable future, since the Polish side will not be prepared voluntarily to hand over parts of its territory, and among our allies there is not one who would be prepared to influence Poles on these lines. . . . Time has not worked for us. . . . It is falsifying the problem if the Federal Government is accused of giving up . . . the German Eastern territories. We cannot dispose with something that has long been at the disposal of history; we cannot give up something we no longer possess. . . . The Federal Republic of Germany has to shoulder the burden of the National Socialist legacy. No Federal Government can win the Second World War after it had taken place. . . . The Federal Republic of Germany is facing a situation which it is not in her power to change. . . . The Federal Republic of Germany has unequivocally undertaken not to question Poland's present western frontier. However, she can make such a declaration only on behalf of herself; she cannot bind an all-German sovereign state which does not yet exist. . . . We would not have been able to conclude the treaty had we not had sufficient evidence that the Polish side was prepared to meet us halfway in the sphere of hu-

man relief, which for us is crucial. [He alluded to the emigration
of German-speaking Polish citizens and to the Polish unilateral
statement]. . . . However, the Federal Government could not expect that the Polish side, by reason of its historical experience,
would be prepared to bestow a minority status on Germans living
in Poland. . . . The Federal Republic of Germany binds herself in
the frontier question in no way to any time limit. . . . A reunified
Germany cannot be bound by the treaty.

THE POLISH INTERPRETATION

The Polish replies to German voices were quick to come. The Polish
newspaper *Życie Warszawy* stated on November 10, 1970:

We do not cast doubts on the sufferings and grief of people who
had to lose their homes twenty-five years ago. However, one cannot make us responsible for this. The guilt is borne by the Third
Reich and the German people who had supported Hitler in its immense majority. The resettlement of those people may in no case
be compared with the murder of six million Poles and with the
horrible martyrdom [of persons] who had to suffer at the hands of
fascist tormentors in the concentration camps. . . . No one in the
German Federal Republic should expect any reparation. Our reparation is our readiness to normalize relations and to begin a new
chapter in the history of both peoples.[18]

While the German government insisted that the treaty was binding
only on the FRG, and that a unified Germany, not bound by it, could
presumably reopen the frontier question, the Polish government no less
vigorously stressed that the treaty finally solved the problem. Polish
Prime Minister Józef Cyrankiewicz took the occasion of the signing of
the treaty to say, "The German Democratic Republic . . . twenty years
ago concluded the Zgorzelec [Görlitz] agreement with People's Poland,
which delimited the Polish-German frontier on the Rivers Oder and
Lusatian Neisse as established in the decisions of the Potsdam Conference. . . . It was also on this basis alone, that is, the irreversibility and
inviolability of the existing western frontier of Poland along the Rivers
Oder and Lusatian Neisse as decided by the Potsdam Conference, that
it proved possible to conclude the present Treaty."[19]

The whole Polish thesis was included in this statement. The Polish Oder-Neisse frontier was fixed by the Potsdam Conference. The two German states could not change this decision but could only admit its irreversibility and its final character. Cyrankiewicz's successor, Prime Minister Piotr Jaroszewicz, also claimed on December 23, 1970, that the Warsaw Treaty "definitely closed the problem of the Polish western frontier on the Oder and Neisse."[20] The German reservations were simply ignored.

However, one of the Polish experts on German problems, Krzysztof Skubiszewski, mentioned the German reservation in an article published by the *American Journal of International Law*.[21] He wrote that "during the negotiations with Poland, the Federal German Government insisted that it could act only in the name of the Federal Republic of Germany. . . . [and thus conveyed] a certain aura of provisionality that purportedly accompanied the settlement of 1970. The moment may come, it is implied, when the Federal Republic will no longer exist, and the German state that takes its place will have its hands free." He interprets this German reservation as intending to leave a reunited Germany free from the usual obligation of a successor state to take over the obligations entered into by its predecessors, in this case the FRG and the GDR. He rejects this thesis, because no reservation by the FRG could possibly change customary international law on state succession. He adds that Poland never accepted this reservation, and that the Warsaw Treaty contains no provision to this effect.

THE VIEWS OF THE WESTERN POWERS

Skubiszewski then proceeds to examine the extent of the rights of the four powers which retain their jurisdiction regarding Berlin and all of Germany. He says that none of the four powers now disputes the validity of the Oder-Neisse frontier. Moreover, the problematic peace conference on Germany would be attended by all former German enemies, including Poland, whose assent to the revision of the frontier would be denied. Then he proceeds to say: "Three among the powers [the USSR, Britain, and France] and the two Germanies have at various times consented to Poland's western frontier. The fourth power, the United States, does not seem to be willing to demand any change in the status quo, and, against the background of consent by the others, it would be surprising if it did." He overlooks the fact that a new determination of Polish frontiers could be made only by unanimous agreement of the four powers and could not be imposed by any one of them separately.

The Polish official *Bulletin* quotes a statement by French Prime Minister Jacques Chaban-Delmas, made on the occasion of his visit to Poland on November 26, 1970: "On its part, the French government committed itself long ago. It did so in 1959 through the far-reaching pronouncement of General de Gaulle, committing France for ever. I reiterate it here. We consider, now and for the future, the establishment of the western frontier of Poland on the Oder and Neisse in its present course as an unquestionable and irrevocable fact."[22] France accepted the Polish thesis.

The same Polish Bulletin quotes the British Foreign Office's view, as published on November 20, 1970: "The Treaty with its accompanying documents . . . enjoys the British Government's full support. They welcome its provisions, including those relating to Poland's western frontier."[23] It also quotes the statement by Foreign Secretary Sir Alec Douglas-Home on December 7, 1970, in the House of Commons. Sir Alec said, "We are glad to see the matter of the Oder-Neisse line settled between the Poles and the Germans." The Parliamentary Under-Secretary for Foreign Affairs, Anthony Royle, added at the same meeting of the House of Commons, "As a European and Potsdam Power, we welcome this Treaty, including the provisions relating to Poland's Western frontier."[24]

President Nixon took the opportunity of his visit to Poland for inserting in the bilateral joint communiqué of May 14, 1972, the following sentence: "Both sides welcomed the treaty between Poland and the Federal Republic of Germany signed on December 7, 1970, including its border provisions."[25]

Neither the British nor the American statement was clear regarding the German reservation that the frontier question could be reopened at a peace conference on Germany. One could interpret them either as assent to the existence of the Oder-Neisse frontier for the duration of the FRG or as recognition of that frontier as final.

AGAIN THE POLISH INTERPRETATION

Skubiszewski in his article denies any validity to the unilateral Bundestag resolution adopted in 1972 on the occasion of approval of the Moscow and Warsaw Treaties (see below). He denies in particular the validity of its paragraph 2 which stated: "The Treaties proceed from the frontiers as actually existing today, unilateral alteration of which they exclude. The Treaties do not anticipate a peace settlement for Germany by treaty and do not create any legal foundation for the frontiers existing today." He says with bitterness: "A curious and unexpected phenomenon during the elaboration of the declaration was the participation of the Soviet ambassador in the working out of the final draft. On the other hand, the Polish government had no part in this compromise."[26] It is true that the Soviet ambassador was invited by the West German political parties to participate in their drafting of the resolution. Moscow assented to this, because it wanted to help Brandt's government in overcoming the difficulties it had met with the opposition, which had at its disposal half of the parliamentary votes. However, the Polish author overlooks the Soviet stand at the time of ratification of the Moscow Treaty by the Presidium of the Supreme Soviet, when the Soviet government made it clear that it was not bound by that particular German resolution but only by the terms of the treaty itself. Its stand did not differ from that of the Polish parliament. His concluding remark is that the adoption by the Bundestag of the resolution "creates some confusion and also some uncertainty as to the West German designs and reliability." He has some right to say so, because the Warsaw Treaty meant to grant the *de jure* recognition of the Oder-Neisse frontier for the duration of the existence of the FRG, while the resolution gave it retrospectively a more narrow meaning of a *de facto* recognition.

The Polish official publication concludes its comments on the Warsaw Treaty by an article written by Józef Winiewicz, the Polish negotiator. He summarized the Polish views:

It is a fact that never in the thousand-year history of her statehood, not even during the Partitions, has Poland endured anything even remotely comparable with the horrors inflicted by German fascism during the Second World War: six million people—22 percent of Poland's population—lost their lives, killed in battle, tortured to death, executed in the streets, exterminated in gas chambers, decimated by forced labor. In the smoking shambles of Warsaw, 800,000 lay dead. In a single city! Human dignity was trampled underfoot. We were stripped of the most elementary rights, treated in fact worse than animals. The whole of Poland was turned to cinders and rubble; 40 percent of our national wealth lay in ruins. . . . Can anyone in all conscience ask us to forget or try to compare their own sufferings in the war (and other nations, Germany among them, had their share) with ours, with Poland's Golgotha? Nevertheless political wisdom . . . bids us tune our plans and actions to the needs of the future. . . . The Treaty unmistakably and very properly turns to the future. . . . In the Treaty both parties unanimously affirm the final nature of the western frontier of Poland as established by the decisions of the Potsdam Conference. . . . The process of normalization will be neither short nor simple. If it is to produce lasting results, it must spread to the mass of public opinion in both countries and the political forces representing it. . . . To the Germans living on the Rhine one cannot resist saying: we are offering you honest, genuine desire to achieve lasting understanding and bring about mutually profitable cooperation. We should like to believe that our good will is reciprocated.[27]

While it is true that actual policies of states are by far more important than the personality of politicians who implement these policies, one cannot deny that Willy Brandt's anti-Nazi record played a certain role in the Polish attitude toward the FRG. He was respected in Warsaw. The Polish Prime Minister paid homage to him on the occasion of the signature of the treaty as "to a man, who from the very moment fascism conquered power grasped the immensity of the misfortunes that it might bring the German people, the nations of Europe and the peace of the world."[28]

RELATIONS WITH THE GDR

1970 was not only the year of the Moscow and Warsaw Treaties. The West German government was moving forward in relations with the GDR and Czechoslovakia. Brandt met his East German counterpart, Prime Minister Willi Stoph, twice. These meetings, though inconclusive, were significant, because it was the first time that the chief executives of the two German states had consented to enter into direct negotiations. Brandt admitted at the first meeting in Erfurt (GDR) in March 1970 that there were two German states but stressed the fact that they were no foreign states to each other. He mentioned the importance of maintaining the present status of Berlin and assured Stoph that any agreement between the FRG and GDR would have the same international force as an agreement concluded between either of them and a third state. "I proceed," he said, "from [the premise] that our relations must be founded on non-discrimination and equality. Neither of us can deal on behalf of the other and neither can represent abroad the other part of Germany. . . . Neither should exercise tutelage over the other."[29]

Willi Stoph did not agree that the two German states should have relations *sui generis,* different from those between either of them and third states, and wanted West German recognition of West Berlin as an independent political entity (a sort of third German state). In spite of this uncompromising East German attitude, Brandt made important concessions, which no previous West German government had been willing to make. He conceded the existence of the two equal German states, abandoned expressly the former claim of the FRG's being the sole spokesman for the whole German nation, and admitted the right of the GDR to have diplomatic relations with third states.

The second meeting took place in Kassel, West Germany, in May 1970. Brandt offered his program for mutual relations, namely, that personal contacts between Western and Eastern Germans should be facilitated, that both states should respect the independence of each other, that neither should represent the other abroad, that citizens of both states should be considered members of the same German nation, that both states should renounce force in mutual relations, that their future agreement would not invalidate the rights of the four powers regarding Berlin and Germany as a whole, that they should respect the forthcoming four-power agreement on Berlin, and that the existing ties of West Berlin with the FRG should be safeguarded. If an agreement were reached, the two states would be represented in their respective capitals by plenipotentiaries of ministerial rank but not by ambassadors, as a sign that the two states were not foreign to each other.[30] Stoph rejected this program, but later on, probably under Soviet pressure, basically accepted it.

German-Czechoslovak negotiations began in March–April, 1970, by contacts in Prague between the high officials of both countries. They were to be continued in the following years.

THE FOUR-POWER AGREEMENT ON BERLIN

Finally, on September 3, 1971, the four powers reached an agreement on the status of Berlin. This dispelled the fears of some among Brandt's followers. Since he conditioned the ratification of the Moscow Treaty on a satisfactory agreement of the four powers on Berlin, they feared that any of the three Western powers might torpedo his Eastern policy by raising demands which the USSR could not possibly accept. Actually the Western powers gave their blessing, so to speak, by making a genuine effort to reach an understanding with the USSR on Berlin.

The Western powers reaffirmed in the agreement their view that, contrary to the constitutions of the FRG and of West Berlin, that city was not a constituent part of the FRG and remained under their supreme jurisdiction. There was nothing new in this stand, but it was the first time that the Western powers confirmed this aspect of West Berlin's status in an agreement with the USSR. The Western powers made another concession by agreeing with the Soviet Union that West German political functions such as visits by the President of the FRG, meetings of the federal government and of the Federal Bundestag, etc. should not be performed in West Berlin. The Soviet government had protested many times against those official manifestations of the FRG's presence in West Berlin and finally scored success. The Western powers committed themselves not to tolerate such West German activities, in contrast to their previous stand. In exchange the Soviet Union also made important concessions. It accepted for the first time the existence of non-political ties between the FRG and West Berlin, the right of the FRG to perform consular services on behalf of West Berlin, and its right to represent the city in non-political international agreements such as treaties of commerce and at non-political conferences and organizations. Even more important was the Soviet commitment not only not to use force regarding the city but to guarantee the security of communications between it and the FRG. Hence the USSR abandoned its former thesis that the problem of these communications belonged within the GDR's jurisdiction because they cut across East German territory. This meant that the Soviet Union would no longer allow the GDR to obstruct those communications whenever the GDR wanted to protest against a particular West German policy. The agreement contained very detailed provisions regarding these communications in order to ensure their safety. West Berliners were allowed by the agreement to visit East Berlin and the GDR on the same conditions as visitors from the FRG and other countries. Additional crossing points were to be opened by the GDR, and the telecommunications of West Berlin were to be extended.[31]

The Soviet concessions strengthened Brandt's hand at home. He could point out that his Eastern policy bore fruit, because the Soviet Union had abandoned its former game of using Berlin as a means of exerting pressure on the FRG and the Western powers, had accepted for the first time that the FRG could exercise its non-political jurisdiction in West Berlin, and had assumed, also for the first time, its own responsibility for uninterrupted communications across East German territory. The former claims of the GDR were simply disregarded by Moscow, eager to smooth its relations with the FRG.

The four-power agreement was initialed on September 3, 1971, but the Soviet Union refused to sign it until such time as the FRG should ratify the Moscow and Warsaw Treaties. In other words, Moscow reciprocated the West German condition for ratification of the treaties by its own refusal to grant its final approval to the four-power agreement on Berlin until it could be sure that the Bundestag assented to the treaties. After the latter Soviet condition was fulfilled by the Bundestag, the USSR and the three Western powers signed the agreement on June 3, 1972, and made it binding.

REASONS FOR BRANDT'S EASTERN POLICY

One should ask at this point why the Brandt-Scheel government decided to accept the territorial and political status quo in Central Europe. The official history of the foreign policy of the FRG mentions as one of the reasons the fear of international isolation of the FRG.[32] This fear was well-founded in the sixties and even more so in 1970. The allies of the FRG were moving toward an improvement in relations with the USSR. If the FRG were to remain the last bastion of the cold war, it would be singled out by the West and the East as the only, but important, obstacle on the road toward detente. Moreover, paralyzed by its bad relations with the Soviet Union and East Europe, the FRG would be taken for granted by its own allies and would have much less voice in Western councils than was warranted by its military and, above all, economic power. The new Eastern policy was expected to provide the FRG with increased independence in foreign policies in regard to both the West and the East. The second reason, not mentioned in the official West German publication, was a decrease of trust in the American military guarantee, because of the American-Soviet nuclear stalemate. Moreover, the United States was proceeding in its policy of detente with the USSR without due consultation of the Western allies, including the FRG. Brandt wanted to be sure that the FRG could safeguard its interests in direct contacts with the USSR. Finally, in 1970 the USA was still fully involved in Southeast Asia and seemed to pay less attention to Western Europe.

All these reasons were considered in Bonn as more important than the preservation of old shibboleths which time had proved to be unrealistic. Since the FRG had no prospects of changing the Central European status quo, the former attitudes and policies looked completely unrealistic. What did the FRG gain in fact by its claim to be the sole spokesman of the whole German nation, by refusing to acknowledge the existence of the other German state, which could not be abolished by a magic wand, by vain efforts to stem the tide of third states' recognition of the GDR, or by advancing territorial claims against Poland while unable to change the Oder-Neisse frontier by force or otherwise?

Finally, West German business was interested almost as much as the Soviet Union in expanding economic relations and in acquiring new markets in Russia and Eastern Europe, at a time when the United States was moving in the direction of becoming in this respect a competitor of both Western Europe and Japan.

Eventually the Christian Democratic opposition had to concede that it had no viable alternative to Brandt's Eastern policy by abstaining in 1972 in the Bundestag's vote on the Moscow and Warsaw Treaties and thus allowing the two treaties to be ratified.

10

The German Ratification Battle

THE BATTLE BEGINS

THE MOSCOW AND WARSAW TREATIES were signed in 1970 but were ratified only in 1972. There were two reasons for this unusual delay. The first one was the *junctim* which the Brandt government made between the ratification and a satisfactory four-power agreement on Berlin. This agreement was concluded only in September 1971. The second reason was the same government's wish to persuade the opposition to vote for the ratification. As the governmental majority, slim to begin with, was gradually melting down, the votes of the opposition were becoming crucial. They were also crucial because West German public opinion was divided on the merits and demerits of the treaties. Finally, the Soviet and Polish partners preferred to see a solid majority in the Bundestag voting for the ratification.

While the governmental majority in the Bundestag was declining (a number of its deputies crossing the aisle because of their opposition to the treaties), the government got an invigorating shot in the arm, thanks to the four-power agreement on Berlin. The opposition's argument that the Western powers looked with disfavor on Brandt's Eastern policy fell to the ground. The conclusion of that agreement, *i.e.,* the fulfillment of Brandt's condition for the ratification, meant that the three Western powers gave their blessing to the treaties. The opposition was placed in an embarrassing position. If they voted against the treaties and prevented their ratification, it would look like a challenge not only to Brandt's government but also to the Western allies. It would also

203

mean a vote against the Berlin agreement, which the USSR would not approve finally without the counterpart, the ratification by the FRG of the two treaties. Yet, the four-power agreement improved the situation of West Berlin and was greeted with satisfaction by the majority of West Germans.

The year 1971 was one of the Brandt government's efforts to offer an interpretation of the treaties which would convince the opposition and public opinion that vital German interests were not sacrificed. Therefore, the government insisted on the narrowest possible interpretation of the treaties, but an interpretation which would not deprive the treaties of their value for the USSR and Poland. This was not an easy task.

The parliamentary battle over the treaties started in 1971 and continued during the first five months of 1972. It was bitter, the opposition fighting against ratification until the last moment when it finally yielded and let ratification take place owing to its abstention from the vote. The weakness of the opposition's stand was its inability to offer a viable alternative Eastern policy. The true choice was between the approval of Brandt's Eastern policy or a return to the former immobility regarding the Soviet Union and its allies.

The year 1971 began in the FRG with recollections of the hundredth anniversary of the founding of a unified German Reich. This anniversary reminded the West Germans of the fact that a unified German state in its three stages (the German Empire, the Weimar Republic, and Nazi Germany) had lasted for only seventy-five years, a short period of time in the long history of the German people. And yet, no German could forget this relatively short period. They thought of it as an apogee of their history. Hence, every government of the FRG had to face the problem of reunification. The difference between Brandt's and former West German governments was rather significant in this respect. The former governments talked about the reunification within a democratic state, which meant the absorption of the GDR by the FRG, although they knew well that such a reunification could not be carried out in the foreseeable future. This was a sort of theoretical dogma, with a corresponding negation of the legitimacy of the GDR and the claim that the FRG could speak on behalf of all Germans. The result was a growing gulf between the two German states.

Brandt thought in more practical terms. What he wanted to prevent was the emergence of two opposite national consciousnesses, the split of the German nation into two hostile parts. His acknowledgment of the existence of two German states was to him a device for preventing the gulf from widening by improving relations with the GDR and thus ensuring more frequent contacts between the two German populations. Knowing the extent of Soviet control over the GDR, he considered the Moscow Treaty as a key treaty. Only the Soviet Union could influence East Berlin in relaxing its restrictive regulations on West and East German personal contacts. He envisaged the process of reunification as a very long one, which required, first of all, the cultivation of a feeling among all Germans that they belonged to one nation though divided into two states. His personal authority in Germany was strengthened by the Nobel Peace Prize, conferred on him in 1971.

THE FIRST BUNDESTAG DEBATE

The first debate on the treaties took place in the Bundestag in January 1971, on the occasion of the Chancellor's message on the state of the nation. The first opposition salvo was fired by Rainer Barzel, chairman of the CDU–CSU parliamentary group. His stand was uncompromising: no recognition of the GDR or of the Oder-Neisse frontier. He claimed that the treaties gave everything to the Russians and the Poles, while leaving the FRG empty-handed. He was opposed to the simultaneous admission of the FRG and the GDR to the United Nations. His stand on the German-Polish frontier was best expressed in his question as to whether Silesia should now be considered a foreign province.[1] What he proposed was to reject the Eastern treaties and start new negotiations in which the FRG would refuse to acknowledge the existing status quo. He must have realized that neither the Soviet Union nor Poland would accept this alternative. In effect, he advocated a return to the former immobility in relations with the Soviet bloc.

Chancellor Brandt warned in his response that a return to the former policies of the fifties and sixties "would find no support among our allies."[2]

The other speakers in the debate were divided along party lines, the Christian Democrats opposing the ratification of the treaties and the Social and Free Democrats supporting the government. The Social Democratic deputy, Dr. Hans Appel, threw light on one of the motivations of Brandt's Eastern policy. He said, "We have not only followed here what our Western Allies have done before us. We, as an equal partner in the Western Alliance, also have ended at last our letting others negotiate and act for us."[3] In other words, by opening channels to the East the Brandt government enabled the FRG to acquire an equal voice in the Western Alliance and to protect its interests in direct contacts with Moscow and other East European capitals. The same was stressed by Herbert Wehner, chairman of the Social Democratic parliamentary group, when he said, "The Eastern Treaties have made it possible for the Federal Republic to participate as an equal partner in the efforts to organize peace."[4]

This first debate on the treaties ended inconclusively, both sides maintaining their positions.

THE OFFICIAL VERSION

The spokesmen for the government took every opportunity throughout the year 1971 to advance arguments for the ratification of the treaties, offering interpretations which might possibly appease the opposition and convince public opinion that the government had obtained the best possible terms under the circumstances. Foreign Minister Walter Scheel defended his government's Eastern policy as practically the only possible one in his May, 1971, interview with the periodical *Aussenpolitik*:

> The Federal Republic should not let itself be guided by fictitious political standards, or, in other words, should not claim for itself an identity which if realistically considered it has not. . . . It seems to us that it is better to contribute to European stability within the 1971 frontiers than to dream about the 1937 frontiers. The "short road" toward the reunification of our country proved through a painful experience not to be practicable. We must begin a "long march.". . . A glance at the sixties points out that the outlook of citizens of the Federal Republic regarding foreign policy has been confronted with a contradiction at least since the end of the fifties. A fictitious standard, that the restoration of unity of our country was possible through a free unification while retaining the claim to the 1937 frontiers, was upheld officially. . . . Claims were upheld which could not be carried out in actual policies. The Federal government, to which I belong, has taken the step to solve this contradiction. We have done this in the conviction that the German people is attached enough to its democratic system to be able to accept the reality.[5]

What he meant was that a realistic policy which broke off from former illusions would not cause, as it had at the time of the Weimar Republic, a nationalistic popular reaction not only against that policy but also against the democratic system itself. The following years proved him right. Brandt's Eastern policy did not weaken at all the democratic foundations of the FRG.

However, it was necessary to convince West German citizens that the Eastern policy did not go beyond what international reality required. The government argued that the two treaties were nothing but the result of a lost war, unleashed by Hitler. The long-delayed payment for that bill had to be made. The then Minister for National Defense, Social Democrat Helmut Schmidt, had the courage to acknowledge German responsibility for the Second World War. Speaking on November 14, 1971, on an occasion of homage to those who perished in the two World Wars, he made a distinction between the meanings of German deaths and those of their adversaries in the Second World War, because that war was an unprovoked German aggression: "The deaths of millions of German men and women had no sense because they were not a sacrifice for a good cause. . . . The deaths of German citizens during the Second World War belong to a different historical category, if compared with the deaths of citizens of states which Hitler attacked. The deaths of Frenchmen, Poles, Russians, Dutchmen and Yugoslavs were not senseless, because those peoples defended their countries."[6]

THE BRANDT-BREZHNEV MEETING

The first fruit of the Eastern policy was the invitation extended by Brezhnev to Chancellor Brandt to meet him in September 1971, in the Crimea. For the first time the Soviet government was ready to talk with the Federal government in the same way it had done for years with its Western allies. It was evident that the FRG, as the consequence of the Eastern treaties, became a valid partner of Moscow, of lesser importance, of course, than the United States but more important than France, formerly the most favored of the state-members of the North Atlantic bloc.

After three days of conversations, Brandt and Brezhnev issued a joint communiqué, dated September 18, 1971. It stressed the importance not only of the Moscow Treaty as the point of departure for better mutual relations between the two countries, but also of the four-power agreement on Berlin. Brezhnev implicitly accepted Brandt's *junctim* between the treaty and the four-power agreement. The two men talked not only about Soviet-German relations but also about more general European problems, such as the projected European Security Conference, in which the United States and Canada would participate, and the possible reduction of armed forces in Europe. They agreed that the relations between the FRG and the GDR should be normalized on the basis of equality, non-discrimination, and mutual respect for their independence, and that both German states should simultaneously be admitted to the United Nations. They promised each other an intensification of cooperation, including economic, and agreed on the usefulness of future mutual consultations on matters of common concern.[7]

After his conversations with Brezhnev, Brandt could say: "The Federal Republic does not participate any longer, as was the case in the former years, only in one-sided consultations, only in Western exchanges of views regarding this very important topic [European security] which has a pivotal significance for the coming years. It now plays an equal role, unlike [in the former period] when [only] our Western allies proceeded for years with Western-Eastern exchanges of views."[8] He had reached his goal of equality with the Western allies in relations with the Soviet Union.

Brandt had to reassure the Western allies that his policy would not lead to a sort of Rapallo, a one-sided cooperation with the Soviet Union. He pointed out quite rightly the difference between the two historical situations. Germany no longer faced a weak Russia as was the case at the time when the Rapallo agreement was concluded.[9] Walter Scheel on his part appeased any imaginable Eastern European fears, especially Polish, that the Moscow Treaty might open an era of German-Soviet cooperation at the expense of Poland, such as the Prussian kings or German emperors and the Russian tsars, as well as Hitler and Stalin in 1939, had carried out. He quite rightly remarked that the circumstances were entirely different, and that "such nightmarish ideas one can encounter in German criticisms rather than in the heads of responsible East European politicians."[10] Of course, the Poles had nothing to fear since the Soviet Union was powerful enough not to need German cooperation at the price of sharing the spoils in Eastern Europe. All of Poland was now a part of the exclusive Soviet sphere of influence. What the opposition leaders were actually saying was not that the Soviet Union was ready to partition Poland with the FRG, but that the Moscow Treaty put a seal of approval on the status quo which placed the Eastern European countries under the Soviet protectorate. Actually, no policy of the FRG could change that situation.

OFFICIAL VOICES

Dr. Paul Frank, Secretary of State at the German Foreign Office, explained the reasons for the Eastern policy in a lecture he gave on October 13, 1971, at the annual meeting of the politically important Society for Eastern European Knowledge.[11] He said that the forthcoming debate in the Bundestag on the ratification of the Moscow and Warsaw treaties would have to end with a decision as to whether the foreign policy of the FRG would or would not take into account the changes which had occurred in the world: "There is nothing worse for the foreign policy of any country than to lose touch with the environment. A policy of immobility, followed out of indolence, or a policy which fails to take into account the dimensions of the world, can result in a situation where one day one finds himself isolated." After this warning he proceeded with an analysis of recent changes in the international environment. First, he mentioned the new balance of power which no longer rested only on the two superpowers but on five centers: the United States, the Soviet Union, China, Japan, and Western Europe, whose power would be strengthened by the expected accession by Britain, Ireland, Denmark, and Norway to the European Economic Community. Second, the objectives of NATO were modified: North Atlantic security was to be ensured not only by military deterrence but also by the reduction of tensions in relations with the Soviet bloc. This new view was evidenced by the American-Soviet SALT negotiations. Third, West German public opinion was affected by the new outlook of the young generation.

He pointed out a fact which could not be overlooked in the formulation of West German policy, the divergences in perspectives between the FRG, saddled with the problem of partition of the country, and its allies. These allies, such as France and the United States, looked at their relations with the Soviet Union in a different light from the FRG. However, the FRG could not ignore the views of its allies, for instance, President Nixon's words about the transition from the era of confrontation to the era of negotiation.

His conclusion was that "since we neither may nor want to wait for cooperation between the East and the West until all controversial problems are settled in a peace treaty, the contractual renunciation of the use of force must be founded on the territorial status quo. . . . At the root of our over-all Eastern and Western policies lies the renunciation of a tactic which would play one [state] against another. It would be unrealistic and to a high degree unreasonable, taking into account the existing power relations and our location in the middle [between the two blocs], to aim in the negotiations at isolating one or another of our Eastern partners. . . . We do not aim either at undermining the security of the Soviet Union." These last three sentences alluded to the Eastern policy of the great coalition which unsuccessfully tried to isolate the GDR and Poland, to loosen the ties between Czechoslovakia and the Eastern bloc, and to reduce Soviet influence in Eastern Europe.

The FRG accepted in the Moscow Treaty the existing European frontiers, including the one between the German states. This raised the question as to whether respect for the latter frontier would not preclude reunification. The government denied this by quoting from the statements made by the Soviet Foreign Minister on July 29, 1970, during his negotiations with Minister Walter Scheel. Gromyko said, "When two states freely decide to unite or to correct their frontiers, as we did several times with Norway, Afghanistan, and Poland, or when states, for instance, lift their common frontier and unite, as Syria and Egypt did, it would not occur to us to criticize, since this would be an expression of sovereignty and would be part of the inalienable rights of states and peoples."[12]

Gromyko must have had his tongue in cheek while making this statement. He knew very well that Poland was forced by superior Soviet power to abandon half of its prewar territory. He failed to remember that the short-lived union between Egypt and Syria was criticized by the then First Secretary Khrushchev. Finally, the Soviet Union had no intention of agreeing to the reunification of the German states and could exercise its veto, using in the last instance its troops stationed in the GDR. As a matter of fact, Gromyko told Minister Scheel on the same day that the respective West German and Soviet positions on reunification were clearly stated but that "we have our own ideas as to how the future German unity should be built up."[13]

In any event, Soviet opposition to reunification was not changed by his statements. Neither was Soviet insistence on the maintenance of the Oder-Neisse frontier. Even if Poland wanted to modify that frontier, which it did not, the Soviet Union would not allow any change since the existence of that frontier was in its own national interest. Chancellor Brandt honestly told German public opinion in his interview with the periodical *Publik* on November 12, 1971, that "after more than twenty-five years of separation and the very different constitutional, economic, legal and social developments [of each part] related to it, one may not bring the two parts [of Germany] together again as simply as was considered possible until the middle fifties. . . . Our population should be told the truth instead of having sand thrown in its eyes. . . . What we have done and what had at last to be done is to come nearer to the realities. The acknowledgment of the existence of two German states belongs to this approach." He alluded to Western reluctance to see a powerful and united Germany again by quoting the well-known anti-communist, Secretary of State John Foster Dulles, who had told him many years ago: "We may quarrel with the Russians regarding a hundred problems, but we are of the same opinion on the hundred and first problem: we shall not again give you the chance to march, united and rearmed, here and there between us two."[14]

MEMORANDUM ON THE WARSAW TREATY

The task of the government in defending the terms of the Warsaw Treaty was much more difficult than arguing in favor of the ratification of the Moscow Treaty. The former treaty pledged the FRG to abandon its former claims against the Oder-Neisse frontier. This was a bitter pill to swallow after many years of West German agitation for the revision of that frontier. The government tried to offer the narrowest possible interpretation of the treaty, leaving intact the right of a united Germany to question the validity of the frontier.

The governmental memorandum of December 13, 1971, on the Warsaw Treaty, submitted to the German parliament, began with these words: "The relations between Germans and Poles have been burdened, above all, by the Second World War. Poland was the first victim of the aggressive war unleashed by Hitler. The war and the national-socialist atrocities, and later the expulsion of the German population from its homeland in the Eastern provinces of the German Reich, have inflicted immeasurable sufferings on both peoples."[15]

The memorandum added that another problem divided the two peoples: "The frontier question unavoidably stood out as a pivotal problem in the negotiations. The agreement between the Federal Republic and the Polish People's Republic could not be reached without an understanding regarding this question. This is why we accepted the wish of the Polish government to deal in the first place in the Treaty with the frontier question. It [the Treaty] proceeded from a sober evaluation of the situation which arose from the consequences of the Second World War and the defeat of the German Reich."[16]

The memorandum insisted that the frontier question was not irrevocably settled in the Warsaw Treaty: "The Polish government signed the Treaty while knowing the legal reservations which the German side in the treaty negotiations constantly stressed regarding the frontier question."[17] These reservations amounted to saying that the treaty, signed only on behalf of the FRG, could bind neither a reunited Germany nor the four powers whose rights remained untouched regarding the final determination of German frontiers. The treaty did not replace the future peace treaty. In other words, the Warsaw Treaty closed the territorial question for the FRG, but left it open for a reunited Germany.

German insistence on the binding force of the treaty only for the FRG was visible in all governmental statements. It suffices to quote from the official governmental statement, made on January 17, 1972, regarding the Moscow and Warsaw Treaties: "The Treaties involve no disposal of German territories. The Federal government would not be empowered to do so since the responsibility of the four powers is reserved regarding Germany as a whole as long as there is no peace-treaty settlement for Germany. The Federal Republic of Germany is not empowered to dispose of those territories because of the reservations made by the three Western powers in the Treaty on Germany. The federal government did nothing more in the Warsaw Treaty than to cease questioning any longer the situation which had been created by the four powers and by factual developments."[18]

However, it was also necessary to appease Polish fears that this interpretation emptied the treaty of any significance. As we have seen, the Polish government interpreted the treaty in the opposite sense, namely that it closed the frontier question for ever. The memorandum of December 13, 1971, included the following sentence regarding the stand of a future reunited Germany: "The reunited Germany, which would declare the peaceful goal of German policy as its fundamental law, could not lose sight of the existing situation which is the point of departure for the German-Polish Treaty. It would have to take into consideration especially the attitude of the three [Western] powers."[19]

Thus, if the three Western powers insisted on the occasion of German reunification on the maintenance of the Oder-Neisse frontier, reunited Germany would have to confirm that frontier. This sentence curiously enough did not mention the fourth power, the Soviet Union, as though its own stand at the time of reunification would play no role. In any event, the statement overlooked an all-important aspect of reunification: would reunification take place within the present distribution of international power or in circumstances entirely different? If the distribution of power were changed radically, for instance because of a great weakening of the Soviet Union, would the Western powers be inclined to insist on the Oder-Neisse frontier as a condition for reunification, or would a powerful reunited Germany be inclined to listen to the other powers?

Chancellor Brandt, in his interview of November 12, 1971, with the periodical *Publik,* stated the reasons for the Federal Republic's abandoning its former opposition to the Oder-Neisse frontier: "We may speak only on behalf of the Federal Republic of Germany regarding the Oder-Neisse frontier, but anyone who knows the world must also know that the revisionist claim would result in nothing else but our isolation and/or a threat to European peace. . . . Moreover, how may one figure out a policy which would obtain the revision of the frontier by peaceful means (only such means may be envisaged) without support by anyone else?"[20]

German official sources insisted on such an interpretation as would mean that the FRG granted in the Warsaw Treaty only *de facto* recognition of existence of the Oder-Neisse frontier. The above-mentioned memorandum stated, for instance, that the recognition of that frontier as the actual Western Polish frontier "had no retroactive force," and that the treaty was so drafted that "the different viewpoints of both sides remain unchanged regarding the legal meaning of the Potsdam Agreement."[21] Thus the federal government rejected the Polish stand that the Potsdam Agreement had fixed definitely the Western Polish frontier. This amounted to saying that there was no legal foundation for the present Western Polish frontier since there was subsequently no other four-power agreement regarding the Polish frontier. The Warsaw Treaty in this interpretation only acknowledged the existing factual situation which had no legal foundation. This interpretation was to be confirmed in the Bundestag's resolution which all parties adopted in 1972 prior to the final vote on ratification of the Eastern treaties.

The government further weakened the Warsaw Treaty by the statement that the Moscow Treaty "did not exclude a peaceful and mutually agreed correction or modification of frontiers," and that the same treaty obligated the FRG only "not to modify the present factual situation by the threat or use of force."[22] If this was true of the Moscow Treaty, which pledged the FRG not to dispute the East German and

Polish frontiers, what did the Warsaw Treaty offer to Poland? The memorandum said that "the Federal Republic of Germany will henceforth no longer question the Oder-Neisse line as the Polish Western frontier. It does not condition its stand on when the peace-treaty settlement for Germany will take place."[23] In other words, the net Polish gain was the end of the official revisionist campaign by the FRG.

The memorandum contained another German reservation, namely, that the Warsaw Treaty did not mean that "we have retrospectively legitimized the expulsions."[24] Since the expulsions of East Germans were approved by the four powers, this statement challenged their right to do so. If the expulsions were illegitimate, did it mean that the federal government upheld the claims of the expellees to the right to return to their former homelands, as the previous German governments had done, or was it only a platonic declaration to appease the expellee organizations?

The federal government insisted on the importance of the counterpart of the Warsaw Treaty, the Polish unilateral "information" that Poland would allow the repatriation of Polish citizens of German nationality. It stressed the improvement which the "information" promised, because Warsaw consented to the departure of not only those Germans who had been allowed formerly to emigrate to the FRG because they had relatives there, but also of other Polish citizens who claimed to be Germans though they had no such relatives.[25] The Parliamentary State Secretary for Foreign Affairs, Karl Moersch, mentioned on February 6, 1972, that the Polish government allowed the repatriation of 26,000 Germans during the year 1971, a sort of anticipated payment for the not yet ratified Warsaw Treaty.[26] These repatriated Germans were immediately accepted as German citizens on their crossing the FRG frontier by virtue of existing German legislation. West German legislation, extending citizenship to all Germans who had been German citizens prior to the end of the Second World War, clashed with Polish legislation which conferred Polish citizenship on the prewar population still remaining in the formerly German territories annexed by Poland. This was another controversial issue between Bonn and Warsaw, although it remained without practical meaning as long as the FRG did not claim the right to protect Polish citizens of German nationality, whom it considered German citizens, until the moment of their crossing the West German frontier.

Chancellor Brandt stretched out his hand to the opposition on December 22, 1971, by proposing to adopt a joint Bundestag resolution on a mutually agreed interpretation of the Moscow and Warsaw Treaties.[27] This conciliatory gesture helped eventually to soften the opposition's stand and allowed for the ratification of both treaties after the adoption of such a resolution.

THE DEBATE IN THE BUNDESRAT

In February 1972 the great debate on the ratification of the Moscow and Warsaw Treaties began in the Bundesrat, the upper chamber of the German parliament, composed of representatives of governments of the eleven states (Länder) which together formed the Federal Republic. The debate was opened by the submission of reports by the committee on foreign relations and the committee on legal matters.[28] The majority of the latter committee (eight state governments out of the eleven) expressed the opinion that the two treaties were not contrary to the Constitution, in particular to its preamble on the reunification of Germany. This meant that the negative vote in the Bundesrat, where the opposition had a majority of one vote, would not require a two-third majority in the Bundestag, required for an amendment of the Constitution. Practically speaking, this opinion of the committee, supported by three Christian Democratic governments, allowed for ratification by a simple majority in the Bundestag. This indicated that the opposition did not want to shut the door and was perhaps ready to let the Bundestag assent to the ratification. If this were the case, the severe criticism of the treaties was not motivated by the desire to nullify them but rather was an appeal to the nationalist-minded portion of the electorate in order to overturn the Brandt-Scheel government in the next general election.

The minority of members of the committee argued that the treaties violated the Constitution whose preamble allegedly imposed on the FRG the duty to seek reunification within the 1937 frontiers. This interpretation of the Constitution, which, as a matter of fact, did not mention any frontiers, would preclude the conclusion of political agreements with the Soviet Union, Poland, and other states of the Soviet bloc. They never would have assented to the view that the 1937 frontiers were still legally valid. Moreover, the great coalition government already had abandoned the former view that Germany should be reunified within those frontiers.

The majority of the committee considered that the treaties did not contain any provisions contrary to the Constitution because it had been enacted a few years after the Potsdam Conference which placed the territories east of the Oder-Neisse Rivers under the Polish or Soviet administration. They interpreted the Constitution in the personal but not the territorial sense. The Constitution envisaged the reunification not of all the territories which had been part of the German Reich in 1937, but only of those territories where Germans now lived and presumably formed the majority of the population. Moreover, the majority of the committee argued that the treaties did not preclude the modification of frontiers by voluntary agreement of the states concerned. Finally, the FRG reserved the final settlement of the frontier question to the peace treaty, which a reunited Germany would negotiate with the four powers and other former enemies. This preserved for a united Germany the right to claim the 1937 frontiers even after the entry into force of the two treaties which left the problem of frontiers open.

The minority claimed that the Warsaw Treaty deprived the Germans still living in Poland of their German citizenship. The majority disagreed. Those Germans, although Polish citizens by virtue of Polish legislation, remained German citizens in the eyes of the FRG. However, they could invoke their German citizenship only after being repatriated to the FRG.

THE OPPOSITION'S ARGUMENTS

The debate developed along party lines. The government and its supporters adopted a defensive position, trying to refute the opposition's arguments by such a restrictive interpretation of the treaties as could meet the opposition half-way. It is necessary, therefore, to begin here with the arguments advanced by the opposition.

The five opposition state governments (the sixth government, that of Baden-Würtemberg, did not undersign the motion) deposed a motion which rejected the ratification of the two treaties, because they allegedly endangered the prospect of German reunification within one state by their acknowledgment of the existence of two German states and the promise to respect the frontier between the FRG and the GDR; because this acknowledgment would make possible the admission of both German states to the United Nations; because the treaties allegedly contained the final approval of the Oder-Neisse frontier and would have a binding force for a reunified Germany; because the Germans still living east of that frontier would be as a result deprived of their German citizenship and would, therefore, lose the right to be protected by the FRG; because the treaties allegedly contained the elements of a peace treaty and hence freed the four powers of their responsibility for Germany as a whole and released the three Western powers of their obligation to seek reunification within a democratic German state; because the four-power agreement on Berlin might be sabotaged by the GDR; because it was uncertain whether the USSR truly renounced its right to intervene by virtue of the enemy clause in the United Nations Charter; because the West German pledge to respect all European frontiers, including those in eastern and southeastern Europe, allegedly strengthened the Soviet hegemony in that part of Europe; because the treaties would not facilitate human contacts and exchange of ideas between Western Europe and the Soviet bloc; and, finally, because the treaties would serve as an argument for the American isolationists and would bring about a reduction of American forces stationed in Europe, and the weakening of NATO. Yet, the same motion paradoxically affirmed the wish of the opposition to reach an understanding with the Soviet Union and Poland, but an understanding which would be based on a mutual renunciation of the use of force and nothing else.[29]

The motion was couched in such demagogic terms that probably even its authors did not take it very seriously. But it appealed to the right wing of the electorate. Some of the arguments did not hold water. Others postulated, in effect, a radical change in the international distribution of power, since neither Poland nor the Soviet Union would have accepted otherwise the demands of the opposition. The motion left in the air the question as to how the FRG could bring about such a radical change in the world's balance of power. However, the opposition, having the numerical majority in the Bundesrat, was able to carry the motion by a majority of one vote. The final decision was left to the Bundestag.

The spokesmen for the opposition state governments advanced arguments in support of the motion which were couched in terms by far more moderate than the wording of the motion itself. It seemed that the opposition did not want to blow up the bridges to the government and left open the possibility of the ratification's being approved by the Bundestag. The representatives of the Christian Democratic governments did not deny that the rejection of the treaties would result in a deterioration in relations with the Soviet bloc although they expressed the hope that the negotiations could be resumed at a more propitious time. They tried to shift the responsibility for non-ratification to the government's shoulders, accusing it of having conducted the negotiations in undue haste and abandoning in the process the former fundamental premises of West German foreign policy. If the propitious time for the negotiations was not the time when the government signed the treaties, when would such a more favorable time come? The opposition claimed that this more propitious time would come when Western Europe formed a strong political union which would support the FRG in its negotiations with the Soviet Union and Poland (negotiating from the position of strength?), and when the Soviet-Chinese quarrel forced the Soviet Union to make concessions to the West. In the meantime, the FRG should only widen its non-political contacts with the Soviet bloc in order to build that bloc's trust in peaceful West German intentions and thus prepare the ground for better treaties than those now under consideration.

This waiting for a more propitious time characterized Adenauer's era, but the twenty-three years that had elapsed since the foundation of the FRG had not brought the expected more favorable time for a settlement with the Soviet bloc. Of course, the FRG could have waited for another twenty-three years, but there were no signs on the international horizon that promised a change of circumstances for the better.

What were the defects in the treaties which the opposition pointed out as the reason for their voting against their ratification? The spokesmen for the opposition state governments maintained that the terms of the treaties were unclear and would lead to different interpretations by the contracting parties. For instance, the government insisted that the obligation to respect the Oder-Neisse frontier did not bind the four powers or a future united Germany, while the Polish government claimed that the Warsaw Treaty confirmed the finality of that frontier. The opposition speakers mentioned, as an example, a statement made by the Polish Vice-Minister for Foreign Affairs and the negotiator of the Warsaw Treaty, Józef Winiewicz, who said in November 1970 in Bonn that the Warsaw Treaty would prevent everyone now and in the future from reopening the frontier question.[30]

However, the opposition did not claim that a united Germany should recover the 1937 frontiers. They admitted that improvement in relations with the Soviet Union and Poland, which they also desired, would demand concessions and sacrifices on the part of the Germans, and that no perfect solution was to be expected.[40] They probably remembered that their own political colleague, the former Chancellor Kurt Kiesinger, had said a few years earlier that he was ready to discuss a compromise territorial settlement with Poland even prior to the conclusion of a peace treaty.

The uncompromising stand was defended only by Alfons Goppel, Prime Minister of Bavaria. He represented the right wing of the opposition, the Christian-Social Union with its Bavarian stronghold. He insisted on the necessity to uphold the claim to the 1937 frontiers, including East Prussia. The revindication of East Prussia, of course, sounded pleasantly in the ears of the expellee organizations whom the Bavarian Prime Minister certainly had in mind. His stand differed even from that of previous Christian Democratic federal governments which usually bypassed that particular problem, because otherwise they would have questioned not only Polish annexation of the southern part of that province but also Soviet annexation of its northern part. The former federal governments usually restricted their territorial quarrel to Poland and its annexation of former German territories east of the Oder-Neisse. Moreover, Goppel overlooked the American-British promise, made at Potsdam, that the two powers would support the Soviet annexation of the Koenigsberg area at the time of a peace conference on Germany. To Goppel the two treaties involved "a concealed recognition of [present] German frontiers."[31]

Another Bavarian representative, Minister Franz Heubl, was also alone in reproaching the government for its failure to reach a bilateral agreement with Poland on the grant to Germans still residing in Poland of minority rights, such as the right to German schools and free cultural activities.[32] His colleagues in the opposition did not mention this revindication, perhaps because they realized that Poland would never agree.

The opposition spokesmen strongly disapproved the recognition of the GDR as another German state and the federal government's assent to its admission to the United Nations. They did not believe that the government's subtle distinction between recognition by international and by constitutional law (as a foreign state or a state of the same nation) would be understood by foreign politicians and lawyers. They warned that, in spite of West German legal reservations, recognition of the GDR as another German state would open the gate to recognition by other states, including the Western allies, who had refrained from such recognition so far only out of friendship for the FRG. This assertion proved to be true since the United States, Britain, and France decided in 1973 to establish regular diplomatic relations with the GDR.

The opposition also claimed that the conclusion of the Eastern treaties by the FRG could be interpreted by such American politicians as Senators Fulbright and Mansfield as an argument for the reduction of American troops stationed in Germany, and this in turn would weaken West German security.

The opposition did not contest that the four-power agreement would improve the situation of West Berlin, but expressed their regret that this agreement did not state that West Berlin was a component part of the FRG. What they knowingly overlooked was the consistent policy of the three Western powers which always had refused to treat West Berlin as another state of the FRG. The only novelty was the confirmation of their stand in an agreement with the Soviet Union.

In spite of their disagreement with the government on the Eastern treaties, the spokesmen of the opposition, including even the representative of the Bavarian state government, promised that their parties would abide by the principle of *"pacta sunt servanda"* in case the treaties were duly ratified. This was an important reassurance for the Soviet Union and Poland. They did not need to fear that a Christian Democratic federal government would denounce the treaties or would refuse to abide by their terms.[33]

The shared apprehension of the governmental and opposition parties was the fear that the debate on the treaties might split German public opinion into two mutually hostile camps for a long time to come and would preclude a bipartisan foreign policy. This grim prospect did not look improbable at that time because not only the parties but also the public were at loggerheads in the hot debate on the merits and demerits of the treaties. At a conference held in 1970, this author heard one of the leaders of the Bavarian C.S.U., Baron von und zu Guttenberg, predicting a sharp and long-term division of the German nation, reminding him of the similar division of the French nation at the time of the Dreyfus affair. Fortunately this somber forecast proved false. However, the durable split might not have been avoided if the treaties had been rejected and a bitter debate in the FRG had continued with increased bitterness. In that case, the Soviet Union would not have been the loser, in spite of the rejection of the treaties. It would have benefitted anyhow from the weakening of the FRG, whose foreign policy could not then have relied on support by at least half of the German population.

MINISTER POSSER'S COLD SHOWER

The important issue dividing the opposition from the government turned on whether the government should have waited for a more propitious time; in other words, did it make concessions to the Soviet Union and Poland which could be avoided later on? Dr. Diether Posser, Minister in the Nordrhein-Westfallen government, responded to this question by drawing the balance-sheet of the foreign policy of the FRG in its attempts to deal with three consequences of the Second World War: (1) the presence of the Soviet army on the Rivers Elbe and Werra in the middle of Germany; (2) the emergence of the GDR and of West Berlin as an entity which was not a part of either of the two German states; and (3) the fate of East German territories from which millions of Germans had fled or had been expelled.[34] He recalled that for a few years in the fifties it seemed that these problems would soon be solved to the FRG's entire satisfaction. In 1947 the American government proclaimed its containment policy, which rested on the assumption that the Soviet Union, already greatly weakened by the Second World War and encircled by American containment, would lose heart and become ready to make concessions. This expectation failed to materialize. The slogan launched in 1952 by the Republican party of a "roll-back" of the Soviet Union to its 1939 frontiers and of "liberation" of Eastern Europe, proved to have been only an electoral slogan. The then Secretary of State, John Foster Dulles, intended, however, to bring about an anti-Soviet revolutionary situation in Eastern Europe by waging psychological warfare in support of anti-Soviet trends among the East European populations. He assigned an important role to the FRG in 1950. He wrote in his book, *War or Peace,* that the FRG could attract the population of the GDR and thus win a crucial strategic position in Central Europe. The result would be the undermining of Soviet influence in Poland, Czechoslovakia, and Hungary.

This American strategy, Posser continued, was supported by Adenauer who hoped to roll back the Soviet Union to its 1939 frontiers. What Adenauer wanted to achieve was not only to unite the GDR with the FRG but also to force the Soviet Union to abandon the whole of Eastern Europe. The argument which seemed to justify this kind of expectation was that of American nuclear strength. That argument lost its meaning, however, at the time when the Soviet Union achieved the capacity for a devastating second strike and the American national territory lost its former invulnerability. Posser quoted what de Gaulle had said in 1965, that the policy of negotiating from a position of strength "was only a dream."

After the FRG had joined NATO, the Soviet government declared that reunification was a problem to be solved by Germans themselves, *i.e.,* by negotiations between the FRG and the GDR. The Adenauer government rejected that view, invoking its claim to speak for all Germans and asking for free elections in East Germany.

Posser further mentioned Adenauer's refusal to listen to Dulles's advice that he should seriously examine the Soviet proposal made in January 1959 to build a confederation of both German states as a first step toward reunification. The negative German policy found its expression in the Hallstein doctrine which threatened to break off relations with any state that recognized the GDR. This doctrine, according to Posser, did not prevent several states from establishing normal relations with the GDR. Finally, the FRG had to abandon the doctrine. After the erection of the wall in the midst of divided Berlin in August 1961, President Kennedy sent General Clay as his emissary. Clay advised the Adenauer government to open negotiations with the GDR. Adenauer rejected this advice. The foreign policy of the FRG continued to deviate from the modified American policy. President Kennedy indicated the American intention to reach a peaceful coexistence with the Soviet Union in his speech of June 10, 1963. On December 17, 1963, President Johnson formulated even more clearly this intention to terminate the cold war. Finally, President Nixon spoke of substituting negotiations for confrontation.

This review of American and West German policies was used by Posser as proof of the thesis that the FRG at first followed the erroneous American policy, but then deviated from the new American outlook by continuing to abide by the "cold war" pattern, already abandoned by the United States. The FRG began to be threatened by international isolation because of its refusal to acknowledge the existence of the GDR and its opinion that reunification was the precondition for the reduction of tensions in Europe, while its Western allies adopted the new view that only the relaxation of tension would make German reunification possible.

Posser further said that in the meantime, a growing number of West Germans started to realize that time was not working for them. The military presence of the Soviet Union in the GDR was if anything strengthened, the GDR was consolidated, while millions of Poles were resettled in the former East German territories. This is why the Brandt-Scheel government decided to take into consideration the international situation as it was, not as the Germans would have liked it to be. This new outlook led to acknowledgment of the existence of the GDR as another German state and the abandonment of former claims against the Oder-Neisse frontier.

Posser argued that the federal government did not and could not renounce its alleged right to the Oder-Neisse territories since the FRG had no common frontier with Poland. It could only reserve the decision on their future fate to the peace treaty. He continued: "The Federal Republic abandoned in the Warsaw Treaty, it is true, its former legal point of view that the Oder-Neisse territories continued to be German and were only administered by the Polish People's Republic." He recalled the Potsdam decision, by virtue of which the Soviet Union got the American and British promise to support its annexation of the Koenigsberg area at a peace conference. At the same time the three powers placed the other German territories east of the Oder-Neisse line, including the former Free City of Danzig, under Polish administration, while excluding these territories from the Soviet zone of occupation and from the jurisdiction of the Allied Control Council. The Soviet Union and Poland interpreted that decision as meaning that the Potsdam Conference had allocated irrevocably to Poland the former German territories east of Oder-Neisse, reserving for the peace conference only the final demarcation of the frontier. Posser added:

The protests by the Western powers against the Polish annexation were becoming each year weaker and finally were silenced. This attitude was decisively influenced by the fact that the Allies had intended, as the results of the Teheran, Yalta and Potsdam conferences prove, not to give back to Germany the Oder-Neisse territories after the termination of Polish administration, but to adjudicate, *i.e.*, to allocate them to Poland. The Western powers not only did not protest against the expulsion of millions of Germans from their homeland but, to the contrary, reached an understanding with the Polish authorities on particulars of transportation and offered the means of transportation. They did not protest against the settlement of Poles in the German Eastern provinces. Nothing speaks for the thesis that the Western powers regarded the expulsion of Germans as something temporary. Today millions of Poles live in the expulsion territories, of whom a large part were born there and consider that land as their homeland. The wrong of the German expulsion cannot and may not be followed by the wrong of a new expulsion. There is no statement of intention, not to mention a guarantee, on the part of the Allies to reestablish Germany within the 1937 frontiers. Moreover, Western politicians of all [political] orientations in growing numbers have been declaring during the last fifteen years that the Oder-Neisse line is the Polish Western frontier. For instance, de Gaulle stressed many times since 1959, the last time on the occasion of his visit to Poland, the final nature of that frontier. We all desire a stronger cooperation with the European countries. This cooperation, including within the E.E.C., cannot be realized if the Federal Republic continues to claim as German the territories which even allied governments consider an integral part of the Polish state. . . . A modification of the territorial situation would be conceivable only by war which we all abhor and which would bring about our ruin. Bertolt Brecht has warned us: "The great Carthage waged three wars. It remained still powerful after the first and still habitable after the second. It could no longer be found after the third war."

After this cold shower administered to his political opponents, Posser did not deny that the Moscow Treaty contained more concessions by the FRG than by the USSR, but reminded the Bundesrat that the FRG was only a part of the defeated former German Reich, while the Soviet Union was one of the victorious great powers. It was not the Soviet Union which had broken the German-Soviet treaties, concluded in 1922 in Rapallo and in 1926 in Berlin, as well as the 1939 non-aggression pact. But it was the Soviet Union which suffered the most during the war unleashed by Germany in violation of those three treaties. It lost more than twenty million of its citizens, more than the combined population of five states of the Federal Republic (Niedersachsen, Hessen, Rheinland-Pfalz, Saarland, and Bremen). This left behind a deep Soviet distrust of German good faith. Yet the Soviet Union made two concessions in the Moscow Treaty: the unconditional renunciation of force, including the right to intervene by virtue of the enemy clause in the United Nations Charter, and Soviet assent to a compromise solution of the problem of West Berlin.

OTHER PRO-GOVERNMENT SPEAKERS

Posser was outspoken both in his criticism of foreign policies of former federal governments and in his realistic outline of the limits within which the FRG could move in foreign affairs. This was helpful to the government, because Posser's speech could swing a large portion of public opinion to its side. The spokesmen of the government, Brandt and Scheel, could not afford to use the same blunt language since they still hoped to persuade the opposition to vote in favor of the treaties, if not in the Bundesrat, then in the Bundestag. They interpreted the two treaties in a way which would appease the opposition critics.

Other spokesmen for the state governments supporting the federal government did not add much to what Posser said. Hans Koschnick, President of the Bremen Senate, pertinently observed that reconciliation with the Soviet Union and Poland, as well as with Israel, was a task much more difficult than reconciliation with the Western countries, because "I do not know whether I should have the courage now to reach an understanding with the Federal Republic of Germany were I a Russian, an Israeli, or a Pole."[35] He was one of those Germans who remembered the Nazi horrors, which the Russians, the Israelis, and the Poles could not easily forget.

The Mayor of West Berlin, Klaus Schütz, who could not cast a vote since the Western powers denied to West Berlin the right to consider itself a constituent part of the FRG, insisted on the importance of the four-power agreement which he considered very beneficial for the population of his city. He advocated the ratification of the treaties as the only way to ensure the entry into force of that agreement.[36]

BRANDT'S AND SCHEEL'S SPEECHES

Chancellor Brandt was one of the two spokesmen of the federal government, Foreign Minister Scheel being the other. Brandt frankly admitted:

A decisive difference between [the policies] of former federal governments, including the one in which I was the Foreign Minister, consists in the fact that we acknowledged in October 1969 the existence of two states on German soil without retrospectively recognizing the division of Germany. I stress in this respect that we could not engage otherwise in an earnest dialog with the states of the Warsaw Pact. There is no state in the world, in any event I do not know of any such state, which shows any tendency to support [the claims to] the 1937 frontiers in a settlement of the German question. . . . It should be made completely clear that the frontiers mentioned in the Moscow Treaty were not recognized, as one [the opposition] maintains, but that it was stated that frontiers should not be encroached upon, that they were inviolable. The statement that no territorial claims would be made . . . neither excludes a free agreement of the concerned on the changing or lifting up of frontiers now existing, nor precludes the carrying out of the German people's right to self-determination. . . . Also Article One of the Warsaw Treaty did not establish any frontier, but the Federal Republic simply declared therein that it would not question any longer the Polish Western frontier. . . . The attitude of the international community regarding the German-Polish frontiers is well known. . . . He who wants to burden the ship of German unity with the load of old frontiers must realize that this ship would never reach the harbor. . . . Our policy must be free of illusions. . . . There is no short road toward German unity. . . . I am still waiting for . . . a true alternative [to his own Eastern policy]. Many critics seem to think that we still should have waited. . . . However, a simple waiting and the repetition of maximal demands are not a successful policy. The others do not wait. We, the Federal Republic and the German people, would fall under the wheels if we did not move ourselves. We would be isolated even among our Western friends, if we did not move in order to protect our interests within the limits of present possibilities.[37]

Brandt's statement that the treaties did not exclude the possibility of changing frontiers by mutual agreement of states concerned probably referred to the inter-German frontier, but could be interpreted by the Poles as applicable also to the Polish frontier.

Foreign Minister Scheel said:

The debate over the East-West policy of the federal government and on the treaties has often developed as though the new ordering of European relations depended on us, on us alone, and as though the international environment moved exclusively according to what we see as our legal position. However, this is not so, because we live and must live in a world which is continuously changing. . . . Since that dramatic [Cuban] crisis the world in the East and in the West has been moving toward what one may call "peaceful coexistence". . . . Should we have waited until such time as other European countries had agreed on the nature of West-Eastern relations over our heads or by bypassing us? This question is addressed to those among us who think that, twenty-five years after the breakdown [of Germany], the moment for negotiations with the East has not yet come. Of course, if the federal government had remained immobile and continued to wait for a favorable time for negotiations, the price would have been simply completion of isolation in the East by the isolation in the West. . . . The Federal Republic of Germany would become an anachronistic island in Europe. . . . Where would the Federal Republic find itself today in the changed East-Western constellation, if it were the only European country to face hostile confrontation with the Soviet Union?[38]

After this justification of the treaties by international circumstances unfavorable to the FRG, Scheel proceeded with his interpretation of the treaties:

> We have not granted a recognition, valid in international law, of the existing frontiers. . . . The Warsaw Treaty has not fulfilled and could not fulfill the original Polish demands and expectations. This is true in particular regarding the reservation of the peace treaty. . . . The treaties do not mention anywhere the recognition [of frontiers]. . . . It was simply said in the Moscow Treaty that the frontiers should not be infringed upon and that they were inviolable; this excludes forcible actions. Also the statement that no territorial claims should be raised . . . excludes neither a free decision of the concerned to agree on a modification or on the lifting up of frontiers nor the exercise by the German people of the right to self-determination. . . . The Warsaw Treaty cannot be called a frontier treaty or be compared to the peace treaty. Article One of this treaty establishes no frontiers. Taking into consideration the existing situation, the Federal Republic of Germany declares only that it will no longer question the Polish Western frontier as it is. The decision of the all-German sovereign [state], therefore, continues to be unprejudiced. . . . It is true that the attitudes of the Polish and the federal governments are not the same regarding the legal meaning of the frontier provision. . . . The Federal Republic of Germany speaks [in the Warsaw Treaty] only for itself and for no one else. . . . It could not decide on frontiers which lie beyond the limits of its own sovereignty.[39]

This interpretation of the Warsaw Treaty could raise in Polish minds the question of what that treaty offered to Poland. If it did not mean the recognition of the Oder-Neisse frontier, even only on behalf of the Federal Republic, as Scheel claimed, and if it meant that the FRG renounced only the use of force for changing that frontier, the Poles could respond that they did not fear any forcible action on the part of the FRG which was separated from Poland by the whole breadth of the GDR and by many Soviet divisions stationed on East German soil. They could find comfort only in that Scheel did not deny that the FRG was foreclosed by the treaty from officially waging a revisionist campaign, as it had done prior to the conclusion of the two Eastern treaties.

Scheel further mentioned the acceptance by the Polish side on November 14, 1970, of the statement made by the West German delegation that the treaty would not cause any person to lose his rights guaranteed by German legislation, *i.e.*, the German citizenship of Germans still residing in Poland, and the property rights of the expellees. What he meant was the right of expellees to West German reparations for their lost property, which reparations had been granted by West German legislation.

Scheel mentioned also the first improvements in relations with the Soviet Union and Poland: the conclusion with the USSR of an agreement on civil air transportation, the erection of consulates in Leningrad and Hamburg, the mutual decision to increase economic and scientific cooperation, and the Polish repatriation of 25,000 Germans to the FRG in the year 1971.

These appeasing speeches by Brandt and Scheel did not convince the opposition state governments which, as we have seen, carried their negative motion. This closed the debate in the Bundesrat and shifted the discussion to the Bundestag which had to say the last word.

THE FEBRUARY DEBATE IN THE BUNDESTAG

The Bundestag debate over the treaties took place during the two sessions of February and May 1972. Every Bundestag deputy was aware of the importance of that debate. The FRG faced for the second time a decisive turn in its foreign policy. The first debate of equal importance took place in the early fifties when Adenauer's government decided to defer to American wishes and to rearm West Germany and let it join the North Atlantic Alliance. The Social Democrats opposed his policy, fearing that it would alienate the Soviet Union and provoke it to veto reunification forever. Adenauer prevailed, and the Social Democrats eventually accepted the FRG's participation in the Western alliance.

This time the parties were divided over whether bridges to the Soviet Union and Eastern Europe should be built on the terms specified in the two treaties. The importance of the debate was heightened by the fact that all West Germans could follow the debate in the Bundestag either on the radio or on television and could ponder the arguments for or against the treaties. The Bundestag speakers were aware that their pronouncements would influence the attitudes of the electorate in the next elections.

Numerous speakers both for the government and the opposition stressed the vital importance of the debate. The Speaker of the Bundestag, Kai-Uwe von Hassel, opened the February debate by stating that "we all know that we shall discuss in the coming days problems and questions which our people has only seldom faced in its history."[40] Foreign Minister Walter Scheel agreed: "This is a great hour for our parliament and our state. . . . The manner and style in which we are going to debate will have significance also for the future of our country. Do we want to conduct this debate in such a way that national division would result in creating a domestic gulf within the Federal Republic? Should the acceptance of the treaties, possibly by a small majority, result in the continuation of the struggle against the treaties, and should the chances offered by them be smothered?"[41]

Former Chancellor Kurt Kiesinger admitted the same on behalf of the opposition: "This is in fact one of the most important, possibly the most important, decision that the Bundestag has had to take since the beginning of its existence."[42] Two other speakers for the opposition, Werner Marx and Franz-Joseph Strauss, said the same. Marx mentioned "the deep gulf torn open by this [Brandt's] policy in this house and outside within the [German] people."[43] Strauss drew attention to Soviet interest in the split within German public opinion: "Brezhnev said at the 24th Party Congress in Moscow that the consequence of these treaties was the polarization of political forces in the Federal Republic."[44] What Brezhnev said was true. The rejection of the treaties would have polarized West German public opinion for years to come. But Strauss did not mention the particular responsibility of the opposition in this respect.

This specter of a permanent division of German public opinion played a somewhat lesser role in the February debate. After all, the government still possessed a slim majority in the Bundestag and seemed able to carry out the approval of the treaties. The opposition could then criticize the government in the next elections without denying the binding force of ratified treaties. It could avoid sharing with the government the responsibility for the treaties without ruining Brandt's Eastern policy. The situation was altogether different during the second debate in May 1972. The government had lost its majority in the meantime. The Bundestag was numerically equally divided between pro-governmental and opposition deputies. In other words, the opposition could easily prevent ratification by its negative vote. This change in the parliamentary situation forced the opposition to face a troublesome fact: it had to assume direct responsibility for ratification or nonratification. As we shall see, the opposition, once confronted with its own responsibility, decided finally to abstain and let the governmental half of the Bundestag assent to the treaties. It was no longer a question of making electoral calculations, but of making a most vital decision about the foreign policy of the country.

The parliamentary debate in February turned around the following main topics: the problem of German reunification and the related question of the attitude to take regarding the GDR; the link, made by both Chancellor Brandt and the Soviet government, between the entry into force of the four-power agreement on Berlin and the ratification of the Moscow and Warsaw Treaties; and the Oder-Neisse frontier. The opposition made an easy game of quoting profusely former statements made in the fifties and early sixties by the Social Democratic and Free Democratic leaders to the effect that they would never recognize the GDR as a state or accept the Oder-Neisse frontier. The spokesmen for these two parties could only reply that they could no longer abide by their former views, which the lapse of twenty-seven years since the end of the Second World War had proved to be unrealistic.

THE OPPOSITION'S ARGUMENTS

The opposition held the treaties to be highly unsatisfactory. The Soviet Union and Poland allegedly got everything they wanted without making any worthwhile concessions to the FRG. This result was due to the inconsiderate haste of the government in negotiating the treaties and in choosing the wrong time for coming to terms with these two countries. The government should have waited for a more propitious time, which would come due to changes which the opposition expected to take place in international circumstances. The spokesmen for the opposition pointed out the following future changes which would force the Soviet Union to be more accommodating: the allegedly growing strength of the North Atlantic Alliance, the future political and military union of Western Europe, and the consequences of the Soviet-Chinese quarrel. All this would allegedly compel the USSR to make concessions to the FRG which it did not make in the present treaties. This amounted to saying that the FRG should wait for a better time when it would be able to negotiate from a position of strength. The opposition's alternative to Brandt's Eastern policy consisted in rejection of the treaties and waiting for that better time. However, it was ready to develop economic, scientific, and technological cooperation with the USSR and Eastern Europe in spite of its negative attitude toward the treaties.

Rainer Barzel reproached the government on grounds that it departed from the premises of former foreign policy of the FRG while having only a slim parliamentary majority. He defined the stand of the opposition with two words: "So nicht!", *i.e.,* nay to the present treaties but willingness to negotiate better treaties instead in international circumstances more favorable for the FRG.[45]

THE GDR

Why is it that the opposition refused to approve the treaties? First of all, it did not agree with the government's recognition of the GDR as another German state, which, it believed, would make future reunification within one democratic German state more difficult. They opposed Brandt's view that the main concern should be the safeguarding of the feeling among all Germans, including the Eastern ones, of belonging to the same German nation. For them the main goal should be reunification within one state. However, Rainer Barzel did not deny that the prospect for such reunification was distant to say the least. Barzel said: "We do not want to make claims that we have sovereign rights in the other part of Germany. . . . We understand by the settlement of the German problem neither annexation nor incorporation of the GDR but a historical process which will culminate in the implementation of the right to self-determination. Indeed, everyone must say that no one today may foresee the particular stages of that process."[46] This did not differ from the government's view, except that the latter considered the recognition of the GDR as a means to accelerate the process or at least prevent the appearance of two different national consciousnesses in West and East Germany. Another opposition spokesman, Richard von Weizsäcker, doubted that recognition of the GDR would help in preserving the unity of the nation and pointed out the statements of Erich Honecker, the First Secretary of the East German Communist Party, to the effect that there were already two mutually opposed German nations, one socialist in the GDR and another "bourgeois" in the FRG.[47]

A SPEECH BY F.-J. STRAUSS

It is worthwhile to mention here the speech by the leader of the Bavarian CSU, Franz-Joseph Strauss. He exerted a great influence on the attitudes of the whole Christian Democratic opposition. Moreover, he would be an important member of a future Christian Democratic government. Strauss, although an opponent of the Eastern treaties, did not speak in such extreme tones as his political friends from the CSU or his admirers, deputies representing the expellee organizations. He agreed with Brandt that "we know that a war for which one bears the guilt and which was lost must be paid for."[48] However, he deduced a very different conclusion: "After what had been done by the German side in destroying the right of self-determination in Middle Europe, in the area [located] between the then Soviet Union and the then German Reich, and after what had happened in oppressing human freedom in the same area, every German policy must legitimize its justification by its contribution to the restoration of the right of nations to self-determination and of human freedom in that area, however much such a policy might be inconvenient and not always and not unconditionally attractive in the eyes of our allies." What he suggested went far beyond what any other Bundestag deputy said. He did not limit himself, as they did, to vindicate the right of self-determination and individual freedoms only for Germans. He appeared in the role of an apostle for the liberation of Eastern Europe from Soviet influence and from their Communist regimes. This reminded one of John Foster Dulles' electoral slogans of rolling back Communism to the Soviet frontiers, a slogan that had long been forgotten by the United States. He did not specify how the FRG, a relatively weak state by comparison to the Soviet Union, could possibly conduct that policy of liberation. Yet he was a practical politician with a nation-wide influence. His stand amounted in practice to refusal to deal with the Soviet Union and the Eastern European Communist governments, which he probably did not seriously mean. That part of his speech was sheer demagogy.

What he really had in mind regarding the Eastern policy was opposition to the treaties and an alternative to be found in waiting for more favorable international circumstances. He expected the change to come because of what he considered the end of a bipolar world and the emergence of a multipolar pattern of international politics. He mentioned China, Japan, and Western Europe as the other three pillars in the new distribution of power. This five-power balance of forces was to result in a condition in which the FRG could extract concessions from the Soviet Union. Therefore, he proposed in effect inaction in the East but an active policy in the West: the strengthening of the North Atlantic Alliance and the building of a political and military union of Western Europe. Insofar as the East was concerned, he proposed the conclusion of agreements on the renunciation of force with the Soviet-bloc countries without the recognition of their territorial possessions, and an economic, scientific, and technological cooperation. All this amounted to the advocacy of a return to Dulles's and Adenauer's concept of negotiating with the Soviet Union from a position of strength, a policy abandoned by the German Western allies.

Strauss seemed at times to depart from this hard line in the same speech. Talking about the Chinese factor, which his political colleagues mentioned as a means to force the Soviet Union eventually to take a more accommodating attitude, he said: "No one believes or thinks that it is possible for Germany to play Moscow and China against each other and to make the Russian bear ready for compromise by using the Chinese stick. . . . This would be stupid. . . . There cannot be a Far Eastern policy as a substitute for the Eastern policy or as an excuse for having no Eastern policy, but the consideration of the existence of a big neighbor on the other frontier of our big partner should have its place in our calculations regarding the whole game of [international] forces." How would or could any federal government deduce a practical policy regarding the USSR and China from these contradictory statements?

He was more accommodating regarding the Oder-Neisse frontier than his political friends in the expellee organizations. He did not mention the 1937 frontiers, but said, "I do not belong to the country of Utopia and am not a devotee of the idea that, in case of a peace conference, at which the German state represented by a legitimate German government would participate as an equal partner, the others would ask us where we would want the German Eastern frontier to be . . . , and that they would defer to our wishes. I do not belong to those Utopians."

His politically rather incoherent speech, which did not offer a practical alternative to Brandt's Eastern policy and which contained a good dose of wishful thinking, ended by the sober admission that the ratification and rejection of the treaties were two evils between which one had to choose. He chose what he called a lesser evil, the vote against the treaties, while conceding that non-ratification would bring about "new tough strains and problems."

Strauss, strangely enough, quoted Hegel's statement which could very well be applied to his own political arguments: "Hegel maintained in his lectures on the philosophy of history that . . . peoples and governments never learned from history and never acted in accordance with the lessons which they should have deduced from history."

Neither Strauss nor the other leaders of the opposition contested the value of the four-power agreement on Berlin. The only exception was Kurt Kiesinger, who regretted that the agreement did not recognize West Berlin as an integral part of the FRG.[49] He was joined by only one opposition backbencher, Franz Amhern, who deplored the fact that the three Western powers confirmed their traditional view regarding West Berlin not being a part of the FRG in an international agreement concluded with the Soviet Union.[50] But the opposition conveniently disregarded the link which the Soviet Union made between the entry into force of the four-power agreement and the ratification of the Eastern treaties.

REUNIFICATION

The accusation that West German recognition of the GDR as another German state would hinder progress toward reunification was buttressed by criticism of Brandt's willingness to see both German states simultaneously admitted to the United Nations. The opposition spokesmen said that third states would disregard Brandt's subtle distinction between the recognition of the GDR as another German state and as a foreign state, especially after the admission of the GDR to the United Nations, all of whose members were considered sovereign. Gerhard Schröder formulated this argument as follows: "What will the consequences be if both parts of Germany become members of the United Nations? What will the consequences be following world-wide recognition of the GDR under the terms of international law? What will the situation be when our partners in the Treaty on Germany, when France, Great Britain, and the United States of America, erect their embassies in East Berlin?"[51] Schröder was not a false prophet. All this happened after the admission of the FRG and the GDR to the United Nations. The subtle legal distinction made by Brandt was simply beyond the limits of the political understanding of the third states.

The opposition did not pretend that reunification was a simple or easily solvable problem. Richard von Weizsäcker, for instance, admitted that the European peoples did not wish "to let arise in the middle of the otherwise weak Central Europe a new and fully sovereign German national state with eighty million inhabitants and with the total [potential] of both economic capacities, each of which is the second strongest within its respective alliance."[52] He knew that this was true not only of the Soviet Union and its allies but also of the West European allies of the FRG.

THE ODER-NEISSE FRONTIER

The recognition of the GDR as another German state and the admission by implication that Germany was to remain divided were hard pills to swallow, but at least Eastern Germany remained under the control of a German though Communist government. No European state raised any claim to the territories of the FRG and the GDR. It was much harder for the opposition to accept that the former Eastern German provinces were to be treated as parts of Poland, perhaps forever. This issue was painful for the whole Bundestag though the government interpreted the treaties as leaving a free hand to a united Germany in reopening the territorial issue. Yet, as we have seen, even Strauss doubted that a peace conference, if it were to be convoked, would defer to German wishes for the revision of the Oder-Neisse frontier.

Former Chancellor Kurt Kiesinger was so much carried away by his criticism of the territorial provisions of both treaties that he unwittingly advanced an argument which could be used by the Soviet Union and Poland in favor of their thesis that the territorial problem was settled once for all. While the government argued that the word "inviolability" of frontiers did not mean that they were irreversible, Kiesinger maintained the opposite interpretation by invoking the meaning of "inviolability" in the Locarno Treaty of 1925. He said that this word meant that Germany accepted its frontiers with France and Belgium as irreversible, which was true. He added that the then Foreign Minister, Gustav Stresemann, for this very reason refused to conclude similar treaties with Poland and Czechoslovakia because he wanted to keep Eastern German frontiers open to revision.[53]

Kiesinger's colleague, Gerhard Schröder, quoted the Polish interpretation of the Warsaw Treaty as meaning German acceptance of the finality of the Oder-Neisse frontier. He adduced, for instance, Gomułka's statement, made on December 3rd, 1970: "The Federal Republic of Germany recognizes in this [Warsaw] Treaty the final character of our Oder-Neisse western frontier."[54]

Another Christian Democratic leader, Werner Marx, pointed out, not without reason, that the government's restricted interpretation of that treaty would force the Poles to become fierce opponents of German reunification: "If I should say, for instance, that the present and all future federal governments would be bound by the statement regarding the Oder-Neisse line as being the Polish western frontier, and that this attitude would be changed for the first time when we shall have an all-German sovereign [state], then I might visualize that Pole who would deduce for himself a politically sensible and correct conclusion that he should worry if such an all-German sovereign [state] were to appear."[55] One could answer him that the Poles not only might worry about the distant and uncertain prospect of a reunified Germany, but had been worried since the foundation of the FRG because of its official revisionist policy. The Warsaw Treaty was to stop this policy.

Marx, like several of his colleagues, mentioned the Soviet and Polish interpretations that the territorial problem was solved for good by the two treaties and asked the government which denied the validity of those interpretations: "Are the frontiers now [still] open, or is the frontier problem settled?"[56] Rainer Barzel added that it would be a different matter if the two treaties stated clearly that they only described the existing frontiers as a temporary *modus vivendi* and made the explicit reservation that the frontier problem was not finally settled.[57]

However, none of the leaders of the opposition, including Strauss, claimed that a united Germany should recover the 1937 frontiers. Such a claim figured only in speeches made by the nationalist right wing deputies, for instance Heinrich Windelen (CSU), who indignantly exclaimed, "The Chancellor signed on December 7th, 1970, in Warsaw a Treaty whose crux consists in the statement that the Oder-Neisse line represents the Western state frontier of the Polish People's Republic. Ladies and gentlemen, East Prussia, Pomerania, East Brandenburg, Upper Silesia and [Lower] Silesia . . . will have to be regarded following the entry into force of that Treaty . . . no longer as the [German] inland but as the territory of another state."[58] His enumeration of all the lost provinces implied that he disagreed with the other opposition leaders and upheld the claim to the 1937 frontiers. It was not even certain that he would be satisfied with those frontiers since he traced back the initial reason for the German-Polish quarrel to the Versailles Treaty with its German-Polish frontier which was unfair in his opinion. He saw the other reason for that quarrel in the alleged Polish mistreatment of the German minority during the interwar period. These were exactly the two reasons invoked by Hitler for justification of his armed attack on Poland on September 1, 1939.

He did not deny the fact of atrocities committed by Germans during the wartime occupation of Poland, but dismissed them rather lightly by saying that the Poles also committed crimes against the Germans. He claimed on the one hand that the non-Communist Poles felt unhappy about the Warsaw Treaty and that Brandt allegedly concluded that treaty "over the heads of the Poles," and, on the other hand, that a free, *i.e.,* non-Communist, Poland would oppose the re-unification of Germany, if the government's interpretation of the Warsaw Treaty were correct and left to a united Germany the right to reopen the territorial problem. So, were the Poles happy or unhappy because of the conclusion of the Warsaw Treaty?

The same line of thought was taken by the representative of expellee organizations, Herbert Czaja. He accused the government of sacrificing the interests of the expellees and of those Germans who still remained in Poland.[59] According to him, the government should have demanded for the latter Germans the rights of a national minority and even the right to protect them because, according to West German legislation, they continued to be German citizens. Obviously, if Brandt were to make such demands, the negotiations with Warsaw would not even have begun. Incidentally, Wolfram Dorn, the Parliamentary State Secretary for Internal Affairs, reposted to Czaja's mentioning the right of expellees to return to their former homelands by quoting Strauss, who said on July 5th, 1970: "If Gomulka and Husak [the respective First Secretaries of the Polish and Czechoslovak Communist parties] were to offer a return to their homelands to the expelled Germans today, with the situation there remaining unchanged, then nobody, except for a handful of desperados and visionaries, would go back."[60]

Czaja said that the total number of Germans in Poland amounted to one million.[61] Another fierce opponent of the treaties, Erich Mende, former leader of Free Democrats who had crossed the aisle and had joined the opposition, outbid Czaja by raising that figure to one and a half million.[62] Both should have known the different figures available at the German Red Cross, which was for years in charge of the repatriation of those Germans to the FRG. The Red Cross statistics start with the figure of one million for the early period which immediately followed the mass flight westward of the East German population and the subsequent expulsions of other millions. The Red Cross estimated that 400,000 of that one million had emigrated to the FRG during the intermediate period. Hence, according to its statistics, 600,000 Germans remained in Poland at the time of Czaja's and Mende's speeches. Even that figure was inflated since it overlooked two facts. First, it treated as Germans all former German citizens who remained east of the Oder-Neisse, while a sizeable portion of them considered themselves Poles, not Germans. Second, it did not take into account the repatriation of those who went to the GDR because their relatives were there.

The opposition maintained its rejection of the treaties till the end of the February debate. It could have washed its hands of any responsibility since the government still had a slim majority. Schröder expressed this attitude in these words: "The federal government must be clearly told that it alone bears the responsibility for a policy which it alone has followed and is following."[63]

Yet the quickly melting down governmental majority might have been the reason for a somewhat milder tone of Barzel's closing speech. He conceded that "we see the realities in Germany, also those which we do not like. We see as well that the GDR exists, but this reality, as it is, is unacceptable for us."[64] This reduced the difference between him and the government to the question of whether it was opportune officially to recognize the GDR which he did not call "another part of Germany." His final stand on frontiers was also milder than in his initial speech. He told the Chancellor that the main point in the controversy was whether the treaties contained only the description of existing frontiers as a sort of a temporary *modus vivendi* or acknowledged their final nature. In fact, the governmental interpretation of the treaties was not far removed from what he desired. Nevertheless he upheld his "So nicht!" because, as he said, "It is better to have no treaties rather than equivocal ones."[65] Other opposition leaders, Gerhard Schröder and Richard Weizsäcker, opted for the alternative of waiting for a time when allegedly better treaties could be concluded.

The opposition speeches produced the impression that its deputies rejected the treaties with varying degrees of conviction.

DEFENSE OF THE TWO TREATIES

The government and its supporters defended the treaties during the February debate in a way which would not close the door to a search for compromise. They tried to appease the fears of the opposition by offering an interpretation of the treaties which would be acceptable to the Christian Democrats. But, first of all, the opposition had to be reminded of the fact that the division of Germany and loss of the former East German provinces were the direct results of the war unleashed by the Germans and lost by them. Hence, the government did nothing else but acknowledge what had taken place twenty-seven years ago and what could not be changed in any foreseeable future. It divorced itself from former illusions that these results of the war could be erased quickly.[66]

At first sight, it might seem strange that Western Germans, especially the older generation, had to have these reminders. But even that generation, to which most of the Bundestag deputies belonged, had almost forgotten the war and its aftermath, seeing the prosperity of the FRG and the rebuilt cities where one could hardly find traces of allied bombing. As one of the Free Democrats, Wolfgang Mischnick, remarked: "Today, twenty-seven years after the end of war, some people are no longer conscious of the devastating effects of the war, of human losses, and of the destruction of cities."[67] These "some people" were actually very many.

It was high time to get rid of illusions that time was working for Germany. The governmental speakers reminded the opposition of what Adenauer had said in the fifties when, encouraged by the cold war and American talk about "the negotiation from the position of strength," he refused to talk with Moscow and hoped that the FRG and the whole West would eventually force the Soviet Union to accept German unification and even the liberation of Eastern Europe.[68] The Vice-Speaker of the Bundestag, Social Democrat Carlo Schmid, compared people who still nourished such illusions to Don Quixote, who also charged against the windmills and fell in the dust and mud. At last, twenty-seven years after the war, one had to accept realities which neither the FRG nor its Western allies could change.[69]

One of those realities was the GDR. The government and its supporters considered that the lack of official relations with the other German state would only deepen the gulf, and hence would strike a death blow to hopes for an eventual reunification and create a cleavage between the West and East Germans. Finally, the respective populations of the two German states might acquire a feeling of belonging to two mutually hostile nations. The most urgent task was to save the feeling of unity of the German nation, even though it was divided into two states.[70]

The Vice-Speaker of the Bundestag, Carlo Schmid (SPD), reminded his colleagues of the Social Democratic fears in the early fifties that Adenauer's decision to join the North Atlantic Alliance would provoke firm Soviet resistance to German reunification. The Western states were more interested in having the FRG as a member of that Alliance than in German reunification. He recalled what a Danish Social Democrat told him at that time: "We prefer to have a half of Germany rather than to have half of the whole Germany!" The West preferred a committed FRG to a reunited but neutral Germany. Schmid pointed out the indifference, to say the least, of Western allies to what the French called "the German quarrels" between the FRG and the GDR. Reunification was conceivable only in a Europe free of the present tensions between the West and the East. The great powers, not only the Soviet Union but also the Western powers, would first look at their own interests before they would allow the Germans to be reunited. Schmid also recalled the apprehension among the European nations that a unified Germany would dangerously upset the European balance of power. He cited the French literary writer, François Mauriac, who said: "I love Germany so much that I cannot have enough of [separate] Germanies." These foreign fears forced the FRG to think, first of all, not about a state reunification but about the saving of unity of the German nation, which had preserved its identity for centuries at a time when Germany was divided into many states.[71]

THE TERRITORIAL QUESTION

The other reality resulting from the Second World War was the Polish frontier on the Oder-Neisse. The pro-government deputies expressed two different ideas. For most of them the territorial problem was not solved by the two treaties because the right to reopen it was reserved for the four great powers and for a reunited Germany. Some deputies believed that the western Polish frontier was there to stay, whatever the legal reservations made by the government. This conviction was in fact more widespread than the speeches would make one believe. Even a number of the Christian Democrats did not expect that the lost territories would ever be returned to Germany.

Foreign Minister Walter Scheel gave the official interpretation of the territorial provisions of both treaties:

> They create no legal foundation for the existing frontiers and do not define any attitude [of the FRG] regarding the origin of those frontiers. They contain, however, certain obligations. The parties to the German-Soviet Treaty undertake to respect the frontiers as inviolable. This means that the frontiers may not be changed by recourse to force. Of course, a peaceful and mutually agreed upon modification of frontiers is not thereby excluded. . . . Further, both parties declared in the German-Soviet Treaty that they had no territorial claims. This corresponds to our former policy. The Federal Republic has not made in the past any territorial claims either regarding the territories beyond the Oder-Neisse or regarding the

territory of the GDR. . . . The statement on frontiers was made more explicit in the German-Polish Treaty. This statement says clearly that the Federal Republic no longer questions the Oder-Neisse line as being the Polish western frontier. This means that the territory on the other side of that frontier is to be considered and respected by the Federal Republic of Germany as Polish territory for the duration of its [the FRG's] existence, although the peace treaty settlement for Germany has not yet been achieved and the rights and responsibilities of the four powers regarding Germany as a whole continue to exist.[72]

This official interpretation of the territorial provisions in the treaties amounted to saying that the FRG rejected the Soviet and Polish point of view that the Potsdam Conference had fixed legally and definitely the Polish western frontier, and that the Potsdam decision represented the legal foundation for the Oder-Neisse frontier. Judged by Scheel's interpretation, the FRG acknowledged the existence of the Oder-Neisse frontier *de facto,* as an existing fact, but not *de jure.* Scheel was not quite truthful when he said that the former governments of the FRG had raised no territorial claims. Those former governments constantly questioned the very right of the GDR to exist and no less constantly disputed the validity of the Oder-Neisse frontier. The value of Brandt's new Eastern policy for the Soviet Union and Poland consisted precisely in abandoning that former stand and recognizing the GDR as a state and the Oder-Neisse frontier as the Polish western frontier. Scheel's mentioning of the peace treaty and the rights of the four powers as well as his reminder in the same speech of the so-called Treaty on Germany concluded with the three Western powers, intended to reassure the opposition that a reunited Germany and the four powers would not be bound by the Moscow and Warsaw Treaties and could reopen the territorial question at the peace conference.

The leader of the Social Democratic group, Herbert Wehner, looked at the problem of the Oder-Neisse frontier in a different light. He warned against the linking of the question of the future German-Polish frontier with the problem of reunification: "He who would like to burden or load the debate [on reunification] with the opening of [the question of] the Oder-Neisse line or who actually does it, builds up a negative guarantee against the concrete discussion of self-determination."[73] Unlike Scheel, he would have preferred not to insist on the right of a reunited Germany to reopen the territorial problem. What he had in mind was that the official interpretation of the treaties as given by Scheel would add a strong reason for Soviet and Polish resistance to a reunification which would coincide with the threat to their territorial integrity.

However, the spokesman for the Free Democrats, Wolfgang Mischnick, sustained the view of his party leader, Walter Scheel. He said that "the frontiers of a reunified Germany may be determined only in a settlement freely arrived at with an all-German government. . . . The German-Soviet Treaty does not prejudice the peace-treaty settlement of German frontiers. . . . You [the opposition] say constantly that inviolability means that the frontiers may not be changed. This is untrue. . . . The [Warsaw] Treaty leaves open the possibility for both the Germans and the Poles to negotiate regarding this question at a time when such a possibility arises in consequences of future developments."[74] His Free Democratic colleague, Ernst Achenbach, reduced the commitment to the obligation not to attempt to change the frontiers by force.[75]

Minister Horst Ehmke, although born in Danzig, interpreted Brandt's Eastern policy in a different way: "I, who lost my homeland in the East, accept not only the peace policy of the federal government but also its concrete component part . . . the territorial status quo. . . . Ladies and gentlemen of the opposition, it is legally incorrect and devoid of any sense of reality to claim, twenty-five years after the collapse [of Germany] and after the end of Hitler's war, that everything is open and that these treaties give away or surrender, among other things, the land beyond the Oder-Neisse. This amounts either to sticking one's head in the sand or, much worse, to hypocrisy."[76]

Minister for the Interior Hans-Dietrich Genscher (FDP) also did not believe that the former East German provinces could be recovered: "It will be as impossible for future governments as it was for former governments since 1945 to bring back these territories to Germany." Responding to Windelen's statement that a territorial settlement favorable to Germany could be easily reached with a non-Communist Poland, Genscher said, "We must abandon this illusion. . . . All Poles are united regarding one question; they are united in their stand that they do not want to give back these territories. We know this not only from the statements made by the politicians in exile. . . . We know this not only, for instance, from [the declarations] by the responsible [leaders] of the Catholic Church in Poland. We know this also from the statements by non-Communist politicians who could talk freely immediately following the end of war or in the last years of the war. . . . There is none among our allies who would support our claim."[77] Minister Erhard Eppler confirmed this view, also stressing the unanimity among all the

Poles, Communist or non-Communist, living in Poland or abroad, re-garding the Oder-Neisse frontier.[78]

The Vice-Speaker and senior of the Bundestag, Professor Carlo Schmid (SPD), had the courage to tell the bitter truth:

According to the Potsdam decisions, East Prussia was to go to Russia, while the territory East of the Oder-Neisse was . . . placed under the Polish administration. These parts of Germany were not subjected to [the jurisdiction of] the [Allied] Control Council; only the rest of Germany with the exception of these parts was so sub-jected. It was clear from the onset that 'Germany' should remain in the future within the frontiers which the Potsdam Agreement had [thus] defined. . . . If you read the papers and memoirs of the participants, you will realize that the settlement in the peace treaty meant only that the [final] adjudication, something similar to the deliverance of the land deed, was reserved. No one meant that the [East German] territory could at some future time be given back to Germany. . . . The powers . . . to the present day have founded their practical policy on the frontier definition by the Potsdam Agreement. . . . Let us not forget that Poland has been partitioned several times. . . . They do not want to become victim again. . . . I have the feeling of guilt regarding that state and that people. Everyone of you should share this feeling. But if you had that feeling, you would be ready to take into account the depth of the Polish trauma. This trauma, whether we like it or not, is made up of the fear that a new partition might again be carried out, the fourth, fifth or sixth partition, and that . . . they could not live in security. . . . The right [to the Oder-Neisse territory] which we have, the moral and historical right, is, as the jurisconsults of the Roman law would say, a naked right, a right that corresponds to an idea but which no more contains any substance. To renounce a naked right is not a renunciation.[79]

This was the only speech during the debate with such strong expression of sympathy for and such understanding of Polish feelings.

SOVIET AND POLISH CONCESSIONS

The spokesmen for the government denied the opposition's allegation that the two treaties conceded everything to the Soviet Union and Po-land without any counter-concessions in favor of the FRG. First of all, they pointed out the four-power agreement on Berlin as a net gain which could not be dissociated from the two treaties and their ratification.[80] Second, they stressed the value of renunciation of the use of force, which was more important for the FRG, the weaker party, than for the USSR, and which included the abandonment by Moscow of its former claim to use force against the FRG by virtue of Articles 53 and 107 of the United Nations Charter.[81] Third, they pointed out that the opening of channels to Moscow and Eastern Europe emancipated the FRG from its inferior status in international politics, paralyzed as it had been, unlike its allies, in relation to the Soviet Bloc. Minister Helmut Schmidt said, "The Federal Republic of Germany has won for its actions the elbow-room necessary from the point of view of its own interests. ... The winning of this elbow-room . . . has been possible only because the whole international politics has started to move and because we have gained in these politics the place due to us."[82] Fourth, the pro-government deputies recalled the Polish promise to allow for the emigration of ethnic Germans and the repatriation in 1971 of the first batch of over 25,000.[83] Minister Walter Scheel went so far as to claim that "the prospect of improvement in our relations with Poland opens to us the possibility of interceding on behalf of those Germans."[84] It is highly doubtful whether Warsaw would have agreed with him, since it considered those Germans as Polish citizens. Scheel also reassured the Bundestag that the Warsaw Treaty did not deprive anybody of the rights due him by virtue of German legislation.[85] This was a reference to those German laws which maintained that all former German citizens still residing east of the Oder-Neisse frontier retained their German citizenship.

THE RIGHT TIME?

Finally, the pro-government speakers had to answer the opposition's claim that the present time was not well chosen for negotiations with Moscow and Warsaw and that it would be better to wait for a more favorable moment. Minister Helmut Schmidt agreed with Franz-Joseph Strauss on the multipolarity of world politics but differed from him regarding the impact of that multipolarity on the situation of the FRG, especially in respect to China: "At the same time that both superpowers want to avoid confrontation and have begun the search for areas of cooperation, there is a trend toward the former bipolarity, as Herr

Strauss has mentioned, being superseded by a new balance with several pillars. . . . But I repeat for the benefit of those who believe that the Chinese factor should be added to the foundation of Eastern policy, that he who wishes to promote the relaxation of tensions in Europe must seek cooperation without bringing to the game new factors of insecurity. . . . He who tells the Soviet Union that he will negotiate with it only when the Soviet Union feels a stronger pressure from the third side, misunderstands the effects of such an attitude on a world power."[86]

Foreign Minister Scheel called the references to the Chinese factor "escapism," a flight from European realities in order to avoid any decision regarding relations with the Soviet bloc.[87] Brandt added that China was not the kind of "wonder weapon" that would solve German problems.[88]

Helmut Schmidt, perhaps recalling the failure of the Eastern policy of the great coalition, warned that "nothing important may happen in the East European area without the cooperation of Moscow. Such is the situation today. . . . It would have been foolish and dangerous to want to hammer in wedges between the [Warsaw] Pact states, dangerous not only for us but also and especially for the peace."[89]

The spokesmen for the governmental majority argued that the treaties were concluded in agreement with the Western allies and corresponded to their policies of reducing tensions in Europe. Foreign Minister Scheel said, "Those treaties, conceived as a part of West European policy and elaborated in a continuous collaboration with our allied partners, announced that restored Western Europe begins to be the master of its own problems. . . . Do you believe that the time and opportunity have come to dig in politically when our friends and allies have chosen movement long ago? Should we go back to the half-overcome dugouts of the cold war, while our most powerful allies have chosen the relaxation of tensions and cooperation?"[90] Minister Helmut Schmidt recalled President Richard Nixon's decision to end the era of confrontation and begin the era of cooperation, this decision being currently evidenced by the SALT negotiations. He also told the opposition that their speeches, if they were made at a NATO ministerial meeting, would not only cause consternation but would start on the same evening the process of German isolation among its own allies.[91]

The rejection of the treaties would mean the refusal to follow the same policy that the Western allies were practicing and a return to the cold war, i.e., to isolation. The right moment was now, and the opposition's alternative of simply waiting longer was no alternative at all.

Scheel told the opposition: "The arguments which the opposition has advanced against the policy of the federal government would be more credible if a realizable alternative were visible."[92] The Chancellor expressed the government's conviction that "twenty-seven years after the end of the war, the time has finally come to place our relations with the Soviet Union and Eastern Europe on a new foundation. Nobody may still say that this is too early."[93]

Deputy Ernst Achenbach (FDP) told the opposition that their past and present policies had always been nothing but waiting: "You were always of the opinion during those long years that the [right] moment had not yet come or that the moment was unfavorable."[94] Minister Horst Ehmke concluded that this waiting for a favorable moment had only one result, the deepening of the division of Germany.[95]

Minister Helmut Schmidt pointed out the consequences of rejection of the treaties: "The consequences would be as follows: the loss of elbow-room for actions by the Federal Republic and the loss for a long time to come of the chance for a treaty policy regarding the East, as well as a crisis within the alliance and in Western Europe, with an impact on the political efficiency of the alliance and effects on relations with the United States of America, for whom the treaties and in particular the Berlin agreement represent important elements in its foreign policy strategy. . . . The alternative to the Eastern policy of the federal government does not consist in waiting."[96]

The debate ended as it had begun in a disagreement between the government and the opposition. Minister Scheel thought, however, that he had discerned a division in the ranks of the opposition. On the one hand, there were those like Strauss and Windelen who believed that the negotiations with the Communist governments amounted to a betrayal of East European peoples, and on the other hand, there were those who were ready to negotiate, like Rainer Barzel. Scheel hoped that Barzel would be able to convince his parliamentary group to abandon its negative position.[97] The May debate was to prove him right, except that Barzel could not help the government to the extent that he wanted to.

REPATRIATION OF ETHNIC GERMANS

The problem of repatriation of ethnic Germans from Poland was often mentioned during the February debate. This problem, as we know, concerns former German citizens still residing east of the Oder-Neisse and asking for permission to emigrate to the FRG. The first difficulty consists in the question of whether they truthfully declared themselves Poles at the time of the registration of the so-called autochthons or did so only because they feared Polish reprisals if they declared themselves ethnic Germans? This brings about the second question: do they revoke their original declaration of being Poles for the valid reason of always having felt themselves to be Germans, or because they want to emigrate to the FRG only because of the attraction of its economic prosperity? The third difficulty consists in the fact that Upper-Silesians (who constitute the immense majority of applicants for emigration) have always belonged to the marginal cases in regard to nationality. Like the Alsatians, they included many people who were never certain to which of the two neighboring nationalities they belonged. They could speak German or Polish at home (usually they bear Polish names) and yet be unsure how they felt regarding their own nationality. The decisive factor for their option was the surrounding circumstances, namely, which of the two nationalities had the upper hand. Such marginal cases, and they were many, were tempted to act as though they were fierce German nationalists during the Nazi period and then declared themselves Poles after the German defeat. The prospect of a well-paid job, a comfortable apartment, and a car in the prosperous FRG might now be the decisive factor for renunciation of Polish nationality and application for emigration.

All this creates problems for both Poland and the FRG. Warsaw does not want to allow for the emigration of those who in fact feel like Poles but want to emigrate for economic reasons. As the officials of the German Red Cross say, the main enemy of repatriation of even ethnic Germans is the Polish Five-Year Plan, the reluctance of Poland to lose skilled manpower, educated or trained by the Polish state. Otherwise, one may assume that Poland would be rather happy to get rid of citizens who are not sure of their nationality or who consider themselves Germans. This would offer two advantages. First, these few hundred thousand people form the last relatively large minority within a homogeneous nation. Their departure would end the problem. Second, the very insistence of the FRG on repatriating them is obvious proof that the FRG does not hope that even a reunified Germany could recover the lost territories. No state wants to repatriate its ethnic countrymen from a contested territory. The Weimar Republic, for instance, encouraged the ethnic Germans to remain in the former Prussian provinces lost to Poland after the First World War.

The FRG has its own problems regarding assimilation of the immigrants, especially the young ones. On the one hand, its active population includes about two and a half million foreign workers (Turks, Greeks, Yugoslavs, Italians, Spaniards, etc.) who form an alien body within the West German population. It would be simpler to assimilate the immigrants from Poland who claim to be Germans. But even this problem of assimilation is not so simple as it might appear at first sight. Older immigrants, who still remember prewar Germany, discover that they have come to a different Germany with changed ways of life. Their image of Germany does not fit into the reality of West German society. Their dialect is different from the German of their new neighbors, who look on them as some kind of aliens. They are somewhat disappointed in their former hopes.

The real problem exists for the younger generation, those under thirty years of age. They have been educated in Polish schools where they never learned German, and they are used to the "socialist" way of life. For them the shock is great. All this is conceded in an official document, issued in 1972 by the West German Ministry for Youth, Family, and Health.[98] It starts with the statement that over fifty percent of immigrants in 1971 were under the age of thirty. They did not know German and could not easily adapt to the "capitalist" way of life. They came with notions inculcated in them at the Polish schools, critical not only of the "capitalist" society but also of Germany as such. They knew nothing about German culture. Moreover, those with higher skills resulting from graduation from the Polish senior high schools or Polish universities discovered that in the FRG they could not acquire jobs which they had in Poland. They had to work hard to get similar German diplomas. Above all, they had to learn German. They realized that their former hopes for a well-paid job, a comfortable apartment, and a car did not easily become realities. Their neighbors usually treated them as aliens. Their complete assimilation requires a long time, a period of difficult and painful adjustment.

While the abovementioned official West German document conceded all these problems of young immigrants, Minister Horst Ehmke cited a brighter aspect of the young generations. He told a congress of West German youth in April 1972 that the young generations of Germans and Poles could begin the process of German-Polish reconciliation much better than their elders, since their minds were not burdened with recollections of the past. Turning to the young Germans, he said: "Youth is not burdened or at least less burdened [by the past]; among other things, it is easier for youth than for the older generation to support efforts at a detente in Europe which starts with the [acceptance of] the territorial status quo."[99] This is true, or at least would be completely true if the young in both countries would reject the resentments and prejudices, communicated to them by parents, teachers, and the mass media. Ehmke was correct in mentioning in this respect the importance of personal contacts between the youths of both countries, and of beginning a series of meetings between the German and Polish historians and geographers who try to revise German and Polish schoolbooks in order to eliminate insofar as possible mutually hostile images of the two nations.

THE MAY DEBATE

The second Bundestag debate on the Eastern treaties began on May 10, 1972. In the meantime, the government lost its parliamentary majority, but the opposition did not gain the majority. It was a strange situation, with each side having exactly the same number of 259 votes. This time the fate of the treaties depended on the opposition. The government had to seek an accommodation with the opposition, while the Christian Democrats were not reluctant to reach a compromise solution. Now both sides of the Bundestag were confronted with equal responsibility for the foreign policy of the FRG.

The May debate had two aspects. One of them was a sort of shadow boxing. The discussion of reports by the Bundestag's foreign relations committee provided the opposition with an opportunity to repeat its former arguments critical of the treaties. If one listened to that public debate, he would not believe that the opposition would allow for ratification. This was a shadow-boxing spectacle. In fact, the government and the leaders of the opposition had been engaged for two weeks prior to the debate in negotiations regarding the wording of a joint resolution which would offer an interpretation of the treaties acceptable to the opposition. The practical question was no longer whether the opposition would continue to say "So nicht!" but rather how the resolution should be drafted so that the opposition would not have to vote against ratification.

THE MOSCOW TREATY

The shadow-boxing part of the May debate was made up of the four reports on the Moscow and Warsaw Treaties (two for the government and two for the opposition) submitted on behalf of the Bundestag's committee of foreign relations. First, Ernst Achenbach (FDP) presented in his report the SPD's and his own party's arguments in favor of ratification of the Moscow Treaty.[100] He claimed that the Soviet Union understood the wish of the FRG to achieve eventually the reunification of all Germans within one state, but conceded that the USSR was not ready to help in fulfilling this West German wish. What was achieved in the treaty was the renunciation of the use of force, including the retraction of the former Soviet claim to the right to use force by virtue of Articles 53 and 107 of the United Nations Charter. While the FRG pledged itself to respect the existing frontiers and not to raise any territorial claims, this did not mean that the Moscow Treaty replaced or prejudged the terms of the future peace treaty to be concluded with a reunited Germany which could reopen the frontier question. "The Federal Republic of Germany . . . has not recognized any frontiers in Article 3."[101] Hence, the treaty did not undermine the validity of the 1952 treaty which the FRG concluded with the three Western powers, and in particular did not invalidate the rights and responsibilities of those powers regarding the problem of reunification, the peace settlement, and the final determination of German frontiers. This was one of the reasons why the FRG could not undertake any obligations in the Moscow Treaty regarding the frontiers of a unified Germany. The Moscow Treaty did not solve German problems, including "a sensible solution of German frontiers."[102] The implication was clear: the Oder-Neisse frontier was not sensible. Finally, Achenbach warned that a change in the present status quo, held unfair by the Germans, would not be possible if the cold war and tensions continued to exist in Europe, because any change depended on the cooperation not only of the Western powers but also of the Soviet Union and its allies.

The opposition report was presented by Bruno Heck (CDU/CSU) who explained why his political friends could not recommend the approval of the Moscow Treaty.[103] He enumerated the opposition requests: first, that the treaty should be interpreted in such a way that it did not replace or prejudice the peace treaty. Second, the normalization of relations in Europe should not be acceptable for the FRG if it were to be separated from the problem of German reunification. He conceded, however, that a workable *modus vivendi* with the GDR should be ensured in a treaty. He spelled out the entire official name of the GDR instead of calling it, as the opposition usually did, "the other part of Germany." His requests corresponded to the government's interpretation of the Moscow Treaty and could be easily accepted by the government. It was obvious that the opposition was ready to reach an understanding with the government.

The only matter that bothered Herr Heck was the divergence between the government's and the Soviet interpretations of the Moscow Treaty. He remarked, not without reason: "The exchange of declarations on the renunciation of force has any sense for the Soviet Union only when the existing territorial situation in Europe is recognized and is not to be questioned in the future. . . . [For the USSR] the results of the Second World War are not to be changed, and the question of frontiers in Europe has been settled finally and irrevocably."[104] He cited statements made by Foreign Minister Andrei Gromyko at the meeting of the Supreme Soviet to the effect that normalization of relations was possible only on the basis of West German recognition of European realities. He saw the risk that the different Soviet and West German interpretations of the Moscow Treaty might create new difficulties in relations between the FRG and the USSR.

THE WARSAW TREATY

Dieter Haack (SPD) submitted the report on the Warsaw Treaty on behalf of his Social Democratic and Free Democratic colleagues.[105] He said that the treaty was not a mere renunciation of the use of force, because

> The treaty with Poland could not and cannot be made without a clear, unequivocal and credible statement by the Federal Republic of Germany regarding the Oder-Neisse frontier. The developments during the last twenty-five years have to be taken into consideration. The former German Eastern territories have been fully integrated within the Polish state during that period of time. The question of the Western frontier is for the Polish state the question of its existence. This frontier is guaranteed by the Eastern alliance. It is regarded as final by all states in the world. Only if the foreign policy of the Federal Republic of Germany takes account of these facts will a German-Polish settlement be possible.[106]

Haack was one of the few deputies who accepted in a public speech the irreversibility of the Oder-Neisse frontier. But he did not contest the legal interpretation by the government that the Warsaw Treaty was binding only on the FRG and not on a reunified Germany or on the four powers. He added, however, that the Warsaw Treaty freed the problem of reunification of, as he said, the "odium" of contesting the existing frontiers and raising territorial claims. He strengthened the validity of his view regarding the Polish western frontier by citing one of the leaders of the opposition, von Weizsäcker, who wrote on April 18, 1972, in the *Frankfurter Allgemeine Zeitung*: "The Oder-Neisse frontier is a question finally settled for all and not the least for our allies."[107]

Haack confirmed the official view that the FRG continued to regard ethnic Germans who were prewar residents in the territory beyond the Oder-Neisse as German citizens, and noticed the Polish willingness to repatriate them to the FRG, including those who had no relatives in West Germany.

Franz-Josef Bach (CDU) presented the counter-report and expressed his colleagues' apprehension regarding the divergent interpretations of the Moscow and Warsaw Treaties by the federal and the Soviet governments.[108] He cited Soviet Foreign Minister Gromyko, who stated at the joint meeting of foreign affairs committees of the two chambers of the Supreme Soviet: "A treaty which would consist only in the obligation of partners to renounce the use or threat of force would be void of any sense for the Soviet Union in a situation where the inviolability of existing frontiers in Europe would be further questioned by the Federal Republic of Germany. The normalization of relations between the Federal Republic of Germany and other countries is possible only if the Federal Republic recognizes and respects European realities."[109] He also quoted another statement by Gromyko: "The frontier question has been solved by the war and the postwar developments in Europe. . . . The unshakability of the Western frontier of the socialist commonwealth is guaranteed by the whole might of the USSR and its allied fraternal states."[110] These quotations were to prove Bach's contention that Moscow and Warsaw considered the two treaties, at variance with the FRG, as a final settlement of the frontier question. He also expressed his unpleasant surprise at hearing what his SPD colleague Dieter Haack said, because Haack had made it "clear that the [Oder-Neisse] frontier was final."[111] It was true that Haack's report deviated from the official position of the government which maintained that acknowledgment of the Oder-Neisse frontier was good only for the duration of the FRG but was not binding on a reunited Germany. Bach concluded sorrowfully that the Warsaw Treaty seemed to be a treaty conceding the loss of East German territories and a frontier treaty rather than an agreement on the renunciation of force.

THE BUNDESTAG RESOLUTION

The two reports on behalf of the opposition ended with refusal to vote for the treaties but were very moderate in their criticism of them, if compared with the speeches made by the opposition during the February debate. In fact, every deputy knew that the government and the opposition were close to an agreement on a joint resolution which would offer an interpretation of the treaties which would allow the opposition to vote for ratification. The leader of the opposition, Rainer Barzel, played the crucial role in trying to help the government and to carry out the Bundestag's approval of the treaties.

The concept of a unilateral interpretive resolution as a condition of ratification was unusual in international practice but had a precedent in the Bundestag's records. In January 1963 Adenauer and de Gaulle concluded a German-French treaty of friendship and cooperation, a sort of political alliance. The Bundestag, including Adenauer's Christian Democrats, was afraid that the United States could interpret that treaty as a proof of the FRG's support for the French policy of challenging American leadership in Western Europe. Hence, the Bundestag adopted a preamble to the treaty, a unilateral interpretation, as a condition for approval of the treaty. That preamble stated the objectives of West German foreign policy, all of them at variance with the foreign policy of the Fifth Republic. The treaty was approved, but de Gaulle drew his own conclusions, namely, that the Bundestag had in fact repudiated the treaty. He responded by abandoning his former idea of close co-operation with the FRG and by improving French relations with the Soviet Union, at that time an adversary of the FRG.

West German leaders had learned on that occasion that the unilateral interpretation of a treaty might be risky. This is why both the government and the opposition consulted Soviet Ambassador Falin on the text of the draft resolution, to be sure that the Soviet Union would not refuse ratification. However, there is no proof that either Bonn or Moscow consulted Warsaw on the text of the resolution or sought its approval. Falin raised objections chiefly against that part of the resolution which stated that the two treaties did not create any legal foundation for the existing frontiers. This resulted in a temporary hitch in the negotiations between the government and the opposition.

It was then, on May 10, 1972, that Chancellor Brandt intervened in an attempt to appease the opposition.[112] First, he mentioned the most important objective of his Eastern policy: "After the Treaties have entered into force, we shall be able to conduct the Eastern policy under conditions similar to those of the other Western countries, no less and no more."[113] Then the Berlin agreement would enter into force, a settlement with the GDR would be achieved, a treaty would be concluded with Czechoslovakia, and diplomatic relations would be established with Hungary and Bulgaria. Relations with the entire Soviet bloc would be normalized. But ratification of the Moscow and Warsaw Treaties was the precondition although "nobody can expect that every sentence and every formula in the treaties will be joyfully welcomed here."[114] Even Brandt did not feel happy, but he thought that the terms of the two treaties had to be accepted because "Germany had lost the war," and because "more than thirty million dead lie between us Germans and the East European peoples on the ruins of the bloody history of the Second World War. Mountains of distrust, lack of knowledge, anxiety, and prejudices arose on the ruins of that bloody history."[115] He assured the opposition that a joint resolution would be founded on the following assumptions:

> There is no difference of opinion with the Soviet side that the [Moscow] Treaty does not make unnecessary the peace conference; the two states are not empowered to do so [to replace a peace settlement] in a bilateral treaty. The Soviet side has once again stressed that the Treaty does not encroach on the rights of the four powers. . . . Taking into account the views and responsibilities of the federal government, it is considered that . . . , although the Treaties do not anticipate the peace-treaty settlement and do not create any legal grounds for the frontiers existing today, this does not mean, of course, any restriction of obligations undertaken by the Federal Republic, especially in the Warsaw Treaty.[116]

He appealed to the opposition to accept the terms of the joint draft resolution and to vote for ratification of the treaties in order, among other things, to make certain that the four-power agreement on Berlin would enter into force. He then assured the Poles of the friendly intentions of his government: "The year 1772 [date of the first partition of Poland] marked the beginning of a policy which questioned the existence of the Polish state. The year 1972, we hope, marks the beginning of an era when Poles may live within secure frontiers. . . . They must know in Poland that we . . . do not want to make political experiments at their expense."[117]

Brandt concluded by saying that there was no alternative to his Eastern policy which the Soviet Union would accept and which the

Western allies would support. The alternative would be an international isolation of the FRG.

Rainer Barzel responded in a conciliatory manner.[118] He appealed for a little more time so that his parliamentary group could make its decision in the full knowledge of what was involved in the resolution. He said that the day of decision would be neither one of triumph nor one of mourning but the day of common sense. He conceded the importance of the four-power agreement on Berlin and agreed with the Chancellor that both sides should seek a compromise in drafting the resolution. He referred to the Soviet ambassador's objections to that part of the resolution to which the opposition attached great importance, namely, that "the Treaties do not replace a peace-treaty settlement for Germany and create no legal grounds for the frontiers existing today."[119] Barzel added, however, that Ambassador Falin had informed him on the same afternoon of his government's decision to retract that objection. According to Barzel, what now remained was to make the joint resolution an official document of the FRG.[120] It was obvious that Barzel himself was ready to vote both for the resolution and approval of the treaties but needed more time to convince his parliamentary group to do the same.

Foreign Minister Scheel reassured the opposition that the problem of the cited part of the draft resolution did not exist since the government shared its point of view and because Ambassador Falin no longer objected to it.[121] However, the Chancellor in a second intervention warned that "the resolution stands [as agreed with the opposition]. But if someone should think that he could change the [Warsaw] Treaty by a resolution, then we have negotiated on false assumptions. . . . It must, therefore, be clearly and unequivocally stated that, insofar as the obligations resulting from the Warsaw Treaty are concerned, the resolution may not be understood as having a meaning regarding the frontier question which would deprecate the treaty."[122]

All in all, the discussion was not unfriendly. It was clear that the two sides intended to reach an agreement. But it took another week to reach it because of dissensions within the CDU/CSU group. Only on May 17, 1972, did the government and the opposition agree on the text of the joint resolution. The government understood all along that Barzel would deliver the approving votes of his political friends for the ratification of the two treaties in exchange for a mutually agreed upon interpretation of those treaties. The CDU/CSU group, however, deserted its leader and finally decided to abstain. It is true that this "Jein" (neither *Ja* nor *Nein*) allowed the governmental half of the

Bundestag to approve the treaties. The stand of the opposition was childish since its abstention implied its responsibility for the ratification of the treaties, and was so understood by German public opinion. The right wing of that opinion denounced the stand of the opposition as a betrayal.

The repudiation by the CDU of its own leader marked the beginning of Barzel's downfall. The defeat of the Christian Democrats in the following elections ended his career as the leader of the CDU and as a candidate for the post of Chancellor. It was significant that the decision of the CDU/CSU group was announced in the Bundestag not by him but by Kurt Kiesinger, who explained on May 17, 1972, that the majority of his group, after the longest and most lively debate in its whole history, decided to abstain in order not to prevent the ratification.[123]

The government had no choice but to accept that decision, although Minister Scheel expressed regret that Barzel's promise was not honored by his own parliamentary group. He added that the joint resolution would be transmitted to the Soviet Ambassador as an official document of the FRG.[124]

THE VOTE

The debate ended with the vote. Two hundred forty-eight deputies voted for approval of the Moscow Treaty, 238 abstained, and ten voted against. The result of the vote on the Warsaw Treaty was somewhat different: 248 deputies voted for, 230 abstained and seventeen voted against. A lesser number of the opposition deputies could prevail on themselves only to abstain on the Treaty with Poland. None of the Christian Democratic deputies dared to disobey the party line (no vote for the treaties), while a number of their colleagues did so in voting against the treaties. Yet a small portion of Christian Democrats privately favored the Warsaw Treaty, including the provision on the Oder-Neisse frontier. They lacked civic courage. Anyhow, the two treaties were approved by the governmental half of the Bundestag with the implicit assent of the other half.

The resolution was adopted by 491 votes, only five deputies abstaining. It stated that the two treaties represented important elements of a *modus vivendi* between the FRG and its Eastern neighbors. However, the obligations undertaken by the FRG "are undertaken in its own name. The treaties are based on the frontiers which exist in fact today and exclude their unilateral modification. The treaties do not anticipate a peace-treaty settlement for Germany and create no legal foundation for the now existing frontiers."[125] The resolution further stated that the treaties did not encroach upon the German right of self-determination, but that "the Federal Republic of Germany neither raises territorial claims nor asks for the modification of frontiers while calling for the implementation of the right of self-determination."[126] The resolution reaffirmed the validity of the 1954 Treaty on Germany concluded with the three Western powers; the rights and responsibilities of the four powers regarding Germany as a whole, including the final settlement of German frontiers; the firm commitment of the FRG to the North Atlantic Alliance; the intention gradually to transform the EEC into a political union of Western Europe and the hope that the Soviet bloc would cooperate with the EEC; the decision to maintain and strengthen West German ties with West Berlin; and, finally, the intention to normalize relations between the FRG and the GDR.

The only controversial part of the resolution was that which denied that the treaties provided a legal basis for the existing frontiers. The Soviet government, eager to bring about the ratification, agreed to that formula but only as a unilateral German interpretation not binding on the Soviet side. The Polish government, not asked to approve the resolution, was not committed even to that extent. It could claim that it did not accept that part of the resolution even as a unilateral West German view. The fact that neither Bonn nor Moscow consulted Warsaw might have been one of the reasons why Warsaw delayed the establishment of diplomatic relations for several months.

The German press mentioned the names of deputies who voted against the Warsaw Treaty. Not surprisingly, the leaders of the expellee organizations—Becher, Czaja, and Hupka—and the right wing nationalists such as Baron von und zu Guttenberg, Windelen, and Mende were among those seventeen deputies who refused to approve the treaty. They were extreme nationalists who could not conceive of any reconciliation with Poland that would require a German sacrifice or concession.

The moderate and serious West German newspaper, *Frankfurter Allgemeine Zeitung,* remarked in its comment on the resolution that the part which denied a legal foundation for the existing frontiers was meant to apply to the future and final settlement of the situation in Germany between the Rhine and the Oder (the lifting of frontiers between the FRG and the GDR at the time of their reunification) but had "no practical relevance for the Polish Western frontiers on the

Oder-Neisse."[127] This was true insofar as the majority of West German politicians of all parties were concerned. Whatever they said for the benefit of the electorate, they did not believe that the Oder-Neisse frontier could be changed, even if Germany were reunified.

Gustav Heinemann, the President of the Republic, signed the documents of ratification on May 23, 1972. Soon after, on June 3, the Foreign Ministers of the four powers signed their 1971 agreement on Berlin which immediately entered into force. On the same day the Soviet, Polish, and West German representatives exchanged the documents of ratification of the two treaties. The most difficult part of Brandt's Eastern policy was completed.

11

Polish and Soviet Ratifications

POLISH DISTRUST

THE POLES watched the debate in West Germany with intense interest during the long period of time which separated the signature of the Warsaw Treaty and its approval by the Bundestag. They knew that the Moscow and Warsaw treaties provoked a stormy debate in West Germany, but they themselves did not feel that a ratified Warsaw Treaty would bring about a honeymoon in their relations with the FRG. The resentment caused by the horrors committed during the German wartime occupation and distrust of German intentions did not suddenly evaporate. This distrust was deepened by the strong Christian Democratic opposition to the Warsaw Treaty during the February debate in the Bundestag.

The mood in Poland was well expressed by Ryszard Frelek, the then director of the Polish Institute of International Affairs. He noted that the Warsaw Treaty could be concluded only because the FRG had signed the Moscow Treaty first.[1] This fact had a double meaning. First, Poland itself could not sign a treaty of normalization of relations with the FRG without Soviet approval. This was known in Warsaw, particularly after Czechoslovakia's experience in 1968. Second, was it conceivable that the FRG would have consented to acknowledge the existence of the Oder-Neisse frontier if the Soviet Union had not guaranteed that frontier?

Frelek reminded the Germans that the treaty did not mean "forgetfulness," "forgiveness," or "reconciliation." "There can be no question

259

of forgetting the Hitlerite crimes." Normalization meant for him, first of all, much more lively economic relations, which would bring about not only greater trade but also cooperation between Polish state enterprises and West German private corporations and West German credits.

Frelek noted that France had recognized the Oder-Neisse frontier as final, while the United States and Britain were of the same opinion and admitted this in informal conversations, although they did not confirm it officially for fear of offending their West German ally. He also remarked that the Warsaw Treaty did not contain any West German reservations regarding the renunciation by the FRG of all territorial claims now and for the future. The Polish frontier on the Oder-Neisse was generally recognized as final, thanks to such factors as the Polish population living in the territories east of that frontier, the existence of the GDR, and the Polish alliance with the Soviet Union. What the FRG renounced was only illusions and dreams.

Daniel Luliński, correspondent in Bonn of *Trybuna Ludu,* the newspaper of the Polish Communist Party (United Polish Workers Party), did his best to maintain the feeling of distrust among his countrymen. He wrote that the anti-Polish mood, spread in the millions of copies of newspapers and periodicals published by the Springer publishing group, could not be effectively counterbalanced by the liberal press with a much smaller circulation or by those television programs which showed the great results obtained by the Poles in rebuilding the war-devastated former East German territories. He mentioned the names of several West German politicians, like Franz-Joseph Strauss and Baron Karl-Theodor von und zu Guttenberg, and of numerous journalists who were opposed to a reconciliation with Poland. While warning that a large part of the West German political elite did not want a true normalization of relations, he conceded that another large part of that elite and of public opinion supported Brandt's policy.[2]

However, Polish readers of scholarly periodicals were reminded of the difference in attitudes between the Weimar Republic and the present-day FRG. The Polish periodical specializing in German affairs, *Przegląd Zachodni,* published in March 1971 a long review of a new West German book on German-Polish relations during the period of 1919–70. It took this opportunity to recall the hostility toward Poland throughout the existence of the Weimar Republic, hostility shared by all political parties. According to the Polish journal, the Weimar politicians wanted more than just the revision of the Versailles frontiers; they questioned even the right of the Polish state to exist. The periodical mentioned as examples not only the well-known opinion of General Hans von Seeckt, commander-in-chief of the Republic's Reichswehr, but also that of Josef Wirth, leader of the Catholic Centrum party and at that time Chancellor, who said in July 1922: "Poland must be finished off. . . . I do not intend to conclude any agreement which would strengthen Poland. . . . I am in this respect completely in agreement with the military circles, in particular with General von Seeckt." The Polish journal also reminded its readers of the tariff war which the Weimar Republic had waged against Poland in order to weaken it economically.[3]

The reader could compare the attitude of the Weimar Republic with Brandt's policy and conclude that a notable change had taken place in the minds of German politicians, a change favorable to Poland. But the Polish press constantly referred to Brandt's opponents as proof that one could not trust the West Germans completely. The same periodical mentioned in another article the influence of West German scholars who had no sympathy for Poland, those associated with the important German Society for the Knowledge of Eastern Europe (*Deutsche Gesellschaft für Osteuropakunde*). These scholars determined school programs insofar as the East European countries, in particular Poland, were concerned, and promoted unfriendly feelings among the young West Germans. The same article mentioned various West German research institutes such as the Herder Institut in Marburg and the Göttinger Arbeitkreis as other examples of scholars working in a spirit unfriendly to Poland. Such scholars (Georg Strobel was especially singled out) were contributors to *Osteuropa,* a monthly published by the abovementioned association. What irritated the Polish commentators most was the *leitmotiv* in the writings of those scholars, denying Polish right to the former East German territories.[4]

THE PERSONALITY OF WILLY BRANDT

Willy Brandt personally was trusted, because, unlike many other West German politicians, he had refused to cooperate with the Nazi regime and did not bear any responsibility for the Nazi policy toward Poland. *Trybuna Ludu* welcomed him on the occasion of his coming to Warsaw to sign the Treaty in these words: "We see in the person of Willy Brandt an eminent politician who is the first Chancellor in the history of the FRG with an anti-fascist past."[5] The same newspaper noted with satisfaction Brandt's thoughtfulness in bringing with him to Warsaw several representative personalities, such as the leaders of the two governmental parties, well-known writers Günther Grass and Siegfried Lenz, Klaus von Bismarck, director of one of the television networks, and spokesmen for various associations such as the labor unions and youth organizations, both Catholic and Protestant. It was understood in Warsaw that he wanted to prove in this way a large West German support for his policy.[6]

POLISH INTERPRETATION OF THE WARSAW TREATY

Polish interpretation of the Warsaw Treaty remained the same prior to and after the ratification. Disregarding statements made by the federal government and the Bundestag resolution, all Polish commentators maintained that the FRG had recognized the Oder-Neisse frontier as final and irrevocable. This interpretation could mislead Polish public opinion, which had not been informed by the mass media of a quite different West German interpretation. Polish commentators simply ignored the Brandt government's official statements to the effect that the FRG did not recognize any legal foundation for the Oder-Neisse frontier, and that the right to reopen the territorial problem was reserved for a reunited Germany and for the four great powers. This ostrich-like attitude was imprudent from the Polish point of view, since it hid from the Poles the risk involved in German reunification. The West German interpretation was more important for Poland than its own, because it defined the German attitude toward the Polish frontier with the implication that a reunited Germany might question the validity of that frontier.

Several comments were published in 1971–72 on the meaning of the Warsaw Treaty. One of them by Adam Daniel Rotfeld appeared in *Sprawy Międzynarodowe,* a monthly published by the Polish Institute of International Affairs. It was typical.[7] Rotfeld claimed that the FRG recognized in the Warsaw Treaty the mutually binding character of the Potsdam decision, while, as we have seen, the West German government in fact denied it. According to the West German interpretation, the description in the treaty of the Polish Western frontier by using the terms of the Potsdam decision did not mean that that decision fixed the frontier finally and irrevocably. By using the terms of the Potsdam decision, the FRG only accepted the description of the present factual situation. This West German understanding of the Warsaw Treaty was further clarified in the Bundestag resolution which denied that the Eastern treaties had created any legal foundation for the existing frontiers. The implication was clear: what was lacking was the legitimacy of the Oder-Neisse frontier, because the Potsdam decision had not provided the legal foundation insofar as the FRG was concerned. Rotfeld was right, however, when he wrote that "the question of frontiers is not and may not become a controversial problem between Poland and the FRG."[8]

Rotfeld mentioned the FRG's reservation of the right of the four great powers regarding the final settlement of German frontiers and also of Article 7 of the Treaty on Germany, concluded by the FRG with the USA, Britain, and France, in which the contracting parties had agreed to postpone the final determination of those frontiers until the peace settlement for Germany. He denied, however, any meaning to that West German reservation, as though he had not read the official West German comments regarding the still outstanding peace treaty to be concluded with a reunified Germany.

Rotfeld was on firmer ground when he denied to the party to a treaty the right to change it by a unilateral interpretation.[9] This disclaimer of any legal significance for Poland of the Bundestag resolution was correct from the point of view of international law but did not reduce the political importance of the resolution.

Rotfeld agreed with the West German statements that the Warsaw Treaty was binding only on the FRG. He said that any other West German stand would not be acceptable to Poland, because it would have meant that the FRG had the right to undertake obligations on behalf of all Germans, including the GDR. But he did not deduce the conclusion made in the FRG, that the treaty left a future united Germany free to reopen the territorial problem. He only discreetly alluded to the West German interpretation: "It seems that the government of the FRG has made some concessions, in particular in its interpretation which has narrowed down the meaning of the treaties, in order to obtain the support of the opposition for the ratification."[10] But he did not care to explain what this more narrow interpretation consisted of. Yet the pertinent published West German documents were available. The Polish reader was left at a loss in trying to understand to what extent the German and Polish interpretations of the Warsaw Treaty differed from each other.

The well-known Polish specialist on German-Polish relations, Professor Alfons Klafkowski, contributed his commentary in the same vein.[11] He began by presenting the Polish view, according to which the Potsdam decision had settled once and for all the question of the Polish frontier on the Oder-Neisse and thus had made unnecessary any further settlement in a peace treaty. He cited Soviet and other East European official views in the same vein, for instance, the Polish-Soviet Treaty of March 5, 1957, on the delimitation of the common frontier in former East Prussia, the Polish-Czechoslovak Treaty of June 13, 1958, on the mutual boundary, the Polish-Soviet Treaty of friendship and mutual assistance, signed on April 8, 1965, whose Article 5 confirmed the inviolability of the Oder-Neisse frontier (the foundation, Klafkowski said, of the Polish-Soviet alliance), etc. His conclusion was that the various treaties concluded by Poland with the USSR and other East European countries strengthened the Polish right to participate in any future decisions regarding Germany as a whole (reunification) and on that occasion to protect its territorial integrity. Like Rotfeld, Klafkowski claimed that "the government of the FRG recognized for the first time in a legal document [the Warsaw Treaty] the binding force of the Potsdam Agreement regarding the Polish-German frontier."[12] He simply did not want to notice the West German statements to the contrary. Since the Potsdam decision was considered by Klafkowski and all other Polish commentators as having irrevocably determined the Polish Western frontier, all that the two German states could do was recognize the finality of that frontier. Thus, the Görlitz and Warsaw Treaties, concluded with the two German states, had only declaratory meaning in the sense of recognition of the frontier existing legally since 1945. It was in this sense that Klafkowski agreed with the West German view that the Warsaw Treaty had not created the legal foundation for the Oder-Neisse frontier. Finally, Klafkowski said that "neither of the two German states tried to insert a conditional formula in the Treaties."[13] This is true insofar as the text of the two treaties was concerned. It is also true that the GDR has never interpreted the Görlitz Treaty in a way different from the Polish view. But it is also true that the official West German documents made the acceptance of the frontier conditional in the sense that its acceptance by the FRG would not at all bind a reunified Germany or the four great powers at the time of a peace conference on Germany.

Adam Rotfeld returned to the question of the Warsaw Treaty in another article, published in April 1972, in *Sprawy Międzynarodowe*.[14] He continued to maintain that the FRG recognized the binding force of the Potsdam decision, because Article One of the treaty described the Western Polish frontier by using the wording of that decision. He acknowledged, nevertheless, the West German reservation that the final settlement of German frontiers should be postponed until a peace settlement, but denied any meaning to that reservation because, as he wrote, neither the Moscow nor the Warsaw Treaty mentioned the future peace settlement. One may add that this did not change the intention formulated by the FRG to postpone the final territorial settlement to a peace treaty to be negotiated principally between a reunified Germany and the four great powers.

Rotfeld was right in writing that the ratification of any treaty might not be made dependent on any conditions formulated unilaterally by one of the contracting parties after the signature of the treaty. The Bundestag resolution, adopted after the publication of his article, was no doubt such a unilateral condition for West German ratification.

Rotfeld did not mention the West German official interpretation of the territorial provisions of the Warsaw Treaty, which was not very different from the later resolution, but leaves the reader guessing about the meaning of what he himself wrote: "It seems that the government of the FRG has made certain concessions, in particular regarding its restrictive interpretation of the meaning of the concluded treaties, in order to gain the opposition's support for the ratification."[15] If *Sprawy Międzynarodowe* had followed the Western usage of publishing readers' letters, not a few of its readers probably would have asked: "What is this restrictive West German interpretation?"

One of the Polish specialists on German problems, Jerzy Sułek, published two articles on the same subject. The first, printed by *Sprawy Międzynarodowe* in June 1972, was obviously written prior to the adoption of the Bundestag resolution.[16] He remarked that Germany did not exist as one state at the time of the conclusion of the Warsaw Treaty. This is why the FRG could act only on its own behalf. The GDR was the only Western neighbor of Poland. Therefore, the Görlitz Treaty, concluded in 1950 with the GDR, was the only one of practical importance, because it confirmed the validity for the Polish neighbor of the common frontier, already finally settled in the Potsdam Agreement. Following the Görlitz Treaty, no "unsolved" or "controversial" frontier existed in relations between the FRG and Poland, which had no common frontier. What existed was something else, namely the refusal for twenty years by the Christian Democratic governments of the FRG to acknowledge the Western Polish frontier. This made impossible the normalization of West German-Polish relations. Sułek was right in his view that the FRG could only wage a campaign against the Polish frontier but could not change it, especially because "the alliance of Poland with the USSR and other socialist countries is a sufficient guarantee of the durability of the Oder-Neisse frontier. We have no fears regarding its security."[17] Except for the fact that the revisionist policy of the FRG prevented the establishment of normal relations with Poland, it was in effect more a political nuisance for Warsaw than anything else.

Sułek repeated the Polish thesis that the FRG recognized the legal validity of the Potsdam decision by consenting to describe the Western Polish frontier in the wording of that decision. While wrong in this respect insofar as West German interpretation was concerned, he was right in saying that "the FRG will not be able to continue the policy of former Christian Democratic governments of regarding 'the former East German territories' as remaining within the 1937 Reich's frontiers and as a part of the German state territory only 'administered' by Poland."[18] This was actually the main Polish gain obtained in the treaty. The former official revisionist policy was to be stopped.

Sułek did not overlook the question of a peace treaty on Germany but argued that such a treaty could be concluded only with the two existing German states, both of which accepted the present Polish frontier and both of which "are formally bound not to demand the revision of the Western Polish frontier."[19] This might be so, except that the West German reservation regarding the peace treaty envisaged that treaty as being negotiated not by the two present German states but by an already reunified German state. Sułek had an answer to this question by holding that a reunified Germany, as a successor state, would have to respect the treaties concluded by its two predecessors.

Sułek's second article, published in August 1972, was written after the adoption of the Bundestag resolution, but strangely enough he did not mention nor discuss it.[20] He repeated once again the official Polish thesis that the Moscow and Warsaw Treaties meant the recognition by the FRG, valid in international law, of the Oder-Neisse frontier as "final and inviolable."[21] Yet he must have read the explanations offered by the West German government during the Bundestag debates, and the text of the resolution which denied the legal foundation for the existing frontiers. For him there was no problem of a future peace settlement since the GDR had settled its problems with the socialist states a long time ago, while the FRG did the same in the Moscow and Warsaw Treaties. The particular problem of the Western Polish frontier was finally solved in those two treaties, especially as the four great powers "today uphold completely their Potsdam stand regarding the Western frontier of Poland. None of these powers demands its modification. . . . This means that the USSR-FRG and PPR-FRG Treaties closed finally the problem of the Polish-German frontier, already solved in Potsdam."[22]

His remark regarding the four powers was exact regarding the Soviet Union and France. He was right too that neither the United States nor Britain was raising any longer the question of validity of the Oder-Neisse frontier, as they had done during the period of the cold war. However, neither of the two officially and publicly stated, even after the conclusion of the two treaties, that they abandoned their right to consider the German frontiers again at the time of a peace settlement.

The only Polish commentator who deviated from the official interpretation and took into account the West German point of view was Krzysztof Skubiszewski who published his commentary in a law journal.[23] He disagreed, however, with the West German view that the Warsaw Treaty contained only a *de facto* recognition of the frontier. He recalled that the preamble to the Treaty had mentioned the two parties' "respect . . . for the sovereignty of all European states within their present frontiers." This meant that the FRG recognized by implication Polish sovereignty over the former East German territory. Recognition of sovereignty could only mean recognition *de jure*.

He was the only one among both the Polish and West German commentators to draw attention to the inadequate description of actual Polish Western frontiers in the Potsdam decision. This description was repeated word by word in Article One of the Warsaw Treaty. The Potsdam decision did not mention expressly the southern part of East Prussia or Stettin which lay west of the River Oder. Skubiszewski added, however, that the records of the Potsdam Conference made it clear that both that part of East Prussia and Stettin were to be placed under Polish administration. (See above Chapter 3.)

While agreeing with the FRG that it had undertaken its obligations in the Warsaw Treaty only on its own behalf and repeating the Polish view that Poland could not accept the former West German claim of being the spokesman for all Germans, he rejected the West German and Soviet views (see above Chapters 8 and 10) that the Eastern treaties did not preclude a peaceful revision of frontiers if agreed upon by the two states concerned. He argued that Article 2 of the Warsaw Treaty, where the parties agreed to settle all controversial issues only by peaceful means, did not apply to the territorial problem, because the FRG renounced all territorial claims now and for the future. The frontier problem was no longer a controversial issue between the FRG and Poland. One may add that the USSR and the FRG had in mind not the Polish Western frontier but the inner frontier between the two German states. If the Soviet government had denied that frontiers could be changed by agreement between the two states concerned, and thus had precluded German reunification, the German government would not have signed the Moscow Treaty.

Skubiszewski stated the truth, overlooked in other comments, when he said that "the federal government left the problem of the German-Polish frontier with a reunified Germany to be rebuilt in the future to the all-German government and to the peace treaty, because it did not consider itself competent to speak on this topic."[24] He also spoke the truth when he stated that the Warsaw Treaty did not invalidate the rights of the four powers regarding Germany as a whole and regarding the final settlement in a peace treaty of the frontiers of a reunited Germany. But he thought that a peace treaty could only confirm the existence of the Oder-Neisse frontier after the lapse of so many years since the Second World War, and in view of Polish resettlement of the former East German territories. Incidentally, the latter view was shared by many West German politicians.

While conceding that the Görlitz and Warsaw Treaties were binding only on the two German states, Skubiszewski invoked international law on succession to claim that a reunified Germany as a successor state would be bound by the two treaties concluded by its predecessors.

His comment was the only one to take into consideration the West German point of view, as expressed not only in the period following the signature of the Warsaw Treaty, but also in the notes addressed to the four great powers at the time of signature. The discussion of the meaning of the Warsaw Treaty could not be dissociated from Polish-Soviet relations since the existence of the Oder-Neisse frontier rested politically not on the treaties concluded with the German states, but on the alliance with the USSR. The Polish Prime Minister Piotr Jaroszewicz said on May 8, 1971: "Poland needs the might of the Soviet Union, because the guarantee of our independence, the inviolability of our frontiers and our security repose on this might."[25]

POLISH RATIFICATION

The parliamentary procedure of approval of the Warsaw Treaty was preceded by a statement of the Political Bureau of the ruling United Polish Workers' Party: "The main obligations in the Treaty between Poland and the FRG concern the recognition, in accordance with the provisions of the Potsdam Agreement, of the Western Polish frontier on the Oder and the Lusatian Neisse as being inviolable and final. The normalization of international relations between the PPR and the FRG is possible only on this basis. . . . The entry into force of the PPR-FRG Treaty means the complete closure of the problem of international law recognition of the Oder-Neisse frontier."[26]

This interpretation, at variance with the West German, set the tone for the debate in the Polish parliament. The debate was opened by one of the secretaries of the Central Committee of the United Polish Workers' Party and head of its Foreign Department, Ryszard Frelek. He repeated the thesis of his party's Political Bureau that the Potsdam Agreement had determined the Polish Oder-Neisse frontier, and that this frontier was confirmed in the Görlitz Treaty with the GDR and recognized as inviolable and irreversible in the Warsaw Treaty. The territorial problem did not exist any longer. The Polish-Soviet alliance guaranteed the security of that frontier and hence the problem of its inviolability did not exist practically. The only question settled in the Warsaw Treaty was the recognition of the frontier by the FRG. Alluding to the Bundestag resolution, Frelek said: "Only and exclusively the Treaty itself has importance from the point of view of international law and only it is binding on both parties. . . . Nothing may undermine the essence and significance of the Treaty. . . . The Bundestag resolution has only a unilateral character and has no binding force in international law."[27]

Frelek was right insofar as Poland was concerned. His government, unlike the Soviet, was not consulted on the text of the resolution and could ignore it officially even as a unilateral West German interpretation. But the fact remained that the resolution, which formulated the other party's unilateral interpretation, could not be politically disregarded.

All the deputies who participated in the debate followed Frelek's point of view. They insisted that only the treaty was binding, while the West German interpretive declarations had no legal significance. For them the FRG recognized in the Warsaw Treaty the finality and irreversibility of the Oder-Neisse frontier. Deputy Witold Jankowski (nonparty) denounced the Bundestag resolution as a symptom of German nationalism and complained of "the different treatment of partners." He thus alluded to the fact that the Polish government, unlike the Soviet, had not been consulted on the wording of the resolution. What he did not mention was another aspect of the same fact, namely, that the Soviet government had not asked Bonn to consult Warsaw also. Deputy Bogdan Waligórski (UPWP) stigmatized those West German interpretations which he deemed contrary to the Warsaw Treaty as acts of bad faith. Deputy Jerzy Bafia (UPWP) also claimed that only the treaty was binding and should be identically interpreted by both parties. This identical interpretation should concede the final closure of the problem of the Oder-Neisse frontier.

Deputy Edmund Osmańczyk (non-party), one of the prewar leaders of the Polish minority in Germany, warned that one should not be in a hurry to trust the intentions of the FRG. Normalization in mutual relations should not be viewed as a radical change in the FRG's attitude toward Poland. Another deputy, Stanisław Rostworowski (non-party), was also distrustful: "The Brandt-Scheel government confirmed the realities, but it is unknown to what extent it did accept them in its innermost mind." Deputy Feliks Barabasz (UPWP) hoped that the treaty would result eventually in a better image of Poland in West German school education and would accelerate the criminal prosecution in the FRG of Nazi war criminals who had committed their offenses in Poland. Edmund Męclewski (non-party) complained that the second postwar West German generation was being brought up in schools in a spirit of hostility to Poles, but he conceded that many West German teachers, scholars, and publishers favored a new, unprejudiced approach to the teaching on Poland.

The past was not forgotten. Deputy Henryk Korotyński (UPWP) recalled the ghost of the German occupation: the loss of 6 million Polish lives, one-fifth of the prewar Polish population. He added that only 123,000 soldiers and 521,000 civilians perished during actual hostilities, while well over five million were murdered by the Germans in summary executions and in prisons and concentration camps. He claimed that the FRG should pay reparations to the surviving Polish victims of Nazi camps and of slave labor in Germany. Deputy Maria Milczarek (UPWP) added to these sad recollections a reminder of the martyrdom of Polish women, in particular of inmates of the Nazi camps in Brzezinka and Ravensbrück. Both she and Stanisław Stomma, representing the Catholic group, worried about the fact that as many as seventeen Bundestag deputies had voted against the Warsaw Treaty. Deputy Witold Jankowski raised the question of incompatibility between the Warsaw Treaty and the functioning of Radio Free Europe on the soil of the FRG.

The debate showed unanimity regarding Polish interpretation of the treaty and no less unanimous denial of any validity to the Bundestag resolution. It also demonstrated the prevailing distrust of the FRG and the feeling that the process of normalization would not be an easy task. It pointed out remaining controversial matters such as the revision of West German schoolbooks, raised among other things by deputies

Edmund Męclewski (non-party) and Wilhelm Szewczyk (UPWP); the activities of the expellee organizations; the existence of Radio Free Europe in Munich; the prosecution of Nazi war criminals before the West German courts; West German legislation (deputy Witold Jankowski) which was based on the assumption that Germany continued to exist within the 1937 frontiers and its incompatibility with the Warsaw Treaty; and reparation for the victims of Nazi concentration camps and slave labor.

The only deputy to express some optimism regarding the future was Bogdan Waligórski (UPWP) who voiced the hope that the young generation of Poles and Germans, who did not remember the war, might create an atmosphere propitious for future Polish-German cooperation. The mood in parliament was expressed best by deputy Wojciech Żukrowski (non-party) to whom the treaty was only a threshold leading to a long and difficult road toward the normalization of relations with the FRG.

Foreign Minister Stefan Olszowski closed the debate:

> The Federal Republic of Germany recognized in this Treaty the Oder-Neisse frontiers as inviolable and final. . . . The reservations in the Bundestag's unilateral resolution have no force from the point of view of international law and in the light of obligations contained in the Treaty. . . . The frontier was determined in the Potsdam Agreement. . . . The German Democratic Republic recognized it . . . in the 1950 Görlitz Treaty. Recognition also by the other German state, the Federal Republic of Germany, completely closes the question. . . . No further decisions or acts are now or in the future needed in this respect. . . . The inviolability of the Oder-Neisse frontier rests on the Polish-Soviet alliance . . . and on the defensive might of the Warsaw Pact. . . . Side by side with the establishment of diplomatic relations, economic and scientific-technological cooperation is one of the important aspects of normalization.

It seemed that the ratification of the treaty took place under unfavorable portents, the two parties attributing almost opposite meanings to the treaty. Strangely enough, however, this did not prevent an improvement in mutual relations even prior to the ratification of the treaty. The Polish daily press and scholarly journals noted both aspects of new Polish-German relations during that period: the existence of controversial issues but also an improvement in the mutual atmosphere. On the whole, the Poles would have agreed with Willy Brandt's characterization of the meaning of the Warsaw Treaty. The Chancellor said in a speech immediately after the signature of the treaty: "Germans and Poles have travelled on a historical road during their many-century neighborhood. It was a difficult road. The years which followed 1939 belonged to the most sinister sectors of that road. . . . Nothing can erase that. . . . I realize that today's act may not fill in the crevasse which was so brutally opened. I know too that an understanding or even more a reconciliation may not be achieved by statesmen, but must mature in the human hearts on both sides."[28]

THE MOOD IN POLAND

The Warsaw Treaty marked only a beginning of normalization, not yet of reconciliation. The Polish press listed in various articles controversial issues such as the need for more vigorous prosecution of the Nazi war criminals residing in West Germany;[29] the subventions granted by some of the West German state governments to the expellee organizations in spite of their anti-Polish propaganda;[30] the functioning of Radio Free Europe on German soil and its propaganda directed against the Polish regime;[31] the vilification of Polish culture in the publications of various West German research institutes;[32] those parts of West German legislation which extended its authority over former East German territories and which held that Germany still remained within its 1937 frontiers (the Polish critics particularly raised objections to West German laws on citizenship, because these laws considered as German citizens those persons who had that citizenship prior to the Second World War and also their descendants, in spite of the fact that a great many of those persons resided in the Polish-annexed former East German territories and now possessed Polish citizenship).[33]

On the other hand, the year 1971 witnessed many reciprocal visits, a new phenomenon in mutual relations. The list of German visitors in 1971 included not only pro-government politicians such as Herbert Wehner (SPD), Minister Georg Leber (SPD), Wolfgang Mischnick (FPD), but also Christian Democrats such as Rainer Barzel and von Bismarck, chairman of the Pomeranian expellee organization. West German business organizations, the Catholic Pax Christi, the Young Socialists, the Evangelical Church and other associations sent their representatives to initiate the first postwar contacts. Poland sent to Bonn a parliamentary delegation which was received by President Heinemann, Chancellor Brandt, Foreign Minister Scheel, and Speaker of the Bundestag von Hassel. Various officials also traveled from one country to the other. This in itself marked a change for the better.

It was perhaps not unrelated to the signature of the Warsaw Treaty that the Polish government granted to the Catholic Church in 1971 the ownership of church buildings and other assets in the former East German territories, assets which the Church could use before but not as their legal owner.

The Polish press noted West German manifestations of a better attitude toward Poland. For instance, the federal government decided in July 1971 to change the names of birthplaces in the passports of citizens of the FRG. The old German names were to be used only in the passports of those citizens who were born east of the Oder-Neisse prior to 1945. Those whose birth dates were later than 1945 would have in their passports the Polish names of their birthplaces with the German names mentioned only in parentheses. Also received with satisfaction was the federal government's decision to annul the former requirement that all maps published in the FRG should represent Germany as existing within the 1937 frontiers, while the Polish and Soviet-annexed territories were to bear the words, "under the Polish respectively Soviet temporary administration." The Polish press also welcomed another decision to the effect that the federal government would stop paying subsidies to the expellee organizations and would no longer send its representatives to their annual meetings. Moreover, the federal government forbade the former practice of naming special trains transporting the expellees to their meetings after cities lost to Poland or to the Soviet Union.

The more friendly attitude of the West German Catholic Church, the usual mainstay of Christian Democrats, was also noted with satisfaction; for instance, the Catholic Pax Christi adopted in November 1971 in the presence of Cardinal Doepfner, president of the German episcopate, a resolution in favor of the ratification of the Warsaw Treaty. The Central Committee of German Catholics adopted a resolution in March 1971 which advocated the revision of German schoolbooks in a sense more favorable to Poland, the payment of reparations to those Poles whose health was permanently impaired by wartime Nazi mistreatment, the intensification of contacts between the German and Polish churches, and the organization of seminars on Poland for German Catholic adults and youth, with the participation of Polish lecturers. The Christian Democratic youth associations such as the *Junge Union* and the *Ring Christlich-Demokratischer Studenten* took a position different from that of their party elders by favoring the recognition of the Oder-Neisse frontier.[34]

The Polish attitude was on the whole rather optimistic regarding the mood in the FRG. However, what interested the Polish press most was the prospect of more lively economic cooperation with the FRG.

SOVIET RATIFICATION

Soviet ratification of the Moscow Treaty followed on the heels of that in the FRG. The discussion took place in the Presidium of the Supreme Soviet. Foreign Minister Andrei Gromyko submitted the report on behalf of the government and did everything possible to dissociate the USSR from the interpretation contained in the Bundestag resolution, which Moscow had approved through its ambassador in Bonn but only as a unilateral West German interpretation without any binding force for the Soviet Union. Gromyko said:

> The purpose and task of the [Moscow] treaty are clear and easy to understand. They are formulated with entire precision in the text of the treaty which leaves no room for any incorrect interpretations. The definition of obligations of the parties regarding the fundamental question of European security, the existing state frontiers in Europe, has a particular importance. . . . The Western frontier of the PPR and the frontier between the GDR and the FRG have been confirmed for the first time in the postwar period in a treaty concluded with the big capitalist state which is at the same time one of the successors of defeated Hitlerite Germany. . . . These provisions constitute the heart of the treaty. . . . The treaty contains the obligation of the parties to renounce the use of force in mutual relations and for the settlement of international problems. These pertinent articles were included in the treaty, while taking into account the fact that the treaty provisions were founded on the inviolability of existing frontiers and excluded the possibility of raising any territorial claims whatsoever. . . . It is self-evident that only the text agreed upon by the parties, *i.e.,* only the treaty itself, may serve as the basis for the interpretation of the treaty as well as for the determination of the extent of its application and of the scope and meaning of the treaty obligations.[35]

It was clear from what Gromyko said that his government considered the acceptance of existing frontiers by the FRG as the most crucial part of the Moscow Treaty. One of the most important members of the Soviet Political Bureau, N. V. Podgornyi, confirmed in his capacity as Chairman of the Presidium of the Supreme Soviet the view of the Foreign Minister. He said, "The treaty clearly defines the inviolability now and in the future of the frontiers of all European states, including the Western frontier of the Polish People's Republic on the Oder and the Neisse and the frontier between the FRG and the GDR. These provisions of the treaty have key importance for the task of strengthening peace and security on the European continent. No European state now exists which would question the stability of European frontiers."[36]

What counted from the Soviet point of view was the fact that West Germany, which had contested for many years the validity of the territorial status quo in Central Europe, finally accepted it. The reservations made in the Bundestag resolution did not matter as long as the FRG agreed to halt its revisionist propaganda. As for the future, including German reunification and the prospect of a reunited Germany asking for the revision of frontiers, Moscow did not need to worry. The Soviet Union was one of the four great powers with the same right as the United States, Britain, and France to participate in the decisions regarding reunification. It could stop by its veto any possible move toward reunification. Above all, it kept several divisions on East German soil, and their presence there guaranteed the survival of the GDR and the security of the Polish Oder-Neisse frontier. The Poles knew this well.

12

Epilogue—The Aftermath

BRANDT'S ELECTORAL VICTORY

THE PREFACE stated that this book would be concerned with postwar relations between Poland and the Federal Republic of Germany. It was also noted that this topic would hardly be understandable without a parallel survey of the attitudes of the Federal Republic toward the whole Soviet bloc since its foundation in 1949 and until and including Brandt's New Eastern Policy, because the Polish problem was only one, though a very important, aspect of those attitudes. But if every aspect of the developments in Polish-German relations following the entry into force of the Warsaw Treaty had to be traced, we would have a never-ending story. Those relations continue to follow their course, the Warsaw Treaty having been the threshold leading to normal relations between the two countries. Hence, we shall look at only a few high points of the years 1973–75.

First of all, we must mention the last stages in the completion of Brandt's Eastern policy which was based on the assumption that the Moscow and Warsaw Treaties would open the gate to the other East European states. Brandt could lead his country through these later stages with no further worry about the opposition. The parliamentary deadlock was broken in the general election held on November 19, 1972. The Social Democrats and the Free Democrats won a resounding victory. The issue of the two treaties did not play a major role, since the opposition bore coresponsibility for their ratification. If it played any role, the majority of the electors approved the treaties by the very fact of

277

voting for the governmental parties. The participation reached a record for any democratic state: 91.2 percent of eligible voters cast their ballots. For the first time in the history of the FRG the Social Democrats did better than the Christian Democrats, while the Free Democrats obtained a respectable portion of ballots. The results were as follows: 45.9 percent for the SPD, 44.8 percent for the Christian Democrats, and 8.4 percent for the Free Democrats. The Brandt-Scheel coalition won a 48-seat majority in the Bundestag.[1]

THE TREATY WITH THE GDR

On November 8, 1973, the two German states initialed a treaty on the normalization of their relations. This treaty stated in Articles 1 and 2 that the two parties would develop normal good-neighborly relations, founded on the United Nations principles of sovereign equality and respect for independence, territorial integrity, and mutual non-discrimination. Article 3 pledged the two states to refrain from the use of force and to respect now and in the future their present frontier. Article 4 stated that neither of them would represent the other internationally or act on its behalf. Article 8 said that the two governments would be represented in each other's capitals by permanent missions.[2]

The parties agreed that they would simultaneously seek admission to the United Nations. The four great powers immediately promised to support their admission.

The FRG abandoned in the treaty its long-held pre-Brandt stand. The Hallstein doctrine and the West German claim to speak on behalf of all Germans were finally buried. The FRG relinquished its former opposition to establishment by third states of diplomatic relations with the GDR. This opened the door to all states interested in having their embassies in East Berlin, including Britain, France, and the United States. Brandt's subtle distinction between the recognition of the GDR as a foreign or as another German state lost its meaning for the third states. However, the four powers stated expressly that the treaty did not encroach upon their own responsibilities and rights regarding Germany as a whole. This meant that the two German states, even if they wanted it, could not be reunited without the assent of the great powers.

The single trace of Brandt's reservation that he would recognize the GDR only as another state of the same German nation consisted in the name of the mutual diplomatic representations: they were to be called permanent missions, not embassies. What he gained was agreement by the GDR that the FRG's mission in East Berlin would also represent the interests of West Berlin. Another gain for the FRG was the East German promise to ease its policy regarding personal contacts between the two populations.

The treaty entered into force on June 21, 1973. The CSU Bavarian government tried to prevent its ratification by submitting to the German Constitutional Court the question of its alleged incompatibility with the Constitution, but it lost its case. In effect, the treaty acknowledged the division of Germany. Poland could only welcome it, since it knew that reunification might reopen the territorial problem.

The two German states were admitted to the United Nations in the fall of 1973. The GDR became a universally recognized member of the international community.

THE TREATY WITH CZECHOSLOVAKIA

The next step in the Eastern policy was the conclusion of the treaty with Czechoslovakia. The two governments signed that treaty on December 11, 1973.[3] Article 1, like Article 1 of the Warsaw Treaty, dealt with the main controversial question, in this case the Munich Agreement by virtue of which Czechoslovakia had lost its Sudetenland in 1938. The protracted controversy as to the exact time the Munich Agreement had become null and void (at the time of its very signature, as the Czechs claimed, or only in March 1939, because of the German occupation of Prague, as the FRG maintained) was solved in a Solomon-like way: "The Federal Republic of Germany and the Czechoslovak Socialist Republic . . . deem the Munich Agreement of 29 September 1938 void with regard to their mutual relations." This wording of Article 1 allows each party to continue to uphold its version of nullity. The prospect of criminal prosecution for treason of former Sudeten Germans, if they should visit Czechoslovakia, was prevented by Article 2, which said that the present treaty would not affect the legal effects on persons of the laws applied in the period between September 30, 1939, and May 9, 1945. In other words, the Sudeten Germans who became German citizens after the annexation of the Sudetenland would not be considered traitors by Czechoslovakia because the latter country retrospectively recognized their acquisition of German citizenship. The Czechoslovak government made one exception in the letter addressed to the other party, namely, that it remained free to prosecute German war criminals. The other articles of the treaty followed the pattern of the Moscow and Warsaw Treaties. They pledged the two parties to settle all their disputes by peaceful means and to renounce the use of force (Article 3), to respect the inviolability of their frontier, and to renounce any territorial claims now and in the future (Article 4).

HUNGARY AND BULGARIA

The conclusion of the treaty with Czechoslovakia ended the cycle of treaties with those East European states with whom the FRG had vital controversies (the recognition of the GDR as a coequal state, the renunciation of claims against the Oder-Neisse frontier, and the settlement of the problem of the Munich Agreement). Hungary and Bulgaria were not divided from the FRG by any quarrels of this kind; hence, it was easy for the West German government to establish diplomatic relations with these two countries in December 1973. The FRG now had at last normalized its relations with the whole Soviet bloc. The objective of Brandt's Eastern policy was fully reached. What remained was day-to-day relations with their usual problems between any capitalist state and the socialist countries.

PRESIDENT NIXON'S VISIT TO WARSAW

President Nixon visited Warsaw in 1972 on his return from Moscow. The President conceded in the joint communiqué issued on June 1, 1972, that "both sides agree that the development of peaceful cooperation among states must be based *on the principles of territorial integrity and inviolability of frontiers* [italics added], noninterference in internal affairs, sovereign equality, independence, and renunciation of the use of threat of use of force. . . . Both sides welcomed the Treaty between Poland and the Federal Republic of Germany, signed on December 7, 1970, including its border provisions."[4] This statement meant American recognition of the Oder-Neisse frontier at least for the duration of the existence of the FRG.

THE VATICAN'S RECOGNITION OF THE ODER-NEISSE FRONTIER

The Holy See went much farther in drawing its own conclusion from the Warsaw Treaty. It solved its controversy with the Polish government radically by the redrawing of the ecclesiastical boundaries of dioceses in Poland to make them conform with the new Polish frontiers. This protracted controversy not only hampered relations between the Polish Catholic Church and the Polish government, but was also an obstacle in establishing workable relations between the Vatican and Poland. The Communist Party had an easy game in accusing the Polish Church of weakness in pressing the Vatican for the redrawing of the ecclesiastical borders, and the Vatican of pro-German sympathies. The Holy See was caught in the crossfire between the two churches, the German insisting on the maintenance of prewar boundaries and the Polish Church asking for their revision in favor of Poland. Pope John XXIII gave the first signs of sympathy for the Polish request, but it was Pope Paul VI who settled the problem, taking the opportunity of the conclusion of the Warsaw Treaty. This was in accordance with the Eastern policy of the Vatican which sought to improve its relations with the whole Soviet bloc, especially with those countries having large Catholic populations. Poland occupied the first place in these preoccupations because the very great majority of its population were Catholics regularly attending church services. Actually the proportion of such Catholics in Poland was much higher than in any other country presumed Catholic. This very fact has made the Church the only political power other than the Communist Party.

The Vatican decided on June 28, 1972, to redraw the ecclesiastical borders of Polish dioceses in accordance with the new western and northern Polish frontiers. The temporary Polish bishops in the Polish-annexed territories were renamed regular bishops. Among other things, the Vatican recognized the Archbishop in Wrocław (formerly Breslau) as a regular head of his archdiocese. He was soon after named a cardinal. The meaning of the Vatican's decision was clear. It recognized the Oder-Neisse frontier as final. Its traditional policy had consisted in waiting for such a redrawing of ecclesiastical borders until a peace treaty should be concluded between the two states concerned. It obviously considered the Warsaw Treaty as a substitute for a peace treaty.

The Primate of Poland, Cardinal Stefan Wyszyński, immediately sent a letter to the Polish Prime Minister, Piotr Jaroszewicz, in which he stressed that the Holy See's decision was the result of efforts by the Polish episcopate, and expressed confidence that the decision would strengthen the position of Poland in the "Recovered Lands." The Polish government also expressed its satisfaction in a public communiqué.

CONTROVERSIAL LEGISLATION

One of the still outstanding Polish-German problems is West German legislation and court decisions which extend the validity of laws of the FRG not only to the GDR but also to the Polish and Soviet-annexed former East German territories.[5] Both the GDR and those former East German territories were included within the concept of the "inland" of Germany, allegedly remaining within the 1937 frontiers. This problem should now be solved by appropriate West German amendments to pertinent legislation and by a new judicial interpretation of what is actually "inland" for the FRG. The FRG is bound by treaties to consider as inland only its own territory within the present frontiers. The treaty concluded with the GDR formally conceded the relinquishment of former claims to East German territory as the West German inland. The Moscow and Warsaw Treaties obliged the FRG to renounce all claims to the former East German territories. Hence, they may no longer be treated as the inland in West German laws and by West German courts.

However, the federal government made a reservation regarding that part of West German legislation which had extended German citizenship to persons residing east of the Oder-Neisse frontiers and who had been German citizens prior to 1945. They were to continue to be considered German citizens. Since they were granted Polish citizenship by Poland, they have a different citizenship for each country. This strange situation results from both the West German constitution and the Imperial German law on citizenship of July 22, 1913, which is considered valid in the FRG. Article 116, Paragraph One of the Constitution states: "Unless otherwise legally stipulated, every person possessing German citizenship is German, including every person who, as refugee or expellee, and his or her spouse and descendants, found refuge on the territory of the German Reich within the frontiers of December 31, 1937." This provision included the pre-1945 population remaining east of the Oder-Neisse frontier since the Constitution mentions their "refuge" within the 1937 frontiers. No specific distinction was made between those persons who were of German or Polish ethnic nationality. The law of July 22, 1913, is considered applicable to all those persons. They and their descendants retain their German citizenship although they live in Poland and now have Polish citizenship. Moreover, the West German law of February 22, 1955, recognized as valid the German citizenship bestowed by Nazi Germany on the so-called *Volksdeutsche*, *i.e.*, on Polish or other citizens of German descent living in the territories occupied by Germany. What occurred during the Second World War was not only a free-will request by such persons to obtain German citizenship, but also the forcible imposition on them of that citizenship. In the latter case they had the choice only of accepting that citizenship or facing death. The law of 1955 took this into consideration by limiting the validity of claim to German citizenship to those persons among the *Volksdeutsche* who now consider themselves ethnic Germans, as proved, among other things, by their daily use of the German language. Moreover, West German legal comments on that law exclude from its application persons to whom Poland or another concerned state had restored their former, prewar citizenship.

In May 1970, the West German government issued a public statement according to which the FRG would treat in fact as German citizens those who had been such citizens prior to 1945, but only if they were to take domicile on its own territory. This interpretation made the whole Polish-German controversy rather academic. The FRG does not make the usual international claim to have the right to extend its consular protection to the pre-1945 German citizens who are now Polish citizens from the Polish point of view. The German Embassy in Warsaw may not raise such claims. This is the reason why the repatriation of Polish citizens of German ethnic nationality is handled by the Red Cross of the two countries. Those pre-1945 German citizens do not need naturalization in the FRG when they cross the West German frontier at the time of their repatriation. They are treated as German citizens once they take domicile in the FRG.

ECONOMIC ASPECTS OF GERMAN-POLISH RELATIONS

The main Polish interest in normal relations with the FRG is economic. This means expanded trade, credits, and more frequent contracts with West German private corporations in order to import the higher German technological knowledge to modernize Polish factories or build new ones with German assistance. Parenthetically, Poland is making its modest reverse contribution by building a sulphuric-acid factory in the FRG, by building ships for West German contractors, and by helping to reconstruct some of the war-damaged German historical buildings, among others, the medieval gate in Munich and one of the oldest and war-damaged cathedrals. It is a bizarre twist of history. The deliberate German destruction of Polish historical buildings, especially in Warsaw, forced the Poles to become internationally known experts in reconstruction of historical buildings and in repairing damaged objects of art. These Polish experts are now helping West Germany.

The important role which the FRG plays in Polish trade is illustrated by the following statistics for the year 1972:[6]

	Polish exports to	Polish imports from
USSR	36.9	29.9
GDR	8.4	11.3
Czechoslovakia	7.4	8.6
FRG	5.4	8.0
Britain	3.8	4.6
Italy	3.8	2.4
Hungary	3.3	4.3
USA	2.6	2.1
France	2.3	2.7

The FRG occupies first place among the non-Communist states. Moreover, German firms and Polish enterprises have concluded 150 contracts for industrial cooperation. Usually these contracts provide for the Polish manufacturing of semi-finished goods which are further processed in Germany. The two governments and their scientific institutions have also concluded agreements for scientific-technological cooperation.

DISPUTED ISSUES

Two issues still dominate German-Polish relations: the repatriation of ethnic Germans to the FRG, and the problem of indemnification by the FRG for the Polish victims of Nazi terror during the Second World War. The latter problem was fully explained in an article published in *Sprawy Międzynarodowe*.[7] The author of that article listed the following categories of persons who should be indemnified: (1) former inmates of concentration camps; (2) the families of Poles killed by the Nazi occupation authorities; (3) other persons whose health was impaired by illegal Nazi treatment; (4) Polish slave laborers forced to work for Germany. His argument was that such victims of the Nazi regime in Poland should receive indemnification similar to that given to the Jews and to the citizens of West European countries who were indemnified by the FRG for damages caused by the Nazi regime. The FRG has so far indemnified only such Poles as had been used by the Nazis as objects of pseudo-medical experiments (140 million German marks). The question of the indemnification of all victims of the Nazi regime was raised for the first time by Party First Secretary Edward Gierek in his speech made in Poznań on March 22, 1972.

The FRG advanced three arguments to justify its negative response: first, the statute limitation because German legislation made December 31, 1969, the ultimate date for applications on behalf of Nazi victims, *i.e.,* prior to the establishment of diplomatic relations with Poland; second, the Polish annexation of the former German territories as a sort of general indemnification; third, German legislation foresaw no indemnification for those Nazi victims who were persecuted for reasons of their nationality but provided it only for the victims of racial persecutions. The Poles evaluate the amount of indemnification claimed as being approximately 1,800 million German marks. The FRG offered a substitute in 1973 in the form of a twenty-year credit of one billion DM repayable in twenty years. This offer was rejected by Warsaw as insufficient.

According to German and Polish sources, 286,000 Polish citizens (prewar German citizens) have applied for permission to emigrate to the FRG because of their ethnic German nationality. Polish sources add that one-third of those applicants withdrew their applications after visiting the FRG and after having been disappointed by the prospects of their future conditions of life in West Germany. In any event, about 55,000 ethnic Germans left Poland between January 1, 1971, and April 1974. At the time of Foreign Minister Walter Scheel's visit to Poland in October 1973, the two governments agreed that the problem of repatriation would be solved entirely within the next three to five years.

The more liberal Polish policy in granting permissions to Polish citizens, including those who intend to resettle in the FRG, to visit the FRG has helped the latter citizens to make clear for themselves what they can expect after taking domicile in the FRG. All in all, 52,000 Polish citizens were allowed to visit the FRG in 1972, and this figure rose to 118,000 in 1974. As has been said, these visits resulted in the withdrawal of one-third of the applications.

The problem of repatriation remained on the Polish-German agenda, among other reasons, because the German government was under heavy pressure by the Christian Democratic opposition constantly to raise this question in talks with the Polish government. For instance, the government was strongly attacked by the opposition, especially its right wing, at the meeting of the Bundestag on March 21, 1974, for allegedly being lax in pressing Warsaw for a quicker repatriation.

The problem of repatriation was complicated not only by the difference between German and Polish figures of ethnic Germans but also by the fate of mixed marriages. Should the families of mixed German-Polish families be allowed to emigrate? Moreover, the ethnic Germans represent skilled labor whose emigration creates economic difficulties for Poland. If one were to consider the 286,000 extant applications as a criterion, the problem of repatriation could be solved within six to seven years if the Polish government were ready to grant permission.

The other aspect of the exchange of visitors has been growing West German tourism to Poland. The figures of that tourism have been constantly increasing: 49,000 in 1971, 69,000 in 1972, 237,000 in 1974. West and East Germans represented the bulk of foreign visitors in 1974.

The growth of mutual tourism represents the brighter aspect of mutual relations. It helps in providing a better knowledge of both countries. Even the refugees and expellees from the former East German territories are able to convince themselves of the great Polish effort in restoring cities and towns from their wartime devastation (Danzig, Stettin, and Breslau are obvious examples) and their Polonization by the postwar influx of Poles.

THE GIEREK-SCHMIDT AGREEMENT

On May 6, 1974, Willy Brandt was forced to resign as Chancellor because of the discovery of a well-camouflaged East German spy among Brandt's close assistants. Brandt remained the leader of his party, while another Social Democrat, Helmut Schmidt, became Chancellor. Although Brandt was deeply involved emotionally in the efforts to achieve a German-Polish reconciliation and although he was highly respected in Poland because of his faultless anti-Nazi record, the change in the chancellorship produced no adverse repercussions in Polish-German relations. As a matter of fact, it was Chancellor Schmidt who was able to settle with Polish First Secretary Gierek the two controversial issues that had poisoned relations between the two countries.

Schmidt and Gierek met in Helsinki on the occasion of the European Conference and agreed on August 1, 1975, to the terms of settlement of the two issues. Gierek promised to allow 120,000 to 125,000 ethnic Germans to emigrate to the FRG over a period of four years. This did not preclude later emigration of the 161,000 applicants for repatriation to the FRG. Gierek also accepted a figure for damages due to the Polish victims of Nazi occupation much lower than the previous claims. He agreed with the West German Chancellor that the FRG would pay $520 million as an indemnity to those victims and, in addition, that it would grant Poland a credit of $400 million at a low interest rate. These two obstacles removed, it would seem that German-Polish relations have entered the stage of full normalization.

NATIONAL RECONCILIATION?

There is no particular reason to fear that normalized relations will encounter unexpected obstacles or be confronted with serious mutual disappointments. Genuine reconciliation between the two nations is a different matter. The bitter history of their relations, especially during the Second World War, cannot be swept under the carpet by the fiat of the two governments. The only hope lies with the new generations who never witnessed the horrors of that war. This change in the hearts of young Germans and young Poles will take place only if their elders, parents and teachers, do not inculcate in their minds the traditional hostile image of the other nation. This is why the mutually agreed upon revision of schoolbooks is so important for future reconciliation.

This goal is easier to state than to accomplish. First of all, the scholars of both countries will never be able to agree completely on one version of history. Even with the best will, they cannot look at, say, the Teutonic Knights, Frederick the Great, or Bismarck in the same manner. But what could be achieved would be the elimination of stereotypes of either nation as contemptible, inferior, aggressive, or impossible to live with as a good neighbor. The second difficulty exists in the FRG. The Polish authorities could easily order a revision of schoolbooks. In the FRG the same matter lies within the jurisdiction of state governments, which might refuse to follow the federal government's advice. Finally, the older generation of scholars, many of whom cooperated with the Nazi regime and who have influenced present school programs insofar as Eastern Europe is concerned, will not capitulate and will do their best to prevent the revision of schoolbooks. This does not mean that the first step should not be made in the form of mutual consultations between Polish and German geographers and historians. This first step has been taken.

Before mentioning what has been done in this respect, it is worthwhile to glance at the German side of the problem. Why is the German aspect more important? If a nation is represented as aggressive, militarist, even immoral, as the Germans often have been depicted in Poland, this does not prejudge its future image. It retains the chance to become better. Moreover, the official Polish ideology, Marxism-Leninism, as well as the alliance with the GDR, acts today as a restraining influence. No nation is inherently bad for a Marxist-Leninist. Only its "ruling classes" are bad if a given nation has a capitalist system. The ruling Polish Party reminds the Poles of the fact that East Germans are good Germans. Moreover, the Polish mass media have conceded since 1969 the existence of reasonable men among West German Social Democrats and Free Democrats with whom Poles may peacefully coexist. In other words, the image of the German is not uniform or hopeless.

The traditional German image of the Poles is different, because it assumes that Poles by nature are inferior in every respect, with no capacity for rational government or economy and, moreover, with an inferior culture. This image of an inborn Polish and generally Slavic inferiority was the precondition for Nazi wartime atrocities. One cannot mobilize one's countrymen against another race, nation, ethnic, or racial minority without first inculcating in their minds the inferiority of that race, nation, or minority. Only such inferior human beings may be discriminated against and persecuted. The superiority image held by one nation, race, or ethnic group has its psychological effect on the other nation, race, or ethnic group. The latter can forget and even forgive atrocities and discriminations. Such wounds are healed by the lapse of time. One does not easily forgive the humiliation of being treated as an inferior human being. This insult to the dignity of the individual and his social group is not forgotten unless the detrimental image is truly abandoned by the other side.

The traditional and not only Nazi image of Polish inferiority persists in West German schools. A Pole becomes an equal only by the saving grace of becoming Germanized. Moreover, the Nazi period is not far away, and the then-widespread notions have left their traces even today. How many West German educators of the older generation did not collaborate with the Nazis in spreading the bad image of Poland?

The problem is well analyzed in a West German book published under the auspices of the Evangelical Academy of West Berlin.[8] The book opens with the remark that many West Germans wondered why Chancellor Brandt knelt in Warsaw before the monument to the exterminated Jews. This gesture seemed to them superfluous or undignified as though it were not the Germans who bore the responsibility for the extermination of Jews, Poles, Russians, and other Eastern Europeans.

The same book reminds the readers of the evil image of Poles, contemptuously called "Polaken," that has a long tradition, antecedent by at least 150 years to the Nazi period. This image has been hammered into the minds of several German generations, among other things, by schoolbooks and school programs. The beginning of that process, which the book calls "brainwashing," is more or less contemporary with the partitions of Poland in the second half of the eighteenth century. The image of the moral and political decomposition of Poland was needed to clothe the partitions with the mantle of high morality. The partitioning powers, including Prussia, proceeded simply with the surgery necessary for the health of Europe. Protests against the extinction of a state whose recorded history had begun in the tenth century were to be silenced by the repulsive image of the Poles who got what they deserved.

Field-Marshal von Knesebeck, in a memo submitted to his Prussian government in 1814, justified his view that Poland should never again be independent by accusing the Poles of being "drunkards, gluttons, servile, and destroyers of everything better and of every other people . . . dissipate, slovenly, easily bought with money, sly and false."[9] This was written after the Poles had enacted in 1791, shortly before the last two partitions, a constitution very progressive for its time, and after they had proved their patriotism by fighting for their independence at Napoleon's side.

Knesebeck wrote his memo in 1814. In 1970 a questionnaire was submitted to schoolboys graduating from high schools in Hamburg. They were asked to express their opinion of Frenchmen, Russians, and Poles. First, these youngsters did not even claim any knowledge of Poland, dismissed as an unimportant neighbor of Russia. Yet they had their image of the Pole, the least sympathetic by comparison to Frenchmen and Russians. The Poles were primitive, brutal, cunning, unfriendly, unreliable, and irascible.[10] Knesebeck would have been proud of these schoolboys.

The evil image of the Pole, originally a Prussian product, began to be widely accepted by other Germans in the second half of the nineteenth century and even more so after the foundation of the German Reich under Prussian auspices in 1871. Bismarck's letter, written in 1848, was typical of the Prussian view of the irreconcilability of German and Polish interests. He said that a restored Poland would want to regain its pre-partition provinces annexed by Prussia. He concluded his letter by saying that the Poles, once they achieved their independence, "shall be our sworn enemies as long as they can not conquer from us the mouth of the Vistula and also every Polish-speaking village in Western and Eastern Prussia, Pomerania, and Silesia."[11] This incompatibility between German interests and Polish independence had a lasting influence on the German image of Poland, up to and including the time of the Weimar Republic. A Bismarck contemporary, Wilhelm Jordan, exclaimed at the German National Assembly in Frankfurt in 1848: "Our right is no other than the right of the stronger, the right of conquest."[12] These statements marked the turning point in German public opinion, which previously had been sympathetic at times to the Polish yearning for independence. It was the task of German historians to popularize the hostile Prussian image of the Pole.[13] Eventually it became generally accepted. It prevailed at the time of the Weimar Republic and it survived after the Second World War. The prejudiced image helped in teaching the so-called *Ostkunde* (knowledge of the East) and in rooting in the minds of school students the belief that they should not be reconciled to the loss of former East German territories, annexed by the unworthy Poles. The textbooks often divided Poland into the part represented by the former East German territories, and the rest, which they called only the Vistula land. They taught that if there were any culture in the East, it was due to hard pioneering German work. It was the Germans who founded the Polish cities, including Cracow, and it was they who changed a country of forests and marshes into a cultivated land. The Poles apparently did nothing.[14] For example, a textbook published in 1967 made it clear that culture ended on the Vistula: "From there on the forest takes over and with it foxes, wolves and all sorts of wild game. Finally the landscape sinks down into a wide marshland. . . . Central Europe ends there."[15] The purpose of this sort of teaching of *Ostkunde* is to instill in young minds their duty to recover from the half-barbaric Poles the land east of the Oder-Neisse which their ancestors had conquered for civilization.[16]

This sort of *Ostkunde* with its insistence on the recovery of the East German territories was approved in December 1956 by the conference of state ministers of culture. Their instruction recommended: "The German East [the lost territories] must be entrusted to the Germans, especially to the youth. Its accomplishments must be rooted in the German consciousness. . . . Germany must be treated as a whole. Middle Germany [the GDR], Berlin, and other territories temporarily under foreign administration must be closely associated in the minds of the youth with the territory of the Federal Republic of Germany." This meant that young Western Germans were to be brought up in the conviction of the illegitimacy not only of the GDR but also of the loss of former East German territories. They should believe that a reconciliation with Poland was impossible until Poland should return the land east of the Oder-Neisse frontier. The same instruction intentionally confused two issues: the territorial quarrel and hostility toward the Communist regime of present-day Poland. Poland not only annexed the former East German territories but on top of everything had an evil regime.[17]

The then federal minister for all-German affairs issued on August 20, 1965, a complementary instruction on geographical names to be used in schoolbooks and maps published in the FRG. He began by stating that the FRG was legally identical with the former German Reich although its actual authority could not be effectively exercised outside of its own territory. "The state territory of the German Reich within its frontiers of December 31, 1937, must be depicted as German state territory until the time of final settlement reserved for the peace treaty. The frontiers valid in international law are those of the German Reich at the date of December 31, 1937." Consequently, the minister required that the GDR be named in textbooks and on maps as "the Soviet Zone of Occupation" or at least as "Middle Germany," the territories east of the Oder-Neisse forming "East Germany." The latter territories should be marked as "the German Eastern territories temporarily under a foreign administration." The word *frontier* should be avoided, and the phrases "demarcation line" or "the Oder-Neisse Line" should be used instead. All the places east of that latter line should bear only German names.[18]

Both the instructions of ministers of culture and of the minister for all-German affairs are contrary now to West German obligations undertaken in the Moscow and Warsaw Treaties. But they and the traditional critical image of Poland, perpetuated by the *Ostkunde*, already have had a detrimental effect on the attitudes of young Germans toward Poland.

If the future generations of Germans and Poles have to find ways to national reconciliation, the problem of school textbooks and school programs will play an immense role. This is why the revision of textbooks is more important than treaties in this respect. Yet this reform in West German education would be a radical departure from the present pattern. Moreover, the scholars of the older generation, who initiated the *Ostkunde,* already have protested against the revision of textbooks. For instance, the Göttinger Arbeitskreis, one of the organizations of this type of scholars, protested against the revision of schoolbooks on July 7, 1971.[19]

The picture also has brighter colors, however. First of all, cultivated public opinion in the FRG showed in the last several years a lively interest in Polish culture. This in itself corrects the former image of Poland. Many translations of Polish literary works were published. Polish modern composers are known because their compositions are played in the FRG. Mass media in many cases try to convey a new image of contemporary Poland. The growing number of German visitors can correct the false image received in school by their own observations.

Finally, the younger generation of German historians has produced scholars on Poland who take a sympathetic view of that country. One of them is Immanuel Geiss, who did not hesitate to write that the anti-Hitler conspirators during the Second World War wanted to negotiate a compromise peace with the Allies which would leave Germany its 1914 frontiers, including the ethnically Polish provinces. He also admits that Germans in the summer of 1939 were not in the majority opposed to war against Poland, but that their only worry was "the fear that the consequence of legitimate German demands addressed to Poland might be the outbreak of the Second World War with unpleasant results for the German Reich." Geiss does not expect much from the older generation of his country but pins his hopes on the young.[20]

Another West German historian sympathetic to Poland is Professor Hans Roos. It is he who told his countrymen, for instance, that Polish King John Sobieski (second half of the seventeenth century) was the best educated among his contemporary European sovereigns. He praises also the high intellectual culture of the last Polish king, Stanisław August Poniatowski. He writes about Polish religious tolerance in pre-partition Poland, greater tolerance than in most of the other European countries. He also pays tribute to the Polish Constitution of May 3, 1791, as the most progressive for its time. He reminds his readers that the Załuski Library in Warsaw was the largest European library in the eighteenth century, while the Polish Commission for Education in the same century was the first European Ministry of Education. His writings give the lie to the traditional German image of pre-partition Poland as a country without culture. He vindicates in a sense the Polish parliamentary regime, founded it is true on the nobility only, by remarking that the nobility or electorate represented 8 percent of the total population, a percentage higher than that of eighteenth-century Britain.[21]

Another historian of the same orientation is Hans Adolf Jacobsen. Jacobsen dwells in his recent book on German-Polish relations on the hostility of the Weimar Republic toward the reborn Polish state.[22] He mentions as one of his examples the foreign policy of Gustav Stresemann, even today a popular figure among the politicians of all West German parties. Stresemann's main objective was the revision of the Versailles German-Polish frontier. What he had in mind was explained by his close collaborator von Dirksen in a conversation he had with British Ambassador Lord d'Abernon: "The German Reich strives to recover Danzig, the corridor with the neighboring districts, a correction of the frontier in the former Posen province, and, above all, the return of Upper Silesia." Jacobsen says that the pro-Soviet Rapallo policy, favored by the military, political, and business elites of the Weimar Republic, had for its goal and justification the settlement of accounts with Poland. Jacobsen hopes that the young generation of his countrymen will start a truly new and friendly policy toward Poland.

All this brings us back to the problem of revision of schoolbooks. This task was defined in February 1972 at a conference held in Warsaw. It was assembled under the auspices of UNESCO and was attended by Polish and German scholars, mainly historians and geographers. This first conference made some progress in trying to synchronize the two versions of mutual thousand-year-old history. For example, both parties agreed that the main reason for the Polish partitions had been not the domestic weakness of the Polish state but the superior might of the partitioning powers. They did not find it difficult to agree on one version of Nazi policy during the Second World War. They disagreed on other subjects such as the role of the medieval Teutonic Order: did it carry on a cultural mission, as the Germans thought, or was it a militaristic order expanding German dominion in the east, as the Poles saw it?

The participants at that first conference were aware of the fact that such conferences might and should produce new versions of mutual history, propitious for reconciliation between the two nations, but also that the final recommendations by scholars could be implemented by the government's fiat only in Poland. These recommendations could be favorably received by the federal government of the FRG, but their implementation would depend on the individual decisions of the various state governments. These governments could heed the scholarly recommendations or ignore them. Moreover, private publishers and authors could not be forced to publish or write in the new spirit.

Other such conferences followed suit, and eventually, in October 1972, the representatives of the German and Polish UNESCO committees signed an agreement which formed a joint commission of scholars to whom was entrusted the task of recommending a revision of schoolbooks in both countries. This commission is to meet twice a year. The schoolbooks under consideration are to be not only in the fields of history and geography but also in civics, foreign languages, and foreign literatures.

In German-Polish relations, considered from the point of view of true reconciliation between the two nations, much will depend on the final product of work by that commission and on the practical implementation of its recommendations. School textbooks and school programs are a very important problem, but, of course, a better mutual atmosphere also could be built by the mass media.

Unless both nations take serious steps in order gradually to discard false images, true reconciliation between Poles and Germans will remain a pipe dream of well-intentioned intellectuals. The proper conclusion for this book is the expression of hope that today's dream might one day become a living reality.

Notes to the Chapters

INTRODUCTION

1. Robert Aron, *Histoire de Vichy: 1940–1944* (Paris: Librairie Arthème Fayard, 1954).

CHAPTER 1

1. The best history of Poland in English is *The Cambridge History of Poland*, 2 vols. (Cambridge: At the University Press, 1950 and 1941).

2. Quoted in Walter Tritsch, *Metternich und Sein Monarch* (Darmstadt: Holle Verlag, 1952), p. 559.

3. These official figures are quoted in Gerard Labuda, *Polska Granica Zachodnia* (Poznań: Wydawnictwo Poznańskie, 1971), p. 224.

4. These official figures are quoted in *ibid.*, p. 225.

5. An excellent history of the Weimar Republic's policy on Poland is V. Kellermann, *Schwarzer Adler—Weisser Adler: Die Polenpolitik der Weimarer Republik* (Köln: Marcus Verlag, 1970).

CHAPTER 2

1. See Gerhard Ritter, *Carl Goerdeler und die deutsche Widerstands-Bewegung* (Stuttgart: Deutsche Verlags Anstalt, 1954).

2. Gerard Labuda, *Polska Granica Zachodnia* (Poznań: Wydawnictwo Poznańskie, 1971), p. 277.

3. *Ibid.*, p. 278.

4. *Ibid.*, p. 280.

5. *Ibid.*

6. Czesław Pilichowski, "Straty nauki i kultury polskiej w okresie II wojny światowej," in *Krajowa Agencja Informacyjna* (March 1973):67–72.

7. *Ibid.*

8. Günther Berndt and Reinhardt Strecker, *Polen: Ein Schauermärchen oder Gehirnwasche für Generationen* (Hamburg: Rowohlt, 1971). For this reason the revision of West German textbooks is of paramount importance for the process of national reconciliation. (See the Epilogue.)

Another example of the biased version of history is provided by the famous *Brockhaus Encyclopedia* where the article on East Prussia does not even mention that East Prussia was conquered by the Teutonic Knights from the medieval Prussian people and that these Knights had settled there at the invitation of a Polish prince. The fact that Ducal (East) Prussia had been held from 1525 until 1657 in fief from Poland after the secularization of the Order is also passed over in silence.

CHAPTER 3

1. For changing Polish views regarding the Western frontier during the second World War, see Edmund Męclewski, *Powrót Polski nad Odrę, Nysę Łużycką, Bałtyk* (Warsaw: Wydawnictwo Ministerstwa Obrony Narodowej, 1971); Gerard Labuda, *Polska Granica Zachodnia* (Poznań: Wydawnictwo Poznańskie, 1971); Włodzimierz T. Kowalski, "The Grand Coalition and Post-war European Security (1943–45)," in *Sprawy Międzynarodowe*, spec. ed. (1970):49–64; Włodzimierz T. Kowalski, "Allied Policy, 1939–1945: Problem of Peace in Post-war Europe," in *Polish Western Affairs* 11, no. 2 (1970):209–33; Marian Orzechowski, "Polish Conceptions of the Polish-German Frontier during World War II," in *Polish Western Affairs* 11, no. 2 (1970):234–70; Ministry of Foreign Affairs, *Bulletin* 1 (Warsaw: November 1970):7–18; and Viktoria Vierheller, *Polen und die Deutschland-Frage: 1939–1949* (Cologne: Verlag Wissenschaft und Politik, 1970).

2. For the Teheran Conference see *Foreign Relations of the United States: The Conferences at Cairo and Teheran, 1943* (Washington, D.C.: U.S. G.P.O., 1961), pp. 510, 512, 594, 598–602, 604, 837–38, 847–48; and Winston S. Churchill, *The Second World War. Closing the Ring* (Boston: Houghton Mifflin, 1951), pp. 362, 394–97, 403, 406.

3. Quoted in Ministry of Foreign Affairs, *Bulletin* 1 (Warsaw: November 1970).

4. Winston S. Churchill, *The Second World War. Triumph and Tragedy* (Boston: Houghton Mifflin, 1953), p. 368.

5. *Foreign Relations of the United States: The Conferences at Malta and Yalta* (Washington, D.C.: U.S. G.P.O., 1955), pp. 846, 848.

6. *Ibid.*, p. 509.

7. Churchill, *Triumph and Tragedy*, p. 372.

8. *Ibid.*, pp. 375–77.

9. *Ibid.*

10. *Foreign Relations of the United States (Malta and Yalta)*, pp. 217–18.

11. *Ibid.*, p. 938.

12. *Foreign Relations of the United States: The Conference of Berlin (the*

Potsdam Conference) (Washington, D.C.: U.S. Government Printing Office, 1960), I:7.

13. *Ibid.,* p. 9.

14. *Ibid.,* p. 13.

15. *Ibid.,* pp. 70, 75, 77.

16. *Ibid.,* pp. 257–58.

17. *Ibid.,* pp. 256–62.

18. *Ibid.,* p. 59.

19. *Ibid.,* p. 715.

20. *Ibid.,* II:1531.

21. *Ibid.,* p. 264.

22. *Ibid.,* I:778.

23. *Ibid.,* p. 781.

24. Quoted in Ministry of Foreign Affairs, *Bulletin* 1 (Warsaw: November 1970):9.

25. *Foreign Relations of the United States (The Conference of Berlin),* I: 585, 742, 746, 750–51.

26. *Ibid.,* II:305–306.

27. *Ibid.,* p. 1138.

28. *Ibid.,* II:209–11, 218.

29. *Ibid.,* pp. 382 and 388.

30. *Ibid.,* p. 217.

31. *Ibid.*

32. *Ibid.,* I:748.

33. *Ibid.,* II:211.

34. *Ibid.,* I:751–54.

35. *Ibid.,* pp. 749–750.

36. *Foreign Relations of the United States (Malta and Yalta),* p. 720.

37. For the Polish arguments, presented prior to and during the Potsdam Conference, see *Foreign Relations of the United States (The Conference of Berlin)* I:757–77; II:332–36, 356–57, and 1517–24.

38. *Ibid.,* II:250.

39. *Ibid.,* p. 251.

40. *Ibid.,* p. 219.

41. *Ibid.,* pp. 211, 219.

42. *Ibid.,* p. 249.

43. *Ibid.,* p. 212.

44. *Ibid.,* p. 248.

45. *Ibid.,* p. 248.

46. *Ibid.,* p. 658.

47. *Ibid.,* pp. 305–306.

48. Churchill, *The Second World War,* p. 672.

49. *Ibid.*, p. 668.

50. *Foreign Relations of the United States (Conference of Berlin),* II:213, 220, 356.

51. *Ibid.*, pp. 208, 212 and 251.

52. *Ibid.*, p. 1150.

53. *Ibid.*, p. 472.

54. *Ibid.*, pp. 1150–51.

55. *Ibid.*, p. 480.

56. *Ibid.*, pp. 520, 534, 539.

57. *Ibid.*, pp. 1507, 1509, 1511.

58. Quoted in Ministry of Foreign Affairs, *Bulletin* 1 (Warsaw: November 1970):17.

59. *Foreign Relations of the United States (Conference of Berlin)* II:1561–62.

CHAPTER 4

1. Quoted in Ministry of Foreign Affairs, *Bulletin 1* (Warsaw: November 1970):18.

2. For the Polish interpretation of the Potsdam decision, see A. Klafkowski, *The Potsdam Agreement* (Warsaw, 1963); idem, *Granica polsko-niemiecka po II wojnie światowej* (Poznań, 1970); Bolesław Wiewióra, *The Polish-German Frontier in the Light of International Law* (Poznań, 1969); Krzysztof Skubiszewski, *Zachodnie Granice Polski* (Gdańsk, 1969).

3. *Statistisches Jahrbuch für das Deutsche Reich. Herausgegeben vom Statistischen Reichsamt, Jahrgang 1941–42* (Berlin, 1942). See also: *Statistisches Jahrbuch für die Bundesrepublik Deutschland 1952,* p. 12.

4. Stanisław Schimitzek, *Truth or Conjecture? German Civilian War Losses in the East* (Warsaw: Zachodnia Agencja Prasowa, 1966), pp. 41–70.

5. *Dokumentation der Vertreibund der Deutschen aus Ostmittel-Europa* (Bundesministerium für Vertriebene), Vol. I/1, p. 6E.

6. For the best Polish analysis of German and Polish population statistics, see Schimitzek, *Truth or Conjecture?* See also Józef Kokot, *The Logic of the Oder-Neisse Frontier* (Poznań: Wydawnictwo Zachodnie, 1959).

7. *Die deutschen Vertreibungsverluste, Bevölkerungsbilanzen für die deutschen Vertreibunsgebiete, 1939–50* (Wiesbaden: Statisches Bundesamt, 1958), pp. 14–16.

8. *Statistisches Jahrbuch für die Bundesrepublik Deutschland, 1960,* p. 78.

9. *Dokumentation,* Vol. I/1, pp. 43, 102 and 155.

10. *Ibid.*, pp. 6, 28E, 39, 41, 44, 46–48, 48E, 50–51, 99, 133, 182, 269, 345, 405, 411, 414, 480 and ff.

11. This figure of five million is given in *ibid.*, p. 24E.

12. *Statistisches Jahrbuch für die Bundesrepublik Deutschland 1960,* p. 79, and *Statistisches Jahrbuch der DDR,* p. 36.

13. On November 20, 1945, the Allied Control Council fixed the following

numbers of Germans to be expelled: 2.5 million from Czechoslovakia, 3.5 million from Poland, and .5 million from Hungary. The Germans from Poland were to be resettled in the following way: 2 million in the Soviet zone of occupation and 1.5 million in the British zone.

14. Edmund Męclewski, *Powrót Polski nad Odrę, Nysę Łużycką, Bałtyk* (Warsaw: Wydawnictwo Ministerstwa Obrony Narodowej, 1971), pp. 463–65.

15. Immanuel Birnbaum in *Die Süddeutsche Zeitung*, July 20, 1973.

16. Henryk Rechowicz, *Polska Zachodnia i Północna* (Warsaw: Wydawnictwo Interpress, 1972), pp. 10–12.

17. For the demographic processes in the northern and western territories see, among others, Edward Rosset, "Demographic Factors Concerning the Repolonization of Western and Northern Territories," in *Polish Western Affairs* 11, no. 1 (1970):66–88; and Rechowicz, *Polska Zachodnia i Północna*, pp. 10–12.

18. *Rocznik Statystyczny 1971* (Warsaw: Główny Urząd Statystyczny), 31: 69, Table 4; and *Rocznik Polityczny i Gospodarczy 1971* (Warsaw: Państwowe Wydawnictwo Ekonomiczne, 1972), pp. 26–39.

19. Męclewski, *Powrót Polski*, p. 722.

20. The data on the maritime activities are taken from Polish Interpress Agency, *Contemporary Poland* 7, no. 5 (1973).

21. For up-to-date data on the present condition of the Polish-annexed territories, see Rechowicz, *Polska Zachodnia i Północna*.

CHAPTER 5

1. U.S. Department of State, *Germany, 1947–1949. The Story in Documents* (Washington, D.C.: U.S. G.P.O., 1950), pp. 7–8.

2. *The Department of State Bulletin*, May 11, 1947, p. 919.

3. *Foreign Relations of the United States 1947, Volume IV, Eastern Europe; The Soviet Union* (Washington, D.C.: U.S. G.P.O., 1972), pp. 426, 427–28.

4. *Ibid.*, p. 428.

5. *Ibid.*, p. 445.

6. Ambassade de France, Service de Presse et d'Information, Nos. 271 and 272, September 11, 1967.

7. For the Soviet stand on the German problem and the Central European status quo, see W. W. Kulski, *The Soviet Union in World Affairs* (Syracuse, N.Y.: Syracuse University Press, 1973), pp. 124–30.

8. Jerzy Sułek and Mieczysław Tomala, *Polska—NRD: Materjały i Dokumenty* (Warsaw: Polski Instytut Spraw Międzynarodowych, 1970), p. 2.

9. *Zeittafel der Vorgeschichte und des Ablaufs der Vertreibung sowie der Unterbringung und Eingliederung der Vertriebenen und Bibliographie zum Vertriebenenproblem* (Bonn: Bundesministerium für Vertriebene, Flüchtlinge und Kriegsgeschädigte, 1959), p. 37.

10. *Ibid.*, p. 43.

11. *Ibid.*

12. Sułek and Tomala, *Polska—NRD*, p. 3.

13. Full text of the treaty in The Ministry of Foreign Affairs, *Bulletin 1* (Warsaw: November 1970):21–23.

14. Sułek and Tomala, *Polska—NRD*, pp. 93–94.

15. *Ibid.*, p. 125.

16. The full text of the Polish-GDR treaty in *ibid.*, pp. 139–43.

17. *Ibid.*, p. 197.

18. *Die Auswärtige Politik der Bundesrepublik Deutschland, Herausgegeben vom Auswärtigen Amt* (Cologne: Verlag Wissenschaft und Politik, 1972), p. 435.

19. *Zeittafel der Vorgeschichte*, p. 117.

20. *Die Auswärtige Politik*, pp. 156–57.

21. *Ibid.*, p. 151.

22. *Ibid.*, p. 183.

23. *Ibid.*, p. 164.

24. *Ibid.*, p. 144.

25. *Ibid.*, p. 26.

26. *Ibid.*, pp. 220–21.

27. *Bulletin des Presse-und Informationsamtes der Bundesregierung*, February 8, 1952, subsequently cited as *Bulletin*.

28. *Bulletin* 26 (1952).

29. *Die Auswärtige Politik*, p. 13.

30. *Ibid.*, p. 44.

31. The text of the treaty in *ibid.*, pp. 208–13.

32. The text of the Paris agreement is reproduced in *ibid.*, pp. 262–66.

33. *Ibid.*, p. 37.

34. *Ibid.*, p. 250.

35. *Ibid.*, p. 254.

36. *Ibid.*, p. 243.

37. *Ibid.*, p. 245.

38. *Ibid.*, p. 277.

39. *Ibid.*, p. 307.

40. *Ibid.*, p. 311.

41. The text of Adenauer's speech in *ibid.*, pp. 308–313.

42. *Ibid.*, p. 308.

43. *Ibid.*, p. 312.

44. *Ibid.*, pp. 314–15.

45. *Ibid.*, pp. 321–22.

46. *Ibid.*, p. 322.

47. Jerzy Sułek, *Stanowisko Rządu NRF wobec Granicy na Odrze i Nysie Łużyckiej: 1949–1966* (Poznań: Instytut Zachodni, 1969), p. 156.

48. *Ibid.*, pp. 156–57.

49. *Ibid.*, p. 157.

50. *Ibid.*, p. 165.
51. *Ibid.*, p. 171.
52. *Die Auswärtige Politik*, pp. 362–63.
53. *Ibid.*, p. 371.
54. *Ibid.*, pp. 408–10.
55. *Ibid.*, p. 49.
56. The full text of the report in *ibid.*, pp. 433–40.
57. *Ibid.*, pp. 61–62.

CHAPTER 6

1. *Die Auswärtige Politik der Bundesrepublik Deutschland* (Cologne: Verlag Wissenschaft und Politik, 1972), p. 470.
2. *Ibid.*, p. 64.
3. *Ibid.*, p. 522.
4. *Ibid.*, p. 496.
5. Boris Meissner, ed., *Die Deutsche Ostpolitik, 1961–1970: Kontinuität und Wandel* (Cologne: Verlag Wissenschaft und Politik, 1970), p. 72.
6. The article in *Foreign Affairs* reproduced in *Die Auswärtige Politik*, pp. 547–52.
7. Meissner, *Die Deutsche Ostpolitik*, p. 101.
8. *Ibid.*, p. 139.
9. *Ibid.*, pp. 141–42.
10. *Ibid.*, p. 140.
11. *Die Auswärtige Politik*, p. 503.
12. *Ibid.*, pp. 505–11.
13. *Ibid.*, p. 507.
14. *Parlamentarisch-Politischer Pressedienst* 221 (November 17, 1964).
15. Meissner, *Die Deutsche Ostpolitik*, p. 149.
16. *Ibid.*, p. 77.
17. *Ibid.*, p. 125.
18. *Ibid.*, p. 138.
19. *Ibid.*, pp. 128–30.
20. *Die Auswärtige Politik*, pp. 517–21.
21. Meissner, *Die Deutsche Ostpolitik*, p. 97.
22. *Die Auswärtige Politik*, p. 525.
23. The text of the notes in *ibid.*, pp. 559–63.
24. The so-called enemy clause in the United Nations Charter refers to Articles 53 and 107. Article 53 states:

"1. The Security Council shall, where appropriate, utilize such regional arrangements or agencies for enforcement action under its authority. But no enforcement action shall be taken under regional arrangements or by regional agencies without the authorization of the Security Council, with the exception of measures against any enemy state, as defined in paragraph 2 of this Article, provided for pursuant to Article 107 or in regional arrangements directed against renewal of aggressive policy on the part of any such state, until such time as the Organization may, on request of the Governments concerned, be charged with the responsibility for preventing further aggression by such a state.

2. The term enemy state as used in paragraph 1 of this Article applies to any state which during the Second World War has been an enemy of any signatory of the Present Charter."

Article 107 says:

"Nothing in the present Charter shall invalidate or preclude action, in relation to any state which during the Second World War has been an enemy of any signatory of the present Charter, taken or authorized as a result of that war by the governments having responsibility for such action."

25. For the Polish comments see Jerzy Sułek, *Stanowisko Rządu NFR wobec Granicy Na Odrze i Nysie Łuzyckiej: 1949–1966* (Poznań: Instytut Zachodni, 1969), pp. 263–66; and Janusz Sobczak, *Polityka Wschodnia NFR w Okresie Rządów Erharda* (Warsaw: 1971).

26. Meissner, *Die Deutsche Ostpolitik,* p. 119.

27. *Ibid.,* pp. 45–48.

28. *Ibid.,* pp. 78–80.

29. *Ibid.,* p. 86.

30. *Ibid.,* p. 131.

31. *Ibid.,* p. 133.

CHAPTER 7

1. "Doepfner zu Aüsserungen Kardinal Wyszynskis über Ostgebiete," in *Der Tagesspiegel,* October 4, 1965.

2. *Die Lage der Vertriebenen und das Verhältnis des deutschen Volkes zu seinen östlichen Nachbarn. Eine Evangelische Denkschrift* (Hanover, 1965).

3. *Die Auswärtige Politik der Bundesrepublik Deutschland* (Cologne: Verlag Wissenschaft und Politik, 1972), p. 573.

4. The full text of Kiesinger's declaration in *ibid.,* pp. 572–76.

5. *Ibid.,* p. 99.

6. Boris Meissner, *Die Deutsche Ostpolitik, 1961–1970: Kontinuität und Wandel* (Cologne: Verlag Wissenschaft und Politik, 1971), p. 214.

7. *Ibid.,* p. 250.

8. *Ibid.,* p. 287.

9. *Ibid.,* p. 236.

10. *Ibid.,* pp. 279–80. Kiesinger made other statements of the same kind on June 17, 1967 (*Auswärtige Politik,* p. 603); March 20, 1967 (Meissner, *Die*

Deutsche Ostpolitik, p. 197); January 27, 1967 (*ibid.,* p. 178); February 28, 1967 (*ibid.,* p. 190); and on April 11, 1969 (*ibid.,* p. 338).

11. Dieter Schwarzkopf, "Die Idee des Gevaltverzichts. Ein Element der neuen Ostpolitik der Bundesrepublik," *Europa Archiv* 24 (1967).

12. See Jerzy Sułek, *Polityka Wschodnia Rządu "Wielkiej Koalicji": 1966–1969* (Warsaw: Polski Instytut Spraw Międzynarodowych, 1972), pp. 30–31.

13. Meissner, *Die Deutsche Ostpolitik,* pp. 257–58.

14. *Ibid.,* p. 179.

15. Sułek, *Polityka Wschodnia Rządu,* p. 31.

16. *Ibid.,* p. 34.

17. Meissner, *Die Deutsche Ostpolitik,* p. 210.

18. *Auswärtige Politik,* p. 602.

19. Meissner, *Die Deutsche Ostpolitik,* pp. 167–68.

20. *Ibid.,* p. 232.

21. *Ibid.,* pp. 251–52.

22. *Ibid.,* p. 182.

23. *Ibid.,* p. 212.

24. *Ibid.,* p. 340.

25. *Auswärtige Politik,* pp. 600–601.

26. *Ibid.,* pp. 612–13.

27. *Ibid.,* pp. 599–600.

28. Meissner, *Die Deutsche Ostpolitik,* p. 164.

29. *Ibid.,* p. 228.

30. *Ibid.,* pp. 235–36.

31. *Ibid.,* pp. 246–47.

32. *Ibid.,* p. 252.

33. *Ibid.,* p. 341.

34. *Ibid.,* p. 353.

35. *Ibid.,* p. 372.

36. *Ibid.,* p. 291.

37. *Ibid.,* p. 203.

38. *Ibid.,* p. 230.

39. *Ibid.,* p. 248. He repeated the same proposal on June 3, 1969 (*ibid.,* p. 356), August 8, 1969 (p. 374), August 10, 1969 (p. 376), and September 11, 1969 (p. 379).

40. *Ibid.,* p. 329.

41. *Ibid.,* p. 318.

42. *Ibid.,* p. 246.

43. *Ibid.,* p. 254.

44. *Ibid.,* p. 372.

45. *Ibid.,* pp. 261–62.

46. Ministry of Foreign Affairs, Department of Press and Information, *Bulletin* 1 (Warsaw: November 1970):27–32.

47. Meissner, *Die Deutsche Ostpolitik,* p. 374.

48. *Ibid.,* pp. 352, 372.

49. *Ibid.,* p. 166.

50. *Ibid.,* p. 208.

51. *Ibid.,* p. 219.

52. *Ibid.,* p. 367.

53. *Ibid.,* p. 183.

54. *Ibid.,* p. 229.

55. *Ibid.,* p. 262.

56. *Ibid.,* p. 247.

57. *Ibid.,* p. 269.

58. Text of the letter in *Pravda,* July 19, 1968.

59. *Pravda,* August 5, 1968.

60. Meissner, *Die Deutsche Ostpolitik,* pp. 279–80.

61. *Auswärtige Politik,* pp. 649–50.

62. Meissner, *Die Deutsche Ostpolitik,* pp. 323–24.

63. *Ibid.,* p. 256.

64. *Ibid.,* p. 347.

65. His statements in that regard on September 4, 1968, December 6, 1968, and on December 29, 1968 (*ibid.,* pp. 286, 325, 333).

66. *Ibid.,* p. 365.

67. *Ibid.,* pp. 191–93.

68. *Ibid.,* pp. 193–94.

69. *Ibid.,* pp. 241–42.

70. *Ibid.,* p. 296.

71. *Ibid.,* p. 328. Another Scheel statement in the same vein on June 17, 1969 (*ibid.,* pp. 361–62).

72. *Ibid.,* p. 363.

73. Sułek, *Polityka Wschodnia Rządu,* pp. 141–43.

CHAPTER 8

1. The full text of Brandt's speech in *Die Auswärtige Politik der Bundesrepublik Deutschland* (Cologne: Verlag Wissenschaft und Politik, 1972), pp. 701–706.

2. Ryszard Wojna, *Spokojnie Płynie Ren* (Warsaw: Czytelnik, 1971).

3. *Die Auswärtige Politik,* pp. 709–10.

4. *Ibid.,* pp. 724–31.

5. Boris Meissner, *Die Deutsche Ostpolitik, 1961–1970* (Cologne: Verlag Wissenschaft und Politik, 1970), pp. 384–88.

6. *Ibid.,* pp. 390–91.

7. *Ibid.,* p. 402–05.

8. *Ibid.,* p. 407.

9. *Ibid.,* pp. 421, 423.

10. *Ibid.,* pp. 428, 430.

11. *Ibid.,* p. 437.

12. *Ibid.,* p. 441.

13. Ministry of Foreign Affairs, *Bulletin* 1 (Warsaw: November 1970):36.

14. *Ibid.,* pp. 38–41.

15. *Ibid.,* pp. 41–48.

16. *Ibid.*

17. *Ibid.*

18. *Bulletin,* Sonderausgabe, Bonn: Presse- und Informationsamt der Bundes-regierung, August 17, 1970, No. 109/A, pp. 1115–17.

19. *Ibid.,* pp. 1119–56.

20. For the text of Articles 53 and 107 of the United Nations Charter see Chapter VI.

21. The German text of the treaty in *Bulletin,* Sonderausgabe, August 17, 1970, p. 1094. The English translation in *New York Times,* August 13, 1970.

22. *Bulletin,* Sonderausgabe, August 17, 1970, p. 1094.

23. *Ibid.,* pp. 1096–98.

24. *Ibid.,* p. 1100.

25. *Ibid.,* p. 1107.

26. *Ibid.,* p. 1110.

27. *Ibid.,* p. 1111.

28. *Ibid.*

29. *Ibid.,* p. 1136.

30. *Ibid.,* pp. 1146–48.

31. *Ibid.,* p. 1148.

CHAPTER 9

1. *Bulletin,* Sonderausgabe, Bonn: Presse- und Informationsamt der Bundes-regierung, December 8, 1970, pp. 1834–75.

2. *Ibid.,* pp. 1830–31.

3. *Ibid.,* pp. 1831–33.

4. *Ibid.,* pp. 1834–75.

5. The two memoranda and the exchange of letters between the bishops of the two countries (only selected parts of the Polish bishops letter) were repro-duced in *ibid.,* pp. 1842–45 and 1848–50.

6. *Ibid.,* p. 1846.

7. *Ibid.,* p. 1850.

8. *Ibid.,* p. 1851.

9. The German text of the treaty in *ibid.,* p. 1815. English translation in *Bulletin* 3 (Warsaw: Ministry of Foreign Affairs, January 1971):5–6.

10. *Bulletin,* Sonderausgabe, December 8, 1970, pp. 1816–17.

11. *Ibid.,* p. 1817. This unilateral Polish statement is not reproduced, interestingly enough, in the Polish official collection of documents relating to the Warsaw Treaty.

12. *Ibid.,* p. 1871.

13. *Ibid.,* pp. 1865–67.

14. *Ibid.,* pp. 1868–69.

15. *Ibid.,* pp. 1870–71.

16. *Ibid.,* p. 1872.

17. *The Treaty between the Federal Republic of Germany and the People's Republic of Poland* (Press and Information Office of the Federal Government, 1971), pp. 41–53.

18. *Bulletin,* Sonderausgabe, 1970, pp. 1861–62.

19. *Bulletin* 3 (Warsaw: Ministry of Foreign Affairs, January 1971):16.

20. *Ibid.,* pp. 17–18.

21. Krzysztof Skubiszewski, "Poland's Western Frontier and the 1970 Treaties," *American Journal of International Law* 67, no. 1 (January 1973):23–43.

22. *Bulletin* 3 (Warsaw: Ministry of Foreign Affairs, January 1971):12.

23. *Ibid.,* p. 11.

24. *Ibid.,* pp. 11–12.

25. *Weekly Compilation of Presidential Documents* 8, no. 23 (June 5, 1972):973–75.

26. Skubiszewski, "Poland's Western Frontier and the 1970 Treaties," *American Journal of International Law* 67, no. 1 (January 1973):32.

27. *Bulletin* 3 (Warsaw: Ministry of Foreign Affairs, January 1971):26–29.

28. *Ibid.,* pp. 17–18.

29. *Die Auswärtige Politik der Bundesrepublik Deutschland* (Cologne: Verlag Wissenschaft und Politik, 1972), pp. 742–48.

30. *Ibid.,* pp. 753–55.

31. The text of the four-power agreement in *The Quadripartite Agreement on Berlin of September 3, 1971* (Bonn: Press and Information Office of the Federal Government, 1971).

32. *Die Auswärtige Politik,* p. 99.

CHAPTER 10

1. *Bulletin* 14 (Presse-und Informationsamt des Bundesregierung, 1971): 132–35 and 155–56.

2. *Ibid.,* p. 135.

3. *Ibid.,* p. 136.

4. *Ibid.*, p. 148.
5. *Bulletin* 78 (1971):832, 835.
6. *Bulletin* 168 (1971):1774.
7. *Bulletin* 136 (1971):1469-70.
8. *Ibid.*, p. 1471.
9. *Ibid.*, p. 1472.
10. *Ibid.*, p. 1474.
11. *Bulletin* 148 (1971):1573-79.
12. Quoted in *Bulletin* 186 (1971):2017.
13. *Ibid.*
14. *Bulletin* 166 (1971):1749, 1751.
15. *Bulletin* 186 (1971):2018.
16. *Bulletin* 186 (1971):2019.
17. *Bulletin* 186 (1971): 2014-15.
18. *Bulletin* 6 (1972):53.
19. *Bulletin* 186 (1971):2019.
20. *Bulletin* 166 (1971):1752.
21. *Ibid.*, 186 (1971):2019-20.
22. *Ibid.*, p. 2017.
23. *Ibid.*, 219-20.
24. *Ibid.*, p. 2020.
25. *Ibid.*
26. *Bulletin* 18 (1972):175.
27. *Bulletin* 192 (1971):2083.
28. *Bulletin* 20 (1972):198-205.
29. *Ibid.*, pp. 251-52.
30. *Bulletin* 20 (1972):221.
31. *Ibid.*, p. 235.
32. *Ibid.*, p. 249.
33. *Ibid.*
34. *Ibid.*, pp. 215-19.
35. *Ibid.*, pp. 236-37.
36. *Ibid.*, pp. 241-44.
37. *Ibid.*, pp. 223-28.
38. *Ibid.*, pp. 244-48.
39. *Ibid.*
40. *Bulletin* 2 (1972):306.
41. *Bulletin* 26 (1972):311.
42. *Ibid.*, p. 344.
43. *Bulletin* 27 (1972):396.
44. *Ibid.*, p. 423.

45. *Bulletin* 26 (1972):318–28.

46. *Ibid.,* pp. 321–22.

47. *Bulletin* 27 (1972):373.

48. *Ibid.,* pp. 419–27.

49. *Bulletin* 26 (1972):336.

50. *Bulletin* 27 (1972):385.

51. *Bulletin* 28 (1972):491.

52. *Bulletin* 27 (1972):377.

53. *Bulletin* 26 (1972):335.

54. *Ibid.,* p. 367.

55. *Bulletin* 27 (1972):391.

56. *Ibid.,* p. 392.

57. *Bulletin* 28 (1972):449.

58. *Bulletin* 27 (1972):409–16.

59. *Bulletin* 28 (1972):462.

60. *Ibid.,* p. 463.

61. *Ibid.,* p. 462.

62. *Ibid.,* p. 483.

63. *Bulletin* 26 (1972):368.

64. *Bulletin* 28 (1972):449.

65. *Ibid.,* p. 452.

66. Speeches by Foreign Minister Walter Scheel (*Bulletin* 26 [1972]:314); Chancellor Willy Brandt (*ibid.,* pp. 341–42); Minister for Inter-German Relations Egon Franke (*Bulletin* 27 [1972]:371); Social Democrat Kurt Mattick (*ibid.,* p. 380); Minister for Special Affairs Horst Ehmke (*ibid.,* pp. 400–401); Minister for National Defense Helmut Schmidt (*ibid.,* p. 429); and Social Democrat Carlo Schmid (*Bulletin* 28 [1972]:468–69).

67. *Bulletin* 26 (1972):348.

68. Kurt Mattick (SPD), *Bulletin* 27 (1972): 380.

69. *Bulletin* 28 (1972):474.

70. Speeches by Chancellor Brandt (*Bulletin* 26 [1972]:307–309); Herbert Wehner, leader of the Social Democratic parliamentary group (*ibid.,* p. 332); Minister Egon Franke (*Bulletin* 27 [1972]:372); Kurt Mattick (SPD) (*ibid.,* pp. 381–83); Minister Horst Ehmke (*ibid.,* p. 407); Minister Helmut Schmidt (*ibid.,* pp. 429–30); Minister Erhard Eppler (*Bulletin* 28 [1972]:457); and Foreign Minister Walter Scheel (*ibid.,* p. 487).

71. *Bulletin* 28 (1972):468–77.

72. *Bulletin* 26 (1972):311–12.

73. *Ibid.,* p. 333.

74. *Ibid.,* pp. 348–50.

75. *Bulletin* 27 (1972):388.

76. *Ibid.,* pp. 401, 403.

77. *Ibid.,* p. 417.

78. *Bulletin* 28 (1972):454–55.

79. *Ibid.,* pp. 469–70, 473–74.

80. Speeches by Chancellor Willy Brandt (*Bulletin* 26 [1972]:307, 341, and *Bulletin* 28 [1972]:446); Foreign Minister Walter Scheel (*Bulletin* 26 [1972]: 311); Herbert Wehner (*ibid.,* pp. 330–31); William Borm (FDP) (*ibid.,* pp. 359–60, 362–63); Rolf Heyen (SPD) (*Bulletin* 27 [1972]:398–99); Minister Horst Ehmke (*ibid.,* pp. 406, 408); Carlo Schmid (*Bulletin* 28 [1972]:474).

81. Speeches by Walter Scheel, *Bulletin* 26 (1972):311, and Minister Helmut Schmidt, *Bulletin* 27 (1972):433.

82. *Bulletin* 27 (1972):433.

83. Speeches by Herbert Wehner, *Bulletin* 26 (1972):333, and Wolfgang Mischnick (FDP), *ibid.,* p. 350.

84. *Ibid.,* p. 312.

85. *Ibid.*

86. *Bulletin* 27 (1972):428, 434.

87. *Bulletin* 26 (1972):317. Also Herbert Wehner (*ibid.,* p. 329) William Borm (FDP) (*ibid.,* p. 361); and Karl Moersch (FDP) (*Bulletin* 27 [1972]:437).

88. *Bulletin* 26 (1972):343.

89. *Bulletin* 27 (1972):430.

90. *Bulletin* 26 (1972):315–16. See also Willy Brandt (*ibid.,* p. 342); Herbert Wehner (*ibid.,* p. 342); and Kurt Mattick (SPD) (*Bulletin* 27 [1972]:379).

91. *Bulletin* 27 (1972):428, 431. See also Willy Brandt, *Bulletin* 26 (1972): 343.

92. *Bulletin* 28 (1972):492.

93. *Bulletin* 26 (1972):343.

94. *Bulletin* 27 (1972):389.

95. *Ibid.,* p. 409.

96. *Ibid.,* pp. 433–434.

97. *Bulletin* 28 (1972):465, 488.

98. *Bulletin* 45 (1972):670–74.

99. *Bulletin* 50 (1972):714–15.

100. *Bulletin* 68 (1972):942–48.

101. *Ibid.,* p. 945.

102. *Ibid.,* p. 947.

103. *Ibid.,* pp. 949–51.

104. *Ibid.*

105. *Ibid.,* pp. 951–54.

106. *Ibid.,* p. 951.

107. *Ibid.,* p. 952.

108. *Ibid.,* pp. 954–56.

109. *Ibid.,* p. 955.

110. *Ibid.,* p. 956.

111. *Ibid.*, p. 955.

112. *Ibid.*, pp. 957–65.

113. *Ibid.*, p. 957.

114. *Ibid.*

115. *Ibid.*, p. 958.

116. *Ibid.*, p. 959.

117. *Ibid.*, pp. 963–64.

118. *Ibid.*, pp. 966–74.

119. *Ibid.*, p. 972.

120. *Ibid.*

121. *Ibid.*, pp. 974–77.

122. *Ibid.*, p. 980.

123. *Bulletin* 72 (1972):1040–41.

124. *Ibid.*, pp. 1045–46.

125. The text of the resolution in *ibid.*, pp. 1047–48.

126. *Ibid.*, p. 1048.

127. *Frankfurter Allgemeine Zeitung*, May 18, 1972, p. 2.

CHAPTER 11

1. Ryszard Frelek, "Podstawa normalizacji," *Sprawy Międzynarodowe* (January 1971):5–14.

2. Daniel Luliński, "Rycerze 'Abendlandu'," *Trybuna Ludu*, June 26, 1971; and *idem*, "Znamienne konfrontacje w NRF," *Trybuna Ludu*, March 9, 1971.

3. Book review of Hans-Adolf Jacobsen, ed., *Misstraurische Nachbarn: Deutsche Politik 1919–1970* (Düsseldorf: Verlag Droste, 1970), in *Przegląd Zachodni* 3 (1971). See also Adam Stanek, "Od Stresemanna do Scheela," *Trybuna Ludu*, March 2, 1971.

4. Anna Wolff-Powęska, "Tematyka polska na łamach miesięcznika Osteuropa (1960–1970)," *Przegląd Zachodni*, April, 1971, pp. 117–28.

5. *Trybuna Ludu*, December 6, 1970.

6. *Ibid.*, December 7, 1970.

7. Adam Daniel Rotfeld, "Wokół ratyfikacji układu PRL-NRF," *Sprawy Międzynarodowe* (April 1972):27–46.

8. *Ibid.*, p. 28.

9. *Ibid.*, p. 31.

10. *Ibid.*, p. 42.

11. Alfons Klafkowski, "Układ Polska-NRF o podstawach normalizacji stosunków jako element uznania status quo w Europie," *Sprawy Międzynarodowe* (September 1971):5–20.

12. *Ibid.*, p. 12.

13. *Ibid.*, p. 19.

14. Rotfeld, "Wokół ratyfikacji układu PRL-NRF," *Sprawy Międzynarodowe* (April 1972):27–46.

15. *Ibid.*, p. 42.

16. Jerzy Sułek, "Główne kierunki politycznej i prawnej interpretacji układu Polska-NRF z 7 grudnia 1970 roku," *Sprawy Międzynarodowe* (June 1972):5–21.

17. *Ibid.*, p. 11.

18. *Ibid.*, p. 13.

19. *Ibid.*, p. 14.

20. Jerzy Sułek, "Porozumienia normalizacyjne z lat 1970–1972 a bezpieczeństwo Europy," *Sprawy Międzynarodowe* (July–August 1972):15–27.

21. *Ibid.*, p. 17.

22. *Ibid.*, p. 19.

23. Krzysztof Skubiszewski, "Zachodnia granica Polski w świetle układów z 1970 roku," *Państwo i Prawo* (March–April 1971):478–87.

24. *Ibid.*, p. 483.

25. *Trybuna Ludu*, May 9, 1971.

26. *Ibid.*, May 20, 1972.

27. Frelek's and other speeches were published in *ibid.*, May 26, 1972.

28. *Ibid.*, December 8, 1970.

29. *Ibid.*, January 28, 1971.

30. *Ibid.*, May 13, 1971.

31. *Ibid.*, May 30, 1971.

32. Michalina Boral, "Polityka kulturalna obu państw niemieckich wobec państw kapitalistycznych i krajów rozwijających się," *Przegląd Zachodni* (September–December 1970):122–205.

33. Lech Janicki, "The Territory and State Citizenship in the Legal Systems of the German Democratic Republic and the German Federal Republic," *Polish Western Affairs* (January 1971):44–86; and Franciszek Sarnecki, "Podstawy stabilizacji pokoju," *Krajowa Agencja Informacyjna* (June 6–12, 1973):II/3–4.

34. Jerzy Sułek, "Chadecja w NRF—Kontynuacja czy zmiana?" *Sprawy Międzynarodowe* (April 1971):5–20.

35. *Pravda*, June 1, 1972.

36. *Ibid.*

CHAPTER 12

1. The electoral results in *Bulletin* 39 (November 21, 1972), of the Press and Information Office of the Government of the Federal Republic of Germany.

2. The text of the treaty and accompanying documents in *Bulletin* 38 (1972), of the Press and Information Office of the Government of the Federal Republic of Germany.

3. The text of the treaty in *Bulletin* 24 (1973), of the Press and Information Office of the Government of the Federal Republic of Germany.

4. The text of the joint communiqué in *Contemporary Poland* 6 (Polish Interpress Agency, June 1972).

5. "Problems of state territory in the legal system of the Federal Republic of Germany," *Contemporary Poland* 10 (October 1972):7–21; and "West-German national status institution," *ibid.*, 11 (October 1972):12–23.

6. "Foreign Trade," *ibid.*, 7–8 (July–August 1973):29.

7. Stanisław Cholewiak, "Odszkodowania wojenne NRF dla obywateli polskich," *Sprawy Międzynarodowe* 4 (1974):99–112.

8. Günther Berndt and Reinhard Strecker, eds., *Polen: Ein Schauermärchen oder Gehirnwäsche für Generationen* (Hamburg: Rowohlt, 1971).

9. *Ibid.*, p. 8.

10. *Ibid.*, pp. 8–9.

11. Quoted in *ibid.*, p. 26.

12. *Ibid.*, p. 27.

13. *Ibid.*, pp. 37–44.

14. Quotations from various current textbooks in *ibid.*, pp. 56–66.

15. Quoted in *ibid.*, p. 64.

16. *Ibid.*, pp. 67–91.

17. The text of the instruction in *ibid.*, pp. 96–102.

18. The text of this instruction in *ibid.*, pp. 102–104.

19. Günther Berndt, "Polen im Westdeutschen Schulbuch," *Stimmen und Begegnungen*, special issue (August 1971):6–7.

20. Immanuel Geiss, "NFR: problemy historji i współczesności," *Sprawy Międzynarodowe* (March 1971):92–102.

21. Zdzisław Grot, "Najnowsze prace profesora H. Roosa z zakresu dziejów Polski," *Przegląd Zachodni* (September 1972):219–21.

22. Hans-Adolf Jacobsen, *Misstrauische Nachbarn: Deutsche Ostpolitik 1919–1970* (Düsseldorf: Droste Verlag, 1970). This book was reviewed by Mieczysław Tomala in *Sprawy Międzynarodowe* (October 1971):140–45.

Bibliography

DOCUMENTS

(presented not in an alphabetical order but according to their subject-matter relationship)

Foreign Relations of the United States: The Conferences at Cairo and Teheran, 1943. Washington, D.C.: U.S. G.P.O., 1961.

Foreign Relations of the United States: The Conferences at Malta and Yalta (1945). Washington, D.C.: U.S. G.P.O., 1955.

Foreign Relations of the United States: The Conference of Berlin (The Potsdam Conference), 1945. Washington, D.C.: U.S. G.P.O., 1960.

Germany 1947–1949: The Story in Documents. Washington, D.C.: Department of State, 1950.

Foreign Relations of the United States 1947. Volume IV: Eastern Europe; The Soviet Union. Washington, D.C.: U.S. G.P.O., 1972.

General de Gaulle's Address in Warsaw on September 11, 1967. New York: Ambassade de France, Service de Presse et d'Information, No. 271, 1967.

Auswärtiges Amt. Die Auswärtige Politik der Bundesrepublik Deutschland. Köln: Verlag Wissenschaft und Politik, 1972.

Meissner, Boris, ed. *Die Deutsche Ostpolitik 1961–1970: Kontinuität und Wandel.* Cologne: Verlag Wissenschaft und Politik, 1970.

Dokumentation der Vertreibung der Deutschen aus Ostmittel Europa. Bonn: Bundesministerium für Vertriebene, 1952.

Die Deutschen Vertreibungsverluste, Bevölkerungsbilanzen für die Deutschen Vertreibungsgebiete: 1939–1950. Wiesbaden: Statistisches Bundesamt, 1958.

Zeittafel der Vorgeschichte und des Ablaufs der Vertreibung sowie der Unterbringung und Eingliederung der Vertriebenen und Bibliographie zum Vertriebenenproblem. Bonn: Bundesministerium für Vertriebene, Flüchtlinge und Kriegsgeschädigte, 1959.

Vertriebenenproblem: Recht auf die Heimat und Selbstbestimmung im Deutschen Parlament von 1949 bis Mitte 1960. Bonn: Bundesministerium für Vertriebene, 1960.

Die Lage der Vertriebenen und das Verhältnis des deutschen Volkes zu seinen ostlichen Nachbarn: Eine Evangelische Denkschrift. Hanover, 1965.

Le Dialogue Germano–Polonais: Des Lettres des Evêques Polonais et Allemands et Prises de Position Internationales. Bonn-Bruxelles-New York: Editions Atlantic-Forum, 1966.

Brandt, Willy. *Reden und Interviews: 1968–1969.* Bonn, 1969.

Treaty between the F.R.G. and the Soviet Union of August 12, 1970. Bulletin No. 109/S.1093, Sonderausgabe. Bonn: Presse-und Informationsamt der Bundesregierung, 1970.

Treaty between the Federal Republic of Germany and the People's Republic of Poland of December 7, 1970. Bulletin No. 171/S.1813. Sonderausgabe. Bonn: Presse-und Informationsamt der Bundesregierung, 1970.

Treaty between the Polish People's Republic and the Federal Republic of Germany concerning the Bases of Normalization of their Mutual Relations. Bulletin No. 3. Warsaw: Polish Institute of International Affairs (Ministry of Foreign Affairs), 1971.

Układy Związku Radzieckiego i Polski z Niemiecką Republiką Federalną: Dokumenty, Przemówienia, Wywiady, Komentarz. Warsaw: Książka i Wiedza, 1972.

Die Ostpolitik der Bundesregierung in einer sich wandelnden Welt: Vertrag von Staatssekretär Dr. Frank. Bulletin No. 148/S.1573. Bonn: Presse-und Informationsamt der Bundesregierung, 1971.

Kommuniqué über den Besuch des Bundeskanzlers in der Sowjetunion vom 16. bis 18. September 1971. Bulletin No. 136/S.1469. Bonn: Presse-und Informationsamt der Bundesregierung, 1971.

Dokumente zur Einleitung des Ratifikationsverfahrens zu den Verträgen von Moskau und Warschau. Bulletin No. 186/S.2013. Bonn: Presse-und Informationsamt der Bundesregierung, 1971.

Bilanz der Deutsch-Polnischen Beziehungen. Bulletin No. 18/S.173. Bonn: Presse-und Informationsamt der Bundesregierung, 1972.

Official Documents and Statements concerning the Polish Western Frontier

(1944–1970) and the Relations with the German Federal Republic. Bulletin No. 1. Warsaw: Polish Institute of International Affairs (Ministry of Foreign Affairs), 1970.

Die Beratung der Ostverträge im Bundesrat am 9. Februar 1972. Bulletin No. 20/S.197. Sonderausgabe. Bonn: Presse-und Informationsamt der Bundesregierung, 1972.

Erste Beratung der Ostverträge im Deutschen Bundestag am 23. Februar 1972. Bulletin No. 26/S.305. Sonderausgabe. Bonn: Presse-und Informationsamt der Bundesregierung, 1972.

Erste Beratung der Ostverträge im Deutschen Bundestag am 24. Februar 1972. Bulletin No. 27/S.369. Sonderausgabe. Bonn: Presse-und Informationsamt der Bundesregierung, 1972.

Erste Beratung der Ostverträge im Deutschen Bundestag am 25. Februar 1972. Bulletin No. 28/S.441. Sonderausgabe. Bonn: Presse-und Informationsamt der Bundesregierung, 1972.

Zweite Beratung der Ostverträge im Deutschen Bundestag am 10. Mai 1972. Bulletin No. 68/S.941. Sonderausgabe. Bonn: Presse-und Informationsamt der Bundesregierung, 1972.

Forsetzung der Zweiten Beratung und Schlussabstimmung der Ostverträge im Deutschen Bundestag am 17. Mai 1972. Bulletin No. 72/S.1037. Sonderausgabe. Bonn: Presse-und Informationsamt der Bundesregierung, 1972.

Eingliederung Junger Aussiedler. Bulletin No. 45/S.665. Bonn: Presse-und Informationsamt der Bundesregierung, 1972, pp. 670–74.

The Quadripartite Agreement on Berlin of September 3, 1971. Bonn: Presse-und Informationsamt der Bundesregierung, 1971.

Basic Treaty between the Federal Republic of Germany and the German Democratic Republic. Bulletin No. 38, 1973. Bonn: Press and Information Office of the Government of the Federal Republic of Germany, 1973.

Treaty between the Federal Republic of Germany and Czechoslovakia of December 11, 1973. Bulletin No. 24, 1973. Bonn: Press and Information Office of the Government of the Federal Republic of Germany, 1973.

Rocznik Polityczny i Gospodarczy 1971. Warsaw: Państwowe Wydawnictwo Ekonomiczne, 1972.

Rocznik Statystyczny 1971. Warsaw: Główny Urząd Statystyczny, 1972.

Statistisches Jahrbuch für das Deutsche Reich: Jahrgang 1941–42. Berlin: Statistisches Reichsamt, 1942.

Statistisches Jahrbuch für die Bundesrepublik Deutschland: 1952. Wiesbaden: Statistisches Bundesamt, 1953.

Statistisches Jahrbuch für die Bundesrepublik Deutschland: 1960. Wiesbaden: Statistisches Bundesamt, 1961.

BOOKS

Adenauer, Konrad. *Erinnerungen: 1945–1963.* 4 vols. Stuttgart: Deutsche Verlags Anstalt, 1965–68.

Ashkenasi, Abraham. *Reformpartei und Aussenpolitik: Die Aussenpolitik der SPD.* Berlin-Bonn-Köln: Westdeutscher Verlag, 1968.

Aster, Sidney. *1939: The Making of the Second World War.* New York: Simon and Schuster, 1973.

Barzel, Rainer. *Gesichtspunkt eines Deutschen.* Düsseldorf: Econ Verlag, 1968.

Baring, Arnulf. *Aussenpolitik in Adenauers Kanzlerdemokratie.* München: R. Oldenburg, 1969.

Basiński, Euzebiusz and Walichnowski, Tadeusz. *Stosunki Polsko-Radzieckie w Latach 1943–1972.* Warsaw: Książka i Wiedza, 1974.

Batowski, Henryk. *Dyplomacja Niemiecka: 1919–1945.* Katowice: Śląski Instytut Naukowy, 1969.

———. *Ostatni Tydzień Pokoju.* Poznań: Wydawnictwo Poznańskie, 1964.

Beck, Joseph. *Dernier Rapport: Politique Polonaise (1926–1939).* Neuchâtel: Editions de la Baconnière, 1951.

Bender, Peter. *Sechs Mal Sicherheit: Befürchtungen in Osteuropa.* Köln-Berlin: Kiepenheur und Witsch, 1970.

———. *Zehn Gründe für die Anerkennung der DDR.* Frankfurt: Fischer Bücherei, 1968.

Berndt, Günther, and Strecker, Reinhard. *Polen: Ein Schauermärchen oder Gehirnwäsche für Generationen.* Hamburg: Rowohlt, 1971.

Besson, Waldemar. *Die Aussenpolitik der Bundesrepublik: Erfahrungen und Masstäbe.* München: R. Piper, 1970.

Binder, Gerhart. *Deutschland seit 1945.* Stuttgart: Seewald Verlag, 1969.

Birnbaum, Immanuel. *Entzweite Nachbarn: Deutsche Politik in Osteuropa.* Frankfurt: H. Scheffler, 1968.

Bluhm, Georg. *Die Oder-Neisse-Linie in der Deutschen Aussenpolitik.* Freiburg: Rombach Verlag, 1963.

Bohmann, Alfred. *Strukturwandel der Deutschen Bevölkerung im Polnischen Staats-und Verwaltungsberich.* Cologne: Verlag Wissenschaft und Politik, 1969.

Bracher, Karl Dietrich, ed. *Nach 25 Jahren: Eine Deutschland-Bilanz.* München: Kindler, 1970.

Brandt, Willy. *Friedenspolitik in Europa.* Frankfurt: Fischer, 1968.

———. *A Peace Policy for Europe.* London: Weidenfeld and Nicolson, 1969.

Carstens, Karl. *Politische Führung: Erfahrungen im Dienste der Bundes-regierung.* Stuttgart: Deutsche Verlags Anstalt, 1971.

Churchill, Winston S. *The Second World War.* 6 vols. Boston: Houghton Mifflin, 1948–53.

Cienciala, Anna M. *Poland and the Western Powers: 1938–1939.* Toronto: University of Toronto Press, 1968.

Contemporary Poland. Warsaw: Polish Interpress Agency, 1973.

Conze, Werner. *Das deutsch-russische Verhältnis im Wandel der modernen Welt.* Göttingen: Vandenhoeck und Ruprecht, 1967.

Cycon, Dieter. *Es Geht um die Bundesrepublik: Eine Kritische Wertung der Aussenpolitik Willy Brandts.* Stuttgart: Seewald Verlag, 1971.

Die Internationale Politik: Jahrbücher der Forschungsinstituts der Deutschen Gesellschaft für Auswärtige Politik. München: R. Oldenburg, 1958–71.

Dębicki, Roman. *Foreign Policy of Poland: 1919–1939.* New York: Praeger, 1962.

Dohrmann, Rudolf. *Versöhnung hat politische Gestalt: Stimmen zur Be-gegnung mit Polen.* Hamburg: Herbert Reich Evangelischer Verlag, 1968.

Domes, Alfred, ed. *Ost-West Polarität.* Cologne: Verlag Wissenschaft und Politik, 1972.

Dönhoff, Marion Gräfin. *Deutsche Aussenpolitik von Adenauer bis Brandt.* Hamburg: Wegner, 1970.

Drzewieniecki, W. M. *The German-Polish Frontier.* Chicago: Polish Western Association of America, 1959.

Ehmke, Horst. *Perspektiven: Sozialdemokratische Politik im Übergang zu den 70-er Jahren.* Reinbek bei Hamburg: Rowohlt, 1969.

—————. *Politik der Praktischen Vernunft: Aufsätze und Referate.* Frankfurt: S. Fischer, 1969.

Fechner, Helmuth. *Deutschland und Polen: 1772–1945.* Würzburg: Holzner Verlag, 1964.

Froese, Leonhard, ed. *Was Soll aus Deutschland Werden? Neue Aspekte zur Deutschlandspolitik.* München: Goldmann, 1968.

Gelberg, Ludwik. *Niemcy po Drugiej Wojnie Światowej: Refleksje o Sytuacji Prawnej.* Wrocław: Zakład Narodowy Imienia Ossolińskich, 1971.

Giełżynski, Wojciech. *Polen Heute.* Wien-Düsseldorf: Econ Verlag, 1973.

Goguel, R., ed. *Polen, Deutschland und die Oder-Neisse Grenze.* Berlin: Rütten und Loening, 1959.

Göttinger Arbeitskreis. *Das Östliche Deutschland: Ein Handbuch.* Würzburg: Holzner Verlag, 1959.

Grossmann, K. R. *Die Ehrenschuld: Kurzgeschichte der Wiedergutmachung.* Berlin: Ullstein, 1967.

Guttenberg, Karl Theodor. *Deutsche Wiedervereinigung und Europäische Mitte*. Cologne, 1967.

────. *Die Neue Ostpolitik: Wege und Irrwege*. Osnabrück: Fromm, 1971.

Heinemann, Gustav W. *Verfehlte Deutschlandpolitik: Irreführung und Selbsttäuschung*. Frankfurt: Stimme Verlag, 1966.

Henderson, Sir Neville. *Failure of a Mission: Berlin 1937–1939*. New York: Putnam's, 1940.

Hanrieder, Wolfram F. *Die Stabile Krise: Ziele und Entscheidungen der Bundesrepublikanischen Aussenpolitik: 1949–1969*. Düsseldorf, 1971.

Henkys, Reinhard, ed. *Deutschland und die Östlichen Nachbarn: Beitrage zu Einer Evangelischen Denkschrift*. Stuttgart: Kreuz Verlag, 1966.

Jacobsen, Hans-Adolf, ed. *Misstrauische Nachbarn: Deutsche Ostpolitik 1919–1970*. Düsseldorf: Droste Verlag, 1970.

────. *National-Sozialistische Aussenpolitik: 1933–1938*. Frankfurt: Alfred Metzner Verlag, 1968.

Jaksch, Wenzel. *Deutsche Osteuropapolitik: Berichte des Bundestagsabgeordneten W. Jaksch*. Bonn: Editions Atlantic Forum, 1963.

────. *Westeuropa-Osteuropa-Sowjetunion: Perspektiven Wirtschaftlicher Zusammenarbeit*. Bonn: Editions Atlantic Forum, 1965.

Kellermann, Volkmar. *Schwarzer Adler—Weisser Adler: Die Polenpolitik der Weimarer Republik*. Cologne: Markus Verlag, 1970.

Kiesinger, Kurt Georg. *Stationen 1949–1969*. Tübingen: R. Wunderlich, 1969.

Klafkowski, Alfons. *The Legal Effects of the Second World War and the German Problem*. Warsaw: Interpress Publishers, 1968.

────. *The Polish-German Frontier After World War II*. Poznań: Wydawnictwo Poznańskie, 1972.

────. *The Potsdam Agreement*. Warsaw: Interpress Publishers, 1963.

────. *Umowa Poczdamska z dnia 2. VIII, 1945 r,: Podstawy Prawne Likwidacji Skutków Wojny Polsko-Niemieckiej z Lat 1939–1945*. Warsaw: Instytut Wydawniczy Pax, 1960.

────. *The Treaty of December 7th, 1970, between Poland and the Federal Republic of Germany: Bases for an Interpretation in the Light of International Law*. Warsaw: Interpress Publishers, 1973.

Kokot, Józef. *The Logic of the Oder-Neisse Frontier*. Poznań: Wydawnictwo Zachodnie, 1959.

Korbel, Josef. *Poland between East and West: Soviet and German Diplomacy toward Poland (1919–1933)*. Princeton, N.J.: Princeton University Press, 1963.

Kowalski, Włodzimierz T. *Walka dyplomatyczna o miejsce Polski w Europie: 1939–1945*. Warsaw: Książka i Wiedza, 1970.

Kraus, Herbert. *Die Oder-Neisse Linie: Eine Völkerrechtliche Studie: Osteuropa und der Deutsche Osten.* Cologne: R. Müller, 1959.

Kwilecki, Andrzej. *Ziemie Zachodnie w Polskiej Literaturze Socjologicznej: Wybór Tekstów.* Poznań: Instytut Zachodni, 1970.

Krasuski, Jerzy; Labuda, Gerard; and Walczak, Antoni W., eds. *Stosunki Polsko-Niemieckie w Historiografii.* Poznań: Instytut Zachodni, 1974.

Kulski, W. W. *The Soviet Union in World Affairs: A Documented Analysis, 1964-1972.* Syracuse, N.Y.: Syracuse University Press, 1973.

Labuda, Gerard. *Polska Granica Zachodnia: Tysiąc Lat Dziejów Politycznych.* Poznań: Wydawnictwo Zachodnie, 1971.

————, et al. *Ziemie Zachodnie w Granicach Macierzy: Drogi Integracji.* Poznań: Wydawnictwo Zachodnie, 1966.

Laeuen, Harald. *Polen nach dem Sturz Gomulkas.* Stuttgart: Seewald Verlag, 1972.

Lemberg, Eugen, and Rhode, Gotthold. *Das Deutsch-Tschechische Verhältnis seit 1948.* Stuttgart: W. Kohlhammer, 1969.

Lipski, Józef. *Diplomat in Berlin: 1933-1939.* New York: Columbia University Press, 1968.

Maass, Johannes. *Dokumentation der Deutsch-Polnischen Beziehungen nach dem Zweiten Weltkrieg.* Bonn, 1960.

Majonica, Ernst. *Möglichkeiten und Grenzen der Deutschen Aussenpolitik.* Stuttgart: W. Kohlhammer, 1969.

Mann, Golo. *Verzicht oder Forderung? Die Deutsche Ostgrenzen.* Freiburg: 1964.

Męclewski, Edmund. *The Return of Poland to the Odra, Lusatian Nysa and the Baltic.* Warsaw: Ministerstwo Obrony Narodowej, 1971. The same in Polish: *Powrót Polski nad Odrę, Nysę Łużycką, Bałtyk.* Warsaw: Ministerstwo Obrony Narodowej, 1971.

Mehnert, K. *Der Deutsche Standort.* Frankfurt: Deutsche Verlags Anstalt, 1971.

Menzel, Eberhard. *Das Annexionsverbot des Modernen Völkerrechts und das Schicksal der Deutschen Ostgebiete.* Würzburg: Holzner Verlag, 1959.

Muszyński, Jerzy, and Skibiński, Jerzy. *Uznanie NRD: Prawne, Polityczne i Gospodarcze Aspekty Międzynarodowej Podmiotowości Niemieckiej Republiki Demokratycznej.* Warsaw: Państwowe Wydawnictwo Naukowe, 1973.

Narr, W. D. *CDU-SPD: Programm und Praxis seit 1945.* Stuttgart: 1966.

Pastusiak, Longin. *USA-NRF: Sojusz i Sprzeczności.* Warsaw: Polski Instytut Spraw Międzynarodowych, 1972.

Piotrowski, Stanisław. *Hans Franks Tagebuch*. Warsaw: Polnischer Verlag der Wissenschaften, 1963.

Pratt, J. W. *Die Frage der Deutschen Ostgrenzen auf den Konferenzen von Teheran bis Potsdam*. München: 1957.

Rabl, Kurt. *Die Gegenwärtige Völkerrechtliche Lage der Deutschen Ostgebiete*. München: Isar Verlag, 1958.

Rasch, Harold. *Bonn und Moskau: Von der Notwendigkeit Deutsch-Sowjetischer Freundschaft*. Stuttgart: Seewald Verlag, 1969.

Rechowicz, Henryk. *Polska Zachodnia i Północna*. Warsaw: Wydawnictwo Interpress, 1972.

Ritter, Gerhard. *Carl Goerdeler und die deutsche Widerstands-Bewegung*. Stuttgart: Deutsche Verlags Anstalt, 1954.

Roegele, Otto B. *Versöhnung oder Haas? Der Briefwechsel der Bischöfe Polens und Deutschlands und Seine Folgen*. Osnabrück, 1966.

Rhode, Gotthold. *Osteuropa*. Stuttgart, 1952.

———. *Geschichte Polens*. Darmstadt: Wissenschaftliche Buchgesellschaft, 1966.

Roos, Hans. *Geschichte der Polnischen Nation: 1916–1960*. Stuttgart: W. Kohlhammer, 1961.

Rosset, Edward. *Bilans Reprodukcji Ludności na Ziemiach Zachodnich i Północnych*. Poznań: Wydawnictwo Poznańskie, 1969.

Roth, P. *Deutschland und Polen*. München: Isar Verlag, 1958.

Rothfels, Hans, and Markert, Werner (eds.). *Deutscher Osten und Slawischer Westen*. Tübingen: J.C.B. Mohr (Paul Siebeck), 1955.

Scharffenorth, Gerda. *Echo und Wirkung in Polen: Bilanz der Ostdenkschrift*. Hamburg: Furche Verlag, 1968.

Scheel, Walter, ed. *Perspektiven Deutscher Politik*. Düsseldorf: Diederichs, 1969.

Schimitzek, Stanisław. *Truth or Conjecture? German Civilian War Losses in the East*. Warsaw: Zachodnia Agencja Prasowa, 1966.

Schmidt, Helmut. *Strategie des Gleigewichts: Deutsche Friedenpolitik und die Weltmachte*. Stuttgart: Seewald Verlag, 1969.

Schmidt, Paul. *Statist auf diplomatischer Bühne: 1923–45*. Bonn: Athenäum Verlag, 1949.

Schneider, Franz. *Grosse Koalition: Ende oder Neubeginn?* München: Deutscher Taschenbuch Verlag, 1969.

Schütz, Wilhelm Wolfgang. *Deutschland Memorandum: Eine Denkschrift und Ihre Folgen*. Frankfurt: 1968.

Schwoller, Wolfgang. *Deutschland—und Aussenpolitik*. Frankfurt: 1968.

Skibiński, Jerzy. *Poland-FRG: Problems of Normalizing Relations*. Warsaw: Interpress Publishers, 1974.

Skubiszewski, Krzysztof. *Wysiedlenie Niemców po 2-ej Wojnie Światowej.* Warsaw: Książka i Wiedza, 1968.

———. *Zachodnia Granica Polski.* Gdańsk: Instytut Bałtycki w Gdańsku, Wydawnictwo Morskie, 1969.

Sobczak, Janusz. *Polityka Wschodnia NRF w Okresie Rządów Erharda.* Warsaw: Polski Instytut Spraw Międzynarodowych, 1971.

———. *Propaganda Zagraniczna Niemiec Weimarskich wobec Polski.* Poznań: Instytut Zachodni, 1973.

Stehle, Hansjacob. *Nachbar Polen.* Frankfurt: S. Fischer, 1968.

———. *The Independent Satellite: Society and Politics in Poland since 1945.* New York: F. A. Praeger, 1965.

Stökl, Günther. *Osteuropa und die Deutschen: Geschichte und Gegenwart einer Spannungsreichen Nachbarschaft.* Oldenburg-Hamburg: 1967.

Strauss, Franz Joseph. *Entwurf für Europa.* Stuttgart: Seewald Verlag, 1966.

———. *Herausforderung und Antwort.* Stuttgart: Seewald Verlag, 1968.

Strobel, Georg. *Deutschland-Polen: Wünsch und Wirklichkeit.* Bonn, Bruxelles, New York: Editions Atlantic Forum, 1969.

Sułek, Jerzy. *Polityka Wschodnia Rządu "Wielkiej Koalicji": 1966–1969.* Warsaw: Polski Instytut Spraw Międzynarodowych, 1972.

———. *Stanowisko Rządu NRF wobec Granicy na Odrze i Nysie Łużyckiej: 1949–1966.* Poznań: Instytut Zachodni, 1969.

———, and Tomala, Mieczysław. *Polska-NRD: Materjały i Dokumenty.* Warsaw: Polski Instytut Spraw Międzynarodowych, 1970.

Szembek, Jean comte. *Journal 1933–1939.* Paris: Plon, 1952.

Szłapczyński, J. and Walichnowski, T. *Ostforschung: The Role of West German Political Science.* Warsaw: Interpress Publishers, 1970.

The Cambridge History of Poland. 2 vols. Cambridge: At the University Press, 1941 and 1950.

Tichy, K. *Die Massenausweisungen nach dem 2. Weltkrieg und das Öffentliche Recht, dargestellt an der Ausweisung der Sudetendeutschen.* Tübingen, 1949.

Tritsch, Walter. *Metternich und Sein Monarch.* Darmstadt: Holle Verlag, 1952.

Urbanek, K. *Das Heimatrecht der Deutschen Ausgetriebenen: Ein Ausspruch des Positiven Völkerrechts.* Dortmund, 1959.

Vierheller, Victoria. *Polen und die Deutschland Frage: 1939–1949.* Cologne: Verlag Wissenschaft und Politik, 1970.

Vogel, R. *Deutschland: Weg nach Israel.* Stuttgart: Seewald Verlag, 1967.

Walczak, Antoni W. *Rodowód Polityki Wschodniej NRF.* Warsaw: Polski Instytut Spraw Międzynarodowych, 1972.

Walichnowski, Tadeusz. *Israel and the German Federal Republic*. Warsaw: Interpress Publishers, 1968.

————. *Status Quo w Europie*. Warsaw: Wydawnictwo Ministerstwa Obrony Narodowej, 1970.

————. *Une Doctrine Inquiétante: La Doctrine Politique de Franz Joseph Strauss*. Warsaw: Editions Interpress, 1969.

————. *Warmia, Mazury, Powiśle: 1939–1945*. Warsaw: Książka i Wiedza, 1972.

————. *Z Dziejów NRF i Austrji: Studja Wybrane*. Warsaw: Ministerstwo Obrony Narodowej, 1973.

Weizsäcker, Ernst. *Erinnerungen*. München: Paul List Verlag, 1950.

Whetten, Lawrence L. *Germany's Ostpolitik: Relations between the Federal Republic and the Warsaw Pact Countries*. New York: Oxford University Press, 1971.

Wiewióra, Bolesław. *Polish-German Frontier from the Standpoint of International Law*. Poznań: Wydawnictwo Zachodnie, 1959.

Wilpert, Friedrich von. *The Oder-Neisse Problem: Towards Fair Play in Central Europe*. Bonn: Editions Atlantic-Forum, 1969.

Windelen, Heinrich. *Für Deutschland und Europa*. Bonn: Editions Atlantic Forum, 1969.

————. *SOS für Europa*. Stuttgart: Seewald Verlag, 1972.

Winiewicz, Józef. *NRD-Istotne Ogniwo Bezpieczeństwa Zbiorowego Europy*. Warsaw: Polski Instytut Spraw Międzynarodowych, 1969.

Wiskemann, Elisabeth. *Germany's Eastern Neighbors: Problems Relating to the Oder-Neisse Line and the Czech Frontier Region*. London: Oxford University Press, 1956.

Wojciechowski, Marian. *Die Polnisch-Deutschen Beziehungen: 1933–1938*. Leiden: Brill, 1971.

Wojna, Ryszard. *Spokojnie Płynie Ren*. Warsaw: Czytelnik, 1971.

ARTICLES

Bender, Peter. "Zehn Gründe für die Anerkennung der DDR." *Monat* 7 (1968).

Berndt, Günther. "Polen im Westdeutschen Schulbuch: 200 Jahre Ignoranz und Ressentiment." *Stimmen und Begegnungen* (Sondernummer 1971): 1–7.

Birrenbach, Kurt. "Aktuelle Fragen der Deutschlandpolitik." *Europa Archiv* 8 (1967).

Blumenfeld, Erik. "Wege zu einer europäischen Friedensordnung." *Europa Archiv* 3 (1967).

Boral, Michalina. "Polityka kulturalna obu państw niemieckich wobec państw kapitalistycznych i krajów rozwijających się." *Przegląd Zachodni* 5–6 (1970):122–205.

Brandt, Willy. "Plädoyer fur die Vernunft: Deutsche Aussenpolitik nach dem 21. August 1968." *Monat* 245 (1969).

————. "German policy toward the East." *Foreign Affairs* 4 (1968).

Cholewiak, Stanisław. "Polityka Wschodnia NRF na tle ogólnej koncepcji polityki zagranicznej SPD." *Sprawy Międzynarodowe* 6 (1974):43–59.

————. "Odszkodowania wojenne NRF dla obywateli polskich." *Sprawy Międzynarodowe* 4 (1974):99–112.

Duckwitz, Georg F. "Gewaltverzicht und Interventionsrecht." *Aussenpolitik* 9 (1968).

————. "The Turning Point in the East." *Aussenpolitik* 4 (1971):363–79.

Ehmke, Horst. "Ostverträge: Perspektiven fur die Jugend." *Bulletin* 50/ S.713. Bonn: Presse- und Informationsamt der Bundesregierung, 1972.

Frelek, Ryszard. "Some thoughts on European security and cooperation: Ideas about Polish foreign policy." *Sprawy Międzynarodowe*. Special ed., 1970.

————. "Podstawa normalizacji." *Sprawy Międzynarodowe* 1 (1971):5–14.

Geiss, Immanuel. "NRF: problemy historji i współczesności." *Sprawy Międzynarodowe* 3 (1971):92–102.

Hierowska-Gorzelik, Barbara. "Rola przesiedlenców w polityce kulturalnej NRF." *Przegląd Zachodni* 5–6 (1970):171–73.

Janicki, Lech. "The Territory and State Citizenship in the Legal Systems of the German Democratic Republic and the German Federal Republic." *Polish Western Affairs* 1 (1971):44–86.

Kersten, Krystyna. "Przemiany struktury narodowościowej Polski po II wojnie światowej: Geneza i wyniki." *Kwartalnik Historyczny* 2 (1969): 337–65.

Kokot, Józef. "The Logic of Potsdam Verified." *Polish Western Affairs* 1 (1971):24–43.

Klafkowski, Alfons. "The Treaty between Poland and the German Federal Republic Concerning the Bases of Normalization of Their Mutual Relations as an Element of the Recognition of the Status Quo in Europe." *Studies on International Relations* 1 (Polish Institute of International Affairs, 1973).

————. "Układ Polska-NRF o podstawach normalizacji stosunków jako element uznania status quo w Europie." *Sprawy Międzynarodowe* 9 (1971):5–20.

Konieczny, J. "Information about Poland's Western Territories in the German Federal Republic." *Polish Western Affairs* 1 (1970):41–66.

Kowalski, Włodzimierz T. "The Grand Coalition and Postwar European Security (1943–1945)." *Sprawy Międzynarodowe,* special ed. (1970): 49–64.

————. "Allied Policy (1939–1945): The Problem of Peace in Postwar Europe." *Polish Western Affairs* 2 (1970):209–33.

Löwenthal, Richard. "Der Einfluss Chinas auf die Entwicklung des Ost-West Konflikts in Europa." *Europa Archiv* 10 (1967).

Mądry, Józef. "Tendencje w ocenianiu kultury polskiej w NRF." *Przegląd Zachodni* 5–6 (1970):210–17.

Meissner, Boris. "The Sowjetunion und Deutschland 1941 bis 1967." *Europa Archiv* 14 (1967):515–31.

Olszyński, Józef. "Handel i kooperacja przemysłowa między Polską i NRF." *Sprawy Międzynarodowe* 5 (1974):21–34.

Orzechowski, Marjan. "Polish Conception of the Polish-German Frontier during World War II." *Polish Western Affairs* 2 (1970):234–70.

Pilichowski, Czesław. "Odszkodowania RFN dla Polaków." *Sprawy Międzynarodowe* 11 (1974):107–18.

————. "Straty nauki i kultury polskiej w okresie II wojny światowej." *Rok Nauki Polskiej* (Polska Agencja Informacyjna, 1973):67–72.

Rosset, Edward. "Demographic Factors Concerning the Re-polonization of Western and Northern Territories." *Polish Western Affairs* 1 (1970): 67–88.

Rotfeld, Adam Daniel. "Wokół ratyfikacji układu PRL-NRF: problemy polityczno-prawne." *Sprawy Międzynarodowe* 4 (1972):27–46.

Sarnecki, Franciszek. "Podstawy stabilizacji pokoju." Krajowa Agencja Informacyjna (June 1973):II/3–4.

Schuster, Richard. "Die Hallstein-Doktrin: ihre rechtliche und politische Bedeutung und die Grenzen ihrer Wirksamkeit." *Europa Archiv* 18 (1963).

Schütz, Klaus. "Unsere Politik gegenüber Polen." *Die Zeit* 26 (1969).

Schwarzkopf, Dieter. "Die Idee des Gewaltverzichts: ein Element der neuen Ostpolitik der Bundesrepublik." *Europa Archiv* 24 (1967).

Skubiszewski, Krzysztof. "Poland's Western Frontier and the 1970 Treaties." *American Journal of International Law* 1 (1973):23–43.

————. "Zachodnia granica Polski w świetle układów z 1970 roku." *Państwo i Prawo* 3–4 (1971):476–87.

Sułek, Jerzy. "Chadecja w NRF: kontynuacja czy zmiana?" *Sprawy Międzynarodowe* 4 (1971):5–20.

————. "Der Normaliesierungsprozess BRD-Polen aus polnischer Sicht." *Deutschland Archiv* 12 (1973):1258–67.

————. "Główne kierunki politycznej i prawnej interpretacji układu Polska-NRF z 7 grudnia 1970 roku." *Sprawy Międzynarodowe* 6 (1972): 5–21.

————. "Normalization agreements of 1970–72 and the European security." *Studies on International Relations* 2 (1973):23–36 (Polish Institute of International Affairs).

————. "Polityka rządu NRF wobec Polski (1966–1969)." *Sprawy Międzynarodowe* 10 (1971):90–104.

————. "Porozumienia normalizacyjne z lat 1970–1972 a bezpieczeństwo Europy." *Sprawy Międzynarodowe* 7–8 (1972):15-27.

————. "The Main Directions of the Political and Legal Interpretation of the Polish–West German Treaty of December 7, 1970." *Studies on International Relations* 1 (1973):56–74 (Polish Institute of International Affairs).

Szłapczyński, Józef. "Główne nurty nauk politycznych w NRF." *Sprawy Międzynarodowe* 3 (1972):78–87.

Winiewicz, Józef. "Der polnische Standpunkt zu problemen der europäischen Sicherheit." *Europa Archiv* (Sonderdruck 1971):847–58.

————. "Ein neues Kapitel." *Polnische Perspektiven* 2 (1971):3–7.

Wróblewski, Tadeusz. "Rola przesiedleńcow w polityce kulturalnej NRF." *Przegląd Zachodni* 5–6 (1970).

Wagner, Wolfgang. "Europäische Politik nach der Tschechoslowakischen Krise." *Europa Archiv* 18 (1968).

Wolff-Powęska, Anna. "Tematyka polska na łamach miesięcznika *Osteuropa* (1960–1970)." *Przegląd Zachodni* 3 (1971):117–28.

Index

This index has two major divisions—of persons and subjects.

PERSONS

327

SUBJECTS

GERMANY AND POLAND

was composed in 10-point Linotype Times Roman and leaded two points,
with display type handset in Beton Open, and
printed letterpress on Perkins & Squier 55-bound Special Book
by Heffernan Press, Inc.;
Smyth-sewn and bound over boards in Columbia Riverside Chambray
by Vail-Ballou Press, Inc.;
and published by

SYRACUSE UNIVERSITY PRESS
Syracuse, New York 13210